Computational Intelligence Methods and Applications

The books in this series explain methods developed in computational intelligence (including evolutionary computing, neural networks, and fuzzy systems), soft computing, statistics, and artificial intelligence, and their applications in domains such as heuristics and optimization; bioinformatics, computational biology, and biomedical engineering; image and signal processing, VLSI, and embedded system design; network design; process engineering; social networking; and data mining.

This series includes monographs, introductory and advanced textbooks, contributed volumes and state-of-the-art collections. Furthermore, it supports Open Access publication mode.

Huaqing Li • Qingguo Lü • Dawen Xia •
Xin Wang • Zheng Wang • Lifeng Zheng • Jun Li •
Liang Ran

Network-System Research and Distributed Composite Algorithm Design

Springer

Huaqing Li
College of Electronic and Information Engineering
Southwest University
Chongqing, China

Dawen Xia
College of Microelectronics and Artificial Intelligence
Kaili University
Kaili, Guizhou, China

Zheng Wang
College of Electronic and Information Engineering
Southwest University
Chongqing, China

Jun Li
College of Electronic and Information Engineering
Southwest University
Chongqing, China

Qingguo Lü
College of Computer Science
Chongqing University
Chongqing, China

Xin Wang
College of Electronic and Information Engineering
Southwest University
Chongqing, China

Lifeng Zheng
College of Computer Science and Engineering
Chongqing University of Technology
Chongqing, China

Liang Ran
College of Electronic and Information Engineering
Southwest University
Chongqing, China

ISSN 2510-1765 ISSN 2510-1773 (electronic)
Computational Intelligence Methods and Applications
ISBN 978-981-95-0910-2 ISBN 978-981-95-0911-9 (eBook)
https://doi.org/10.1007/978-981-95-0911-9

This Springer imprint is published by the registered company Springer Nature Singapore Pte Ltd.
The registered company address is: 152 Beach Road, #21-01/04 Gateway East, Singapore 189721, Singapore

Preface

With the rapid development of communication and computer technology, emerging services like cloud computing, Internet of Things, and social networks have led to an unprecedented growth in the types and scale of data in human society. Consequently, the world has entered the era of big data characterized by networking. In this context, distributed optimization methods that rely on parallel computing and distributed storage have emerged as a research focus for achieving system optimization goals. Such methods utilize intelligent agents that interact with neighbors to collaboratively optimize the system using only their own cost function. Distributed optimization is an ideal optimization tool due to its decentralized, strong robustness, and low communication cost characteristics. Moreover, it aligns with the trend of network information intelligent systems moving toward distributed autonomous management.

Analysis and synthesis including primal-dual splitting algorithm, asynchronous algorithm, uncoordinated step sizes, fixed-point iteration, proximal operator, randomized block coordinate, forward-backward splitting method, operator splitting scheme, and model predictive control are intensively studied. This monograph mainly investigates distributed optimization algorithms and applications in networked control systems. In general, the following problems are investigated in this monograph: (1) Distributed primal-dual splitting algorithm for multi-block separable optimization; (2) Distributed primal-dual fixed point algorithm for multi-block separable optimization; (3) Distributed triple proximal splitting algorithm for nonsmooth composite optimization; (4) Distributed dual operator splitting algorithm for nonsmooth composite optimization; (5) Distributed primal-dual forward-backward splitting algorithm for nonsmooth composite optimization; (6) Distributed algorithm for constrained optimization with asynchrony and delays; (7) Distributed model predictive control algorithm for optimal output consensus of high-order multi-agent systems; (8) Distributed dual proximal gradient algorithms for nonsmooth constrained composite optimization; (9) Distributed proximal splitting algorithm for composite constrained convex optimization. Among the topics, simulation results including some typical real applications are presented to illustrate the effectiveness and the practicability of the distributed optimization algorithms proposed in the previous parts.

This book is suitable for undergraduate and graduate students majoring in computer science and technology, artificial intelligence, electrical engineering, etc., and as a reference material for researchers and technologists in related fields.

Acknowledgements This work was supported in part by the Fundamental Research Funds for the Central Universities under Grant SWU-XDJH202312, in part by the National Natural Science Foundation of China under Grants 62573364, 62173278, 62576053, 62302068, and 62462013, in part by the Chongqing Science Fund for Distinguished Young Scholars under Grant 2024NSCQ-JQX0103, in part by the Natural Science Foundation of Chongqing (Innovation and Development Joint Fund) under Grant CSTB2025NSCQ-LZX0085, in part by the Science and Technology Innovation Talent Team Project of Data Science and Computing Intelligence of Guizhou Province under Grant QKHRC-CXTD2025038, and in part by the Key Project of Engineering Research Center of Micro-nano and Intelligent Manufacturing of Ministry of Education under Grant WZG202501.

Chongqing, China Huaqing Li

Contents

List of Figures

Chapter 1
Introduction

Along with the rapid development of information technology, human beings have moved from the information technology era to the data technology era, and gradually entered the ternary world of "human-machine-object" integration. In particular, with the integration of data-driven agents into the physical scene, the interaction of information acquisition, transmission and processing constitutes a complex multidimensional system that deeply integrates communication, control and optimization—networked systems. The core of this type of system is that the networked system composed of many agents can efficiently accomplish certain global goals through mutual collaboration, while making decisions according to different preferences, thus solving large-scale complex problems that are difficult for individual agents to handle, with strong anti-interference and environmental adaptability. In addition, the network structure of such systems requires participating agents to access only their own local information. This may be due to the consideration of security and privacy issues in the network, or simply due to the fact that the network is too large, making it practically impossible or very inefficient to aggregate global information to the central agents. As advances in wireless communication technologies, microelectronic and microelectromechanical technologies, and integrated perceptual computing systems, the application scenarios of networked systems continue to expand.

With the rapid increase in computing power and storage capacity of agents, it has become a trend to deploy advanced optimization algorithms on distributed agents in networked systems. A typical example is the distributed optimization framework: multi-agents in a network collaborate to solve a global optimization task through local computation and local communication. Distributed optimization frameworks have greater advantages over centralized optimization frameworks in terms of scalability, robustness, privacy, etc., and are more suitable for application scenarios of large-scale networked systems. For example, SchedulerX, a new-generation distributed task scheduling platform developed by Alibaba, provides scheduling task orchestration and distributed batch processing by adopting the technology

H. Li et al., *Network-System Research and Distributed Composite Algorithm Design*, Computational Intelligence Methods and Applications,
https://doi.org/10.1007/978-981-95-0911-9_1

of distributing massive data to multi-agents for execution through the master-slave model. MoXing, a distributed training acceleration framework developed by Huawei Cloud's ModelArts team, accelerates the distributed deep learning training process by building in a variety of advanced distributed optimization strategies that enable hardware, software, and algorithms to work together to optimize the training process. MoXing itself does not directly manifest itself as a centered or decentralized distributed architecture, but rather relies on an underlying distributed training framework (Parameter Server or Ring-allreduce) to realize distributed training. As a popular research direction across multiple disciplines with wide applicability and important application prospects, distributed optimization of networked systems has become a key driving force for breakthroughs in computer science, control science, artificial intelligence, big data analysis and other cutting-edge fields.

However, the current distributed algorithms are mainly designed for the optimization of a single function, and do not focus on solving the composite (smooth + non-smooth function + coupled function, etc.) constrained (non-linear inequality constraints, coupled equality constraints, set constraints, etc.) optimization problems that are widespread in the real-world applications such as model predictive control, large energy market generation planning, and so on, which have weak usability. Not only that, the growth rate of actual data size has long far exceeded the growth rate of hardware capacity, further challenging the performance of algorithms. Therefore, it is of great research value to design high-performance distributed optimization algorithms to effectively solve composite constrained optimization problems. In addition, in the actual optimization process of the algorithm, the complexity and variability of the networked system will also cause far-reaching and complex impact. In the networked system, the unidirectional transmission of information between agents without feedback, the dynamic change of neighboring agents, and the maintenance of data consistency all greatly challenge the application efficiency of distributed optimization algorithms. Therefore, it is particularly important to conduct research on distributed optimization in complex network environments. This not only helps to enhance the performance of algorithms in practical applications, but also promotes the development of networked systems, which is of great significance in enhancing the performance of algorithms, optimizing the user experience as well as promoting the technological advancement in related fields.

This book focuses on designing high-performance algorithms for solving more practical and complex optimization problems (multi-block optimization, composite optimization, constrained optimization, optimization with diversity objective functions, etc.) in the context of distributed optimization in networked systems and their successful application to real-world applications (model predictive control, smart grids, etc.). It will introduce readers to the latest and advanced techniques in "Network-System Research and Distributed Composite Algorithm Design", and help them develop their own novel distributed algorithms that have practical applications. Readers may be particularly interested in the book on consensus and optimization protocols, forward-backward splitting methods, proximal gradient methods, primal-dual methods, fixed point methods, asynchronous communication/computaion mechanisms, randomized block coordinate techniques, operator splitting schemes, uncoordinated step sizes strategies, etc., in the process of distributed optimization in various networked systems.

The main contents of this book include the following aspects: 1. In Chap. 2, we propose a synchronous distributed primal-dual splitting algorithm and its asynchronous version in light of the randomized block-coordinate method to solve the distributed optimization problem, where each local objective function involves a Lipschitz-differentiable convex function, a nonsmooth convex function, and a linear composite nonsmooth convex function; 2. In Chap. 3, we propose a distributed primal-dual fixed point algorithm and its randomized asynchronous iterative distributed algorithm to solve the distributed optimization problem, where the objective is to minimize the sum of a twice differentiable convex function and two possibly nonsmooth convex functions, one of which is composed of a bounded linear operator; 3. In Chap. 4, we propose a distributed triple proximal splitting algorithm with uncoordinated step sizes to solve the distributed optimization problem, where the target is to minimize the sum of local objective functions consisting of a Lipschitz-differentiable convex function and two possibly nonsmooth convex functions, one of which contains a bounded linear operator; 4. In Chap. 5, we propose a synchronous distributed dual operator splitting algorithm and its asynchronous version based on the randomized block coordinate descent technique to solve the distributed optimization problem, where the local objective function is composed of two possibly nonsmooth functions with one being strongly convex and the other being proper closed convex; 5. In Chap. 6, we propose a distributed primal-dual forward-backward splitting algorithm to solve the distributed optimization problem, where the problem involves a sum of a differentiable convex function with Lipschitz continuous gradient and two nonsmooth convex functions with a linear operator; 6. In Chap. 7, we propose an asynchronous distributed primal-dual forward-backward splitting algorithm to solve the distributed composite optimization problem over an undirected network with equality constraints, where the problem includes a smooth term and two possibly nonsmooth terms; 7. In Chap. 8, we propose a synchronous distributed model predictive control algorithm and its asynchronous version to solve the model predictive control problem with an application to the optimal output consensus of high-order multi-agent systems. The algorithm allows uncoordinate step sizes depending on local information, which improves the flexibility of multi-agent systems; 8. In Chap. 9, we propose a synchronous distributed dual proximal gradient algorithm and its asynchronous version based on the randomized block-coordinate method to solve a class of totally nonsmooth constrained composite optimization problems, where the mutual goal of agents in the system is to optimize a sum of two separable nonsmooth functions consisting of a strongly-convex function and another convex (not necessarily strongly-convex) function; 9. In Chap. 10, we propose a synchronous full-distributed primal-dual proximal splitting algorithm and its randomized version through subsets of activated agents to solve a class of distributed convex optimization problems subject to local feasible sets, equality and inequality constraints, where the global objective function consists of a sum of locally smooth convex functions and nonsmooth regularization terms. Finally, Chap. 11 summarizes the full book and discusses further future research work.

Chapter 2
Distributed Primal-Dual Splitting Algorithm for Multi-Block Separable Optimization

Abstract This chapter considers the distributed structured optimization problem of collaboratively minimizing the global objective function composed of the sum of local objective functions. Each local objective function involves a Lipschitz-differentiable convex function, a nonsmooth convex function, and a linear composite nonsmooth convex function. For such problems, a synchronous distributed primal-dual splitting (S-DPDS) algorithm is developed with uncoordinated step sizes. Then, its asynchronous version in light of the randomized block-coordinate method (A-DPDS) is proposed. Further, the convergence results show the relaxed range and concise form of the acceptable parameters, which indicates that the algorithms are conducive to the selection of parameters in practical applications. Finally, the efficiency of S-DPDS and A-DPDS algorithms is testified by numerical experiments.

Keywords Distributed optimization · Primal-dual splitting algorithm · Asynchronous algorithm · Uncoordinated step sizes

2.1 Introduction

In this chapter, a class of multi-block separable optimization problems is studied in the following form:

$$\min_{x \in \mathbb{R}^n} f(x) + g(x) + h(Bx), \tag{2.1}$$

where functions f, g and h are three proper lower semi-continuous convex functions, and f is a Lipschitz-differentiable convex function, while B is a linear mapping. Such a structure is universal, thus the separable functions model is widely applied in various convex optimization problems involving machine learning [1], medical image reconstruction [2] and image processing [3]. For the structured optimization problem, researchers have made great achievements in centralized optimization. For instance, Combettes and Pesquet in [4] first proposed a fully

H. Li et al., *Network-System Research and Distributed Composite Algorithm Design*, Computational Intelligence Methods and Applications,
https://doi.org/10.1007/978-981-95-0911-9_2

splitting scheme for solving monotone operator inclusion problem. Based on this, various algorithms were proposed in [5–8] to solve the problem (2.1).

However, although there are numerous distributed optimization results, the results based on operator splitting in distributed optimization are limited. If we start from a more abstract problem model, then all distributed optimization algorithms are to solve the following problem:

$$\min_{x_1,\ldots,x_m} \sum_{i=1}^{m} F_i(x_i). \tag{2.2}$$

The existing distributed algorithms for solving the above problem mostly involve gradient descent methods and primal-dual algorithms. The gradient descent algorithm was first studied in [9] to solve distributed convex optimization problems over time-varying networks. After that, based on Nesterov's gradient algorithm, the fast distributed algorithm was proposed in [10], and a dual averaging sub-gradient method was proposed in [11]. Asynchronous distributed optimization has gotten a lot of attention lately. For example, [12] proposed a robust distributed asynchronous algorithm framework. The authors in [13] addressed distributed optimization with asynchronous updates and unreliable communications. However, these algorithms struggle to handle problem (2.1).

For $F_i = f_i + g_i$, two excellent and independent algorithms were proposed in [14] and [15]. These two algorithms cover some advanced algorithms and main difference between them is that f_i in [14] is convex and f_i in [15] is strongly convex. In [16], the authors presented a distributed version of AFBA [6] to solve the distributed optimization problem $F_i = g_i + h_i \circ B_i$, where f_i is missing. Latafat et al. in [17] creatively proposed a Triangularly Preconditioned Primal-Dual Algorithm (TriPD) to solve problem (2.1) and derive corresponding asynchronous distributed version named TriPD-Dist. However, the parameter condition satisfying the convergence of TriPD-Dist algorithm is not succinct because there is coupling relationship among the parameters. Based on these observations, one thing of great research significance is how to design distributed algorithms to solve this kind of multi-block composite problem, and consider the more common network structure or communication situation, so as to efficiently solve a larger range of problems. This problem motivates our research in this chapter.

In this chapter, the more specific and potential distributed problem (2.1) is considered. Compared with the existing works, the contributions are mainly reflected in the following aspects:

(i) The centralized PDFP algorithm [7] is extended to a distributed form. Specially, the proposed distributed algorithm uses uncoordinated step sizes, which has been widely used in distributed algorithms recently, such as [18, 19]. This means that the algorithm is completely distributed, which only needs the information interaction among neighboring agents in the iterative process.
(ii) By applying the randomized block-coordinate method, the synchronous algorithm can be evolved into an asynchronous version, namely A-DPDS. In

each iteration of the A-DPDS algorithm, only a subset of agents is randomly activated. The asynchronous implementation of the algorithm can eliminate the influence of global clock and improve the robustness. Meanwhile, the A-DPDS algorithm uses independent step sizes.

(iii) Theoretical results and simulation experiments show the advantages of proposed algorithms, especially compared with TriPD-Dist [16]. From the convergence results, the parameters condition is more concise and clear, which is more conducive to the practical application. However, the convergence results of TriPD-Dist are not very clear in form. From the simulation results, the proposed algorithms can achieve a more accurate solution in fewer iterations than TriPD-Dist.

2.2 Preliminaries

2.2.1 *Notation*

The symbol $\mathbb{N}$ represents the set of natural numbers. Let $\rho_{\max}(\cdot)$ denote the spectral radius for matrices. The Euclidean norm of a vector $x \in \mathbb{R}^n$ is represented as $\|\cdot\|$. For a positive definite matrix P, we define the scalar product of the vector x as $x^{\mathrm{T}}Px$ and the induced norm $\|x\|_P = \sqrt{x^{\mathrm{T}}Px}$. An undirected graph $\mathcal{G} = (\mathcal{V}, \mathcal{E})$ consists of a set $\mathcal{V} = \{1, \ldots, m\}$ of all agents and a set $\mathcal{E} \subseteq \mathcal{V} \times \mathcal{V}$ of all edges. $\text{blkdiag}\{P_i\}_{i\in\mathcal{V}}$ is used to represent a block diagonal matrix with m matrices P_i as diagonal components. Let $\mathcal{N}_i = \{j \mid (i, j) \in \mathcal{E}\}$ denote the neighborhood of i-th agent. The undirected graph $\mathcal{G}$ is connected if there exists at least one path between any two distinct vertices. Denote an indicator function of a nonempty set C as $\delta_C(x) = 0$, when $x \in C$, and $\delta_C(x) = \infty$, otherwise. When an operator $T : \mathbb{R}^n \to \mathbb{R}^n$ satisfies $\|Tx - Ty\| \leq \|x - y\|$ for all $x, y \in \mathbb{R}^n$, the operator is nonexpansive. If $\|Tx - Ty\|^2 \leq (Tx - Ty)^{\mathrm{T}}(x - y)$ for all $x, y \in \mathbb{R}^n$, the operator is firmly nonexpansive. The symbol dom_f denotes the effective domain of f, and the interior of a convex subset is defined as $\text{ri}(\cdot)$. Let $\mathrm{X}_0(\mathbb{R}^n)$ be the collection of all proper lower semi-continuous convex functions from $\mathbb{R}^n$ to $(-\infty, +\infty]$. The proximity operator of a function $f \in \mathrm{X}_0(\mathbb{R}^n)$ related to $\|\cdot\|_P$ is defined by

$$\text{prox}_{P^{-1}f}(x) = \underset{y\in\mathbb{R}^n}{\arg\min}\left\{f(y) + \frac{1}{2}\|x - y\|_P^2\right\}. \tag{2.3}$$

Let ∂f be the subdifferential of f, i.e.,

$$\partial f(x) = \left\{v \in \mathbb{R}^n \mid (y - x)^{\mathrm{T}} v \leq f(y) - f(x),\ \forall y \in \mathbb{R}^n\right\}, \tag{2.4}$$

and $f^{\otimes}$ be the convex conjugate function of f. The following definitions and lemmas will be used.

Definition 2.1 The operator T is σ_T-strongly monotone if there exists some $\sigma_T > 0$ such that

$$(Tx - Ty)^{\mathrm{T}} (x - y) \geq \sigma_T \|x - y\|^2, \ x, y \in \mathbb{R}^n. \tag{2.5}$$

Definition 2.2 For a given initial value $z_0 \in \mathbb{R}^n$ and $k \in \mathbb{N}$, the Picard sequence of operator T is defined as $z_{k+1} = Tz_k$.

Lemma 2.3 ([20]) *Let $f \in \mathrm{X}_0 (\mathbb{R}^n)$ and $x, y \in \mathbb{R}^n$, then it holds that*

$$y \in \partial f(x) \Leftrightarrow x = \mathrm{prox}_f (x + y) \Leftrightarrow y = \left(I - \mathrm{prox}_f\right)(x + y). \tag{2.6}$$

Lemma 2.4 ([7]) *The sequence $\{z_k\}$ generated by the fixed point iteration $z_{k+1} = Tz_k$ converges to a fixed point z^* of the operator T if $\{z_k\}$ and T satisfy (i) T is continuous; (ii) $\left\{||z_k - z^*||^2\right\}$ is non-increasing; (iii) $\lim\limits_{k\to\infty} \|z_{k+1} - z_k\|^2 = 0$.*

2.2.2 *Model of Optimization Problem*

Consider a network with m agents, where each agent has three local objective functions. According to problem (2.1), in the distributed case, $f(x) = \sum_{i=1}^m f_i(x_i)$, $g(x) = \sum_{i=1}^m g_i(x_i)$, and $h(Bx) = \sum_{i=1}^m h_i(B_i x_i)$, then we can get the following distributed optimization problem:

$$\begin{aligned} \min_{x_i \in \mathbb{R}^{n_i}} & \sum_{i=1}^m f_i(x_i) + g_i(x_i) + h_i(B_i x_i), \\ \text{s.t.} \quad & A_{ij} x_i + A_{ji} x_j = b_{(i,j)}, \quad (i, j) \in \mathcal{E}. \end{aligned} \tag{2.7}$$

The linear constraint on the edges specifies the coupling relationship between the variables of adjacent agents, where $A_{ij} \in \mathbb{R}^{l(i,j) \times n_i}$ and $A_{ji} \in {}^{l(i,j) \times n_i}$ are two linear mappings and $b_{(i,j)} \in \mathbb{R}^{l(i,j)}$ for $j \in \mathcal{N}_i$, and this edge-based constraint is also considered in [21]. There is a special case that we let $A_{ij} = I$ if $i > j$ and $A_{ij} = -I$ if $i < j$, and take $b_{(i,j)} = 0$, the problem will degenerate into consensus optimization.

Remark 2.5 The most important feature of the model is that it contains three different objective functions. This kind of model has great advantages in dealing with multi-constraint distributed problems through problem transformation. For example, the fusion lasso problem [26] naturally has nonsmooth terms. The economic dispatch problem in power system [27] is usually not a consensus optimization problem, and the linear operator will be generated when the problem is transformed. For the distributed model predictive control [28], the smoothness cannot be guaranteed when the indicator function is used as the penalty function. Therefore the model has a very wide application prospect.

Assumption 2.1 *The undirected graph $\mathcal{G}$ is connected.*

Assumption 2.2 *For $i = 1, \ldots, m$:*

(i) $f_i : \mathbb{R}^{n_i} \to \mathbb{R}$ *is differentiable on* $\mathbb{R}^{n_i}$ *with* $1/\beta_i$*-Lipschitz continuous gradient for* $\beta_i \in [0, +\infty)$*, i.e.,*

$$\beta_i \|\nabla f_i(x) - \nabla f_i(y)\| \leq \|x - y\|, \quad \forall x, y \in \mathbb{R}^{n_i}; \tag{2.8}$$

(ii) $g_i : \mathbb{R}^{n_i} \to \bar{\mathbb{R}}$ *and* $h_i : \mathbb{R}^{r_i} \to \bar{\mathbb{R}}$ *are two convex nonsmooth functions, and* $B_i \in \mathbb{R}^{r_i \times n_i}$ *is a linear mapping;*

(iii) Problem (2.7) *has at least one solution and there exists* $x_i \in \operatorname{ri} \operatorname{dom}_{g_i}$ *such that* $B_i x_i \in \operatorname{ri} \operatorname{dom}_{h_i}$ *for* $i \in \mathcal{V}$ *and* $A_{ij}x_i + A_{ji}x_j = b_{(i,j)}$ *for* $(i, j) \in \mathcal{E}$*.*

Next, we make an equivalent transformation to problem (2.7) for subsequent algorithm derivation. Define the linear operator $N_{(i.j)} : x \to (A_{ij}x_i, A_{ji} x_j)$, where $N_{(i.j)} \in \mathbb{R}^{2l_{(i,j)} \times \sum_{i=1}^{m} n_i}$. By stacking $N_{(i.j)}$, on can get $N : x \to \left(N_{(i,j)}x\right)_{(i,j)\in\mathcal{E}}$, where $N \in \mathbb{R}^{\sum_{(i,j)\in\mathcal{E}} 2l_{(i,j)} \times \sum_{i=1}^{m} n_i}$. Meanwhile, we can get the following equality:

$$N^{\mathrm{T}}N = \sum_{(i,j)\in\mathcal{E}} N_{(i,j)}^{\mathrm{T}} N_{(i,j)} = \operatorname{diag}\left\{\sum_{j\in\mathcal{N}_i} A_{ij}^{\mathrm{T}} A_{ij}\right\}_{i\in\mathcal{V}}. \tag{2.9}$$

Considering the set $C_{(i,j)} = \left\{(e_1, e_2) \in \mathbb{R}^{2l_{(i,j)}} \middle| e_1 + e_2 = b_{(i.j)}\right\}$, we can write problem (2.7) equivalently as

$$\min_{x_i \in \mathbb{R}^{n_i}} \sum_{i=1}^{m} f_i(x_i) + g_i(x_i) + h_i(B_i x_i) + \sum_{i=1}^{m} \sum_{(i,j)\in\mathcal{E}} \delta_{C_{(i,j)}}\left(N_{(i,j)}x\right). \tag{2.10}$$

By defining $B = \operatorname{blkdiag}\{B_i\}_{i\in\mathcal{V}} \in \mathbb{R}^{\sum_{i=1}^{m} r_i \times \sum_{i=1}^{m} n_i}$, and $C = \times_{(i,j)\in\mathcal{E}} C_{(i,j)}$, (2.10) can be globally represented as

$$\min_{x\in\mathbb{R}^n} f(x) + g(x) + h(Bx) + \delta_C(Nx), \tag{2.11}$$

where $x = \operatorname{col}\{x_i\}_{i=1}^{m}$, $f(x) = \sum_{i=1}^{m} f_i(x_i)$, $g(x) = \sum_{i=1}^{m} g_i(x_i)$, $h(Bx) = \sum_{i=1}^{m} h_i(B_i x_i)$, and $\delta_C(Nx) = \sum_{i=1}^{m} \sum_{j\in\mathcal{N}_i} \delta_{C_{(i,j)}}\left(N_{(i,j)}x\right)$.

2.3 Algorithm Development

In this section, we develop S-DPDS and A-DPDS algorithms for solving the problem (2.11). First, we derive a centralized algorithm for the problem (2.11) from the perspective of fixed point iteration. Then, by setting operator and step sizes matrices, the distributed form of the centralized algorithm is developed. Further, the asynchronous version of S-DPDS algorithm is designed by introducing randomized block-coordinate method.

Define v^*, $\tilde{v}^*$ and x^* as the optimal solution, $\mathcal{S}$ is the set of primal-dual solutions, and $z^* = (v^*, \tilde{v}^*, x^*) \in \mathcal{S}$. Meanwhile, define the following operators:

$$T_0\left(v^*, \tilde{v}^*, x^*\right) = \operatorname{prox}_{\Sigma g}\begin{pmatrix} x^* - \Sigma \nabla f\left(x^*\right) \\ -(\mathrm{H}B)^{\mathrm{T}} v^* - (\tilde{\mathrm{H}}N)^{\mathrm{T}} \tilde{v}^* \end{pmatrix}, \tag{2.12}$$

$$T_1\left(v^*, \tilde{v}^*, x^*\right) = \left(I - \operatorname{prox}_{\Gamma^{-1}h}\right)\left(BT_0\left(v^*, \tilde{v}^*, x^*\right) + v^*\right), \tag{2.13}$$

$$\tilde{T}_1\left(v^*, \tilde{v}^*, x^*\right) = \left(I - \operatorname{prox}_{\tilde{\Gamma}^{-1}\delta_C}\right)\left(NT_0\left(v^*, \tilde{v}^*, x^*\right) + \tilde{v}^*\right), \tag{2.14}$$

$$T_2\left(v^*, \tilde{v}^*, x^*\right) = \operatorname{prox}_{\Sigma g}\begin{pmatrix} x^* - \Sigma \nabla f\left(x^*\right) \\ -(\mathrm{H}B)^{\mathrm{T}} T_1\left(v^*, \tilde{v}^*, x^*\right) \\ -(\tilde{\mathrm{H}}N)^{\mathrm{T}} \tilde{T}_1\left(v^*, \tilde{v}^*, x^*\right) \end{pmatrix}, \tag{2.15}$$

$$T\left(v^*, \tilde{v}^*, x^*\right) = \left(T_1\left(v^*, \tilde{v}^*, x^*\right), \tilde{T}_1\left(v^*, \tilde{v}^*, x^*\right), T_2\left(v^*, \tilde{v}^*, x^*\right)\right), \tag{2.16}$$

where Σ, Γ, and $\tilde{\Gamma}$ denote centralized step sizes, H and $\tilde{\mathrm{H}}$ are intermediate parameters obtained by Σ, Γ and $\tilde{\Gamma}$.

The following lemma introduces the reason why we deduce the algorithm from the perspective of fixed point ineration.

Lemma 2.6 *Supposing that x^* is a solution to* (2.11), *$\mathcal{S}$ is the set of primal-dual solutions to* (2.11). *Then, we have*

$$v^* = T_1\left(v^*, \tilde{v}^*, x^*\right), \tag{2.17}$$

$$\tilde{v}^* = \tilde{T}_1\left(v^*, \tilde{v}^*, x^*\right), \tag{2.18}$$

$$x^* = T_2\left(v^*, \tilde{v}^*, x^*\right), \tag{2.19}$$

i.e., $z^* = (v^*, \tilde{v}^*, x^*)$ is a fixed point of T. Meanwhile, if z^* is a fixed point of T, then x^* is a solution to (2.11).

Proof Under Assumption 2.2(iii), according to the first-order optimal condition of (2.11), we get

$$0 \in \Sigma \nabla f\left(x^*\right) + \Sigma \partial g\left(x^*\right) + \Sigma B^{\mathrm{T}} \partial h\left(Bx^*\right) + \Sigma N^{\mathrm{T}} \partial \delta_C\left(Nx^*\right), \tag{2.20}$$

where x^* denotes an optimal solution. According to the composition of the corresponding step sizes matrices, we can deduce

$$\Sigma B^{\mathrm{T}} = B^{\mathrm{T}} \mathrm{H} \Gamma^{-1} = (\mathrm{H}B)^{\mathrm{T}} \Gamma^{-1}, \; \Sigma N^{\mathrm{T}} = N^{\mathrm{T}} \tilde{\mathrm{H}} \tilde{\Gamma}^{-1} = (\tilde{\mathrm{H}}N)^{\mathrm{T}} \tilde{\Gamma}^{-1}, \tag{2.21}$$

then we can further get

$$
\begin{aligned}
0 \in & \Sigma \nabla f\left(x^*\right)+\Sigma \partial g\left(x^*\right)+(\mathrm{H} B)^{\mathrm{T}} \Gamma^{-1} \partial h\left(B x^*\right) \\
& +(\tilde{\mathrm{H}} N)^{\mathrm{T}} \tilde{\Gamma}^{-1} \partial \delta_C\left(N x^*\right) .
\end{aligned} \tag{2.22}
$$

Let $v^* \in \Gamma^{-1} \partial h\left(B x^*\right)$ and $\tilde{v}^* \in \tilde{\Gamma}^{-1} \partial \delta_C\left(N x^*\right)$. By using (2.6), we have

$$
v^*=\left(I-\operatorname{prox}_{\Gamma^{-1} h}\right)\left(B x^*+v^*\right), \tag{2.23}
$$

$$
\tilde{v}^*=\left(I-\operatorname{prox}_{\tilde{\Gamma}^{-1} \delta_C}\right)\left(N x^*+\tilde{v}^*\right), \tag{2.24}
$$

$$
x^*=\operatorname{prox}_{\Sigma g}\left(x^*-\Sigma \nabla f\left(x^*\right)-(\mathrm{H} B)^{\mathrm{T}} v^*-(\tilde{\mathrm{H}} N)^{\mathrm{T}} \tilde{v}^*\right). \tag{2.25}
$$

Combining (2.23)–(2.25) yields that

$$
v^*=\left(I-\operatorname{prox}_{\Gamma^{-1} h}\right)\left(B \operatorname{prox}_{\Sigma g}\left(\begin{array}{l}
x^*-\Sigma \nabla f\left(x^*\right) \\
-(\mathrm{H} B)^{\mathrm{T}} v^* \\
-(\tilde{\mathrm{H}} N)^{\mathrm{T}} \tilde{v}^*
\end{array}\right)+v^*\right), \tag{2.26}
$$

$$
\tilde{v}^*=\left(I-\operatorname{prox}_{\tilde{\Gamma}^{-1} \delta_C}\right)\left(N \operatorname{prox}_{\Sigma g}\left(\begin{array}{l}
x^*-\Sigma \nabla f\left(x^*\right) \\
-(\mathrm{H} B)^{\mathrm{T}} v^* \\
-(\tilde{\mathrm{H}} N)^{\mathrm{T}} \tilde{v}^*
\end{array}\right)+\tilde{v}^*\right). \tag{2.27}
$$

According to the above results, we can get $v^*=T_1\left(v^*, \tilde{v}^*, x^*\right)$, $\tilde{v}^*=\tilde{T}_1\left(v^*, \tilde{v}^*, x^*\right)$, and $x^*=T_2\left(v^*, \tilde{v}^*, x^*\right)$. Therefore, for $z^*=\left(v^*, \tilde{v}^*, x^*\right)$, one has $z^*=T z^*$. On the contrary, if we have the fixed point iteration $z^*=T z^*$, we can prove that x^* meets the first-order optimality condition of problem (2.11) from the reverse and thus we can obtain the conclusion that x^* is an optimal solution to the problem (2.11). ■

Based on Lemma 2.6 and Definition 2.2, we can obtain a component form of Picard sequence of operator T, i.e., the centralized form of S-DPDS algorithm is as follows:

$$
y_{k+1}=\operatorname{prox}_{\Sigma g}\left(x_k-\Sigma \nabla f\left(x_k\right)-(\mathrm{H} B)^{\mathrm{T}} v_k-(\tilde{\mathrm{H}} N)^{\mathrm{T}} \tilde{v}_k\right), \tag{2.28a}
$$

$$
v_{k+1}=\left(I-\operatorname{prox}_{\Gamma^{-1} h}\right)\left(B y_{k+1}+v_k\right), \tag{2.28b}
$$

$$
\tilde{v}_{k+1}=\left(I-\operatorname{prox}_{\tilde{\Gamma}^{-1} \delta_C}\right)\left(N y_{k+1}+\tilde{v}_k\right), \tag{2.28c}
$$

$$
x_{k+1}=\operatorname{prox}_{\Sigma g}\left(\begin{array}{l}
x_k-\Sigma \nabla f\left(x_k\right) \\
-(\mathrm{H} B)^{\mathrm{T}} v_{k+1}-(\tilde{\mathrm{H}} N)^{\mathrm{T}} \tilde{v}_{k+1}
\end{array}\right), \tag{2.28d}
$$

where y is an intermediate variables. The operator form of the above algorithm is written as $z_{k+1} = Tz_k$, where $z_k = (v_k, \tilde{v}_k, x_k)$. Let $u_k = \Gamma v_k$, $\tilde{u}_k = \tilde{\Gamma}\tilde{v}_k$, and use Moreau's identity [22] for (2.28b), then (2.28) can be rewritten as

$$\begin{aligned} y_{k+1} &= \mathrm{prox}_{\Sigma g}\left(x_k - \Sigma\nabla f(x_k) - \Sigma B^{\mathrm{T}} u_k - \Sigma N^{\mathrm{T}}\tilde{u}_k\right), \\ u_{k+1} &= \mathrm{prox}_{\Gamma h^{\otimes}}\left(\Gamma B y_{k+1} + u_k\right), \\ \tilde{v}_{k+1} &= \left(I - \mathrm{prox}_{\tilde{\Gamma}^{-1}\delta_C}\right)\left(N y_{k+1} + \tilde{v}_k\right), \\ x_{k+1} &= \mathrm{prox}_{\Sigma g}\left(x_k - \Sigma\nabla f(x_k) - \Sigma B^{\mathrm{T}} u_{k+1} - \Sigma N^{\mathrm{T}}\tilde{u}_{k+1}\right). \end{aligned} \tag{2.29}$$

We define $v^* = \mathrm{col}\left\{v_i^*\right\}_{i=1}^m$, $\tilde{v}^* = \mathrm{col}\{\tilde{v}^*_{(i,j)}\}_{(i,j)\in\mathcal{E}}$, and $x^* = \mathrm{col}\left\{x_i^*\right\}_{i=1}^m$. Meanwhile, we define the positive parameters γ_i and λ_i for each agent $i \in \mathcal{V}$, and $\tilde{\lambda}_{(i,j)}$ for $(i,j) \in \mathcal{E}$. Then, we decompose the step sizes of the centralized algorithm into following step sizes matrices:

$$\Sigma = \mathrm{blkdiag}\left\{\gamma_i I_{n_i}\right\}_{i\in\mathcal{V}},\ \Gamma = \mathrm{blkdiag}\left\{\frac{\lambda_i}{\gamma_i} I_{r_i}\right\}_{i\in\mathcal{V}}, \tag{2.30a}$$

$$\mathrm{H} = \mathrm{blkdiag}\left\{\lambda_i I_{r_i}\right\}_{i\in\mathcal{V}},\ \tilde{\Gamma} = \mathrm{blkdiag}\left\{\tilde{\lambda}_{(i,j)}\tilde{\gamma}_{(i,j)}^{-1}\right\}_{(i,j)\in\mathcal{E}}, \tag{2.30b}$$

$$\tilde{\mathrm{H}} = \mathrm{blkdiag}\left\{\lambda_{(i,j)} I_{2l_{(i,j)}}\right\}_{(i,j)\in\mathcal{E}}, \tag{2.30c}$$

where $\tilde{\gamma}_{(i,j)} = \mathrm{blkdiag}\left\{\gamma_i I_{l_{(i,j)}}, \gamma_j I_{l_{(i,j)}}\right\}$. Then, we start the derivation of the distributed algorithm. We set two auxiliary variables for individual edge constraint, i.e., we consider $\tilde{v}_{(i,j)} = \left(\tilde{v}_{(i,j),i},\ \tilde{v}_{(i,j),j}\right)$, where $\tilde{v}_{(i,j),i}$ and $\tilde{v}_{(i,j),j}$ are updated by agent i and j. Then, we can convert the summation of edges to the summation of agents

$$\sum_{i=1}^{m}\sum_{(i,j)\in\mathcal{E}}\left(\left(N_{(i,j)}x\right)^{\mathrm{T}}\tilde{u}_{(i,j)}\right) = \sum_{i=1}^{m}\left(x_i^{\mathrm{T}}\sum\nolimits_{j\in\mathcal{N}_i}\left(A_{ij}^{\mathrm{T}}\tilde{u}_{(i,j),i}\right)\right). \tag{2.31}$$

Then, we multiply $\tilde{\Gamma}$ from the left to (2.28c) to get the decomposition form of (2.29) as follows:

$$\begin{aligned} y_i^{k+1} &= \mathrm{prox}_{\gamma_i g_i}\begin{pmatrix} x_i^k - \gamma_i\nabla f_i\left(x_i^k\right) \\ -\gamma_i B_i^{\mathrm{T}} u_i^k - \gamma_i \sum\limits_{j\in\mathcal{N}_i} A_{ij}^{\mathrm{T}}\tilde{u}^k_{(i,j),i} \end{pmatrix}, \\ u_i^{k+1} &= \mathrm{prox}_{\frac{\lambda_i}{\gamma_i}h_i^{\otimes}}\left(\frac{\lambda_i}{\gamma_i}B_i y_i^{k+1} + u_i^k\right), \end{aligned}$$

$$\tilde{u}_{(i,j)}^{k+1} = \tilde{u}_{(i,j)}^{k} + \tilde{\lambda}_{(i,j)} \tilde{\gamma}_{(i,j)}^{-1} \begin{pmatrix} N_{(i,j)} y^{k+1} \\ -\operatorname{prox}_{\frac{\tilde{\gamma}_{(i,j)}}{\tilde{\lambda}_{(i,j)}} \delta_{C_{(i,j)}}} \begin{pmatrix} \frac{\tilde{\gamma}_{(i,j)}}{\tilde{\lambda}_{(i,j)}} \tilde{u}_{(i,j)}^{k} \\ +N_{(i,j)} y^{k+1} \end{pmatrix} \end{pmatrix},$$

$$x_i^{k+1} = \operatorname{prox}_{\gamma_i g_i} \begin{pmatrix} x_i^k - \gamma_i \nabla f_i \left(x_i^k\right) \\ -\gamma_i B_i^{\mathrm{T}} u_i^{k+1} - \gamma_i \sum_{j \in \mathcal{N}_i} A_{ij}^{\mathrm{T}} \tilde{u}_{(i,j),i}^{k+1} \end{pmatrix}. \tag{2.32}$$

We can get the following equivalent transformation according to the definition of indicator function:

$$\begin{aligned}
&\operatorname{prox}_{\frac{\tilde{\gamma}_{(i,j)}}{\tilde{\lambda}_{(i,j)}} \delta_{C_{(i,j)}}} \left(\frac{\tilde{\gamma}_{(i,j)}}{\tilde{\lambda}_{(i,j)}} \tilde{u}_{(i,j)}^{k} + N_{(i,j)} y^{k+1} \right) \\
&= \underset{e \in \mathbb{R}^{2l(i,j)}}{\arg\min} \left\{ \delta_{C_{(i,j)}}(e) + \frac{1}{2\tilde{\lambda}_{(i,j)}} \left\| e - \begin{pmatrix} \frac{\tilde{\gamma}_{(i,j)}}{\tilde{\lambda}_{(i,j)}} \tilde{u}_{(i,j)}^{k} \\ +N_{(i,j)} y^{k+1} \end{pmatrix} \right\|_{\tilde{\gamma}_{(i,j)}^{-1}}^{2} \right\} \\
&= \underset{e \in C_{(i,j)}}{\arg\min} \left\{ \frac{1}{2\tilde{\lambda}_{(i,j)}} \left\| e - \left(\frac{\tilde{\gamma}_{(i,j)}}{\tilde{\lambda}_{(i,j)}} \tilde{u}_{(i,j)}^{k} + N_{(i,j)} y^{k+1} \right) \right\|_{\tilde{\gamma}_{(i,j)}^{-1}}^{2} \right\} \\
&= \underset{e \in C_{(i,j)}}{\arg\min} \left\| e - \left(\frac{\tilde{\gamma}_{(i,j)}}{\tilde{\lambda}_{(i,j)}} \tilde{u}_{(i,j)}^{k} + N_{(i,j)} y^{k+1} \right) \right\|_{\tilde{\gamma}_{(i,j)}^{-1}}^{2} \\
&= \operatorname{proj}_{C_{(i,j)}} \left(\frac{\tilde{\gamma}_{(i,j)}}{\tilde{\lambda}_{(i,j)}} \tilde{u}_{(i,j)}^{k} + N_{(i,j)} y^{k+1} \right).
\end{aligned} \tag{2.33}$$

Combining this with the fact that the projection of $u_1,\ u_2 \in \mathbb{R}^{l(i,j)}$ onto the set $C_{(i,j)}$ is

$$\operatorname{proj}_{C_{(i,j)}} (u_1, u_2) = \frac{1}{2} \left(u_1 - u_2 + b_{(i,j)}, u_2 - u_1 + b_{(i,j)} \right). \tag{2.34}$$

The third equality of (2.32) can be rewritten as

$$\tilde{u}_{(i,j),i}^{k+1} = \tilde{u}_{(i,j),i}^{k} + \frac{\tilde{\lambda}_{(i,j)}}{\gamma_i} \begin{pmatrix} A_{ij} y_i^{k+1} \\ -\frac{1}{2} \begin{pmatrix} \left(\frac{\gamma_i}{\tilde{\lambda}_{(i,j)}} \tilde{u}_{(i,j),i}^{k} + A_{ij} y_i^{k+1} \right) \\ - \begin{pmatrix} \frac{\gamma_i}{\tilde{\lambda}_{(i,j)}} \tilde{u}_{(i,j),j}^{k} \\ +A_{ji} y_j^{k+1} \end{pmatrix} + b_{(i,j)} \end{pmatrix} \end{pmatrix}, \tag{2.35a}$$

$$\tilde{u}_{(i,j),j}^{k+1} = \tilde{u}_{(i,j),j}^{k} + \frac{\tilde{\lambda}_{(i,j)}}{\gamma_j} \begin{pmatrix} A_{ji} y_j^{k+1} \\ -\frac{1}{2} \begin{pmatrix} \left(\frac{\gamma_j}{\tilde{\lambda}_{(i,j)}} \tilde{u}_{(i,j),j}^{k} + A_{ji} y_j^{k+1} \right) \\ - \begin{pmatrix} \frac{\gamma_j}{\tilde{\lambda}_{(i,j)}} \tilde{u}_{(i,j),i}^{k} \\ +A_{ij} y_i^{k+1} \end{pmatrix} + b_{(i,j)} \end{pmatrix} \end{pmatrix}. \tag{2.35b}$$

Then we can get the following fully distributed Algorithm 1.

Algorithm 1 S-DPDS: For each agents $i \in \mathcal{V}$

Initialization : for each agent $i \in \mathcal{V}$, $x_i^0 \in \mathbb{R}^{n_i}$, $u_i^0 \in \mathbb{R}^{r_i}$, and $\tilde{u}_{(i,j),i}^0 \in \mathbb{R}^{l(i,j)}$ for $j \in \mathcal{N}_i$.
For $k = 0, 1, \ldots,$ **do** :

1. $y_i^{k+1} = \text{prox}_{\gamma_i g_i}\begin{pmatrix} x_i^k - \gamma_i \nabla f_i\left(x_i^k\right) - \gamma_i B_i^{\mathrm{T}} u_i^k \\ -\gamma_i \sum_{j\in\mathcal{N}_i} A_{ij}^{\mathrm{T}} \tilde{u}_{(i,j),i}^k \end{pmatrix},$
2. $u_i^{k+1} = \text{prox}_{\frac{\lambda_i}{\gamma_i} h_i^{\otimes}}\left(\frac{\lambda_i}{\gamma_i} B_i y_i^{k+1} + u_i^k\right),$
3. $\tilde{u}_{(i,j),i}^{k+1} = \frac{1}{2}\frac{\tilde{\lambda}_{(i,j)}}{\gamma_i}\left(A_{ij} y_i^{k+1} + A_{ji} y_j^{k+1} - b_{(i,j)}\right) + \frac{1}{2}\left(\tilde{u}_{(i,j),i}^k + \tilde{u}_{(i,j),j}^k\right), \; \forall j \in \mathcal{N}_i,$
4. $x_i^{k+1} = \text{prox}_{\gamma_i g_i}\begin{pmatrix} x_i^k - \gamma_i \nabla f_i\left(x_i^k\right) - \gamma_i B_i^{\mathrm{T}} u_i^{k+1} \\ -\gamma_i \sum_{j\in\mathcal{N}_i} A_{ij}^{\mathrm{T}} \tilde{u}_{(i,j),i}^{k+1} \end{pmatrix}.$
5. Send $A_{ij} y_i^{k+1}$, $\tilde{u}_{(i,j),i}^{k+1}$ to j for $j \in \mathcal{N}_i$.
6. Until the $\left\| x_i^{k+1} - x_i^k \right\|$ approaches zero.

End
Output: the primal variable x_i^{k+1} as the optimal solution x_i^*.

When communication happens, i.e., in each iteration process, each agent will receive information from its neighbors, including $A_{ij} y_i^{k+1}$, $\tilde{u}_{(i,j),i}^{k+1}$ to j for $j \in \mathcal{N}_i$, and also send the above two information to its neighbors. The following assumption is a sufficient condition for the convergence of Algorithm 1.

Assumption 2.3 *The step sizes satisfy the following conditions:*

$$\begin{aligned} &0 < \gamma_i < 2\beta_i, 0 < \lambda_i < \frac{1}{\left(1+\frac{1}{\mu_i}\right)\gamma_i^2 \rho_{\max}\left(B_i B_i^{\mathrm{T}}\right)}, \\ &0 < \tilde{\lambda}_{(i,j)} < \frac{1}{(1+\mu_i)\gamma_i^2 \rho_{\max}\left(\sum_{j\in\mathcal{N}_i} A_{ij}^{\mathrm{T}} A_{ij}\right)}, \end{aligned} \tag{2.36}$$

where $\mu_i > 0$.

The range of parameter convergence in Assumption 2.3 comes from the sufficient condition obtained by the convergence proof of Algorithm 1. The step sizes γ_i, λ_i and $\tilde{\lambda}_{(i,j)}$ of each agent are only related to the corresponding strong convexity parameter β_i, linear operator B_i, constant u_i, and matrix A_{ij}. In the above parameter range, the algorithm can converge, but the optimal convergence parameter value is usually difficult to obtain, because it is related to the nature of the actual problem. Next, we develop the asynchronous version of Algorithm 1.

Definition 2.7 First, we define a partitioning of the vector of the variables $(v, \tilde{v}, x)$ into m blocks of coordinates. Then, let $\boldsymbol{P}_i \in \mathbb{R}^{(n+r+l)} \times \mathbb{R}^{(n+r+l)}$ for $i \in \mathcal{V}$ denote a diagonal matrix with elements 0–1 and call it a coordinate matrix, where n, r, and l represent the dimensions of primal-dual variables x, v, and $\tilde{v}$ respectively. In the matrix $\boldsymbol{P}_i$ corresponding to each agent i, only the i-th block on its diagonal is the identity matrix I, and all the other blocks are zero matrices. Furthermore, let $\xi^k \in \mathbb{R}^m$ be a ϕ-valued activation vector, then the value of ξ_i^k corresponding to i-th block is 1 when it is updated. We suggest that the readers look for more details in [17].

Assumption 2.4 *For* $i = 1, \ldots, m$:

(i) The sum of the activation matrix $\boldsymbol{P}_i$ *is identity matrix, i.e.,* $\sum_i^m \boldsymbol{P}_i = I$*;*
(ii) $\left(\xi^k\right)_{k\geq 0}$ *is a sequence of independent identically distributed* ϕ*-valued vectors with probability* $p_i = \mathbb{P}\left(\xi_i^k = 1\right) > 0, k \geq 0$.

In general, multiple blocks can be activated, so the existence of Assumption 2.4(i) is to facilitate the expression of multiple blocks activated state. Assumption 2.4(ii) is to ensure the randomness of activation. Then we can define the probability matrix $\Pi = \sum_{i=1}^m p_i \boldsymbol{P}_i$.Further, we define conditional expectation as $\mathbb{E}[\cdot\,|\mathcal{F}_k]$ and its abbreviation as $\mathbb{E}_k[\cdot]$, where $\mathcal{F}_k$ denotes the filtration generated by $\left(\xi^1, \ldots, \xi^k\right)$. Let matrix $E_k = \sum_{i=1}^m \xi_i^k \boldsymbol{P}_i$ map the elements of $\left(\mathbb{R}^{n+r}, \mathcal{F}_{k-1}\right)$ to $\left(\mathbb{R}^{n+r}, \mathcal{F}_k\right)$.

Algorithm 2 A-DPDS

Initialization : for each agent $i \in \mathcal{V}$, $x_i^0 \in \mathbb{R}^{n_i}$, $u_i^0 \in \mathbb{R}^{r_i}$, and $\tilde{u}_{(i,j),i}^0 \in \mathbb{R}^{l(i,j)}$ for $j \in \mathcal{N}_i$.
For $k = 0, 1, \ldots,$ **do** : Each agent $i \in \mathcal{V}$ is activated independently with probability p_i. For each activated agent, the update steps in Algorithm 1 are performed. For agents that are not activated, the last values update remain unchanged.
End
Output : the primal variable x_i^{k+1} as the optimal solution x_i^*.

The randomized block-coordinate mechanism adopted in this algorithm can cover some common random activation mechanisms. In particular, the step sizes of asynchronous algorithm are also assumed to meet the Assumption 2.3.

Next, we give a global form of asynchronous algorithm for the subsequent convergence analysis. First, we define the intermediate variable $\hat{z} = (\hat{v}, \hat{\tilde{v}}, \hat{x}) = Tz$ to represent the intermediate variables, and then we always use $(v, \tilde{v}, x)$ to represent the current update state of the system. Further, we get the global form of asynchronous algorithm, i.e.,

$$z_{k+1} = z_k + E_{k+1}\left(Tz_k - z_k\right). \tag{2.37}$$

2.4 Convergence Analysis

In this section, the convergence results of S-DPDS and A-DPDS algorithms are presented. We first use the following lemmas to establish the convergence of S-DPDS algorithm.

Lemma 2.8 *Supposing that Assumptions 2.1 and 2.2 hold, then there exist the following inequalities:*

$$\|v_{k+1} - v^*\|_{\mathbf{H}}^2 \leq \|v_k - v^*\|_{\mathbf{H}}^2 - \|v_{k+1} - v_k\|_{\mathbf{H}}^2 + 2(v_{k+1} - v^*)^\top \mathbf{HB}(y_{k+1} - x^*), \tag{2.38}$$

$$\|\tilde{v}_{k+1} - \tilde{v}^*\|_{\tilde{\mathbf{H}}}^2 \leq \|\tilde{v}_k - \tilde{v}^*\|_{\tilde{\mathbf{H}}}^2 - \|\tilde{v}_{k+1} - \tilde{v}_k\|_{\tilde{\mathbf{H}}}^2 + 2(\tilde{v}_{k+1} - \tilde{v}^*)^\top \tilde{\mathbf{H}N}(y_{k+1} - x^*). \tag{2.39}$$

$$\begin{aligned}\left\|x_{k+1} - x^*\right\|_{\Sigma^{-1}}^2 \leq& \left\|x_k - x^*\right\|_{\Sigma^{-1}}^2 - \|x_{k+1} - y_{k+1}\|_{\Sigma^{-1}}^2 - \|x_k - y_{k+1}\|_{\Sigma^{-1}}^2 \\ &+ 2(x_{k+1} - y_{k+1})^{\mathrm{T}} \Sigma^{-1} \left(\Sigma \nabla f(x_k) + (\mathrm{H}B)^{\mathrm{T}} v_k + (\tilde{\mathrm{H}}N)^{\mathrm{T}} \tilde{v}_k\right) \\ &- 2\left(x_{k+1} - x^*\right)^{\mathrm{T}} \Sigma^{-1} \left(\Sigma \nabla f(x_k) + (\mathrm{H}B)^{\mathrm{T}} v_{k+1} + (\tilde{\mathrm{H}}N)^{\mathrm{T}} \tilde{v}_{k+1}\right) \\ &+ 2\left(g\left(x^*\right) - g\left(y_{k+1}\right)\right).\end{aligned} \tag{2.40}$$

Proof To prove that (2.38) holds, we apply the firmly nonexpansive property of $I - \mathrm{prox}_{\Gamma^{-1}h}$, (2.28b), and (2.23) to obtain

$$\left\|v_{k+1} - v^*\right\|_{\mathrm{H}}^2 \leq \left(v_{k+1} - v^*\right)^{\mathrm{T}} \mathrm{H}\left(\left(B y_{k+1} + v_k\right) - \left(B x^* + v^*\right)\right). \tag{2.41}$$

It is further concluded that

$$\left(v_{k+1} - v^*\right)^{\mathrm{T}} \mathrm{H}\left(v_{k+1} - v_k\right) \leq \left(v_{k+1} - v^*\right)^{\mathrm{T}} \mathrm{H}B\left(y_{k+1} - x^*\right). \tag{2.42}$$

Combining the results above and (2.72), we have

$$\begin{aligned}&\left\|v_{k+1} - v^*\right\|_{\mathrm{H}}^2 \\ =& \left\|v_k - v^*\right\|_{\mathrm{H}}^2 - \|v_{k+1} - v_k\|_{\mathrm{H}}^2 + 2\left(v_{k+1} - v^*\right)^{\mathrm{T}} \mathrm{H}\left(v_{k+1} - v_k\right) \\ \leq& \left\|v_k - v^*\right\|_{\mathrm{H}}^2 - \|v_{k+1} - v_k\|_{\mathrm{H}}^2 + 2\left(v_{k+1} - v^*\right)^{\mathrm{T}} \mathrm{H}B\left(y_{k+1} - x^*\right).\end{aligned} \tag{2.43}$$

Similarly, by combining (2.28c) and (2.24), we can get (2.39). Next, we prove (2.40). Using (2.6) for (2.28d) yields

$$\Sigma^{-1}\left(x_k - \Sigma \nabla f(x_k) - (\mathrm{H}B)^{\mathrm{T}} v_{k+1} - (\tilde{\mathrm{H}}N)^{\mathrm{T}} \tilde{v}_{k+1} - x_{k+1}\right) \in \partial g(x_{k+1}). \tag{2.44}$$

By applying the subdifferential property (2.4), we have

$$\left(x^* - x_{k+1}\right)^\top \varSigma^{-1} \begin{pmatrix} x_k - \varSigma\nabla f(x_k) \\ -(HB)^\top v_{k+1} - (\tilde{H}\mathrm{N})^\top \tilde{v}_{k+1} - x_{k+1} \end{pmatrix}$$

$$\leq g(x^*) - g(x_{k+1}). \tag{2.45}$$

which implies

$$\begin{aligned}
&(x_{k+1} - x^*)^\mathrm{T} \varSigma^{-1}(x_{k+1} - x_k) \\
\leq &- (x_{k+1} - x^*)^\mathrm{T} \varSigma^{-1} \left(\varSigma\nabla f(x_k) + (\mathrm{H}B)^\mathrm{T} v_{k+1} + (\tilde{\mathrm{H}}N)^\mathrm{T} \tilde{v}_{k+1}\right) \\
&+ g(x^*) - g(x_{k+1}).
\end{aligned} \tag{2.46}$$

Meanwhile, we have

$$\begin{aligned}
\left\|x_{k+1} - x^*\right\|^2_{\varSigma^{-1}} =& \|x_k - x^*\|^2_{\varSigma^{-1}} - \|x_{k+1} - x_k\|^2_{\varSigma^{-1}} \\
&+ 2\left(x_{k+1} - x^*\right)^\mathrm{T} \varSigma^{-1}(x_{k+1} - x_k)\,.
\end{aligned} \tag{2.47}$$

Similar to the derivation of (2.46), for (2.28a), we get

$$\begin{aligned}
&(x_{k+1} - y_{k+1})^\mathrm{T} \varSigma^{-1}(x_k - y_{k+1}) \\
\leq &(x_{k+1} - y_{k+1})^\mathrm{T} \varSigma^{-1} \left(\varSigma\nabla f(x_k) + (\mathrm{H}B)^\mathrm{T} v_k + (\tilde{\mathrm{H}}N)^\mathrm{T} \tilde{v}_k\right) \\
&+ g(x_{k+1}) - g(y_{k+1}).
\end{aligned} \tag{2.48}$$

Therefore, one has

$$\begin{aligned}
&- \|x_{k+1} - x_k\|^2_{\varSigma^{-1}} \\
= &- \|x_{k+1} - y_{k+1}\|^2_{\varSigma^{-1}} - \|x_k - y_{k+1}\|^2_{\varSigma^{-1}} \\
&+ 2(x_{k+1} - y_{k+1})^\mathrm{T} \varSigma^{-1}(x_k - y_{k+1}) \\
\leq &- \|x_{k+1} - y_{k+1}\|^2_{\varSigma^{-1}} - \|x_k - y_{k+1}\|^2_{\varSigma^{-1}} \\
&+ 2\left[g(x_{k+1}) - g(y_{k+1})\right] \\
&+ 2(x_{k+1} - y_{k+1})^\mathrm{T} \varSigma^{-1} \left(\varSigma\nabla f(x_k) + (\mathrm{H}B)^\mathrm{T} v_k + (\tilde{\mathrm{H}}N)^\mathrm{T} \tilde{v}_k\right).
\end{aligned} \tag{2.49}$$

Taking the two inequalities above back to (2.47), we get(2.40). ■

Lemma 2.9 *Suppose that Assumptions 2.1 and 2.2 hold. For* $z = (v, \tilde{v}, x)$, *we have*

$$
\begin{aligned}
&\left\| z_{k+1} - z^* \right\|_P^2 \\
&\leq \left\| z_k - z^* \right\|_P^2 - \| v_{k+1} - v_k \|^2_{\mathrm{H}\left(I - BU_1 \Sigma \Sigma^{\mathrm{T}} (\mathrm{H}B)^{\mathrm{T}}\right)} \\
&\quad - \| \tilde{v}_{k+1} - \tilde{v}_k \|^2_{\tilde{\mathrm{H}}\left(I - NU_2 \Sigma \Sigma^{\mathrm{T}} (\tilde{\mathrm{H}}N)^{\mathrm{T}}\right)} \\
&\quad - \left\| \begin{matrix} (x_{k+1} - y_{k+1}) + (\mathrm{H}B\Sigma)^{\mathrm{T}} (v_{k+1} - v_k) \\ + (\tilde{\mathrm{H}}N\Sigma)^{\mathrm{T}} (\tilde{v}_{k+1} - \tilde{v}_k) \end{matrix} \right\|^2_{\Sigma^{-1}} \\
&\quad - \left\| x_k - y_{k+1} - \left(\Sigma \nabla f(x_k) - \Sigma \nabla f(x^*) \right) \right\|^2_{\Sigma^{-1}} \\
&\quad - \left\| \nabla f(x_k) - \nabla f(x^*) \right\|^2_{2\beta - \Sigma},
\end{aligned}
\tag{2.50}
$$

where $P = \text{blkdiag}\{\mathrm{H}, \tilde{\mathrm{H}}, \Sigma^{-1}\}$ *is positive definite,* $U_1 = \text{blkdiag}\{(1 + (1/\mu_i)) I_{n_i}\}_{i \in \mathcal{V}}$, *and* $U_2 = \text{blkdiag}\left\{(1 + \mu_i) I_{n_i}\right\}_{i \in \mathcal{V}}$.

Proof Summing (2.38), (2.39), and (2.40), and rearranging the terms get

$$
\begin{aligned}
&\left\| x_{k+1} - x^* \right\|^2_{\Sigma^{-1}} + \left\| \tilde{v}_{k+1} - \tilde{v}^* \right\|^2_{\tilde{\mathrm{H}}} + \left\| v_{k+1} - v^* \right\|^2_{\mathrm{H}} \\
&\leq \left\| v_k - v^* \right\|^2_{\mathrm{H}} + \left\| \tilde{v}_k - \tilde{v}^* \right\|^2_{\tilde{\mathrm{H}}} + \left\| x_k - x^* \right\|^2_{\Sigma^{-1}} - \| v_{k+1} - v_k \|^2_{\mathrm{H}} \\
&\quad - \| \tilde{v}_{k+1} - \tilde{v}_k \|^2_{\tilde{\mathrm{H}}} - \| x_{k+1} - y_{k+1} \|^2_{\Sigma^{-1}} - \| x_k - y_{k+1} \|^2_{\Sigma^{-1}} \\
&\quad + 2 \begin{pmatrix} (v_{k+1} - v^*)^{\mathrm{T}} (\mathrm{H}B\Sigma) \\ + (\tilde{v}_{k+1} - \tilde{v}^*)^{\mathrm{T}} (\tilde{\mathrm{H}}N\Sigma) \end{pmatrix} \Sigma^{-1} (y_{k+1} - x_{k+1}) \\
&\quad + 2 (x_k - y_{k+1})^{\mathrm{T}} \Sigma^{-1} \left(\Sigma \nabla f(x_k) - \Sigma \nabla f(x^*) \right) \\
&\quad - 2 \left(x_k - x^* \right)^{\mathrm{T}} \Sigma^{-1} \left(\Sigma \nabla f(x_k) - \Sigma \nabla f(x^*) \right) \\
&\quad + 2 \begin{pmatrix} \begin{pmatrix} -\Sigma \nabla f(x^*) \\ -(\mathrm{H}B)^{\mathrm{T}} v^* - (\tilde{\mathrm{H}}N)^{\mathrm{T}} \tilde{v}^* \end{pmatrix}^{\mathrm{T}} \Sigma^{-1} (y_{k+1} - x^*) \\ + g(x^*) - g(y_{k+1}) \end{pmatrix} \\
&= \left\| v_k - v^* \right\|^2_{\mathrm{H}} + \left\| \tilde{v}_k - \tilde{v}^* \right\|^2_{\tilde{\mathrm{H}}} + \left\| x_k - x^* \right\|^2_{\Sigma^{-1}} - \| v_{k+1} - v_k \|^2_{\mathrm{H}} \\
&\quad - \| \tilde{v}_{k+1} - \tilde{v}_k \|^2_{\tilde{\mathrm{H}}} - \| x_{k+1} - y_{k+1} \|^2_{\Sigma^{-1}} - \| x_k - y_{k+1} \|^2_{\Sigma^{-1}} \\
&\quad + \left\| \begin{matrix} (\mathrm{H}B\Sigma)^{\mathrm{T}} (v_{k+1} - v_k) \\ + (\tilde{\mathrm{H}}N\Sigma)^{\mathrm{T}} (\tilde{v}_{k+1} - \tilde{v}_k) \end{matrix} \right\|^2_{\Sigma^{-1}} + \| y_{k+1} - x_{k+1} \|^2_{\Sigma^{-1}} \\
&\quad - \left\| y_{k+1} - x_{k+1} - (\mathrm{H}B\Sigma)^{\mathrm{T}} (v_{k+1} - v_k) - (\tilde{\mathrm{H}}N\Sigma)^{\mathrm{T}} (\tilde{v}_{k+1} - \tilde{v}_k) \right\|^2_{\Sigma^{-1}}
\end{aligned}
$$

$$
\begin{aligned}
&+\|x_k-y_{k+1}\|_{\Sigma^{-1}}^2+\left\|\Sigma\nabla f(x_k)-\Sigma\nabla f\left(x^*\right)\right\|_{\Sigma^{-1}}^2\\
&-\left\|x_k-y_{k+1}-\left(\Sigma\nabla f(x_k)-\Sigma\nabla f\left(x^*\right)\right)\right\|_{\Sigma^{-1}}^2\\
&-2\left(x_k-x^*\right)^{\mathrm{T}}\left(\nabla f(x_k)-\nabla f\left(x^*\right)\right)\\
&+2\left(\begin{pmatrix}-\Sigma\nabla f(x^*)\\-(\mathrm{H}B)^{\mathrm{T}}v^*-(\tilde{\mathrm{H}}N)^{\mathrm{T}}\tilde{v}^*\end{pmatrix}^{\mathrm{T}}\Sigma^{-1}(y_{k+1}-x^*)\atop +g(x^*)-g(y_{k+1})\right).
\end{aligned}\tag{2.51}
$$

Combining (2.25) with (2.6) yields

$$\Sigma^{-1}\left(-\Sigma\nabla f\left(x^*\right)-(\mathrm{H}B)^{\mathrm{T}}v^*-(\tilde{\mathrm{H}}N)^{\mathrm{T}}\tilde{v}^*\right)\in\partial g\left(x^*\right).\tag{2.52}$$

Applying the property of subdifferential, we obtain

$$\left(y_{k+1}-x^*\right)^{\mathrm{T}}\Sigma^{-1}\begin{pmatrix}-\Sigma\nabla f(x^*)\\-(\mathrm{H}B)^{\mathrm{T}}v^*\\-(\tilde{\mathrm{H}}N)^{\mathrm{T}}\tilde{v}^*\end{pmatrix}+\left(g\left(x^*\right)-g\left(y_{k+1}\right)\right)\leq 0.\tag{2.53}$$

On the other hand, combining the Assumption 2.2(i) and Definition 2.1, so we get

$$-\left(\nabla f(x_k)-\nabla f\left(x^*\right)\right)^{\mathrm{T}}\left(x_k-x^*\right)\leq-\left\|\nabla f(x_k)-\nabla f\left(x^*\right)\right\|_{\boldsymbol{\beta}}^2,\tag{2.54}$$

where $\boldsymbol{\beta}=\text{blkdiag}\{\beta_i I_{n_i}\}_{i\in\mathcal{V}}$. For $||(\mathrm{H}B\Sigma)^{\mathrm{T}}(v_{k+1}-v_k)+(\tilde{\mathrm{H}}N\Sigma)^{\mathrm{T}}(\tilde{v}_{k+1}-\tilde{v}_k)||_{\Sigma^{-1}}^2$ by using the inequality $\|a_i+b_i\|^2\leq(1+(1/\mu_i))\|a_i\|^2+(1+\mu_i)\|b_i\|^2$ for $\mu_i>0$ and any $a_i,\ b_i\in\mathbb{R}^{n_i}$, we can obtain (2.50). ■

Lemma 2.10 *Suppose that Assumptions 2.1–2.3 hold. The sequence* $\{||z_k-z^*||_P^2\}$ *is non-increasing and* $\lim_{k\to\infty}\|z_{k+1}-z_k\|_P^2=0$.

Proof We can easily conclude that $\{||z_k-z^*||_P^2\}$ is non-increasing if Assumption 2.3 holds. Summing (2.50) over k from 0 to n to get

$$
\begin{aligned}
&\left\|z_{n+1}-z^*\right\|_P^2\\
\leq&\left\|z_0-z^*\right\|_P^2-\sum_{k=0}^{n}\|v_{k+1}-v_k\|_{\mathrm{H}\left(I-BU_1\Sigma\Sigma^{\mathrm{T}}(\mathrm{H}B)^{\mathrm{T}}\right)}^2\\
&-\sum_{k=0}^{n}\|\tilde{v}_{k+1}-\tilde{v}_k\|_{\tilde{\mathrm{H}}\left(I-NU_2\Sigma\Sigma^{\mathrm{T}}(\tilde{\mathrm{H}}N)^{\mathrm{T}}\right)}^2\\
&-\sum_{k=0}^{n}\left\|\begin{matrix}(x_{k+1}-y_{k+1})+(\mathrm{H}B\Sigma)^{\mathrm{T}}(v_{k+1}-v_k)\\+(\tilde{\mathrm{H}}N\Sigma)^{\mathrm{T}}(\tilde{v}_{k+1}-\tilde{v}_k)\end{matrix}\right\|_{\Sigma^{-1}}^2
\end{aligned}\tag{2.55}
$$

$$
\begin{aligned}
&-\sum_{k=0}^{n}\left\|x_k-y_{k+1}-\left(\Sigma\nabla f\left(x_k\right)-\Sigma\nabla f\left(x^*\right)\right)\right\|_{\Sigma^{-1}}^2\\
&-\sum_{k=0}^{n}\left\|\nabla f\left(x_k\right)-\nabla f\left(x^*\right)\right\|_{2\beta-\Sigma}^2.
\end{aligned}
$$

By letting n to infinity, we infer that if there is at least one term tending to infinity in the summation terms of the above inequality, then the right side of the inequality tends to negative infinity, and because the non-negative norm $\|z_{n+1}-z^*\|_P^2$ will not be less than or equal to negative infinity, we know that none of the terms tending to infinity on the right side of the inequality exist, that means,

$$
\sum_{k=0}^{\infty}\|v_{k+1}-v_k\|_{\mathrm{H}\left(I-BU_1\Sigma\Sigma^{\mathrm{T}}(\mathrm{H}B)^{\mathrm{T}}\right)}<\infty, \tag{2.56}
$$

$$
\sum_{k=0}^{\infty}\|\tilde{v}_{k+1}-\tilde{v}_k\|_{\tilde{\mathrm{H}}\left(I-NU_2\Sigma\Sigma^{\mathrm{T}}(\tilde{\mathrm{H}}N)^{\mathrm{T}}\right)}<\infty, \tag{2.57}
$$

$$
\sum_{k=0}^{\infty}\left\|\begin{array}{l}(x_{k+1}-y_{k+1})+(\mathrm{H}B\Sigma)^{\mathrm{T}}(v_{k+1}-v_k)\\+(\tilde{\mathrm{H}}N\Sigma)^{\mathrm{T}}(\tilde{v}_{k+1}-\tilde{v}_k)\end{array}\right\|<\infty, \tag{2.58}
$$

$$
\sum_{k=0}^{\infty}\left\|x_k-y_{k+1}-\left(\Sigma\nabla f\left(x_k\right)-\Sigma\nabla f\left(x^*\right)\right)\right\|<\infty, \tag{2.59}
$$

$$
\sum_{k=0}^{\infty}\left\|\nabla f\left(x_k\right)-\nabla f\left(x^*\right)\right\|<\infty. \tag{2.60}
$$

Thus, we get

$$
\lim_{k\to\infty}\|v_{k+1}-v_k\|_{\mathrm{H}\left(I-BU_1\Sigma\Sigma^{\mathrm{T}}(\mathrm{H}B)^{\mathrm{T}}\right)}=0, \tag{2.61}
$$

$$
\lim_{k\to\infty}\|\tilde{v}_{k+1}-\tilde{v}_k\|_{\tilde{\mathrm{H}}\left(I-NU_2\Sigma\Sigma^{\mathrm{T}}(\tilde{\mathrm{H}}N)^{\mathrm{T}}\right)}=0, \tag{2.62}
$$

$$
\lim_{k\to\infty}\left\|\begin{array}{l}(x_{k+1}-y_{k+1})+(\mathrm{H}B\Sigma)^{\mathrm{T}}(v_{k+1}-v_k)\\+(\tilde{\mathrm{H}}N\Sigma)^{\mathrm{T}}(\tilde{v}_{k+1}-\tilde{v}_k)\end{array}\right\|=0, \tag{2.63}
$$

$$
\lim_{k\to\infty}\left\|x_k-y_{k+1}-\left(\Sigma\nabla f\left(x_k\right)-\Sigma\nabla f\left(x^*\right)\right)\right\|=0, \tag{2.64}
$$

$$
\lim_{k\to\infty}\left\|\nabla f\left(x_k\right)-\nabla f\left(x^*\right)\right\|=0. \tag{2.65}
$$

From (2.64) and (2.65), we have

$$
\lim_{k\to\infty}\|x_k-y_{k+1}\|=0. \tag{2.66}
$$

Meanwhile, $I{-}BU_1\Sigma\Sigma^{\mathrm{T}}(\mathrm{H}B)^{\mathrm{T}}$ and $I{-}NU_2\Sigma\Sigma^{\mathrm{T}}(\tilde{\mathrm{H}}N)^{\mathrm{T}}$ are symmetric positive definite under Assumption 2.3. Therefore, (2.61) and (2.62) imply that

$$\lim_{k\to\infty}\|v_{k+1}-v_k\|=0,\ \lim_{k\to\infty}\|\tilde{v}_{k+1}-\tilde{v}_k\|=0. \tag{2.67}$$

Combine (2.63) with (2.67) to obtain $\lim_{k\to\infty}\|x_{k+1}-y_{k+1}\|=0$. Therefore, from (2.66) and the above equality, we have

$$\lim_{k\to\infty}\|x_{k+1}-x_k\|^2=0. \tag{2.68}$$

Finally, (2.67) and (2.68) yield that $\lim_{k\to\infty}\|z_{k+1}-z_k\|^2=0$. ■

According to Lemmas 2.4 and 2.10, we get the following theorem that establishes the convergence for Algorithm 1.

Theorem 2.11 *Supposing that Assumptions 2.1 and 2.3 hold, we have that* $\{z_k\}$ *converges to a fixed point of* T*, and* $\{x_k\}$ *converges to a solution to* (2.7).

Proof The operator T is continuous because it is nonexpansive. Meanwhile, the result of Lemma 2.10 shows that the sequence $\left\{||z_k-z^*||_P^2\right\}$ is non-increasing and $\lim_{k\to\infty}\|z_{k+1}-z_k\|_P^2=0$. Applying Lemma 2.4, we conclude that the sequence $\{z_k\}$ converges to a fixed point of the operator T. Then based on Lemma 2.6, we can get that $\{x_k\}$ converges to a solution to (2.7). ■

We give the convergence results of asynchronous algorithm in the following theorem.

Theorem 2.12 *Supposing that Assumptions 2.1 and 2.4 hold, the sequence* $\{z_k\}_{k\geq k_0}$, $k_0\in\mathbb{N}$, *generated by Algorithm 2 is* $\Pi^{-1}P$ *stochastic Fejér monotonicity [24, Th. 2.5] relative to the solution set* $\mathcal{S}$*, i.e.,*

$$\begin{aligned}&\mathbb{E}\left[\left\|z_{k+1}-z^*\right\|_{\Pi^{-1}P}^2\right]\\&\leq\left\|z_k-z^*\right\|_{\Pi^{-1}P}^2-\|v_{k+1}-v_k\|_{\mathrm{H}(I-BU_1\Sigma\Sigma^{\mathrm{T}}(\mathrm{H}B)^{\mathrm{T}})}^2\\&\quad-\|\tilde{v}_{k+1}-\tilde{v}_k\|_{\tilde{\mathrm{H}}\left(I-NU_2\Sigma\Sigma^{\mathrm{T}}(\tilde{\mathrm{H}}N)^{\mathrm{T}}\right)}^2-\left\|\nabla f\left(x_k\right)-\nabla f\left(x^*\right)\right\|_{2\boldsymbol{\beta}-\Sigma}^2.\end{aligned} \tag{2.69}$$

Therefore, the sequence $\{z_k\}_{k\geq k_0}$, $k_0\in\mathbb{N}$, *converges almost surely to some* $z^*\in\mathcal{S}$.

Proof According to the definition of ξ^k, we have

$$\begin{aligned}\mathbb{E}\circ(E_{k+1})&=\sum_{\varepsilon\in\phi}\left(\xi^{k+1}=\varepsilon\right)\sum_{j=1}^m\xi_j\boldsymbol{P}_j=\sum_{j=1}^m\sum_{\varepsilon\in\phi}\left(\xi^{k+1}=\varepsilon\right)\varepsilon_j\boldsymbol{P}_j\\&=\sum_{j=1}^m\sum_{\varepsilon\in\phi,\varepsilon_j=1}\left(\xi^{k+1}=\varepsilon\right)\boldsymbol{P}_j=\sum_{j=1}^m p_j\boldsymbol{P}_j=\Pi.\end{aligned} \tag{2.70}$$

Meanwhile, E_k is a diagonal matrix with diagonal elements are 0 or 1, thus E_k is self-adjoint and idempotent. Combining with the above results, for asynchronous algorithm (2.37), we get

$$\begin{aligned}
&\mathbb{E}\left[\left\|z_{k+1}-z^*\right\|_{\Pi^{-1}P}^2\right]\\
=&\mathbb{E}\left[\left\|z_k+E_{k+1}\left(Tz_k-z_k\right)-z^*\right\|_{\Pi^{-1}P}^2\right]\\
=&\mathbb{E}\left[\begin{array}{l}\|z_k-z^*\|_{\Pi^{-1}P}^2+\|E_{k+1}\left(Tz_k-z_k\right)\|_{\Pi^{-1}P}^2\\ +2(z_k-z^*)^{\mathrm{T}}\Pi^{-1}P\left(E_{k+1}\left(Tz_k-z_k\right)\right)\end{array}\right]\\
=&\left\|z_k-z^*\right\|_{\Pi^{-1}P}^2+\|Tz_k-z_k\|_P^2+2\left(z_k-z^*\right)^{\mathrm{T}}P(Tz_k-z_k)\,.
\end{aligned} \tag{2.71}$$

For $a,\ b,\ c\in\mathbb{R}^{n+r+l}$ and a positive definite matrix $\mathrm{K}\in\mathbb{R}^{(n+r+l)\times(n+r+l)}$, there holds that

$$2(a-b)^{\mathrm{T}}\mathrm{K}\,(c-b)=\|c-b\|_{\mathrm{K}}^2+\|a-b\|_{\mathrm{K}}^2-\|a-c\|_{\mathrm{K}}^2\,, \tag{2.72}$$

then according to Lemma 2.9, we can derive

$$\begin{aligned}
&\mathbb{E}\left[\left\|z_{k+1}-z^*\right\|_{\Pi^{-1}P}^2\right]\\
=&\left\|z_k-z^*\right\|_{\Pi^{-1}P}^2+\left\|Tz_k-z^*\right\|_P^2-\left\|z_k-z^*\right\|_P^2\\
\le&\left\|z_k-z^*\right\|_{\Pi^{-1}P}^2-\|v_{k+1}-v_k\|_{\mathrm{H}\left(I-BU_1\Sigma\Sigma^{\mathrm{T}}(\mathrm{H}B)^{\mathrm{T}}\right)}^2\\
&-\|\tilde{v}_{k+1}-\tilde{v}_k\|_{\tilde{\mathrm{H}}\left(I-NU_2\Sigma\Sigma^{\mathrm{T}}(\tilde{\mathrm{H}}N)^{\mathrm{T}}\right)}^2-\left\|\nabla f\left(x_k\right)-\nabla f\left(x^*\right)\right\|_{2\boldsymbol{\beta}-\Sigma}^2\,.
\end{aligned} \tag{2.73}$$

Therefore, under Assumption 2.3, we can know that the sequence generated by inequality (2.69) is stochastic Fejér monotonicity. Due to the space limitation, we can refer to [23, Th. 3] for the remaining proof process. ■

2.5 Numerical Experiments

This section provides the performance evaluation of Algorithms 1 and 2 by solving the following quadratic programming problem:

$$\begin{aligned}
&\min_{x_1,\ldots,x_m}\sum_{i=1}^{m}f_i\left(x_i\right)=x_i^{\mathrm{T}}Q_ix_i+w_i^{\mathrm{T}}x_i,\\
&\text{s.t.}\ \ a_i^{\mathrm{T}}x_i\le d_i,\quad i=1,\ldots,m,
\end{aligned} \tag{2.74}$$

$$x_i^m \le x_i \le x_i^M, \quad i = 1, \ldots, m,$$
$$A_{ij} x_i + A_{ji} x_j = b_{(i,j)}, \quad i = 1, \ldots, m, \ (i,j) \in \mathcal{E},$$

where the network model is a connected graph with five agents, $x_i \in \mathbb{R}^2$ is decision variable, the elements in diagonal matrix $Q_i \in \mathbb{R}^{2\times 2}$ and $w_i \in \mathbb{R}^2$ are uniformly randomly distributed in $[1, 3]$ and $[-5, 5]$, respectively. In the inequality constraint $a_i^{\mathrm{T}} x_i \le d_i$, components of a_i are generated uniformly in $[0, 10]$ and components of d_i in $[-5, 5]$. We define the set $X_i = \left\{ e \in \mathbb{R}^2 \left| x_i^m \le e \le x_i^M \right. \right\}$ to represent the box constraint of each agent, where components of x_i^m are generated uniformly in $[-8, -5]$ and components of x_i^M in $[5, 8]$. Meanwhile, we let $A_{ij} = I$ when $i < j$, $A_{ij} = -I$ when $i > j$, and $b_{(i,j)} = 0$ for $j \in \mathcal{N}_i$.

Similar to the derivation of (2.10), by defining $\mathcal{D}_i = \left\{ e \left| a_i^{\mathrm{T}} e \le d_i \right. \right\}$, indicator function $\delta_{\mathcal{D}_i}(I_i x_i)$ and $\delta_{X_i}(x_i)$, we can obtain the following equivalent form of (2.74):

$$\min_{x_i \in \mathbb{R}^2} \sum_{i=1}^{m} f_i(x_i) + \delta_{X_i}(x_i) + \delta_{D_i}(I_i x_i) + \sum_{i=1}^{m} \sum_{(i,j)\in\mathcal{E}} \delta_{C_{(i,j)}}\left(N_{(i,j)} x\right), \tag{2.75}$$

therefore, we can use S-DPDS and A-DPDS algorithms to solve the problem (2.74). In Fig. 2.1, we compare Algorithm 1 with Algorithm 2 under different activation probability p_i, mainly by describing the optimality gap $(1/m) \sum_{i=1}^{m} \left\| x_i^k - x^* \right\|$ of the algorithms versus the number of iterations. Figure 2.2 depicts the performance comparison of some existing algorithms that can solve quadratic programming problem (2.74) from the perspective of multi-block composition. Among them, DPGA-W [25] is an algorithm based on ADMM and combined with the weight matrix of edges. For different algorithms, we try to tune its step sizes to make its performance as optimal as possible. The final results prove that our algorithms have better performance than other algorithms.

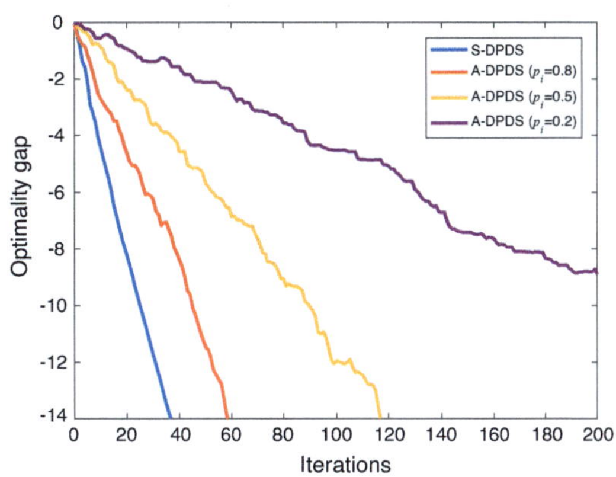

Fig. 2.1 Performance comparison of S-DPDS and A-DPDS algorithms with $p_i = 0.8, 0.5, 0.2$ respectively

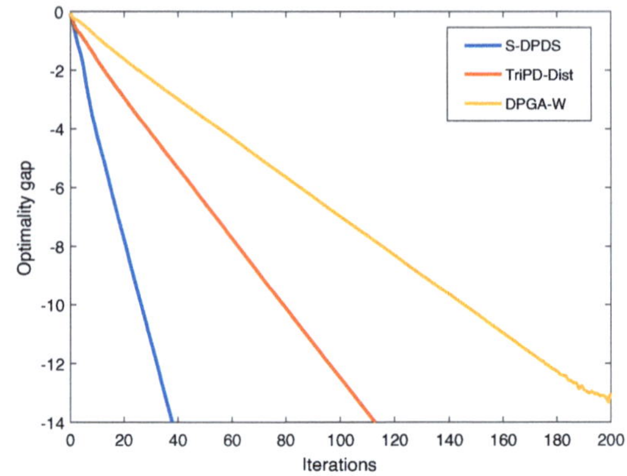

Fig. 2.2 Performance comparison between S-DPDS and other distributed composite optimization algorithms

2.6 Conclusion

This chapter has developed two distributed primal-dual splitting algorithms, S-DPDS and A-DPDS, to deal with structural optimization model. The two algorithms are fully distributed algorithms because of the consideration of uncoordinated parameters. We also has used the algorithms to solve a quadratic programming problem, and compared them other similar algorithms to verify the efficiency of our algorithms.

Chapter 3
Distributed Primal-Dual Fixed Point Algorithm for Multi-Block Separable Optimization

Abstract This chapter considers distributed optimization by a group of agents over an undirected network. The objective is to minimize the sum of a twice differentiable convex function and two possibly nonsmooth convex functions, one of which is composed of a bounded linear operator. A novel distributed primal-dual fixed point algorithm is proposed based on an adapted metric method, which exploits the second-order information of the differentiable convex function. Further, by incorporating a randomized coordinate activation mechanism, we propose a randomized asynchronous iterative distributed algorithm that allows each agent to randomly and independently decide whether to perform an update or remain unchanged at each iteration, and thus alleviates the communication cost. Moreover, the proposed algorithms adopt non-identical step sizes to endow each agent with more independence. Numerical simulation results substantiate the feasibility of the proposed algorithms and the correctness of the theoretical results.

Keywords Adapted metric method · Completely distributed · Primal-dual fixed point algorithm · Nonsmooth convex function · Randomized asynchronous iterative

3.1 Introduction

In this chapter, we keep focusing on solving the multi-block separable optimization problem in Chap. 1. To reiterate, the problem is shown as follows:

$$\min_{x \in \mathbb{R}^n} \quad f(x) + g(x) + h(Bx), \tag{3.1}$$

where functions f, g, and h are three properly closed convex functions (g and h may be nonsmooth), and B is a bounded linear mapping. The proximal mappings associated with h and g are efficiently computable [29]. The wide application of problem (3.1) involves machine learning, image reconstruction, and signal processing. Here, we give some examples. A popular example of problem (3.1)

H. Li et al., *Network-System Research and Distributed Composite Algorithm Design*, Computational Intelligence Methods and Applications,
https://doi.org/10.1007/978-981-95-0911-9_3

lies in the fused lasso problem [3, 26] that contains a ℓ_1 regularization and a penalty term. The optimization problem is formulated as $\min_{x\in\mathbb{R}^n} \|Cx - c\|^2/2 + \gamma_1\|x\|_1 + \gamma_2\|Bx\|_1$, where $C \in \mathbb{R}^{m\times n}$, $c \in \mathbb{R}^m$, $B \in \mathbb{R}^{(n-1)\times n}$, $\gamma_1 > 0$, and $\gamma_2 > 0$. Another useful example is the image restoration problem with total variation regularization and nonnegative constraint [8]. The optimization problem is $\min_{x\in\mathbb{R}^n} \|Cx - c\|^2/2 + \delta_J(x) + \gamma_1\|Bx\|_1$, where $C \in \mathbb{R}^{m\times n}$ denotes the linear forward projection operator, $c \in \mathbb{R}^m$ denotes the measured data with noise, δ_J denotes the indicator function of the closed convex set J, $\gamma_1 > 0$ denotes the regularization parameter, and B denotes a discrete gradient operator. In distributed optimization, we consider a network of m agents and assume that each agent has access to its own private function of the form (3.1). Then, the distributed form of problem (3.1) can be formulated as

$$\min_{x\in\mathbb{R}^n} \sum_{i=1}^{m} f_i(x) + g_i(x) + h_i(B_i x),$$

where f_i, g_i, and h_i are three properly closed convex functions (g_i and h_i are possible nonsmooth), and B_i is a linear mapping.

In the past decade, several algorithms were developed to address problem (3.1). In the seminal work, Combettes et al. [4] designed a fully splitting algorithm derived from the forward-backward-forward scheme [30]. Then, Condat [5] proposed a primal-dual splitting algorithm based on the classical operator splitting algorithms [31, 32]. Chen et al. [7] employed the ideas in [33, 34] to develop a primal-dual fixed point algorithm. Recently, a three-term splitting algorithm, called asymmetric forward-backward-adjoint splitting algorithm, was presented by [6], which covered [5] as a special case. Yan [8] gave a generalization of both Chambolle-Pock algorithm [35] and proximal alternating predictor-corrector [33], namely the primal-dual three operator splitting algorithm. It has the same range of acceptable parameters as [7] and performs the same complexity in each iteration as [5] and [6].

Furthermore, many efforts have been made to improve these algorithms. Bot et al. [36] introduced the inertial schemes [37, 38] and proposed an inertial primal-dual splitting algorithm that could accelerate the algorithm in [4]. To achieve an acceleration of [5], Li et al. [39] adopted the Quasi-Newton and the over-relaxation strategies. In addition, Wen et al. [40] designed a preconditioned version of [5], which was also a generalization of [41]. Utilizing appropriate quadratic approximation on the objective function, Tang et al. [42] developed a primal-dual fixed point algorithm (PDFP_AM) in a way reminiscent of Quasi-Newton methods [43–45]. The PDFP_AM algorithm can be viewed as an extension of [7] with an adapted metric method [43], where an appropriate approximation of the second derivative of f is employed to replace a step parameter in the gradient descent step.

For the algorithms [4–8, 36, 39, 40, 42], we have to accept the fact that they are limited to solving problem (3.1) in a centralized fashion, where the data related to the local private information needs to be transmitted to the central coordinator. From the aspect of practical applications, exploring distributed versions of these algorithms is worthy of studying, since a distributed structure has superiorities in scalability, robustness, and privacy protection compared with its centralized counterparts. In the existing works, distributed methods in dealing with problems similar to (3.1) have been well developed. In the distributed framework, methods are aimed to solve the optimization problem $\min_{x\in\mathbb{R}^n} \sum_{i=1}^{m} F_i(x)$ over a network of m agents, and each agent $i \in \{1, \cdots, m\}$ has access to its own local objective function F_i. To solve this problem, Nedic et al. [9] proposed a distributed subgradient method, and Duchi et al. [11] extended [9] to the projected one based on dual averaging of subgradients. Subsequent works have investigated variations considering acceleration [10], in time-varying networks [46, 47], and in stochastic setting [48]. Shi et al. [49] proposed a novel method (EXTRA) with a cumulative correction term in the iteration of distributed gradient descent, which can linearly converge to the exact solution of the problem with a constant step size. To avoid the uncoordinated execution of distributed algorithms due to the lack of global clocks, some asynchronous works [12, 50, 51] have also been well developed. Parikh et al. [52] focused on a composite formulation of F_i, i.e., $F_i = S_i + R_i$, and given a general method for solving this problem. However, due to a central agent is needed at each iteration to accumulate the value of the agents' variables, the algorithm in [52] can only be viewed as a parallel algorithm rather than a distributed one. Based on the idea of [5], Bianchi et al. [53] proposed a distributed primal-dual algorithm and presented its application to distributed optimization. Taking the advantages of proximal operations for the nonsmooth terms, Shi et al. [54] extended EXTRA [49] to deal with the problem of composite nonsmooth optimization, and established an improved convergence. Similarly, Li et al. [18] proposed NIDS algorithm by combining EXTRA [49] and proximal operations, which achieved the same convergence as [54] and could employ a larger step size. Recently, some advances have been made to deal with problem (3.1) in a distributed manner. By studying the distributed form of problem (3.1) and introducing equality constraints, Latafat et al. [17] exploited fully distributed synchronous and asynchronous algorithms, and achieved linear convergence rates under the condition that the local objective functions are quadratic growth or piecewise linear-quadratic.

Notice that the primal variable in [17] was updated by a gradient descent step. For distributed gradient-based algorithms, although several novel works [55, 56] have been shown to converge linearly, their convergence rates are slow when there is a large spread in eigenvalues of the function's Hessian matrix [57, 60]. This issue can be corrected in the centralized optimization by using the Newton step that incorporates the second-order Hessian matrix information into the descent computation. However, this method cannot be directly used in distributed form due to the non-sparse of the inverse of Hessian matrix. Some methods such as the primal-dual algorithms [58, 59], the penalty-based algorithms [60, 61], etc., designed the distributed approximations of Newton steps, and achieved faster convergence than their associated first-order algorithms. Despite the advances in distributed Newton-based methods, it is usually expensive to compute the exact Hessian information [57, 60]. Motivated by this fact, we aim to develop a way reminiscent of Quasi-Newton methods to solve problem (3.1) in a distributed setting. This is done by using the idea of the adapted metric method in [42, 43], where an adequate quadratic form is employed to approximate the objective function. Our contributions are as follows:

(i) Based on the adapted metric method, we design and discuss a new distributed primal-dual fixed point algorithm, termed as D-PDFP_AM, which is a distributed extension of the centralized algorithm in [42]. D-PDFP_AM is completely distributed, where not only the iterations are performed locally, but also the step sizes of each agent are based only on local information. Owning to such a distributed structure, D-PDFP_AM is more practical than the traditional centralized algorithms [4–8, 36, 39, 40, 42] to solve large-scale problems in formation control [62, 63], model predictive control [64, 65], economic dispatch [66, 67], etc.
(ii) Motivated by Latafat et al. [17], a randomized asynchronous iterative distributed primal-dual algorithm based on the randomized coordinate activation mechanism is developed. Unlike the algorithms in [57–60, 62] requiring all agents to be activated per iteration, the execution of the proposed algorithm only wakes up a random subset of agents to perform updates (inactive agents remain unchanged) at each iteration, which removes the requirement of the global clock and effectively reduces the iteration cost.
(iii) Compared with the gradient-based algorithm [17] that only uses the first-order information of the objective function, we incorporate an adapted metric method [42, 43] into the distributed primal-dual fixed point algorithm and can perform better to exploit the second-order information of the differentiable convex function.

3.2 Preliminaries

In this section, we introduce some notations, formulate the distributed constrained optimization problem, and give some necessary definitions and lemmas.

3.2.1 Notation

All vectors are defaulted to be columns. Denote the n-dimensional Euclidean space by $\mathbb{R}^n$. Let $I_n \in \mathbb{R}^{n\times n}$ be the identity matrix and Id be the identity operator. The notation $\mathbb{N}^+$ denotes the set of positive integers. The relative interior of a set A is denoted by ri A. Denote the set of all $l \times l$ positive definite symmetric matrices by $Z_{++}(l)$. Define $\lambda_{\min}(B)$ and $\lambda_{\max}(B)$ as the minimum eigenvalue and the spectral radius of a real symmetric matrix B, respectively. The symbol col $\{(a_i)_{i=1}^m\}$ denotes the column vector composed of vectors $a_1, a_2, \cdots, a_m$. We define $\langle \cdot, \cdot \rangle$, $\|\cdot\|$, and $(\cdot)^{\mathrm{T}}$ as the inner product, the Euclidean norm, and the transpose of a vector or matrix, respectively. For a vector x, its C-weighted norm is defined as $\|x\|_C = \sqrt{\langle x, Cx\rangle}$, where C is a positive definite matrix. For an operator $T : \mathbb{R}^m \to \mathbb{R}^n$ that maps each point $x \in \mathbb{R}^m$ to a subset $Tx \in \mathbb{R}^n$, the resolvent of T is denoted by $(\mathrm{Id} + T)^{-1}$. Let D be a nonempty set. The projector onto D is denoted by $\mathcal{P}_D$, and the indicator function of D is denoted by δ_D, i.e., $\delta_D = 0$ if $d \in D$ and $\delta_D = +\infty$ otherwise. Define $\Gamma_0(\mathbb{R}^n)$ as the collection of all proper, lower semi-continuous functions. Denote $f \in \Gamma_0(\mathbb{R}^n)$. The symbol dom f denotes the domain of f. Then, its subdifferential is denoted by $\partial f : \mathbb{R}^n \to \mathbb{R}^n$, i.e., $\partial f(a) = \{b | \forall c \in \mathbb{R}^n, f(a) + \langle b, c - a\rangle \le f(c)\}$, and the proximity operator of f relative to $\|\cdot\|_V$ is denoted by prox_f^V, i.e., $\mathrm{prox}_f^V(a) = \arg\min_{b \in \mathbb{R}^n}\{f(b) + (1/2)\|a - b\|_V^2\}$, where V is a symmetric positive definite matrix.

3.2.2 Model of Optimization Problem

The underlying communication network is denoted by an undirected network $\mathcal{G} = (\mathcal{V}, \mathcal{E})$, where $\mathcal{V} = \{1, \cdots, m\}$ represents the set of agents and $\mathcal{E} \subseteq \mathcal{V} \times \mathcal{V}$ denotes the set of edges. Denote the neighbors set of agent i by $\mathcal{N}_i = \{j | (i, j) \in \mathcal{E}\}$. Consider a network of m agents. The goal of the agents is to cooperatively solve the following constrained optimization problem:

$$\begin{aligned} \min_{x \in \mathbb{R}^n} \quad & \sum_{i=1}^{m} f_i(x_i) + g_i(x_i) + h_i(B_i x_i), \\ \text{s.t.} \quad & A_{ij} x_i + A_{ji} x_j = b_{(i,j)}, (i, j) \in \mathcal{E}, \end{aligned} \tag{3.2}$$

where $x_i \in \mathbb{R}^{n_i}$, $x = \mathrm{col}\{(x_i)_{i=1}^m\}$, and $n = \sum_{i=1}^m n_i$. The notation (i, j) represents the unordered pair of i and j, and ij denotes the edge of i and j.

Remark 3.1 The formulated problem (3.2) can be frequently found in many practical application scenarios, e.g., the problems of formation control of a group of robots [62, 63], distributed model predictive problems [64, 65], distributed economic dispatch problems [66, 67], etc. The existing work [17] is based on the first-order methods to deal with problem (3.2) in a distributed setting and it fails to use the second-order information of the objective function. Thus, designing a way reminiscent of Quasi-Newton methods [42, 43] will have far-reaching implications.

Assumption 3.1 *For* $i = 1, \cdots, m$,

(i) $f_i : \mathbb{R}^{n_i} \to \mathbb{R}$ *is convex, twice differentiable, and its gradient is* $(1/\beta_i)$*-Lipschitz continuous, for some* $\beta_i > 0$; $g_i : \mathbb{R}^{n_i} \to (-\infty, +\infty]$ *and* $h_i : \mathbb{R}^{r_i} \to (-\infty, +\infty]$ *are proper, lower-semicontinuous convex functions;* $B_i : \mathbb{R}^{n_i} \to \mathbb{R}^{r_i}$ *is a bounded linear mapping;*

(ii) *For* $j \in \mathcal{N}_i$, $A_{ij} \in \mathbb{R}^{n_i} \to \mathbb{R}^{l(i,j)}$ *and* $b_{(i,j)} \in \mathbb{R}^{l(i,j)}$;

(iii) *The set of solutions to problem* (3.2) *is nonempty, and there is* $x_i \in$ *ri dom* g_i *such that* $L_i x_i \in$ *ri dom* h_i, $i \in \mathcal{V}$ *and* $A_{ij} x_i + A_{ji} x_j = b_{(i,j)}$, $(i, j) \in \mathcal{E}$.

Let $r = \sum_{i=1}^{m} r_i$ and $l = \sum_{(i,j)\in\mathcal{E}} 2l_{(i,j)}$. Let $N_{(i,j)} : x \mapsto \left(A_{ij}x_i, A_{ji}x_j\right) \in \mathbb{R}^{2l_{(i,j)}\times n}$ be the bounded linear operator. By stacking $N_{(i,j)}$, we obtain $N : x \mapsto \left(N_{(i,j)}x\right)_{(i,j)\in\mathcal{E}} \in \mathbb{R}^{l\times n}$. The transpose of N is denoted by $N^{\mathrm{T}} : \left(w_{(i,j)}\right)_{(i,j)\in\mathcal{E}} \mapsto \hat{x} = \sum_{(i,j)\in\mathcal{E}} N_{(i,j)}^{\mathrm{T}} w_{(i,j)}$, where $\hat{x}_i = \sum_{j\in\mathcal{N}_i} A_{ij}^{\mathrm{T}} w_{(i,j),i}$ and $\hat{x} = \mathrm{col}\left\{\left(\hat{x}_i\right)_{i=1}^{m}\right\}$. Here, we set $w_{(i,j)} = \left(w_{(i,j),i}, w_{(i,j),j}\right) \in \mathbb{R}^{2l_{(i,j)}}$. Define $C_{(i,j)} = \left\{(h_1, h_2) \in \mathbb{R}^{l_{(i,j)}} \times \mathbb{R}^{l_{(i,j)}} \,\middle|\, h_1 + h_2 = b_{(i,j)}\right\}$. Then, problem (3.2) can be rewritten as

$$\min_{x\in\mathbb{R}^n} \sum_{i=1}^{m} \left(f_i\left(x_i\right) + g_i\left(x_i\right) + h_i\left(B_i x_i\right)\right) + \sum_{i=1}^{m} \sum_{(i,j)\in\mathcal{E}} \delta_{C_{(i,j)}}\left(N_{(i,j)}x\right). \tag{3.3}$$

Define $C = \prod_{(i,j)\in\mathcal{E}} C_{(i,j)}$, $B = \mathrm{blkdiag}\left\{\left(B_i\right)_{i=1}^{m}\right\} = \mathrm{blkdiag}\left\{B_1, \cdots, B_m\right\}$, $\hat{B}x = (Bx, Nx) =: \left(\hat{\mathrm{v}}, \hat{\mathrm{w}}\right) \in \mathbb{R}^{n_p}$ with $n_p = r + l$, $f(x) = \sum_{i=1}^{m} f_i\left(x_i\right)$, $g(x) = \sum_{i=1}^{m} g_i\left(x_i\right)$, $\hat{h}\left(\hat{\mathrm{v}}, \hat{\mathrm{w}}\right) = h\left(\hat{\mathrm{v}}\right) + \delta_C\left(\hat{\mathrm{w}}\right)$, and $h\left(\hat{\mathrm{v}}\right) = \sum_{i=1}^{m} h_i\left(\hat{v}_i\right)$. Then, we can rewrite problem (3.3) as the following compact form:

$$\min_{x\in\mathbb{R}^n} f(x) + g(x) + \hat{h}(\hat{B}x). \tag{3.4}$$

3.2.3 Necessary Definitions and Lemmas

Here we give some important definitions and lemmas.

Definition 3.2 ([22]) Consider an operator $T : \mathbb{R}^n \to \mathbb{R}^n$. Then, (i) T is nonexpansive if $\|Ta - Tb\| \leq \|a - b\|, \forall a, b \in \mathbb{R}^n$, and T is firmly nonexpansive if $\|Ta - Tb\|^2 + \|(a - Ta) - (b - Tb)\|^2 \leq \|a - b\|^2, \forall a, b \in \mathbb{R}^n$; (ii) Suppose that the fixed point set of T is nonempty, i.e., $\mathrm{Fix}(T) \neq \emptyset$. If T satisfies $\|Ta - b\| \leq \|a - b\|, \forall a \in \mathbb{R}^n, b \in \mathrm{Fix}(T)$, then T is quasi-nonexpansive.

Definition 3.3 ([22]) Consider an operator $T : \mathbb{R}^n \to \mathbb{R}^n$. Then, T is β-Lipschitz continuous if there exists some $\beta > 0$ such that $\|Ta - Tb\| \leq \beta \|a - b\|$, $\forall a, b \in \mathbb{R}^n$.

Lemma 3.4 ([22]) *Let $f \in \Gamma_0(\mathbb{R}^n)$ and $\lambda > 0$. Then,* $\mathrm{prox}_{\lambda f}$ *and* $\left(\mathrm{Id} - \mathrm{prox}_{\lambda f}\right)$ *are firmly nonexpansive. Further, one has*

$$prox_{\lambda f} = (Id - \lambda\partial f)^{-1}, \tag{3.5}$$

$$a = prox_f(b) \Leftrightarrow b - a \in \partial f(a), \forall b \in \mathbb{R}^n, \tag{3.6}$$

$$b \in \partial f(a) \Leftrightarrow a = prox_f(a + b)$$

$$\Leftrightarrow b = \left(Id - prox_f\right)(a+b), \forall a, b \in \mathbb{R}^n, \tag{3.7}$$

$$a = prox_{\lambda f}(a) + \lambda prox_{\frac{1}{\lambda}f^*}\left(\frac{1}{\lambda}a\right), \forall a \in \mathbb{R}^n. \tag{3.8}$$

Lemma 3.5 ([68]) *Let $f \in \Gamma_0(\mathbb{R}^n)$ and $\beta > 0$. If f is twice differentiable with $(1/\beta)$-Lipschitz continuous gradient, one has $\langle \nabla f(a) - \nabla f(b), a - b\rangle \geq \beta\|\nabla f(a) - \nabla f(b)\|^2, \forall a, b \in \mathbb{R}^n$.*

Lemma 3.6 ([22]) *Let $A \in Z_{++}(k)$. Then, for all $a, b, c \in \mathbb{R}^k$, one has $2\langle a-b, A(a-c)\rangle = \|a-b\|_A^2 + \|a-c\|_A^2 - \|c-b\|_A^2$.*

3.3 Algorithm Development

In this section, we will propose synchronous version and randomized asynchronous iterative version distributed primal-dual fixed point algorithms to deal with problem (3.2).

3.3.1 Synchronous Version of D-PDFP_AM Algorithm

Motivated by the derivations of [42, 43], we utilize the second-order Taylor expansion of $f_i(x_i)$ at the recent iterative point x_i^k, i.e.,

$$f_i(x_i) \approx f_i\left(x_i^k\right) + \left\langle \nabla f_i\left(x_i^k\right), x_i - x_i^k\right\rangle + \frac{1}{2}\left\langle x_i - x_i^k, H_i^k\left(x_i - x_i^k\right)\right\rangle, \tag{3.9}$$

where $H_i^k \in Z_{++}(n_i)$ approximates $\nabla^2 f_i$. Define $H^k = \text{blkdiag}\left\{\left(H_i^k\right)_{i=1}^m\right\}$. Then, problem (3.4) can be approximated by

$$\min_{x \in \mathbb{R}^n} \frac{1}{2}\left\|x - x^k + \left(H^k\right)^{-1}\nabla f\left(x^k\right)\right\|_{H^k}^2 + g(x) + \hat{h}(\hat{B}x). \tag{3.10}$$

Under the condition that $\hat{h}(\hat{B}x) = h(Bx)$, Tang et al. [42] utilized a way reminiscent of Quasi-Newton methods to design a primal-dual fixed point algorithm (PDFP_AM) for solving problem (3.10) in a centralized way. PDFP_AM [42] relied on an adaptive metric method [43] and performed better by exploiting the second-order information of the differentiable convex function than the gradient-based algorithm [7], which inspired our interest to design a novel distributed primal-dual fixed point algorithm. Using $\text{prox}_{\hat{h}^*}(\hat{\text{v}}, \hat{\text{w}}) = (\text{prox}_{h^*}(\hat{\text{v}}), \text{prox}_{\delta_C^*}(\hat{\text{w}}))$, the Moreau equality (3.8), and $\text{prox}_{\delta_C}(\cdot) = \mathcal{P}_C(\cdot)$, the PDFP_AM algorithm in [42] becomes

$$\begin{aligned}\tilde{y}_i &= H_i^{-1}\text{prox}_{g_i \circ H_i^{-1}}\Big(H_i x_i - H_i^{-1}\nabla f_i(x_i) \\ &\quad -\lambda_i H_i^{-1} B_i^{\mathrm{T}} v_i - \gamma_{(i,j)} H_i^{-1}(N^{\mathrm{T}} w)_i\Big), \qquad (3.11a)\\ \tilde{v}_i &= \Big(I - \text{prox}_{\frac{1}{\lambda_i} h_i}\Big)(B_i \tilde{y}_i + v_i), \qquad (3.11b)\\ \tilde{w}_{(i,j)} &= w_{(i,j)} + N_{(i,j)}\tilde{y} - \mathcal{P}_{C_{(i,j)}}\left(w_{(i,j)} + N_{(i,j)}\tilde{y}\right), \qquad (3.11c)\\ \tilde{x}_i &= H_i^{-1}\text{prox}_{g_i \circ H_i^{-1}}\Big(H_i x_i - H_i^{-1}\nabla f_i(x_i) \\ &\quad -\lambda_i H_i^{-1} B_i^{\mathrm{T}} \tilde{v}_i - \gamma_{(i,j)} H_i^{-1}(N^{\mathrm{T}} \tilde{w})_i\Big). \qquad (3.11d)\end{aligned}$$

where $\gamma_{(i,j)}$ denotes the weight of edge (i, j) and λ_i represents the step size of agent i. Then, for $a_1, a_2 \in \mathbb{R}^{l_{(i,j)}}$, one obtains

$$P_{C_{(i,j)}}(a_1, a_2) = \frac{1}{2}\big(a_1 - a_2 + b_{(i,j)}, -a_1 + a_2 + b_{(i,j)}\big). \qquad (3.12)$$

Then, it follows from (3.11c) and (3.12) that

$$\begin{aligned}\tilde{w}_{(i,j)} &= w_{(i,j)} + N_{(i,j)}\tilde{y} - \mathcal{P}_{C_{(i,j)}}\left(w_{(i,j)} + N_{(i,j)}\tilde{y}\right) \qquad (3.13)\\ &= \begin{pmatrix} \frac{1}{2}\left(w_{(i,j),i} + w_{(i,j),j}\right) + \frac{1}{2}\left(A_{ij} y_i + A_{ji} y_j - b_{(i,j)}\right), \\ \frac{1}{2}\left(w_{(i,j),i} + w_{(i,j),j}\right) + \frac{1}{2}\left(A_{ij} y_i + A_{ji} y_j - b_{(i,j)}\right) \end{pmatrix}.\end{aligned}$$

Thus, the iteration (3.11) gives rise to Algorithm 3. Each agent $i \in \mathcal{V}$ has its own local primal variable $x_i \in \mathbb{R}^{n_i}$, dual variable $v_i \in \mathbb{R}^{r_i}$, and edge variable $w_{(i,j),i} \in \mathbb{R}^{l_{(i,j)}}$. The dual variable $v_i \in \mathbb{R}^{r_i}$ is related to the linear mapping B_i, and the edge variable $w_{(i,j),i} \in \mathbb{R}^{l_{(i,j)}}$ corresponds to the constraint. The updates in Algorithm 3 show that agent i only needs to exchange the updated information $A_{ij}x_i$, $w_{(i,j),i}$ to its neighbors $j \in \mathcal{N}_i$ and keeps other variables private.

Let $\lambda_i > 0$, $\gamma_{(i,j)} > 0$, and $H_i \in Z_{++}(n_i)$, for $i = 1, \cdots, m$, $j \in \mathcal{N}_i$. Define $\Gamma = \text{blkdiag}\{(\gamma_{(i,j)} I_{2l_{(i,j)}})_{(i,j)\in\mathcal{E}}\}$ as the edge weight matrix, and $\Lambda = \text{blkdiag}\left\{(\lambda_i I_{r_i})_{i=1}^m\right\}$ as the step size matrix. We introduce the following operators:

$$T_0(v, w, x) = H^{-1}\text{prox}_{g\circ H^{-1}}(Hx - H^{-1}(\nabla f(x) + (\Lambda B)^{\mathrm{T}} v + (\Gamma N)^{\mathrm{T}} w), \qquad (3.14)$$

$$T_1(v, w, x) = \left(\text{Id} - \text{prox}_h^{\Lambda}\right)(B \circ T_0(v, w, x) + v), \qquad (3.15)$$

$$T_2(v, w, x) = \left(\text{Id} - \text{prox}_{\delta_C}^{\Gamma}\right)(N \circ T_0(v, w, x) + w), \qquad (3.16)$$

$$T_3(v, w, x) = H^{-1}\text{prox}_{g\circ H^{-1}}(Hx - H^{-1}(\nabla f(x) + (\Lambda B)^{\mathrm{T}}$$

$$\circ T_1(v,w,x) + (\Gamma N)^{\mathrm{T}} \circ T_2(v,w,x))), \tag{3.17}$$

$$T(v,w,x) = (T_1(v,w,x), T_2(v,w,x), T_3(v,w,x)). \tag{3.18}$$

Algorithm 3 Synchronous version of D-PDFP_AM: for each agents $i = 1, \cdots, m$

1: **Input:** $x_i^0 \in \mathbb{R}^{n_i}$, $y_i^0 \in \mathbb{R}^{n_i}$, $v_i^0 \in \mathbb{R}^{r_i}$, $w_{(i,j),i} \in \mathbb{R}^{l(i,j)}$, $c_i > 0$, $H_i \in Z_{++}(n_i)$, $\left\| H_i^{-1} \right\|_2 < \sqrt{2\beta_i}$, $0 < \lambda_i < 1/((1+(1/c_i))\lambda_{\max}(B_i(H_i^{-1})^2 B_i^{\mathrm{T}}))$, and $\lambda_{\min}(H_i^2)/(1+c_i) - \lambda_{\max}(\sum_{j\in\mathcal{N}_i} \gamma_{(i,j)} A_{ij}^{\mathrm{T}} A_{ij}) > 0$, for $i = 1, \cdots, m$, $j \in \mathcal{N}_i$.

2: **for** $k = 0, 1, \cdots$ **do**

3: Local update:

$$y_i^{k+1} = H_i^{-1}\mathrm{prox}_{g_i \circ H_i^{-1}}(H_i x_i^k - H_i^{-1}(\nabla f_i\left(x_i^k\right) + (\lambda_i B_i)^{\mathrm{T}} v_i^k + \sum_{j\in\mathcal{N}_i} \gamma_{(i,j)} A_{ij}^{\mathrm{T}} w_{(i,j),i}^k)),$$

$$v_i^{k+1} = (I - \mathrm{prox}_{\frac{1}{\lambda_i} h_i})\left(B_i y_i^{k+1} + v_i^k\right),$$

$$w_{(i,j),i}^{k+1} = \frac{1}{2}(w_{(i,j),i}^k + w_{(i,j),j}^k) + \frac{1}{2}\left(A_{ij} y_i^{k+1} + A_{ji} y_j^{k+1} - b_{(i,j)}\right),$$

$$x_i^{k+1} = H_i^{-1}\mathrm{prox}_{g_i \circ H_i^{-1}}(H_i x_i^k - H_i^{-1}(\nabla f_i\left(x_i^k\right) + (\lambda_i B_i)^{\mathrm{T}} v_i^{k+1} + \sum_{j\in\mathcal{N}_i} \gamma_{(i,j)} A_{ij}^{\mathrm{T}} w_{(i,j),i}^{k+1})).$$

4: Transmission of information:

5: Send $A_{ij} x_i^{k+1}$, $w_{(i,j),i}^{k+1}$ to agent j, $\forall j \in \mathcal{N}_i$.

6: **end for**

7: **end for**

Remark 3.7 As shown in Algorithm 3, we propose a fully distributed algorithm, where not only the iterations are performed locally, but also the step sizes λ_i, $\gamma_{(i,j)}$, H_i, $i \in \mathcal{V}$, $j \in \mathcal{N}_i$ are based only on local information. Compared with the traditional centralized algorithms [4–8, 36, 39, 40, 42], it has superiority in addressing large-scale problems, e.g., formation control [62, 63], model predictive [64, 65], economic dispatch [66, 67], etc.

Remark 3.8 Algorithm 3 adopts the adapted metric method [42, 43]. Compared with [7] using a gradient descent step with a step parameter γ, our algorithm employs an adapted metric step H^{-1} to replace γ in the gradient descent step, where H is a suitable approximation of the second derivative of function f. It is worth mentioning that Algorithm 3 performs better to exploit the second-order information of the objective function than the first-order method [17].

3.3.2 Randomized Asynchronous Iterative Version of D-PDFP_AM Algorithm

In this subsection, we propose the randomized asynchronous iterative version of D-PDFP_AM algorithm based on the randomized coordinate activation mechanism in [17]. Specifically, only a random subset of agents is activated, update their variables, communicate with their neighbors, and go idle (the inactive agents remain unchanged) at every iteration. Furthermore, after performing an update, the updated values will be shared with their neighbors. This results in the following iteration:

$$\begin{aligned}\bar{y}_i^k &= H_i^{-1}\mathrm{prox}_{g_i \circ H_i^{-1}}(H_i x_i^k - H_i^{-1}(\nabla f_i\left(x_i^k\right) + (\lambda_i B_i)^{\mathrm{T}} v_i^k \\ &\quad + \sum_{j\in\mathcal{N}_i} \gamma_{(i,j)} A_{ij}^{\mathrm{T}} w_{(i,j),i}^k)),\end{aligned} \tag{3.19a}$$

$$\bar{v}_i^k = (I - \mathrm{prox}_{\frac{1}{\lambda_i}h_i})\left(B_i \bar{y}_i^k + v_i^k\right), \tag{3.19b}$$

$$\bar{w}_{(i,j),i}^k = \frac{1}{2}\left(w_{(i,j),i}^k + w_{(i,j),j}^k\right) + \frac{1}{2}\left(A_{ij}\bar{y}_i^k + A_{ji}\bar{y}_j^k - b_{(i,j)}\right), \tag{3.19c}$$

$$\begin{aligned}\bar{x}_i^k &= H_i^{-1}\mathrm{prox}_{g_i \circ H_i^{-1}}(H_i x_i^k - H_i^{-1}(\nabla f_i\left(x_i^k\right) + (\lambda_i B_i)^{\mathrm{T}} \bar{v}_i^k \\ &\quad + \sum_{j\in\mathcal{N}_i} \gamma_{(i,j)} A_{ij}^{\mathrm{T}} \bar{w}_{(i,j),i}^k)),\end{aligned} \tag{3.19d}$$

$$v_i^{k+1} = v_i^k + \phi_i^{k+1}\left(\bar{v}_i^k - v_i^k\right), \tag{3.19e}$$

$$w_{(i,j),i}^{k+1} = w_{(i,j),i}^k + \phi_i^{k+1}\left(\bar{w}_{(i,j),i}^k - w_{(i,j),i}^k\right), \tag{3.19f}$$

$$x_i^{k+1} = x_i^k + \phi_i^{k+1}\left(\bar{x}_i^k - x_i^k\right), \tag{3.19g}$$

where at the k-th iteration, the activation variable ϕ_i^{k+1} is 1 if agent i is activated, and 0 otherwise. Denote $\bar{y}^k = \mathrm{col}\left\{\left(\bar{y}_i^k\right)_{i=1}^m\right\} \in \mathbb{R}^n$, $y^k = \mathrm{col}\left\{\left(y_i^k\right)_{i=1}^m\right\} \in \mathbb{R}^n$, $\bar{v}^k = \mathrm{col}\left\{\left(\bar{v}_i^k\right)_{i=1}^m\right\} \in \mathbb{R}^r$, $v^k = \mathrm{col}\left\{\left(v_i^k\right)_{i=1}^m\right\} \in \mathbb{R}^r$, $\bar{w}^k = \mathrm{col}\{ (\bar{w}_{(i,j)}^k)_{(i,j)\in\mathcal{E}}\} \in \mathbb{R}^l$, $w^k = \mathrm{col}\{ (w_{(i,j)}^k)_{(i,j)\in\mathcal{E}}\} \in \mathbb{R}^l$, $\bar{x}^k = \mathrm{col}\left\{\left(\bar{x}_i^k\right)_{i=1}^m\right\} \in \mathbb{R}^n$, and $x^k = \mathrm{col}\left\{\left(x_i^k\right)_{i=1}^m\right\} \in \mathbb{R}^n$. Then, we partition the vectors x^k, v^k, and w^k into m, m, and $2\,|\mathcal{E}|$ blocks of coordinates, respectively, where $|\mathcal{E}|$ represents the number of edges in graph $\mathcal{G}$.

For $i = 1, \cdots, m$, we define a diagonal matrix $u_i \in \mathbb{R}^{(r+l+n)\times(r+l+n)}$ with 0-1 diagonal entries, which is used to select a subset of the coordinates to be updated. Let $\varphi = \{0, 1\}^m$ be a binary string of length m, whose elements are m-dimensional column vectors. Let a φ-valued random activation vector $\mathcal{S}^{k+1}$ be adopted to select which blocks of coordinates will be activated at the k-th iteration. The notation $\mathcal{S}_i^{k+1}$ represents the i-th element of the vector $\mathcal{S}^{k+1}$, and the i-th block is activated if $\mathcal{S}_i^{k+1} = 1$.

Assumption 3.2 ([6])

(i) The 0-1 diagonal matrices $\{u_i\}_{i=1}^m$ *satisfy* $\sum_{i=1}^m u_i = I$;
(ii) $\{\mathcal{S}^{k+1}\}$ *is a sequence of independent and uniformly distributed* φ*-valued random vectors with* $P_i := \mathbb{P}\left(\mathcal{S}_i^1 = 1\right) > 0$, *for* $i = 1, \cdots, m$.

Remark 3.9 The first condition in Assumption 3.2 ensures that the coordinate blocks are not overlap. The second one guarantees that each coordinate block is activated with a positive probability.

Denote the diagonal coordinate activation probability matrix by $\mathcal{J} = \sum_{i=1}^m P_i u_i$. By using $U^k = \left(v^k, w^k, x^k\right)$, $\bar{U}^k = \left(\bar{v}^k, \bar{w}^k, \bar{x}^k\right)$, $E^{k+1} = \sum_{i=1}^m \mathcal{S}_i^{k+1}$ u_i, and the operator T in (3.18), we get the compact form of iteration (3.19):

$$\bar{U}^k = TU^k, \tag{3.20}$$

$$U^{k+1} = U^k + E^{k+1}\left(\bar{U}^k - U^k\right). \tag{3.21}$$

According to above analysis, we present a randomized asynchronous iterative version of D-PDFP_AM in Algorithm 4. At each iteration, each agent $i \in \mathcal{V}$ is activated randomly, and independently from others with probability $P_i > 0$, and the active agents perform their local updates as steps 1–4 in Algorithm 4. Then, these agents transmit the required information $A_{ij}x_i$, $w_{(i,j),i}$ to their neighbors and eventually return to an idle state.

Remark 3.10 By incorporating a randomized coordinate activation mechanism [17] into Algorithm 3, we obtain the randomized asynchronous iterative distributed algorithm. At each iteration, each agent $i \in \mathcal{V}$ is activated independently with probability $P_i > 0$, and only a subset of randomly activated agents performs updates (the other inactive agents remain unchanged). Compared with the algorithms [55–60, 62] requiring all agents to be activated per iteration, Algorithm 4 can effectively reduce iteration cost. In addition, Algorithm 4 can activate multiple agents per iteration, which is more practical than the asynchronous algorithms [50, 70] with a single agent activation.

3.4 Convergence Analysis

In this section, we begin to illustrate the convergence analysis of Algorithms 3 and 4. Firstly, a basic relation between the optimal solution to problem (3.4) and the fixed point of Algorithm 3 are presented as follows.

Algorithm 4 Randomized asynchronous iterative version of D-PDFP_AM

Input: $x_i^0 \in \mathbb{R}^{n_i}$, $y_i^0 \in \mathbb{R}^{n_i}$, $v_i^0 \in \mathbb{R}^{r_i}$, $w_{(i,j),i} \in \mathbb{R}^{l(i,j)}$, $c_i > 0$, $H_i \in Z_{++}(n_i)$, $\left\|H_i^{-1}\right\|_2 < \sqrt{2\beta_i}$, $0 < \lambda_i < 1/((1+(1/c_i))\lambda_{\max}(B_i(H_i^{-1})^2 B_i^{\mathrm{T}}))$, and $\lambda_{\min}(H_i^2)/(1+c_i) - \lambda_{\max}(\sum_{j\in\mathcal{N}_i}\gamma_{(i,j)}A_{ij}^{\mathrm{T}}A_{ij}) > 0$, for $i = 1, \cdots, m$, $j \in \mathcal{N}_i$.

for $k = 0, 1, \cdots$ **do**

Each agent $i = 1, \cdots, m$ is activated independently with probability $P_i > 0$.

for all activated agents **do**

Local update:

$$
\begin{aligned}
y_i^{k+1} &= H_i^{-1}\mathrm{prox}_{g_i \circ H_i^{-1}}(H_i x_i^k - H_i^{-1}(\nabla f_i\left(x_i^k\right) + (\lambda_i B_i)^{\mathrm{T}} v_i^k \\
&\quad + \sum_{j\in\mathcal{N}_i}\gamma_{(i,j)}A_{ij}^{\mathrm{T}} w_{(i,j),i}^k)),\\
v_i^{k+1} &= (I - \mathrm{prox}_{\frac{1}{\lambda_i}h_i})\left(B_i y_i^{k+1} + v_i^k\right),\\
w_{(i,j),i}^{k+1} &= \frac{1}{2}(w_{(i,j),i}^k + w_{(i,j),j}^k) + \frac{1}{2}\left(A_{ij}y_i^{k+1} + A_{ji}y_j^{k+1} - b_{(i,j)}\right),\\
x_i^{k+1} &= H_i^{-1}\mathrm{prox}_{g_i \circ H_i^{-1}}(H_i x_i^k - H_i^{-1}(\nabla f_i\left(x_i^k\right) + (\lambda_i B_i)^{\mathrm{T}} v_i^{k+1} \\
&\quad + \sum_{j\in\mathcal{N}_i}\gamma_{(i,j)}A_{ij}^{\mathrm{T}} w_{(i,j),i}^{k+1})).
\end{aligned}
$$

Transmission of information:

Send $A_{ij}x_i^{k+1}$, $w_{(i,j),i}^{k+1}$ to agent j, $\forall j \in \mathcal{N}_i$.

end for

end for

Lemma 3.11 *Let Assumption 3.1 hold. Suppose that* x^* *is an optimal solution to problem* (3.4). *Then, there exist* $v^* \in \mathbb{R}^r$ *and* $w^* \in \mathbb{R}^l$ *such that* (v^*, w^*, x^*) *is a fixed point of* T *in* (3.18), *i.e.,*

$$
\begin{cases}
v^* = T_1(v^*, w^*, x^*),\\
w^* = T_2(v^*, w^*, x^*),\\
x^* = T_3(v^*, w^*, x^*).
\end{cases}
\tag{3.22}
$$

Conversely, if (v^*, w^*, x^*) *is a fixed point of* T *in* (3.18), *then,* x^* *is an optimal solution to problem* (3.4).

Proof According to the first-order optimal condition of problem (3.4), one has

$$
\begin{aligned}
&0 \in \nabla f(x^*) + \partial g(x^*) + \partial(h\circ B)(x^*) + \partial(\delta_C \circ N)(x^*)\\
&\Leftrightarrow 0 \in H^{-1}\nabla f(x^*) + H^{-1}\partial g(x^*) + H^{-1}B^{\mathrm{T}}\partial h(Bx^*)\\
&\quad + H^{-1}N^{\mathrm{T}}\partial\delta_C(Nx^*)
\end{aligned}
$$

$$\Leftrightarrow -H^{-1}\nabla f(x^*) - H^{-1}(\Lambda B)^{\mathrm{T}}\partial(\Lambda^{-1}h)(Bx^*)$$
$$- H^{-1}(\Gamma N)^{\mathrm{T}}\partial(\Gamma^{-1}\delta_C)(Nx^*)$$
$$\in H^{-1}\partial g(x^*) = \partial(g \circ H^{-1})(Hx^*). \tag{3.23}$$

Let $v^* \in \partial\left(\Lambda^{-1}h\right)(Bx^*)$ and $w^* \in \partial\left(\Gamma^{-1}\delta_C\right)(Nx^*)$. Then, (3.23) is equivalent to

$$Hx^* = \mathrm{prox}_{g\circ H^{-1}}\left(Hx^* - H^{-1}\nabla f(x^*) - H^{-1}(\Lambda B)^{\mathrm{T}}v^* - H^{-1}(\Gamma N)^{\mathrm{T}}w^*\right). \tag{3.24}$$

By using Lemma 3.4, it holds that

$$v^* \in \partial\left(\Lambda^{-1}h\right)\left(Bx^*\right) \Leftrightarrow v^* = \left(\mathrm{Id} - \mathrm{prox}_h^{\Lambda}\right)\left(Bx^* + v^*\right), \tag{3.25}$$

$$w^* \in \partial\left(\Gamma^{-1}\delta_C\right)\left(Nx^*\right) \Leftrightarrow w^* = \left(\mathrm{Id} - \mathrm{prox}_{\delta_C}^{\Gamma}\right)\left(Nx^* + w^*\right). \tag{3.26}$$

Further, substituting (3.24) into (3.25) and (3.26) respectively, we obtain

$$v^* = \left(\mathrm{Id} - \mathrm{prox}_h^{\Lambda}\right)\Big(BH^{-1}\mathrm{prox}_{g\circ H^{-1}}\Big(Hx^* - H^{-1}\nabla f\left(x^*\right)$$
$$- H^{-1}(\Lambda B)^{\mathrm{T}}v^* - H^{-1}(\Gamma N)^{\mathrm{T}}w^*) + v^*), \tag{3.27}$$
$$w^* = \left(\mathrm{Id} - \mathrm{prox}_{\delta_C}^{\Gamma}\right)\Big(NH^{-1}\mathrm{prox}_{g\circ H^{-1}}\Big(Hx^* - H^{-1}\nabla f\left(x^*\right)$$
$$- H^{-1}(\Lambda B)^{\mathrm{T}}v^* - H^{-1}(\Gamma N)^{\mathrm{T}}w^*) + v^*), \tag{3.28}$$

which implies that $v^* = T_1(v^*, w^*, x^*)$ and $w^* = T_2(v^*, w^*, x^*)$. Moreover, it follows from (3.24) that

$$Hx^* = \mathrm{prox}_{g\circ H^{-1}}(Hx^* - H^{-1}(\nabla f(x^*) + (\Lambda B)^{\mathrm{T}}T_1(v^*, w^*, x^*)$$
$$+ (\Gamma N)^{\mathrm{T}}T_2(v^*, w^*, x^*)). \tag{3.29}$$

Therefore, $v^* = T_1(v^*, w^*, x^*)$, $w^* = T_2(v^*, w^*, x^*)$, and $x^* = T_3(v^*, w^*, x^*)$. Conversely, if (v^*, w^*, x^*) is a fixed point of T, it is deduced that x^* satisfies the first-order optimal condition of problem (3.4). Thus, x^* is also an optimal solution to problem (3.4). ■

From Lemma 3.11, it is shown that the sequence $\{v^{k+1}, w^{k+1}, x^{k+1}\}$ generated by Algorithm 3 is a fixed point iterative algorithm. In what follows, an important inequality that presents the quasi-nonexpansive of T will be given. Denote $C = \mathrm{blkdiag}\{((1 + 1/c_i) I_{n_i})_{i=1}^m\}$, $\bar{C} = \mathrm{blkdiag}\{((1 + c_i) I_{n_i})_{i=1}^m\}$, $M = \Lambda - \Lambda BH^{-1}CH^{-1}(\Lambda B)^{\mathrm{T}}$, and $P = \Gamma - \Gamma NH^{-1}\bar{C}H^{-1}(\Gamma N)^{\mathrm{T}}$, where

$c_i > 0$, $i \in \mathcal{V}$. Let $0 < \lambda_i < 1/((1 + (1/c_i))\lambda_{\max}(B_i(H_i^{-1})^2 B_i^{\mathrm{T}}))$, $\lambda_{\min}(H_i^2)/(1 + c_i) - \lambda_{\max}(\sum_{j \in N_i} \gamma_{(i,j)} A_{ij}^{\mathrm{T}} A_{ij}) > 0$, $\gamma_{(i,j)} > 0$, $i \in \mathcal{V}$, and $j \in \mathcal{N}_i$, such that M and P are symmetric positive semi-definite matrices. Consider the semi-norms $\|v\|_M = \sqrt{\langle v, Mv \rangle}$ and $\|w\|_P = \sqrt{\langle w, Pw \rangle}$. Then, we define the norm $\|v, w, x\|_{\Lambda,\Gamma,H^2} = \sqrt{\|v\|_\Lambda^2 + \|w\|_\Gamma^2 + \|x\|_{H^2}^2}$.

Lemma 3.12 *Let Assumption 3.1 hold. Suppose that $u^* = (v^*, w^*, x^*)$ is a fixed point of T in* (3.18) *and the sequence $u^k = \left(v^k, w^k, x^k\right)$ is generated by Algorithm 3. Then, one gets*

$$
\begin{aligned}
&\left\| T\left(u^k\right) - u^* \right\|_{\Lambda,\Gamma,H^2}^2 \\
\leq &\left\| u^k - u^* \right\|_{\Lambda,\Gamma,H^2}^2 - \left\| T_1\left(u^k\right) - v^k \right\|_M^2 - \left\| T_2\left(u^k\right) - w^k \right\|_P^2 \\
&- \Big\| H\left(T_3\left(u^k\right) - T_0\left(u^k\right)\right) + H^{-1}\left((\Lambda B)^{\mathrm{T}} T_1\left(u^k\right) - (\Lambda B)^{\mathrm{T}} v^k\right) \\
&+ H^{-1}\left((\Gamma N)^{\mathrm{T}} T_2\left(u^k\right) - (\Gamma N)^{\mathrm{T}} w^k\right) \Big\|^2 \\
&- \left\| H\left(x^k - T_0\left(u^k\right)\right) - H^{-1}\left(\nabla f\left(x^k\right) - \nabla f\left(x^*\right)\right) \right\|^2 \\
&- \left\| \nabla f\left(x^k\right) - \nabla f\left(x^*\right) \right\|_{2\beta - (H^{-1})^2}^2 .
\end{aligned}
\tag{3.30}
$$

Proof See Appendix A for detailed proof. ■

We give the convergence result of Algorithm 3 as follows.

Theorem 3.13 *Let Assumption 3.1 hold. Suppose that $0 < \lambda_i < 1/((1 + (1/c_i))\lambda_{\max}(B_i(H_i^{-1})^2 B_i^{\mathrm{T}}))$, $\lambda_{\min}(H_i^2)/(1 + c_i) - \lambda_{\max}(\sum_{j \in \mathcal{N}_i} \gamma_{(i,j)} A_{ij}^{\mathrm{T}} A_{ij}) > 0$, $\left\| H_i^{-1} \right\|_2 < \sqrt{2\beta_i}$, $\gamma_{(i,j)} > 0$, and $c_i > 0$, for $i = 1, \cdots, m$, $j \in \mathcal{N}_i$. Let the sequence $\left\{u^k\right\} = \left\{\left(v^k, w^k, x^k\right)\right\}$ be generated by Algorithm 3, and the operator T be defined in* (3.18). *Then, one holds that*

(i) The operator T is continuous;
(ii) For any $u^* \in \mathrm{Fix}(T)$, $\lim_{k \to +\infty} \{\|u^k - u^*\|_{\Lambda,\Gamma,H^2}^2\}$ exists;
(iii) The sequence $\left\{u^k\right\}$ converges to a fixed point of T and $\left\{x^k\right\}$ converges to an optimal solution to problem (3.4).

Proof See Appendix B for detailed proof. ■

Next, we present a lemma that is important to the convergence analysis of Algorithm 4.

Lemma 3.14 *Let Assumption 3.2 hold. Suppose that $\mathcal{F}^k$ is the filtration generated by $\left(\mathcal{S}^1, \cdots, \mathcal{S}^k\right)$. According to the definitions of u_i and E^{k+1}, it follows that*

(i) For any $q \in \mathbb{N}^+$, $\left(E^{k+1}\right)^q = E^{k+1}$;
(ii) The conditional expectation $\mathbb{E}\left[E^{k+1}|\mathcal{F}^k\right] = \mathcal{J}$.

Proof *(i)* Notice that $u_i u_j = 0$ if $i \neq j$, and $u_i u_j = u_i$ if $i = j$. For $q = 2$, it has

$$\begin{aligned}\left(E^{k+1}\right)^2 = \left(\sum_{i=1}^{m} \mathcal{S}_i^{k+1} u_i\right)^2 &= \sum_{i=1, i\neq j}^{m} \mathcal{S}_i^{k+1} u_i \mathcal{S}_j^{k+1} u_j + \sum_{i=1}^{m} \left(\mathcal{S}_i^{k+1} u_i\right)^2 \\ &= \sum_{i=1}^{m} \mathcal{S}_i^{k+1} u_i = E^{k+1}.\end{aligned} \tag{3.31}$$

Assume that $\left(E^{k+1}\right)^d = E^{k+1}$ for $q = l$ $(l > 3)$. Then, one has

$$\left(E^{k+1}\right)^{d+1} = \left(E^{k+1}\right)^d E^{k+1} = \left(E^{k+1}\right)^2 = E^{k+1}, \tag{3.32}$$

for $q = l + 1$. Thus, $\left(E^{k+1}\right)^q = E^{k+1}$, for any $q \in \mathbb{N}^+$.

(ii) Let $\mathbb{E}_k[\cdot]$ be the abbreviation of $\mathbb{E}\left[\cdot|\mathcal{F}^k\right]$. Denote the conditional expectation of E^{k+1} by $\mathbb{E}_k \circ \left(E^{k+1}\right)$. Then, it can be achieved that

$$\begin{aligned}\mathbb{E}_k \circ \left(E^{k+1}\right) &= \sum_{e\in\varphi} P\left(\mathcal{S}^{k+1} = e\right) \sum_{i=1}^{m} e_i u_i \\ &= \sum_{i=1}^{m} \sum_{e\in\varphi, e_i=1} P\left(\mathcal{S}^{k+1} = e\right) u_i \\ &= \sum_{i=1}^{m} P_i u_i = \mathcal{J}.\end{aligned} \tag{3.33}$$

This completes the proof. ■

In the following, the convergence result of Algorithm 4 will be shown.

Theorem 3.15 *Let Assumptions 3.1 and 3.2 hold. Suppose that x^* is an optimal solution to problem* (3.4). *The sequences $\left\{U^k\right\} = \left\{\left(v^k, w^k, x^k\right)\right\}$ and $\left\{\bar{U}^k\right\} = \left\{\left(\bar{v}^k, \bar{w}^k, \bar{x}^k\right)\right\}$ are generated by Algorithm 4. Under the same parameter conditions* *as Theorem 3.13, for all* U^*, *the following Fejér-type inequality holds:*

$$\mathbb{E}_k\left[\left\|U^{k+1}-U^*\right\|^2_{\mathcal{J}^{-1}T_s}\right] \leq \left\|U^k-U^*\right\|^2_{\mathcal{J}^{-1}T_s}, \tag{3.34}$$

where $T_s = blkdiag\left\{\Lambda, \Gamma, H^2\right\}$. *Consequently,* $\left\{U^k\right\}$ *converges to* U^*.

Proof See Appendix C for detailed proof. ■

3.5 Numerical Examples

In this section, we use two simulations to verify the effectiveness of Algorithms 3 and 4.

3.5.1 Distributed Constrained Quadratic Programming

This simulation will be conducted over a network consisting of five agents, which is shown in Fig. 3.1. We consider the following distributed constrained quadratic programming problem:

$$\begin{aligned} \min_{x\in\mathbb{R}^n} \ & \sum_{i=1}^{m} f_i\left(x_i\right) = \tfrac{1}{2}\|K_i x_i - r_i\|^2, \\ \text{s.t.} \ & {a_i}^{\mathrm{T}} x_i \leq b_i, \\ & x_i^{\min} \leq x_i \leq x_i^{\max}, \\ & A_{ij}x_i + A_{ji}x_j = C_{(i,j)}, \quad (i,j) \in \mathcal{E}, \end{aligned} \tag{3.35}$$

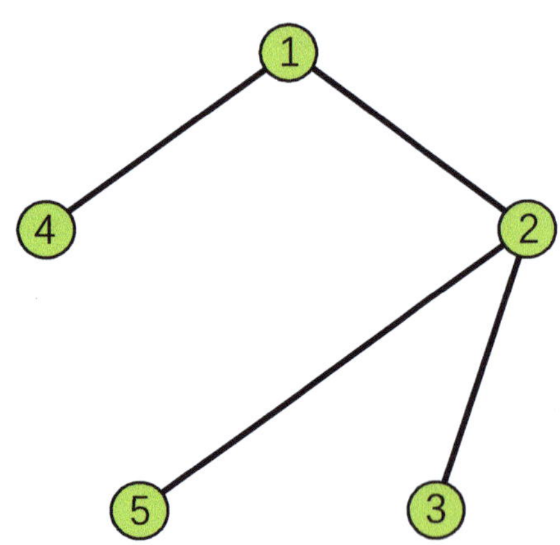

Fig. 3.1 Undirected network

where $x_i \in \mathbb{R}^{n_i}$, $x = \text{col}\left\{(x_i)_{i=1}^m\right\}$, $n = \sum_{i=1}^m n_i$, $K_i \in \mathbb{R}^{l_i \times n_i}$, $r_i \in \mathbb{R}^{l_i}$, $a_i \in \mathbb{R}^{n_i}$, $b_i \in \mathbb{R}$, $x_i^{\min} \in \mathbb{R}^{n_i}$, and $x_i^{\max} \in \mathbb{R}^{n_i}$. It is worth noting that when $A_{ij} = I$, $A_{ji} = -I$, and $C_{(i,\,j)} = 0$, the third constraint in problem (3.35) becomes a consensus constraint.

Firstly, we need to convert problem (3.35) into the form of (3.2). Define the sets $\mathcal{D}_i = \left\{z \left| a_i^{\mathrm{T}} z \le b_i \right.\right\}$ and $X_i = \left\{z \left| x_i^m \le z \le x_i^M \right.\right\}$. Then, by introducing the indicator functions $\delta_{X_i}(x_i)$ and $\delta_{\mathcal{D}_i}(x_i)$, problem (3.35) is equivalent to

$$
\begin{aligned}
\min_{x \in \mathbb{R}^n} \; & \sum_{i=1}^{m} f_i(x_i) + \delta_{X_i}(x_i) + \delta_{\mathcal{D}_i}(x_i), \\
\text{s.t.} \; & A_{ij} x_i + A_{ji} x_j = C_{(i,\,j)}, \quad (i,\,j) \in \mathcal{E}.
\end{aligned}
\tag{3.36}
$$

In the experiment, we set $A_{ij} = I$, $A_{ji} = -I$, and $C_{(i,\,j)} = 0$. Assume that K_i is a positive definite diagonal matrix with $n_i = l_i = 5$ for $i = 1, \cdots, 5$. We randomly select appropriate system parameters. Specifically, for $i = 1, \cdots, 5$, let $K_i = \text{diag}\{\kappa_1, \kappa_2, \kappa_3, \kappa_4, \kappa_5\}$, $r_i = (\iota_1, \iota_2, \iota_3, \iota_4, \iota_5)^{\mathrm{T}}$, $a_i = (\eta_1, \eta_2, \eta_3, \eta_4, \eta_5)^{\mathrm{T}}$, $b_i \in (-5, 5)$, $x_i^{\min} = (\tau_1, \tau_2, \tau_3, \tau_4, \tau_5)^{\mathrm{T}}$, and $x_i^{\max} = (\xi_1, \xi_2, \xi_3, \xi_4, \xi_5)^{\mathrm{T}}$, where $\kappa_j \in (1, 3)$, $\iota_j \in (-5, 5)$, $\eta_j \in (0, 10)$, $\tau_j \in (-5, -2)$, and $\xi_j \in (5, 8)$, for $j = 1, \cdots, 5$. We employ the proposed algorithms and the TriPD-Dist algorithm [17] to solve problem (3.35). Parameter setting: $c_1 = 0.560$, $c_2 = 0.041$, $c_3 = 2.120$, $c_4 = 2.120$, $c_5 = 2.120$, $\lambda_1 = 2.2435$, $\lambda_2 = 0.2461$, $\lambda_3 = 4.2467$, $\lambda_4 = 4.2467$, $\lambda_5 = 4.2467$, $\gamma_{(i,j)} = 2$, and $H_i = 2.5 I_5$, where $i \in \{1, \cdots, 5\}$ and $j \in \mathcal{N}_i$. Based on the conditions of the step size parameters given in [17], we set the parameters of the TriPD-Dist algorithm as $\sigma_1 = 2.1230$, $\sigma_2 = 1.6781$, $\sigma_3 = 2.1098$, $\sigma_4 = 2.1606$, $\sigma_5 = 1.7615$, $\tau_1 = 0.0954$, $\tau_2 = 0.0897$, $\tau_3 = 0.1188$, $\tau_4 = 0.1167$, $\tau_5 = 0.1359$, and $k_{(i,j)} = 2$, $i \in \{1, \cdots, 5\}$, $j \in \mathcal{N}_i$.

The evolutions of x_i^k, $i \in \{1, \cdots, 5\}$ at each dimension are shown in Fig. 3.2a, b, and we can observe that the optimal solution x^* can be achieved by the proposed algorithms. This simulation follows the results of Theorems 3.13 and 3.15 that both consensus and optimization can be realized. In Fig. 3.2c, we plot the evolutions of residual for Algorithm 3, Algorithm 4, and the TriPD-Dist algorithm with the number of iterations, where the residual is defined by $\log_{10}\left((1/m)\sum_{i=1}^m \left\|x_i^k - x^*\right\|\right)$. It is depicted from Fig. 3.2c that Algorithm 3 performs better than Algorithm 4 and the TriPD-Dist algorithm. In addition, Fig. 3.2c also verifies that the greater the probability P_i is selected, the faster the convergence of Algorithm 4 can achieve.

3.5.2 Distributed Economic Dispatch Problem

In this simulation, we study the economic dispatch problem on the IEEE 118-bus test system [67] as shown in Fig. 3.3, where the test system contains 54 generators. The communication between generators adopts the bus data given in [71]. The

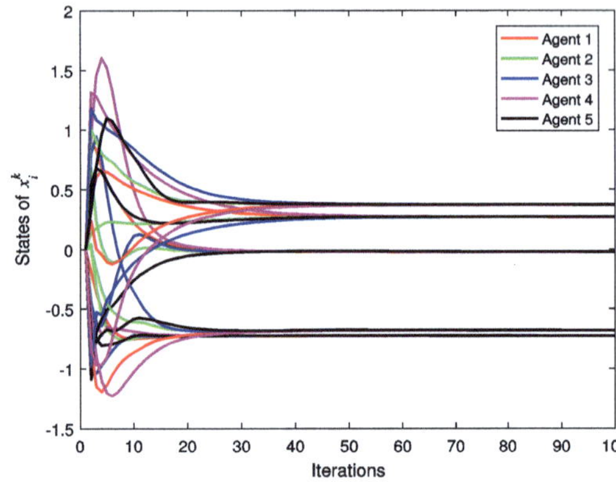

(a)

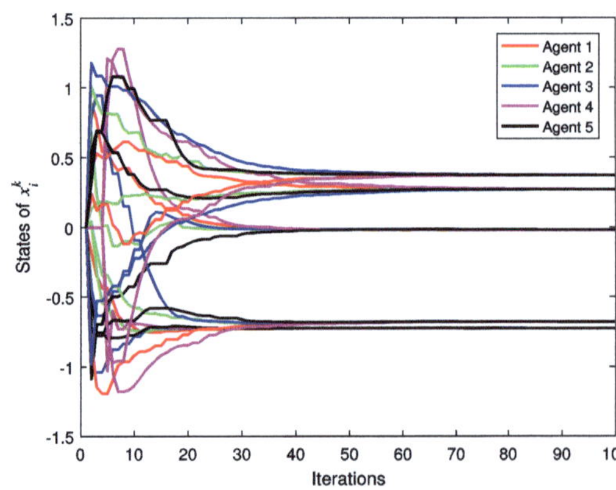

(b)

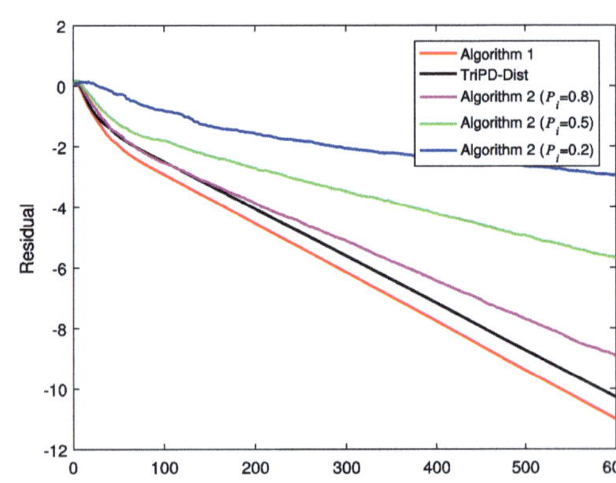

(c)

Fig. 3.2 The simulation results of Algorithms 3 and 4, and the TriPD-Dist algorithm [17]. (**a**) Algorithm 3. (**b**) Algorithm 4 ($P_i = 0.8$). (**c**) Evolutions of residual with iterations

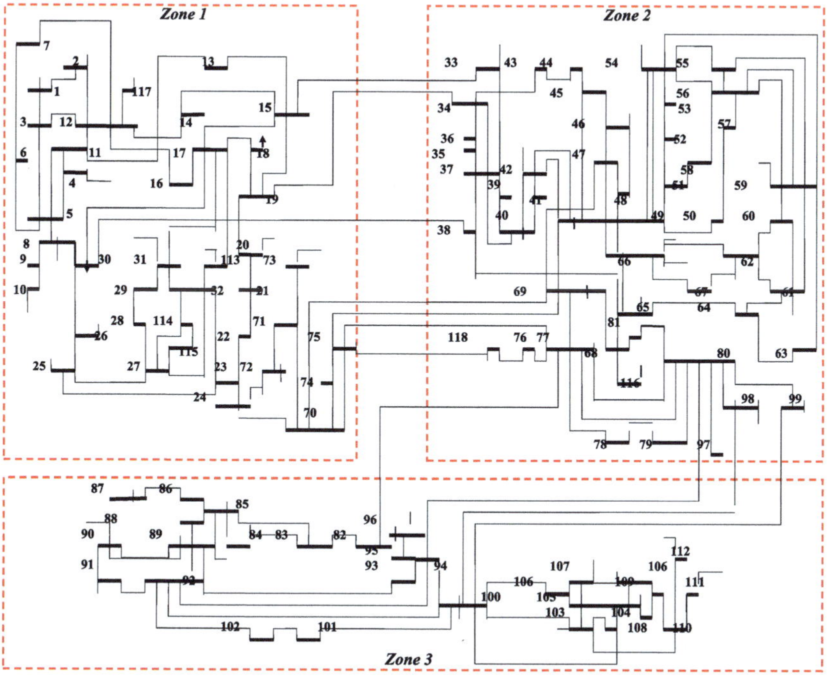

Fig. 3.3 IEEE 118-bus test system

traditional distributed economic dispatch problem can be formulated as follows:

$$\min_{p\in\mathbb{R}^m} \sum_{i=1}^{m} C_i\left(p_i\right), \quad \text{s.t.} \quad \sum_{i=1}^{m} p_i = D, \quad p_i^{\max} \le p_i \le p_i^{\min}, \tag{3.37}$$

where m is the number of generators. For generator $i = 1, \cdots, m$, C_i is the generation cost function, p_i denotes the power generation, $p = \operatorname{col}\left\{(p_i)_{i=1}^{m}\right\}$, $p_i^{\max}$ and $p_i^{\min}$ are the maximum and minimum generation capacities. D represents the total load of the test system.

Define the set $J_i = \left\{z | p_i^{\min} \le z \le p_i^{\max}\right\}$ and the indicator function $\delta_{J_i}\left(p_i\right)$. The Lagrangian function of problem (3.37) can be written as $f\left(p, \zeta\right) = \sum_{i=1}^{m} C_i\left(p_i\right) + \zeta \sum_{i=1}^{m}\left(D_i - p_i\right)$, where $p \in \left[p_1, \cdots, p_m\right]^{\mathrm{T}}$, ζ is the Lagrangian multiplier, and $D_i \in \mathbb{R}$ is virtual local demand at generator i such that $\sum_{i=1}^{m} D_i = D$. The Lagrangian dual problem of (3.37) is $\max_{\zeta\in\mathbb{R}}\min_{p\in\mathbb{R}^m} \; f\left(p, \zeta\right)$, and we convert it into

$$\min_{\zeta\in\mathbb{R}} f\left(\zeta\right) \triangleq \sum_{i=1}^{m} f_i\left(\zeta\right), \tag{3.38}$$

where $f_i(\zeta) = \max_{p_i \in \mathbb{R}^m} \left\{ \zeta p_i - C_i(p_i) - \delta_{J_i}(p_i) \right\} - \zeta D_i$. Finally, problem (3.38) is reformulated as

$$\min_{\zeta_i \in \mathbb{R}} \sum_{i=1}^{m} f_i(\zeta_i), \quad \text{s.t. } A_{ij}\zeta_i + A_{ji}\zeta_j = 0, \quad (i, j) \in \mathcal{E}, \tag{3.39}$$

where $A_{ij} = 1$ if $i < j$ and $A_{ij} = -1$ if $i > j$. Here, $g_i(\zeta_i) = 0$ and $h_i(B_i\zeta_i) = 0$. The generation cost function C_i is defined as a quadratic cost function $C_i(p_i) = c_i p_i^2 + b_i p_i + a_i$, where the cost coefficients $a_i \in [6.78, 74.33]$ (\$), $b_i \in [8.3391, 37.6968]$ (\$/MW), and $c_i \in [0.0024, 0.0697]$ $(\$/\text{MW}^2)$. The generation capacity of generator i satisfies $p_i \in \left[p_i^{\min}, p_i^{\max}\right]$ (MW), where $p_i^{\min} \in [5, 150]$ (MW) and $p_i^{\max} \in [150, 400]$ (MW). The total load of the test system is 4242MW. In this simulation, we set the relevant parameters as follows: $H_i \in (11, 11.1)$, $\gamma_{(i,j)} \in (2.9, 3)$, for $i = 1, \cdots, m$, $j \in \mathcal{N}_i$. As depicted in Fig. 3.4a–c, the generators gradually achieve the optimal generations, the total generation converges to the total demand, and ζ_i, $i \in \mathcal{V}$ converges to the optimal value. The similar results are presented in Fig. 3.4d–f by using Algorithm 4.

Remark 3.16 The distributed economic dispatch problem is a special case of problem (3.2) for verifying the effectiveness and practicality of the proposed algorithms, and more complex problems [62–65] can also be resolved by the proposed algorithms.

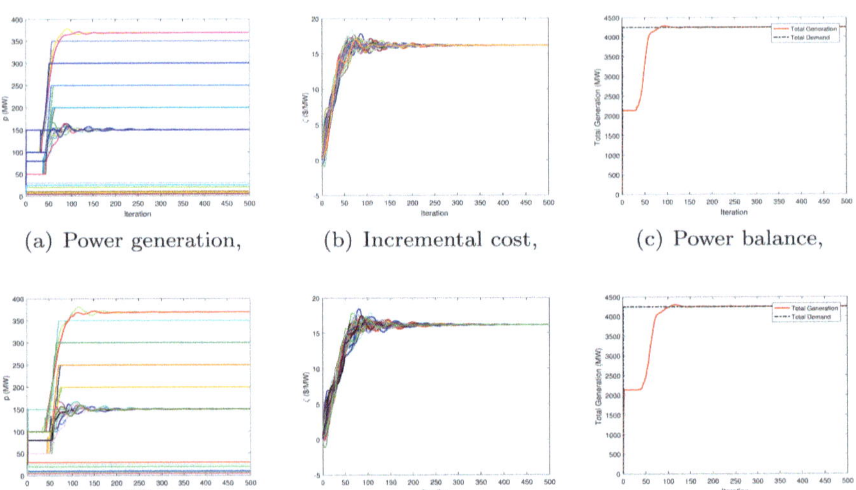

(a) Power generation, (b) Incremental cost, (c) Power balance,

(d) Power generation, (e) Incremental cost, (f) Power balance.

Fig. 3.4 **(a)**–**(c)** are generated by Algorithm 3, **(d)**–**(f)** are generated by Algorithm 4 with $P_i = 0.8$

3.6 Conclusion

This chapter has studied a distributed optimization problem where a group of networked agents cooperatively minimize the sum of the private objective functions with edge-based constraint. Fully distributed primal-dual fixed point algorithms have been proposed. The main features of the algorithms include the adoption of the adapted metric method, the incorporation of the randomized coordinate activation mechanism, and uncoordinated step sizes. It has been rigorously proved that these algorithms converge to the optimal solution under some moderate conditions.

Appendix

Appendix A: Proof of Lemma 3.12

Suppose that Assumption 3.1 hold. Then, there exists the following inequalities:

$$\begin{aligned}\left\|v_{k+1}-v^*\right\|_{\mathrm{H}}^2 \leq &\left\|v_k-v^*\right\|_{\mathrm{H}}^2-\left\|v_{k+1}-v_k\right\|_{\mathrm{H}}^2\\ &+2\left(v_{k+1}-v^*\right)^{\mathrm{T}}\mathrm{H}B\left(y_{k+1}-x^*\right),\end{aligned} \tag{3.40}$$

$$\begin{aligned}\left\|\tilde{v}_{k+1}-\tilde{v}^*\right\|_{\tilde{\mathrm{H}}}^2 \leq &\left\|\tilde{v}_k-\tilde{v}^*\right\|_{\tilde{\mathrm{H}}}^2-\left\|\tilde{v}_{k+1}-\tilde{v}_k\right\|_{\tilde{\mathrm{H}}}^2\\ &+2\left(\tilde{v}_{k+1}-\tilde{v}^*\right)^{\mathrm{T}}\tilde{\mathrm{H}}N\left(y_{k+1}-x^*\right),\end{aligned} \tag{3.41}$$

$$\begin{aligned}&\left\|x_{k+1}-x^*\right\|_{\Sigma^{-1}}^2\\ \leq&\left\|x_k-x^*\right\|_{\Sigma^{-1}}^2-\left\|x_{k+1}-y_{k+1}\right\|_{\Sigma^{-1}}^2-\left\|x_k-y_{k+1}\right\|_{\Sigma^{-1}}^2\\ &+2(x_{k+1}-y_{k+1})^{\mathrm{T}}\Sigma^{-1}\left(\Sigma\nabla f(x_k)+(\mathrm{H}B)^{\mathrm{T}}v_k+(\tilde{\mathrm{H}}N)^{\mathrm{T}}\tilde{v}_k\right)\\ &-2\left(x_{k+1}-x^*\right)^{\mathrm{T}}\Sigma^{-1}\left(\Sigma\nabla f(x_k)+(\mathrm{H}B)^{\mathrm{T}}v_{k+1}+(\tilde{\mathrm{H}}N)^{\mathrm{T}}\tilde{v}_{k+1}\right)\\ &+2\left(g\left(x^*\right)-g\left(y_{k+1}\right)\right).\end{aligned} \tag{3.42}$$

Summing (3.40)–(3.42), and rearranging the terms get

$$\begin{aligned}&\left\|x_{k+1}-x^*\right\|_{\Sigma^{-1}}^2+\left\|\tilde{v}_{k+1}-\tilde{v}^*\right\|_{\tilde{\mathrm{H}}}^2+\left\|v_{k+1}-v^*\right\|_{\mathrm{H}}^2\\ \leq&\left\|v_k-v^*\right\|_{\mathrm{H}}^2+\left\|\tilde{v}_k-\tilde{v}^*\right\|_{\tilde{\mathrm{H}}}^2+\left\|x_k-x^*\right\|_{\Sigma^{-1}}^2-\left\|v_{k+1}-v_k\right\|_{\mathrm{H}}^2\\ &-\left\|\tilde{v}_{k+1}-\tilde{v}_k\right\|_{\tilde{\mathrm{H}}}^2-\left\|x_{k+1}-y_{k+1}\right\|_{\Sigma^{-1}}^2-\left\|x_k-y_{k+1}\right\|_{\Sigma^{-1}}^2\end{aligned}$$

$$
\begin{aligned}
&+2\begin{pmatrix}(v_{k+1}-v^*)^{\mathrm{T}}(\mathrm{H}B\Sigma)\\+(\tilde{v}_{k+1}-\tilde{v}^*)^{\mathrm{T}}(\tilde{\mathrm{H}}N\Sigma)\end{pmatrix}\Sigma^{-1}(y_{k+1}-x_{k+1})\\
&+2(x_k-y_{k+1})^{\mathrm{T}}\Sigma^{-1}\left(\Sigma\nabla f(x_k)-\Sigma\nabla f\left(x^*\right)\right)\\
&-2\left(x_k-x^*\right)^{\mathrm{T}}\Sigma^{-1}\left(\Sigma\nabla f(x_k)-\Sigma\nabla f\left(x^*\right)\right)\\
&+2\begin{pmatrix}\begin{pmatrix}-\Sigma\nabla f(x^*)\\-(\mathrm{H}B)^{\mathrm{T}}v^*-(\tilde{\mathrm{H}}N)^{\mathrm{T}}\tilde{v}^*\end{pmatrix}^{\mathrm{T}}\Sigma^{-1}(y_{k+1}-x^*)\\+g(x^*)-g(y_{k+1})\end{pmatrix}\\
&=\left\|v_k-v^*\right\|_{\mathrm{H}}^2+\left\|\tilde{v}_k-\tilde{v}^*\right\|_{\tilde{\mathrm{H}}}^2+\left\|x_k-x^*\right\|_{\Sigma^{-1}}^2-\|v_{k+1}-v_k\|_{\mathrm{H}}^2\\
&-\|\tilde{v}_{k+1}-\tilde{v}_k\|_{\tilde{\mathrm{H}}}^2-\|x_{k+1}-y_{k+1}\|_{\Sigma^{-1}}^2-\|x_k-y_{k+1}\|_{\Sigma^{-1}}^2\\
&+\left\|\begin{matrix}(\mathrm{H}B\Sigma)^{\mathrm{T}}(v_{k+1}-v_k)\\+(\tilde{\mathrm{H}}N\Sigma)^{\mathrm{T}}(\tilde{v}_{k+1}-\tilde{v}_k)\end{matrix}\right\|_{\Sigma^{-1}}^2+\|y_{k+1}-x_{k+1}\|_{\Sigma^{-1}}^2\\
&-\left\|y_{k+1}-x_{k+1}-(\mathrm{H}B\Sigma)^{\mathrm{T}}(v_{k+1}-v_k)-(\tilde{\mathrm{H}}N\Sigma)^{\mathrm{T}}(\tilde{v}_{k+1}-\tilde{v}_k)\right\|_{\Sigma^{-1}}^2\\
&+\|x_k-y_{k+1}\|_{\Sigma^{-1}}^2+\left\|\Sigma\nabla f(x_k)-\Sigma\nabla f\left(x^*\right)\right\|_{\Sigma^{-1}}^2\\
&-\left\|x_k-y_{k+1}-\left(\Sigma\nabla f(x_k)-\Sigma\nabla f\left(x^*\right)\right)\right\|_{\Sigma^{-1}}^2\\
&-2\left(x_k-x^*\right)^{\mathrm{T}}\left(\nabla f(x_k)-\nabla f\left(x^*\right)\right)\\
&+2\begin{pmatrix}\begin{pmatrix}-\Sigma\nabla f(x^*)\\-(\mathrm{H}B)^{\mathrm{T}}v^*-(\tilde{\mathrm{H}}N)^{\mathrm{T}}\tilde{v}^*\end{pmatrix}^{\mathrm{T}}\Sigma^{-1}(y_{k+1}-x^*)\\+g(x^*)-g(y_{k+1})\end{pmatrix}.
\end{aligned}
\tag{3.43}
$$

Combining (3.29) with Lemma 3.4 yields

$$
\Sigma^{-1}\left(-\Sigma\nabla f\left(x^*\right)-(\mathrm{H}B)^{\mathrm{T}}v^*-(\tilde{\mathrm{H}}N)^{\mathrm{T}}\tilde{v}^*\right)\in\partial g\left(x^*\right).
$$

Applying the property of subdifferential, we obtain

$$
\left(y_{k+1}-x^*\right)^{\mathrm{T}}\Sigma^{-1}\begin{pmatrix}-\Sigma\nabla f(x^*)\\-(\mathrm{H}B)^{\mathrm{T}}v^*\\-(\tilde{\mathrm{H}}N)^{\mathrm{T}}\tilde{v}^*\end{pmatrix}+\left(g\left(x^*\right)-g\left(y_{k+1}\right)\right)\le 0.
$$

On the other hand, combining the Assumption 3.1(i) and Definition 2.1, so we get

$$-\left(\nabla f\left(x_k\right)-\nabla f\left(x^*\right)\right)^{\mathrm{T}}\left(x_k-x^*\right) \leq -\left\|\nabla f\left(x_k\right)-\nabla f\left(x^*\right)\right\|_{\boldsymbol{\beta}}^2,$$

where $\boldsymbol{\beta}=\operatorname{blkdiag}\left\{\beta_i I_{n_i}\right\}_{i \in \mathcal{V}}$. Further, for the term $\|(\mathrm{H}B\Sigma)^{\mathrm{T}}(v_{k+1}-v_k)+(\tilde{\mathrm{H}}N\Sigma)^{\mathrm{T}}(\tilde{v}_{k+1}-\tilde{v}_k)\|_{\Sigma^{-1}}^2$ by using the inequality $\|a_i+b_i\|^2 \leq (1+(1/\mu_i))\|a_i\|^2+(1+\mu_i)\|b_i\|^2$ for $\mu_i>0$ and any $a_i,\ b_i \in \mathbb{R}^{n_i}$, we can obtain (3.30). ■

Appendix B: Proof of Theorem 3.13

We can easily conclude that $\left\{\|T_k-T^*\|_P^2\right\}$ is non-increasing. Sum (3.30) over k from 0 to n to get

$$\begin{aligned}
&\left\|T\left(u^k\right)-u^*\right\|_P^2 \\
&\leq \left\|u_0-u^*\right\|_P^2-\sum_{k=0}^n\left\|v_{k+1}-v_k\right\|_{\mathrm{H}\left(I-BU_1\Sigma\Sigma^{\mathrm{T}}(\mathrm{H}B)^{\mathrm{T}}\right)}^2 \\
&\quad-\sum_{k=0}^n\left\|\tilde{v}_{k+1}-\tilde{v}_k\right\|_{\tilde{\mathrm{H}}\left(I-NU_2\Sigma\Sigma^{\mathrm{T}}(\tilde{\mathrm{H}}N)^{\mathrm{T}}\right)}^2 \\
&\quad-\sum_{k=0}^n\left\|\begin{array}{l}(x_{k+1}-y_{k+1})+(\mathrm{H}B\Sigma)^{\mathrm{T}}(v_{k+1}-v_k) \\ +(\tilde{\mathrm{H}}N\Sigma)^{\mathrm{T}}(\tilde{v}_{k+1}-\tilde{v}_k)\end{array}\right\|_{\Sigma^{-1}}^2 \\
&\quad-\sum_{k=0}^n\left\|x_k-y_{k+1}-\left(\Sigma\nabla f\left(x_k\right)-\Sigma\nabla f\left(x^*\right)\right)\right\|_{\Sigma^{-1}}^2 \\
&\quad-\sum_{k=0}^n\left\|\nabla f\left(x_k\right)-\nabla f\left(x^*\right)\right\|_{2\boldsymbol{\beta}-\Sigma}^2.
\end{aligned}$$

By letting n to infinity, we infer that if there is at least one term tending to infinity in the summation terms of the above inequality, then the right side of the inequality tends to negative infinity, and because the non negative norm $\left\|T\left(u^k\right)-u^*\right\|_P^2$ will not be less than or equal to negative infinity, we know that none of the terms tending to infinity on the right side of the inequality exists, that means,

$$\begin{aligned}
&\sum_{k=0}^{\infty}\|v_{k+1}-v_k\|_{\mathrm{H}(I-BU_1\Sigma\Sigma^{\mathrm{T}}(\mathrm{H}B)^{\mathrm{T}})}<\infty,\\
&\sum_{k=0}^{\infty}\|\tilde{v}_{k+1}-\tilde{v}_k\|_{\tilde{\mathrm{H}}\left(I-NU_2\Sigma\Sigma^{\mathrm{T}}(\tilde{\mathrm{H}}N)^{\mathrm{T}}\right)}<\infty,\\
&\sum_{k=0}^{\infty}\left\|\begin{array}{l}(x_{k+1}-y_{k+1})+(\mathrm{H}B\Sigma)^{\mathrm{T}}(v_{k+1}-v_k)\\ +(\tilde{\mathrm{H}}N\Sigma)^{\mathrm{T}}(\tilde{v}_{k+1}-\tilde{v}_k)\end{array}\right\|<\infty,\\
&\sum_{k=0}^{\infty}\|x_k-y_{k+1}-(\Sigma\nabla f(x_k)-\Sigma\nabla f(x^*))\|<\infty,\\
&\sum_{k=0}^{\infty}\|\nabla f(x_k)-\nabla f(x^*)\|<\infty.
\end{aligned}$$

Thus, we get

$$\lim_{k\to\infty}\|v_{k+1}-v_k\|_{\mathrm{H}(I-BU_1\Sigma\Sigma^{\mathrm{T}}(\mathrm{H}B)^{\mathrm{T}})}=0, \tag{3.44}$$

$$\lim_{k\to\infty}\|\tilde{v}_{k+1}-\tilde{v}_k\|_{\tilde{\mathrm{H}}\left(I-NU_2\Sigma\Sigma^{\mathrm{T}}(\tilde{\mathrm{H}}N)^{\mathrm{T}}\right)}=0, \tag{3.45}$$

$$\lim_{k\to\infty}\left\|\begin{array}{l}(x_{k+1}-y_{k+1})+(\mathrm{H}B\Sigma)^{\mathrm{T}}(v_{k+1}-v_k)\\ +(\tilde{\mathrm{H}}N\Sigma)^{\mathrm{T}}(\tilde{v}_{k+1}-\tilde{v}_k)\end{array}\right\|=0, \tag{3.46}$$

$$\lim_{k\to\infty}\left\|x_k-y_{k+1}-\left(\Sigma\nabla f(x_k)-\Sigma\nabla f\left(x^*\right)\right)\right\|=0, \tag{3.47}$$

$$\lim_{k\to\infty}\left\|\nabla f(x_k)-\nabla f\left(x^*\right)\right\|=0. \tag{3.48}$$

From (3.47) and (3.48), we have

$$\lim_{k\to\infty}\|x_k-y_{k+1}\|=0. \tag{3.49}$$

Meanwhile, $I-BU_1\Sigma\Sigma^{\mathrm{T}}(\mathrm{H}B)^{\mathrm{T}}$ and $I-NU_2\Sigma\Sigma^{\mathrm{T}}(\tilde{\mathrm{H}}N)^{\mathrm{T}}$ are symmetric positive definite. Therefore, (3.44) and (3.45) imply that

$$\lim_{k\to\infty}\|v_{k+1}-v_k\|=0,\ \lim_{k\to\infty}\|\tilde{v}_{k+1}-\tilde{v}_k\|=0. \tag{3.50}$$

Combine (3.46) with (3.50) to obtain $\lim_{k\to\infty}\|x_{k+1}-y_{k+1}\|=0$. Therefore, from (3.49) and the above equality, we have

$$\lim_{k\to\infty}\|x_{k+1}-x_k\|^2=0. \tag{3.51}$$

Finally, (3.50) and (3.51) yield $\left\|T\left(u^k\right)-u^*\right\|_P^2$. Moreover, The operator T is continuous because it is nonexpansive. The sequence $\left\|u^k-u^*\right\|_P^2$ is non-increasing and $\left\|T\left(u^k\right)-u^*\right\|_P^2$. Applying Lemma 3.12, we conclude that the sequence $\{u_k\}$ converges to a fixed point of the operator T. Then based on Lemma 3.11, we can get that $\{x_k\}$ converge to a solution to (3.2). ■

Appendix C: Proof of Theorem 3.15

According to the definition of S^k, we have

$$\begin{aligned}\mathbb{E}\circ(E_{k+1}) &= \sum_{\varepsilon\in\phi}\left(S^{k+1}=\varepsilon\right)\sum_{j=1}^{m} S_j \boldsymbol{P}_j = \sum_{j=1}^{m}\sum_{\varepsilon\in\phi}\left(S^{k+1}=\varepsilon\right)\varepsilon_j \boldsymbol{P}_j \\ &= \sum_{j=1}^{m}\sum_{\varepsilon\in\phi,\varepsilon_j=1}\left(S^{k+1}=\varepsilon\right)\boldsymbol{P}_j = \sum_{j=1}^{m} p_j \boldsymbol{P}_j = \Pi.\end{aligned}$$

Meanwhile, E_k is a diagonal matrix with diagonal element is 0 or 1, so E_k is self-adjoint and idempotent. Combining with the above results, we get

$$\begin{aligned}&\mathbb{E}\left[\left\|T\left(u^k\right)-u^*\right\|_{\Pi^{-1}P}^2\right] \\ &= \mathbb{E}\left[\left\|u_k+E_{k+1}\left(Tu_k-u_k\right)-u^*\right\|_{\Pi^{-1}P}^2\right] \\ &= \mathbb{E}\begin{bmatrix}\|u_k-u^*\|_{\Pi^{-1}P}^2+\|E_{k+1}\left(Tu_k-u_k\right)\|_{\Pi^{-1}P}^2 \\ +2(u_k-u^*)^{\mathrm{T}}\Pi^{-1}P\left(E_{k+1}\left(Tu_k-u_k\right)\right)\end{bmatrix} \\ &= \left\|u_k-u^*\right\|_{\Pi^{-1}P}^2+\mathbb{E}\left[\|Tu_k-u_k\|_{(E_{k+1})^2\Pi^{-1}P}^2\right] \\ &\quad +\mathbb{E}\left[2\left(u_k-u^*\right)^{\mathrm{T}}\Pi^{-1}P\left(E_{k+1}\left(Tu_k-u_k\right)\right)\right] \\ &= \left\|u_k-u^*\right\|_{\Pi^{-1}P}^2+\|Tu_k-u_k\|_P^2+2\left(u_k-u^*\right)^{\mathrm{T}}P(Tu_k-u_k).\end{aligned}$$

For $a,\ b,\ c\in\mathbb{R}^{n+r+l}$ and a positive definite matrix $\mathrm{K}\in\mathbb{R}^{(n+r+l)\times(n+r+l)}$, there holds that

$$2(a-b)^{\mathrm{T}}\mathrm{K}\,(c-b)=\|c-b\|_{\mathrm{K}}^2+\|a-b\|_{\mathrm{K}}^2-\|a-c\|_{\mathrm{K}}^2, \tag{3.52}$$

then according to Lemma 3.12, we can derive

$$
\begin{aligned}
&\mathbb{E}\left[\left\|T\left(u^k\right)-u^*\right\|_{\Pi^{-1}P}^2\right] \\
&=\left\|u_k-u^*\right\|_{\Pi^{-1}P}^2+\left\|Tu_k-u^*\right\|_P^2-\left\|u_k-u^*\right\|_P^2 \\
&\leq\left\|u_k-u^*\right\|_{\Pi^{-1}P}^2-\left\|v_{k+1}-v_k\right\|_{\mathrm{H}\left(I-BU_1\Sigma\Sigma^{\mathrm{T}}(\mathrm{H}B)^{\mathrm{T}}\right)}^2 \\
&\quad-\left\|\tilde{v}_{k+1}-\tilde{v}_k\right\|_{\tilde{\mathrm{H}}\left(I-NU_2\Sigma\Sigma^{\mathrm{T}}(\tilde{\mathrm{H}}N)^{\mathrm{T}}\right)}^2 \\
&\quad-\left\|\nabla f\left(x_k\right)-\nabla f\left(x^*\right)\right\|_{2\boldsymbol{\beta}-\Sigma}^2 .
\end{aligned}
$$

Therefore, we can know that the sequence generated by inequality (3.34) is stochastic Fejér monotonicity. Due to the space limitation, we can refer to [23, Th. 3] for the remaining proof process.

Chapter 4
Distributed Triple Proximal Splitting Algorithm for Nonsmooth Composite Optimization

Abstract In this chapter, we consider a class of distributed nonsmooth composite optimization problems over undirected graphs. The global optimization problem is to minimize the sum of local objective functions consisting of a Lipschitz-differentiable convex function and two possibly nonsmooth convex functions, one of which contains a bounded linear operator. The goal is to solve the global optimization problem through distributed computation and communication over a network of agents without a central coordinator. Through using triple proximal splitting operators to deal with the nonsmooth terms, we propose a novel distributed algorithm with uncoordinated step sizes where the step sizes with independent upper bounds are also distributed for agents or edges over the communication network. Furthermore, we establish the sublinear convergence rates for the proposed algorithm in terms of the first-order optimality residual in a non-ergodic sense. Simulation experiments on a constrained quadratic programming problem and an optimal load sharing problem are carried out to verify the correctness of the theoretical results.

Keywords Distributed optimization · Nonsmooth function · Primal-dual algorithm · Proximal operator · Uncoordinated step size · Fixed-point iteration

4.1 Introduction

In this chapter, we aim to solve a distributed nonsmooth composite optimization problem over undirected graphs with the form of

$$\min_{x_1,\ldots,x_m} \sum_{i=1}^{m} f_i(x_i) + g_i(x_i) + h_i(A_i x_i), \tag{4.1}$$

under constraints related to edges. Here, $f_i : \mathbb{R}^{n_i} \to \mathbb{R}$ is a Lipschitz-differentiable convex function while $g_i : \mathbb{R}^{n_i} \to \bar{\mathbb{R}} \triangleq \mathbb{R} \cup \{+\infty\}$ and $h_i : \mathbb{R}^{n_i} \to \bar{\mathbb{R}}$ are two proper lower semi-continuous convex functions (possibly nonsmooth). f_i, g_i, and h_i are local objective functions to agent i, and A_i is a bounded linear operator.

H. Li et al., *Network-System Research and Distributed Composite Algorithm Design*, Computational Intelligence Methods and Applications,
https://doi.org/10.1007/978-981-95-0911-9_4

Note that though the possibly nonsmooth functions g_i and h_i have the proximal property, the sum of them may not. In fact, this composite optimization problem is summarized from a wide range of problems in the field of machine learning (for example, the distributed fused LASSO problem [26]), resource allocation [72–74], etc. Similar to general distributed optimization studies, we assume that each agent has a local memory and computational unit to process information independently and can only communicate with its neighbors. Under these conditions, the goal of all agents is to cooperatively seek an optimal solution to the global optimization problem through local computations and communications.

As a parallel computational model, distributed optimization splits a complex centralized problem into a series of simple subproblems, which has great significance in relieving the pressure of processors with limited computing resources. Traditionally, distributed optimization methods focused on general problems with single function, and then some effective algorithms over multi-agents systems were developed, see [9, 75–88]. The consensus strategy of multi-agent systems was considered in [9, 75, 76]. Quite a few works adopt gradient descent strategy including projected subgradient algorithms [80], primal-dual subgradient algorithms [81–83], and algorithms based on the Alternating Direction Method of Multipliers (ADMM) [84–86], etc. The application scenarios of multi-agent systems in the engineering field were presented in [87, 88].

In this chapter, we mainly devote ourselves to distributed nonsmooth optimization. Nonsmooth terms may come from regularization or penalty methods for constraints, which are deeply studied in engineering fields such as the L_1-minimization [89] and the constrained DOCO problem [90]. So far, distributed nonsmooth optimization works can be roughly divided into two typical categories. The first one is based on nonsmooth analysis theory [91] which results in a series of algorithms [92–97]. However, the subgradients of the nonsmooth terms are discontinuous and may cause violent vibration in the systems, which is unacceptable especially for multiagent dynamical systems [98]. Meanwhile, the nonsmooth terms also make it more difficult to establish the convergence of algorithms in theory. These situations result in the algorithms of the second category which consider the composite optimization problems and utilize the proximal splitting operator to estimate the subgradient of the nonsmooth functions designed for multiagent systems. Previous works on proximal splitting methods include some centralized algorithms [4–6, 8, 99] and distributed proximal gradient algorithms [18, 25, 54, 100, 101] such as PG-ADMM in [25, 100] for optimization problems with nonsmooth local objective function. Although the works above have achieved some important results for nonsmooth optimization problems, the distributed nonsmooth composite optimization problem studied in this chapter still cannot be solved completely due to the uncertainly proximal property of the nonsmooth part $g_i + h_i(A_i \cdot)$ [98]. In recent years, several distributed nonsmooth composite optimization problems have been directly considered [17, 98]. Such problems are gradually becoming a new research hotspot.

Compared with the recent nonsmooth discrete-time works [18, 25, 54, 92, 93, 96, 100, 101], this chapter studies the nonsmooth composite optimization problem considering the partially smooth property and process the uncertainly proximal property of nonsmooth terms with multiple proximal splitting operators. Compared with the existing works [4–6, 8, 99] on nonsmooth composite optimization focusing on centralized results, the proposed distributed algorithm has superiorities in network robustness and overcomes the limit of computing resources. The contributions of the chapter are summarized as follows:

(i) The studied nonsmooth composite optimization problem considers a summation structure to employ the partial smooth property. Compared with the common nonsmooth optimization problem, the composite structure with two nonsmooth terms can include more optimization scenarios with multiple constraints (e.g., machine learning [26], resource allocation [72–74], and model predictive control [65]).
(ii) Based on the primal-dual strategy, we transform the target problem into an unconstrained problem with three nonsmooth terms and propose a distributed optimization algorithm. The novel algorithm uses proximal splitting operators to estimate the subgradients of the nonsmooth terms and allows decision variables to possess uncoordinated dimensions, which can be applied to more distributed optimization problems rather than just the consensus ones.
(iii) The proposed algorithm has a fully distributed structure by employing the uncoordinated step sizes which are also distributed with regard to agents or edges. Particularly, each uncoordinated step size has its own upper bound instead of global restriction.
(iv) We provide the convergence analysis of the proposed algorithm through the nonexpansive property of the operator defined by one iteration and the optimality conditions from the primal-dual Lagrangian function. Moreover, a sublinear convergence rate $o(1/k)$ is established in terms of the first-order optimality residual in a non-ergodic sense, which is a slightly faster result compared to the ergodic rate $O(1/k)$.

4.2 Preliminaries

In this section, we start by presenting the basic knowledge of graph theory and the notations throughout this chapter. Then, with some necessary assumptions, we formulate the distributed optimization problem and transform it into an unconstrained one.

4.2.1 Notation

Throughout the chapter, we use lowercase letters to denote column vectors and uppercase letters to denote matrices. $\mathbb{R}^n$ represents the set of all the n-dimensional real vectors while $\mathbb{R}^{n\times m}$ indicates the set of all n-rows and m-columns real matrices. Let I_n be the n-dimensional identity operator defined on a real space, and for simplicity, we do not specify its dimensions when it is clear from the context. For a solvable optimization problem, its solution set is $\mathcal{S}$. diag$\{a\}$ generates a diagonal matrix with vector a's elements as diagonal elements and $\odot$ denotes the Hadamard product. For arbitrary matrices M and N, blkdiag $\{M, N\}$ represents the block diagonal matrix with the diagonal blocks M and N. We denote by $M^\top$ the transpose of matrix M. When M is a symmetric positive definite matrix, we define $\langle x, y\rangle_M = \langle x, My\rangle$, the induced norm $\|x\|_M = \sqrt{\langle x, x\rangle_M}$, and the maximum eigenvalue $\tau_{\max}(M)$. For an extended-real-valued function f, dom$f$ represents its domain. We use ∂f to indicate the subdifferential of f and f^* to denote the conjugate function of f, which implies that $f^*(y) = \sup_{x\in\mathbb{R}^n}\{\langle y, x\rangle - f(x)\}$. In addition, considering a positive constant γ and a symmetric positive definite matrix Γ, the proximal mapping of f is defined by the resolvent of $\gamma\partial f$ as $\mathrm{prox}_{\gamma f}(y) = (I+\gamma\partial f)^{-1}(y) = \arg\min_x f(x) + \frac{1}{2\gamma}\|x-y\|^2$, while the proximal mapping related to $\|\cdot\|_\Gamma$ is determined by the resolvent of $\Gamma^{-1}\partial f$ as $\mathrm{prox}_f^\Gamma(y) = \left(I+\Gamma^{-1}\partial f\right)^{-1}(y) = \arg\min_x f(x) + \frac{1}{2}\|x-y\|_\Gamma^2$.

4.2.2 *Model of Optimization Problem*

Consider an undirected graph $\mathcal{G} = (\mathcal{V}, \mathcal{E})$ with m agents. The goal of all agents is to cooperatively solve the nonsmooth composite optimization problem formulated as follows:

$$\min_{x_1,\ldots,x_m\in\mathbb{R}^n} \sum_{i=1}^m \left[f_i(x_i) + g_i(x_i) + h_i(A_i x_i)\right], \tag{4.2a}$$

$$\text{s.t.} \quad \omega_{ij}x_i + \omega_{ji}x_j = b_{(i,j)}, \qquad (i,j)\in\mathcal{E}, \tag{4.2b}$$

where $x_i \in \mathbb{R}^{n_i}$ is the local decision variable and $A_i : \mathbb{R}^{n_i} \to \mathbb{R}^{r_i}$ is a bounded linear operator. f_i, g_i and h_i are local objective functions only known by agent i. $\omega_{ij} : \mathbb{R}^{n_i} \to \mathbb{R}^{l_{(i,j)}}$ and $\omega_{ji} : \mathbb{R}^{n_j} \to \mathbb{R}^{l_{(i,j)}}$ are two bounded linear operators and $b_{(i,j)} \in \mathbb{R}^{l_{(i,j)}}$ for any $j \in \mathcal{N}_i$. Here, $l_{(i,j)}$ represents the value of dimension of $b_{(i,j)}$. (4.2b) contains equality constraints representing the coupling of all edges $(i,j)\in\mathcal{E}$ over the network.

Remark 4.1 Noticing that when $\omega_{ij} = I$, $\omega_{ji} = -I$, and $b_{(i,j)} = 0$, (4.2b) is reduced to the classical consensus constraint. The consensus constraint is generally used to decompose a problem with a summation structure into distributed subproblems [9]. However, for problems with naturally distributed structures, such as resource allocation, consensus constraints cannot describe the coupling relationship over networks. In addition, (4.2b) allows different x_i to take different dimensions instead of the same dimension limited by consensus constraints, which meets the requirement of decision variables in formation control [17] transformed from different inputs of agents. Therefore, (4.2b) is a more general coupling constraint formulation. We make the following necessary assumptions.

Assumption 4.1 *For each agent $i \in \mathcal{V}$,*

(i) The local function f_i is a proper lower semi-continuous convex function and differentiable with Lipschitz continuous gradients. Let $1/\beta_i$ ($\beta_i > 0$) be the Lipschitz constant of ∇f_i, then we have

$$\beta_i \|\nabla f_i(x_i) - \nabla f_i(y_i)\|^2 \leq \langle x_i - y_i, \nabla f_i(x_i) - \nabla f_i(y_i) \rangle . \tag{4.3}$$

(ii) The local functions g_i and h_i are two proper convex and possibly nonsmooth functions;
(iii) There exists $x_i \in dom\ g_i$ such that $A_i x_i \in dom\ h_i$. Meanwhile, the set of solutions to problem (4.2) is nonempty;
(iv) Graph $\mathcal{G}$ is undirected and connected.

Remark 4.2 The assumption that the nonsmooth cost function contains a partially smooth term is not uncommon in distributed nonsmooth optimization [18, 25, 54, 100]. However, most works on distributed nonsmooth optimization consider the smooth + nonsmooth structure, where proximal gradients are difficult to calculate when nonsmooth terms are complex. Therefore, we further divide the nonsmooth term into two parts with and without the linear operator. In fact, the smooth + nonsmooth + nonsmmoth with a linear operator structure has been studied in centralized nonsmooth optimization, but rarely studied in distributed optimization.

Since the strong convex property is not supposed in Assumption 4.1, problem (4.2) may have multiple optimal solutions. To describe this phenomenon, we define $\mathcal{S}$ as the set of optimal solutions. Note that problem (4.2) is an optimization problem with equality constraints. Next, we introduce a penalty function to transform it into an unconstrained problem. Firstly, for the global variable $\mathrm{x} = col(x_1, \ldots, x_m)$, define a linear operator:

$$N_{(i,j)} : \mathrm{x} \mapsto \left((\omega_{ij} x_i)^\top, (\omega_{ji} x_j)^\top \right)^\top . \tag{4.4}$$

Then, we introduce the following indicator function:

$$\delta_C(e) = \begin{cases} 0, & e \in C, \\ +\infty, & e \notin C, \end{cases} \tag{4.5}$$

and the set $C_{(i,j)} = \left\{ \left(z_1^\top, z_2^\top\right)^\top | z_1 + z_2 = b_{(i.j)} \right\}$. Let $C = C_{(i,j)}$ and $e = N_{(i,j)}\mathrm{x}$. Thus, we can define the constraint over an edge into a penalty function

$\delta_{C_{(i,j)}}\left(N_{(i,j)}\mathrm{x}\right)$ and further reformulate the problem (4.2) as

$$\min_{x_1,\ldots,x_m} \sum_{i=1}^{m} \left(f_i\left(x_i\right) + g_i\left(x_i\right) + h_i\left(A_i x_i\right)\right) + \sum_{i=1}^{m} \sum_{(i,j)\in\mathcal{E}} \delta_{C_{(i,j)}}\left(N_{(i,j)}\mathrm{x}\right). \tag{4.6}$$

The penalty function $\delta_{C_{(i,j)}}\left(N_{(i,j)}\mathrm{x}\right)$ is a convex nonsmooth term in unconstrained optimization problem (4.6), and also a composite function containing a linear operator which has a similar structure to $h_i\left(A_i x_i\right)$. This special structure will be utilized to develop a new distributed optimization algorithm in the next section.

4.2.3 *Communication Network*

We introduce some basic knowledge on graph theory which is instrumental to illustrate the communication network. Let $\mathcal{G} = (\mathcal{V}, \mathcal{E})$ denote an undirected graph with m agents, where $\mathcal{V} = \{1, 2, \ldots, m\}$ represents the agents set and $\mathcal{E} \subset \mathcal{V} \times \mathcal{V}$ represents the edges set. $\mathcal{N}_i$ denotes the set of all neighbors of agent i and $(i, j) \in \mathcal{E}$ denotes the edge between agent i and agent j. Here, (i, j) is an unordered pair while i and j are ordered. In this chapter, we assume that edges of the graph are undirected with no self-loops.

4.2.4 *Motivating Scenarios*

The composite structure allows problem (4.2) to cover many optimization scenarios, especially for problems with complex constraints. Here, we provide two practical examples for demonstration.

4.2.4.1 Constrained Regression Problem

Logistic regression problems are widely employed in machine learning. Inspired by [102], we also consider the inequality constraints to avoid some seriously deviated estimations. Coupling constraint (4.2b) should reduce to the consensus constraint to solve the problem in a distributed manner. The explicit formulation of the constrained distributed logistic regression problem is described as follows:

$$\begin{aligned} \min_{x_1,\ldots,x_m} \ & \frac{1}{m}\sum_{i=1}^{m} f_i\left(x_i\right) + \kappa_1 \|x_i\|_1, \\ \text{s.t.} \ & M_i x_i \leq w_i, \ i \in \mathcal{V}, \\ & x_i - x_j = 0, \ (i, j) \in \mathcal{E}, \end{aligned} \tag{4.7}$$

where $f_i(x_i) = \frac{1}{e_i}\sum_{i=1}^{e_i} \ln\left(1 + \exp\left(-b_{ij}c_{ij}^{\top}x_i\right)\right) + \kappa_2\|x_i\|^2$, $x_i \in \mathbb{R}^n$. For each agent $i \in \mathcal{V}$, e_i represents the number of samples allocated to agent i, $c_{ij} \in \mathbb{R}^n$ is the j-th sample and $b_{ij} \in \mathbb{R}$ is the j-th label. The regularization term $\kappa_1\|x_i\|_1$ imposes sparsity of the optimal solution while $\kappa_2\|x_i\|^2$ is used to avoid overfitting. κ_1 and κ_2 are two positive parameters. We use the indicator function as the penalty function for the inequality constraint such that problem (4.7) can be rewritten as

$$\begin{aligned} &\min_{x_1,\ldots,x_m} \frac{1}{m}\sum_{i=1}^{m} f_i(x_i) + \kappa_1\|x_i\|_1 + \delta_{\mathcal{C}_i}(M_i x_i), \\ &\text{s.t.} \quad x_i - x_j = 0, \quad (i,j) \in \mathcal{E}, \end{aligned} \tag{4.8}$$

where $\mathcal{C}_i = \{y_i | y_i \leq w_i\}$. Thus, the constrained distributed logistic regression problem is covered by problem (4.2). In fact, if $f_i(x_i) = \|L_i x_i - c_i\|^2$ in problem (4.7) where L_i represents the matrix of the data and c_i denotes the label, it can also become another well-known problem in machine learning, the constrained LASSO problem [103].

4.2.4.2 Optimal Load Sharing Problem

The optimal load sharing problem is a typical resource allocation problem to decide the most efficient generation allocation meeting the load demands. Considering the generation capacities and transmission line delivering limits, it can be established as

$$\begin{aligned} &\min_{p_1,\cdots,p_m} \sum_{i=1}^{m} C_i(p_i), \\ &\text{s.t.} \quad p_i = \sum_{l=1}^{N} H_{il}v_l + D_i, i \in \mathcal{V}, \\ &\qquad p_i^{\min} \leq p_i \leq p_i^{\max}, \quad i \in \mathcal{V}, \\ &\qquad v_l^{\min} \leq v_l \leq v_l^{\max}, \quad l \in \mathcal{E}, \end{aligned} \tag{4.9}$$

where i belongs to the bus set and l belongs to the transmission line set. C_i is the generation cost function, $p_i \in \mathbb{R}^n$ is the generator output, and D_i is the demand on the bus i. $v_l \in \mathbb{R}^n$ denotes the power on the transmission line l and H_{il} indicates that the power flows in or out bus i with taking -1 or 1, respectively. To process the edge variable v_l at an agent, define $v_i^l \in \mathbb{R}^n$ on bus i and $v_j^l \in \mathbb{R}^n$ on bus j, $i, j \in \mathcal{N}_l$ as the estimation of the power flow v_l on the transmission line connecting buses i and j, where $v_i^l = v_j^l = v_l$. Then, through setting v_i^l as the decision variable, the following equivalent form of the optimal load sharing problem [72] is given as

$$
\begin{aligned}
\min_{v} \quad & \sum_{i=1}^{m} C_i \left(\sum_{l=1}^{N} H_{il} v_i^l + D_i \right), \\
\text{s.t.} \quad & p_i^{\min} \leq \sum_{l=1}^{N} H_{il} v_i^l + D_i \leq p_i^{\max}, \quad i \in \mathcal{V}, \\
& v_l^{\min} \leq v_i^l \leq v_l^{\max}, \ \ i \in \mathcal{N}_l, \ \ l \in \mathcal{E}, \\
& v_i^l = v_j^l, i, j \in \mathcal{N}_l, \ \ l \in \mathcal{E}.
\end{aligned}
\tag{4.10}
$$

Let $x_i = (v_i^1, v_i^2, ..., v_i^N)^\top$, $x^{\min} = (v_1^{\min}, ..., v_N^{\min})^\top$, $x^{\max} = (v_1^{\max}, ..., v_N^{\max})^\top$, $H_i = (H_{i1}, H_{i2}, ..., H_{iN})^\top$, and $\bar{H}_i = (|H_{i1}|, |H_{i2}|, ..., |H_{iM}|)^\top$. For $i, j \in \mathcal{V}, i \neq j$, define linear mappings $L_i x_i = H_i^\top x_i$ and $U_{ij} = \text{diag}\{\bar{H}_i \odot \bar{H}_j\}$ when $i < j$ while $U_{ij} = \text{diag}\{-\bar{H}_i \odot \bar{H}_j\}$ when $i > j$. Thus, problem (4.10) can be rewritten as

$$
\begin{aligned}
\min_{x_1, \cdots, x_m \in \mathbb{R}^n} \quad & \sum_{i=1}^{m} C_i \left(L_i x_i + D_i \right), \\
\text{s.t.} \quad & p_i^{\min} - D_i \leq L_i x_i \leq p_i^{\max} - D_i, \ \ i \in \mathcal{V}, \\
& x_i^{\min} \leq x_i \leq x_i^{\max}, \ \ i \in \mathcal{V}, \\
& U_{ij} x_i + U_{ji} x_j = 0, \quad (i, j) \in \mathcal{E}.
\end{aligned}
\tag{4.11}
$$

Here, we just use the optimal load sharing problem as an example of problem (4.2) and provide necessary steps. One can refer to [72] for detailed transformation process. Letting $\tilde{C}_i(x_i) = C_i(L_i x_i + D_i)$ for $i \in \mathcal{V}$ and using the indicator function as the penalty functions, the optimal load sharing problem is finally equivalent to

$$
\min_{x_1, \cdots, x_m \in \mathbb{R}^n} \sum_{i=1}^{m} \left[\tilde{C}_i(x_i) + \delta_{X_i}(x_i) + \delta_{C_i}(L_i x_i) \right], \tag{4.12a}
$$

$$
\text{s.t.} \quad U_{ij} x_i + U_{ji} x_j = 0, \quad (i, j) \in \mathcal{E}, \tag{4.12b}
$$

which can be covered by problem (4.2). Note that (4.12b) can be described by (4.2b) but not by the consensus constraint.

4.3 Algorithm Development

In this section, we briefly introduce the development of the distributed algorithm whose local update flows for each agent are provided in Algorithm 5. Employing a proximal splitting operator to estimate the subgradients of nonsmooth terms is

Algorithm 5 TPUS

Initialization: For all agents $i \in \mathcal{V}$, $u_i^0 \in \mathbb{R}^{r_i}$, $\tilde{u}_i^0 \in \mathbb{R}^{n_i}$, $\tilde{s}_i^0 \in \mathbb{R}^{n_i}$, and $s_{(i,j),i}^0 \in \mathbb{R}^{l_{(i,j)}}$ for any $j \in \mathcal{N}_i$.

For $k = 0, 1, \ldots, i \in \mathcal{V}$ and $j \in \mathcal{N}_i$ **do:**

$$x_i^k = \text{prox}_{\gamma_i g_i}\left(\tilde{u}_i^k + \tilde{s}_i^k\right), \tag{4.13a}$$

$$\begin{aligned} u_i^{k+1} = \text{prox}_{\sigma_i h_i^*}\Bigg(& \left(I - 2\gamma_i \sigma_i A_i A_i^\top\right) u_i^k \\ & + 2\sigma_i A_i \left(x_i^k - \tilde{u}_i^k - \frac{1}{2}\gamma_i \nabla f_i\left(x_i^k\right)\right)\Bigg), \end{aligned} \tag{4.13b}$$

$$\begin{aligned} s_{(i,j),i}^{k+1} = & \frac{1}{2} s_{(i,j),i}^k - \gamma_i \rho_{(i,j)} \sum_{z \in \mathcal{N}_i} \omega_{ij} \omega_{iz}^\top s_{(i,z),i}^k \\ & + \frac{1}{2} s_{(i,j),j}^k - \gamma_j \rho_{(i,j)} \sum_{z \in \mathcal{N}_j} \omega_{ji} \omega_{jz}^\top s_{(j,z),j}^k \\ & + \rho_{(i,j)} \omega_{ij} \left(x_i^k - \tilde{s}_i^k - \frac{1}{2}\gamma_i \nabla f_i\left(x_i^k\right)\right) \\ & + \rho_{(i,j)} \omega_{ji} \left(x_j^k - \tilde{s}_j^k - \frac{1}{2}\gamma_j \nabla f_j\left(x_j^k\right)\right) \\ & - \frac{1}{2} \rho_{(i,j)} b_{(i,j)}, \end{aligned} \tag{4.13c}$$

$$\tilde{u}_i^{k+1} = \frac{1}{2} x_i^k - \frac{1}{2}\gamma_i \nabla f_i\left(x_i^k\right) - \gamma_i A_i^\top u_i^{k+1}, \tag{4.13d}$$

$$\tilde{s}_i^{k+1} = \frac{1}{2} x_i^k - \frac{1}{2}\gamma_i \nabla f\left(x_i^k\right) - \gamma_i \sum_{j \in \mathcal{N}_i} \omega_{ij}^\top s_{(i,j),i}^{k+1}. \tag{4.13e}$$

Agent i sends the local information x_i^k, γ_i, $\nabla f_i\left(x_i^k\right)$, ω_{ij}, $s_{(i,j),i}^k$, and $\tilde{s}_i^k$ to agent j for $j \in \mathcal{N}_i$, and then broadcasts ω_{ji}, $s_{(j,i),j}^k$.

Until $\left\| x_i^{k+1} - x_i^k \right\|$ approaches zero.

End

Output: The sequence $\left(x_i^k\right)_{k=1}^\infty$ to estimate an optimal solution $x_i^* \in \mathcal{S}$ at agent i.

an effective method in nonsmooth optimization problems. However, the coupling between functions and linear operators $h_i\left(A_i \cdot\right)$, $\delta_{C_{(i,j)}}\left(N_{(i,j)} \cdot\right)$ cannot be processed directly by proximal operators. To deal with this, based on [22, Proposition 19, 20] we establish the Lagrangian function of the optimization problem (4.6) as follows:

$$\mathcal{L} = \sum_{i=1}^m \left(f_i\left(x_i\right) + g_i\left(x_i\right) - h_i^*\left(u_i\right) + \left(A_i x_i\right)^\top u_i\right)$$

$$+\sum_{i=1}^{m}\sum_{(i,j)\in\mathcal{E}}\left(\left(N_{(i,j)}\mathrm{x}\right)^{\top}s_{(i,j)}-\delta^{*}_{C_{(i,j)}}\left(s_{(i,j)}\right)\right), \tag{4.14}$$

where $x_i \in \mathbb{R}^{n_i}$ is the primal variable and both $u_i \in \mathbb{R}^{r_i}$ and $s_{(i,j)} \in \mathbb{R}^{2l_{(i,j)}}$ are the dual variables. Note that in (4.14), the variables $s_{(i,j)}$ depend on edges (i, j) rather than agent i and x is not yet distributed, which does not meet the requirements of distributed operation. Therefore, the next is to split them by agents $i \in \mathcal{V}$.

The edge-based variable $s_{(i,j)}$ for $(i, j) \in \mathcal{E}$ cannot be computed locally by single agent i or j. To solve this problem, we employ two new dual variables $(s_{(i,j),i}^{\top}, s_{(i,j),j}^{\top})^{\top}$ instead of $s_{(i,j)}$. Here, $s_{(i,j),i} \in \mathbb{R}^{l_{(i,j)}}$ is maintained by agent i and $s_{(i,j),j} \in \mathbb{R}^{l_{(i,j)}}$ is maintained by agent j. Thus, the second term of (4.14) results in

$$\begin{aligned}
&\sum_{i=1}^{m}\sum_{(i,j)\in\mathcal{E}}\left(\left(N_{(i,j)}\mathrm{x}\right)^{\top}s_{(i,j)}-\delta^{*}_{C_{(i,j)}}\left(s_{(i,j)}\right)\right)\\
=&\sum_{i=1}^{m}\sum_{(i,j)\in\mathcal{E}}\left(\left(\omega_{ij}x_i\right)^{\top}s_{(i,j),i}+\left(\omega_{ji}x_j\right)^{\top}s_{(i,j),j}\right)-\sum_{i=1}^{m}\sum_{(i,j)\in\mathcal{E}}\delta^{*}_{C_{(i,j)}}\left(s_{(i,j)}\right)\\
=&\sum_{i=1}^{m}\sum_{j\in\mathcal{N}_i}\left(\left(\omega_{ij}x_i\right)^{\top}s_{(i,j),i}-\delta^{*}_{C_{(i,j)}}\left(s_{(i,j)}\right)\right).
\end{aligned} \tag{4.15}$$

Hence, the Lagrangian function (4.14) can be rewritten as

$$\begin{aligned}
\mathcal{L}=&\sum_{i=1}^{m}\left(f_i\left(x_i\right)+g_i\left(x_i\right)-h_i^{*}\left(u_i\right)+\left(A_ix_i\right)^{\top}u_i\right)\\
&+\sum_{i=1}^{m}\sum_{j\in\mathcal{N}_i}\left(\left(\omega_{ij}x_i\right)^{\top}s_{(i,j),i}-\delta^{*}_{C_{(i,j)}}\left(s_{(i,j)}\right)\right).
\end{aligned} \tag{4.16}$$

Notice that $s_{(i,j)}$ still exists in (4.16). We will eliminate this term with the process of designing our algorithm.

For any $(i, j) \in \mathcal{E}$, define $\mathrm{s} \in \mathbb{R}^{\sum_{(i,j)\in\mathcal{E}} 2l_{(i,j)}}$ stacked by $s_{(i,j)}$ and $N \in \mathbb{R}^{\sum_{(i,j)\in\mathcal{E}} 2l_{(i,j)}\times\sum_{i=1}^{m} n_i}$ stacked by $N_{(i,j)}$, which means that $N : \mathrm{x} \to \left(N_{(i,j)}\mathrm{x}\right)_{(i,j)\in\mathcal{E}}$ exists. Then based on (4.16) and using the proximal operators to estimate nonsmooth terms, we first propose the following updates to solve problem (4.6):

$$x_i^k = \mathrm{prox}_{\gamma_i g_i}\left(\tilde{u}_i^k + \tilde{s}_i^k\right), \tag{4.17a}$$

$$u_i^{k+1} = \text{prox}_{\sigma_i h_i^*}\left[\begin{array}{l}\left(I - 2\gamma_i\sigma_i A_i A_i^\top\right) u_i^k \\ +2\sigma_i A_i\left(x_i^k - \tilde{u}_i^k - \frac{1}{2}\gamma_i \nabla f_i\left(x_i^k\right)\right)\end{array}\right], \tag{4.17b}$$

$$s_{(i,j)}^{k+1} = \text{prox}_{\rho_{(i,j)}\delta^*_{C_{(i,j)}}}\left[\begin{array}{l} Y_{(i,j)}\left(I - 2\text{P}N\Gamma N^\top\right)\text{s}^k \\ +2\rho_{(i,j)}N_{(i,j)} \\ \times\left(\text{x}^k - \tilde{\text{s}}^k - \frac{1}{2}\Gamma\nabla f\left(\text{x}^k\right)\right)\end{array}\right], \tag{4.17c}$$

$$\tilde{u}_i^{k+1} = \frac{1}{2}x_i^k - \frac{1}{2}\gamma_i\nabla f_i\left(x_i^k\right) - \gamma_i A_i^\top u_i^{k+1}, \tag{4.17d}$$

$$\tilde{s}_i^{k+1} = \frac{1}{2}x_i^k - \frac{1}{2}\gamma_i\nabla f\left(x_i^k\right) - \gamma_i\sum_{j\in\mathcal{N}_i}\omega_{ij}^\top s_{(i,j),i}^{k+1}, \tag{4.17e}$$

for $i \in \mathcal{V}$ and $(i, j) \in \mathcal{E}$, where γ_i, σ_i, and $\rho_{(i.j)}$ are positive constant step sizes, $\text{P} = \text{blkdiag}\left\{\rho_{(i,j)} I_{2l_{(i,j)}}\right\}$ and $\Gamma = \text{blkdiag}\left\{\gamma_i I_{n_i}\right\}$ are symmetric positive definite matrices and $Y_{(i,j)} : \text{s} \mapsto s_{(i,j)}$ is a mapping that converts a global variable to a local variable.

Notice that the conjugate function $\delta^*_{C_{(i.j)}}$ in (4.17c) does not always have explicit expressions. To ensure that the update flows can be computed by single agent i, we apply the Moreau decomposition $I = \text{prox}_{\gamma f} + \gamma\text{prox}_{\gamma^{-1} f^*}\left(\gamma^{-1} I\right)$ from [22] to rewrite (4.17c) as

$$\begin{aligned} s_{(i,j)}^{k+1} =& \text{prox}_{\rho_{(i,j)}\delta^*_{C_{(i.j)}}}\left(\mathcal{K}_{(i,j)}\right) + \rho_{(i,j)}\text{prox}_{\rho_{(i,j)}^{-1}\delta_{C_{(i,j)}}}\left(\rho_{(i,j)}^{-1}\mathcal{K}_{(i,j)}\right) \\ =& s_{(i,j)}^{k+1} + \rho_{(i,j)}\text{prox}_{\rho_{(i,j)}^{-1}\delta_{C_{(i,j)}}}\left(\rho_{(i,j)}^{-1}\mathcal{K}_{(i,j)}\right), \end{aligned} \tag{4.18}$$

where

$$\mathcal{K}_{(i,j)} = Y_{(i,j)}\left(I - 2\text{P}N\Gamma N^\top\right)\text{s}^k + 2\rho_{(i,j)}N_{(i,j)}\left(\text{x}^k - \tilde{\text{s}}^k - (1/2)\Gamma\nabla f\left(\text{x}^k\right)\right).$$

Next, we analyze the last term on the right side of (4.18). Expanding the proximal operator, there exist the following equalities:

$$\begin{aligned} &\text{prox}_{\rho_{(i,j)}^{-1}\delta_{C_{(i,j)}}}\left[\rho_{(i,j)}^{-1}\mathcal{K}_{(i,j)}\right] \\ =& \arg\min_{y\in C_{(i,j)}}\left\{0 + \frac{\rho_{(i,j)}}{2}\left\|y - \rho_{(i,j)}^{-1}\mathcal{K}_{(i,j)}\right\|^2\right\} \\ =& \arg\min_{y\in C_{(i,j)}}\left\{\left\|y - \rho_{(i,j)}^{-1}\mathcal{K}_{(i,j)}\right\|\right\}. \end{aligned} \tag{4.19}$$

Here, we define a projection $\mathcal{P}_{C_{(i,j)}}$ onto $C_{(i,j)}$ such that

$$\mathcal{P}_{C_{(i,j)}}\left(\rho_{(i,j)}^{-1}\mathcal{K}_{(i,j)}\right) = \arg\min_{y\in C_{(i,j)}}\left\{\left\|y - \rho_{(i,j)}^{-1}\mathcal{K}_{(i,j)}\right\|\right\}. \tag{4.20}$$

Recall the definition of set $C_{(i,j)}$. For two arbitrary vectors $a_1 \in \mathbb{R}^{l(i,j)}$ and $a_2 \in \mathbb{R}^{l(i,j)}$, their corresponding projection z_1 and z_2 on $C_{(i,j)}$ should satisfy $z_1 + z_2 = b_{(i.j)}$. Hence, we can obtain the explicit expression of $\mathcal{P}_{C_{(i,j)}}$ as the following formulation:

$$\mathcal{P}_{C_{(i,j)}}\begin{pmatrix} a_1 \\ a_2 \end{pmatrix} = \frac{1}{2}\begin{pmatrix} a_1 - a_2 + b_{(i,j)} \\ a_2 - a_1 + b_{(i,j)} \end{pmatrix}. \tag{4.21}$$

Rearranging (4.18) with substituting (4.19) and (4.20) into it, we can obtain the update rules for both the dual variables $s_{(i,j),i}$ and $s_{(i,j),j}$ below:

$$\begin{pmatrix} s_{(i,j),i}^{k+1} \\ s_{(i,j),j}^{k+1} \end{pmatrix} = \mathcal{K}_{(i,j)} - \rho_{(i,j)}\text{prox}_{\rho_{(i,j)}^{-1}\delta_{C_{(i,j)}}}\left(\rho_{(i,j)}^{-1}\mathcal{K}_{(i,j)}\right). \tag{4.22}$$

Note that their update flows have similar structures in which i and j just swap roles. Therefore, for each agent $i \in \mathcal{V}$, we only need to compute $s_{(i,j),i}$ in one iteration. Here, we give the expanded form for $s_{(i,j),i}$ as follows:

$$\begin{aligned} s_{(i,j),i}^{k+1} =& s_{(i,j),i}^{k} - 2\gamma_i\rho_{(i,j)}\sum_{z\in\mathcal{N}_i}\omega_{ij}\omega_{iz}s_{(i,z),i}^{k} \\ &+ 2\rho_{(i,j)}\omega_{ij}\left(x_i^k - \tilde{s}_i^k - \frac{1}{2}\gamma_i\nabla f_i(x_i^k)\right) \\ &- \frac{\rho_{(i,j)}}{2}\begin{bmatrix} \rho_{(i,j)}^{-1}s_{(i,j),i}^{k} - 2\gamma_i\sum_{z\in\mathcal{N}_i}\omega_{ij}\omega_{iz}^{\top}s_{(i,z),i}^{k} \\ +\omega_{ij}x_i^k - \omega_{ij}\tilde{s}_i^k - \frac{1}{2}\gamma_i\omega_{ij}\nabla f_i(x_i^k) \\ -\rho_{(i,j)}^{-1}s_{(i,j),j}^{k} + 2\gamma_j\sum_{z\in\mathcal{N}_j}\omega_{ji}\omega_{jz}^{\top}s_{(j,z),j}^{k} \\ -2\omega_{ji}x_j^k - \omega_{ji}\tilde{s}_j^k - \frac{1}{2}\gamma_j\omega_{ji}\nabla f_j(x_j^k) \\ +b_{(i,j)} \end{bmatrix}, \end{aligned} \tag{4.23}$$

which results in (4.13c). Replacing (4.17c) with (4.13c), we thus propose the distributed Triple Proximal splitting algorithm with Uncoordinated Step sizes (TPUS) stated in Algorithm 5. The step size condition is provided in the following assumption.

Assumption 4.2 (Step Size Condition of Algorithm 5) *For each* $i \in \mathcal{V}$ *and* $(i, j) \in \mathcal{E}$, *there exist proper parameters* γ_i, σ_i, *and* $\rho_{(i,j)}$ *satisfying the following inequality:*

$$\gamma_i < \min\left(2\beta_i, \frac{1}{2\sigma_i \tau_{\max}\left(A_i A_i^\top\right)}, \frac{1}{2\tau_{\max}\left(\sum_{j\in\mathcal{N}_i} \rho_{(i,j)}\omega_{ij}^\top \omega_{ij}\right)}\right), \tag{4.24}$$

where the linear operators ω_{ij} *and* A_i *are defined in Sect. 4.2.2.*

Remark 4.3 TPUS allows the step sizes γ_i, σ_i to be set locally at agent i for $i \in \mathcal{V}$. $\rho_{(i,j)}$ for $(i, j) \in \mathcal{E}$ can be considered as the parameter of the communication link (i, j). It is set at agent i and agent j independently first and then kept the same by only one communication. Thus, each agent can select their own parameters rather than being restricted with global ones, which cancels the several communication steps balancing the global step size before algorithms start. In the subsequent convergence analysis, we also prove that the upper bound of each local step size is also distributed, which makes the feasible range of parameters expanded actually.

4.4 Convergence Analysis

In this section, we present the convergence analysis for Algorithm 5. We first formulate a compact form of TPUS and then find a fixed point which is also an optimal solution to problem (4.6). For explicit illustration, we introduce the following notations:

$$\begin{aligned}
&\mathrm{x} = col\left(x_1, \ldots, x_m\right), && \tilde{\mathrm{u}} = col\left(\tilde{u}_1, \ldots, \tilde{u}_m\right),\\
&\tilde{\mathrm{s}} = col\left(\tilde{s}_1, \ldots, \tilde{s}_m\right), && \mathrm{u} = col\left(u_1, \ldots, u_m\right),\\
&A = \mathrm{blkdiag}\left\{A_i\right\}, && \mathrm{B} = \mathrm{blkdiag}\left\{\beta_i I_{n_i}\right\},\\
&\Sigma = \mathrm{blkdiag}\left\{\sigma_i I_{r_i}\right\}, && \Gamma = \mathrm{blkdiag}\left\{\gamma_i I_{n_i}\right\},\\
&\mathrm{P} = \mathrm{blkdiag}\left\{\rho_{(i,j)} I_{2l_{(i,j)}}\right\}, && C = \times_{(i,j)\in\mathcal{E}} C_{(i,j)},
\end{aligned} \tag{4.25}$$

for $i \in \mathcal{V}$ and $(i, j) \in \mathcal{E}$. $\times$ denotes the Cartesian product here. Meanwhile, we also define a series of functions $f(\mathrm{x}) = \sum_{i=1}^m f_i(x_i)$, $g(\mathrm{x}) = \sum_{i=1}^m g_i(x_i)$, $h(A\mathrm{x}) = \sum_{i=1}^m h_i(A_i x_i)$, and $\delta_C(N\mathrm{x}) = \sum_{i=1}^m \sum_{(i,j)\in\mathcal{E}} \delta_{C_{(i,j)}}\left(N_{(i,j)}\mathrm{x}\right)$. Then the iterations of TPUS can be rewritten in a compact form as

$$\mathrm{x}^k = \mathrm{prox}_g^{\Gamma^{-1}}\left(\tilde{\mathrm{u}}^k + \tilde{\mathrm{s}}^k\right), \tag{4.26a}$$

$$\mathrm{u}^{k+1} = \mathrm{prox}_{h^*}^{\Sigma^{-1}}\left[\begin{array}{l}\left(I - 2\Sigma A\Gamma A^\top\right)\mathrm{u}^k\\ +2\Sigma A\left(\mathrm{x}^k - \tilde{\mathrm{u}}^k - \frac{1}{2}\Gamma\nabla f\left(\mathrm{x}^k\right)\right)\end{array}\right], \tag{4.26b}$$

$$\mathrm{s}^{k+1} = \mathrm{prox}_{\delta_C^*}^{\mathrm{P}^{-1}} \begin{bmatrix} \left(I - 2\mathrm{P}N\Gamma N^\top\right)\mathrm{s}^k \\ +2\mathrm{P}N\left(\mathrm{x}^k - \tilde{\mathrm{s}}^k - \frac{1}{2}\Gamma\nabla f\left(\mathrm{x}^k\right)\right) \end{bmatrix}, \tag{4.26c}$$

$$\tilde{\mathrm{u}}^{k+1} = \frac{1}{2}\mathrm{x}^k - \frac{1}{2}\Gamma\nabla f\left(\mathrm{x}^k\right) - \Gamma A^\top \mathrm{u}^{k+1}, \tag{4.26d}$$

$$\tilde{\mathrm{s}}^{k+1} = \frac{1}{2}\mathrm{x}^k - \frac{1}{2}\Gamma\nabla f\left(\mathrm{x}^k\right) - \Gamma N^\top \mathrm{s}^{k+1}. \tag{4.26e}$$

We continue to present some definitions appearing in the latter analysis. Firstly, define the following matrices:

$$\begin{aligned} M &= \Sigma^{-1}\left(I - 2\Sigma A\Gamma A^\top\right), \\ H &= \mathrm{P}^{-1}\left(I - 2\mathrm{P}N\Gamma N^\top\right), \\ D &= \mathrm{blkdiag}\{M, H, 2\Gamma^{-1}, 2\Gamma^{-1}\}, \\ \tilde{D} &= \mathrm{blkdiag}\{M, H, 2\Gamma^{-1} - \mathrm{B}^{-1}, 2\Gamma^{-1} - \mathrm{B}^{-1}\}, \end{aligned} \tag{4.27}$$

where M, D, and $\tilde{D}$ are positive definite block diagonal matrices and H is a positive definite symmetric matrix. The specific parameter conditions for them are supplied in Assumption 4.2. Then from (4.26a)–(4.26c), we define

$$\begin{aligned} \mathrm{q}_g\left(\mathrm{x}^k\right) &= \Gamma^{-1}\left(\tilde{\mathrm{u}}^k + \tilde{\mathrm{s}}^k - \mathrm{x}^k\right) \in \partial g\left(x^k\right), \\ \mathrm{q}_{h^*}\left(\mathrm{u}^{k+1}\right) &= M\mathrm{u}^k - \Sigma^{-1}\mathrm{u}^{k+1} + 2A\left(\mathrm{x}^k - \tilde{\mathrm{u}}^k - \frac{1}{2}\Gamma\nabla f\left(\mathrm{x}^k\right)\right), \\ \mathrm{q}_{\delta_C^*}\left(\mathrm{s}^{k+1}\right) &= H\mathrm{s}^k - \mathrm{P}^{-1}\mathrm{s}^{k+1} + 2N\left(\mathrm{x}^k - \tilde{\mathrm{s}}^k - \frac{1}{2}\Gamma\nabla f\left(\mathrm{x}^k\right)\right). \end{aligned} \tag{4.28}$$

Note that $\mathrm{q}_g\left(\mathrm{x}^k\right) \in \partial g\left(\mathrm{x}^k\right)$, $\mathrm{q}_{h^*}\left(\mathrm{u}^k\right) \in \partial h^*\left(\mathrm{u}^k\right)$, and $\mathrm{q}_{\delta_C^*}\left(\mathrm{s}^k\right) \in \partial\delta_C^*\left(\mathrm{s}^k\right)$. The lowercase letter z is used to represent the column vector consisting of the dual variables and the auxiliary variables in (4.26b)–(4.26e), i.e., $\mathrm{z} = col\left(\mathrm{u}, \mathrm{s}, \tilde{\mathrm{u}}, \tilde{\mathrm{s}}\right)$. In this subsection, we consider two inputs of (4.26) with two groups of vectors $(\mathrm{x}_1, \mathrm{u}_1, \mathrm{s}_1, \tilde{\mathrm{u}}_1, \tilde{\mathrm{s}}_1)$ and $(\mathrm{x}_2, \mathrm{u}_2, \mathrm{s}_2, \tilde{\mathrm{u}}_2, \tilde{\mathrm{s}}_2)$. Because x^k is determined by u^k and s^k that can be eliminated from the iteration, iteration (4.26) is essentially an operator for z^k. We briefly denote the two inputs as $\mathrm{z}_1 = col\left(\mathrm{u}_1, \mathrm{s}_1, \tilde{\mathrm{u}}_1, \tilde{\mathrm{s}}_1\right)$ and $\mathrm{z}_2 = col\left(\mathrm{u}_2, \mathrm{s}_2, \tilde{\mathrm{u}}_2, \tilde{\mathrm{s}}_2\right)$. In addition, one iteration is seen as an operator T, leading to $\mathrm{z}^{k+1} = T\mathrm{z}^k$. When Assumption 4.2 is satisfied, based on the following lemmas and theorems, T is a nonexpansive operator so that TPUS can converge to a fixed point.

Based on the global variables defined above, the compact form of the Lagrangian function (4.16) is

$$\mathcal{L} = f(\mathrm{x}) + g(\mathrm{x}) + \left(\mathrm{u}^\top (A\mathrm{x}) - h^*(\mathrm{u})\right) + \left(\mathrm{s}^\top (N\mathrm{x}) - \delta_C^*(\mathrm{s})\right), \tag{4.29}$$

from which the optimality condition is given.

Lemma 4.4 (Optimality Conditions) *Under Assumption 4.1,* x^* *is an optimal solution, i.e,* $\mathrm{x}^* \in \mathcal{S}$*, if the following conditions hold:*

$$\begin{cases} 0 \in \nabla f(\mathrm{x}^*) + \partial g(\mathrm{x}^*) + A^\top \mathrm{u}^* + N^\top \mathrm{s}^*, \\ 0 \in A\mathrm{x}^* - \partial h^*(\mathrm{u}^*), \\ 0 \in N\mathrm{x}^* - \partial \delta_C^*(\mathrm{s}^*). \end{cases} \tag{4.30}$$

Proof From the Karush-Kuhn-Tucker(KKT) condition associated with the Lagrangian function (4.29) for the decision variable x and dual variables u, s, respectively, the first-order optimality conditions hold. ■

Based on Lemma 4.4, the relation between the fixed point of the proposed algorithm and an optimal solution to the objective optimization problem can be established.

Lemma 4.5 *Define* $(\mathrm{x}^*, \mathrm{u}^*, \mathrm{s}^*, \tilde{\mathrm{u}}^*, \tilde{\mathrm{s}}^*)$ *as the fixed point of the operator* T *and denote* $\mathrm{z}^* = col(\mathrm{u}^*, \mathrm{s}^*, \tilde{\mathrm{u}}^*, \tilde{\mathrm{s}}^*)$*. When Assumption 4.1 holds,* $\mathrm{x}^* = \mathrm{prox}_{\Gamma g}(\tilde{\mathrm{u}}^* + \tilde{\mathrm{s}}^*)$ *is an optimal solution.*

Proof Substituting the fixed point z^* and x^* into iterations (4.26a)–(4.26e), we can obtain a series of equality relations. Firstly, by combining (4.26d) and (4.26e), we have

$$\tilde{\mathrm{u}}^* + \tilde{\mathrm{s}}^* - \mathrm{x}^* + \Gamma \nabla f\left(\mathrm{x}^*\right) + \Gamma A^\top \mathrm{u}^* + \Gamma N^\top \mathrm{s}^* = 0. \tag{4.31}$$

Noticing that from (4.26a) it holds $\tilde{\mathrm{u}}^* + \tilde{\mathrm{s}}^* - \mathrm{x}^* = \Gamma \partial g(\mathrm{x}^*)$, thus, we get

$$\partial g\left(\mathrm{x}^*\right) + \nabla f\left(\mathrm{x}^*\right) + A^\top \mathrm{u}^* + N^\top \mathrm{s}^* = 0. \tag{4.32}$$

Meanwhile, combining (4.26b) and (4.26d), we obtain

$$\partial h^*\left(\mathrm{u}^*\right) = -2A\Gamma A^\top \mathrm{u}^* + 2A\left(\frac{1}{2}\mathrm{x}^* + \Gamma A^\top \mathrm{u}^*\right) = A\mathrm{x}^*. \tag{4.33}$$

Similarly, based on (4.26c) and (4.26e), we have

$$\partial \delta_C^*\left(\mathrm{s}^*\right) = N\mathrm{x}^*. \tag{4.34}$$

It is worth noting that (4.32)–(4.34) are the optimality conditions in Lemma 4.4. Therefore, $x^* \in \mathcal{S}$ is an optimal solution. Then, the following lemmas give the convergence analysis framework of the proposed algorithm with two inputs. ■

Lemma 4.6 *Under Assumption 4.1 and considering the iterations on (4.26a)–(4.26e) with two inputs* $z_1 = col\left(u_1, s_1, \tilde{u}_1, \tilde{s}_1\right)$ *and* $z_2 = col\left(u_2, s_2, \tilde{u}_2, \tilde{s}_2\right)$*, then the following equality holds:*

$$
\begin{aligned}
&\left\langle u_1^{k+1} - u_2^{k+1}, q_{h^*}\left(u_1^{k+1}\right) - q_{h^*}\left(u_2^{k+1}\right)\right\rangle \\
&+\left\langle s_1^{k+1} - s_2^{k+1}, q_{\delta_C^*}\left(s_1^{k+1}\right) - q_{\delta_C^*}\left(s_2^{k+1}\right)\right\rangle \\
&+\left\langle x_1^k - x_2^k, q_g\left(x_1^k\right) - q_g\left(x_2^k\right) + \nabla f\left(x_1^k\right) - \nabla f\left(x_2^k\right)\right\rangle \\
=&\frac{1}{2}\left\|z_1^k - z_2^k\right\|_D^2 - \frac{1}{2}\left\|z_1^{k+1} - z_2^{k+1}\right\|_D^2 - \frac{1}{2}\left\|z_1^k - z_1^{k+1} - z_2^k + z_2^{k+1}\right\|_D^2 \\
&+\left\langle \nabla f\left(x_1^k\right) - \nabla f\left(x_2^k\right), \tilde{u}_1^k - \tilde{u}_1^{k+1} - \tilde{u}_2^k + \tilde{u}_2^{k+1}\right\rangle \\
&+\left\langle \nabla f\left(x_1^k\right) - \nabla f\left(x_2^k\right), \tilde{s}_1^k - \tilde{s}_1^{k+1} - \tilde{s}_2^k + \tilde{s}_2^{k+1}\right\rangle,
\end{aligned} \tag{4.35}
$$

where D is defined in (4.27).

Proof For simplicity, we first analyze the three terms on the left side of (4.35) separately. For the first term, with (4.26d), we have

$$
\begin{aligned}
&\left\langle u_1^{k+1} - u_2^{k+1}, q_{h^*}\left(u_1^{k+1}\right) - q_{h^*}\left(u_2^{k+1}\right)\right\rangle \\
=&\left\langle \begin{array}{l} u_1^{k+1} - u_2^{k+1}, M u_1^k - \Sigma^{-1} u_1^{k+1} \\ +2A\left(x_1^k - \tilde{u}_1^k - \frac{1}{2}\Gamma \nabla f\left(x_1^k\right)\right) \end{array}\right\rangle \\
&-\left\langle \begin{array}{l} u_1^{k+1} - u_2^{k+1}, M u_2^k - \Sigma^{-1} u_2^{k+1} \\ +2A\left(x_2^k - \tilde{u}_2^k - \frac{1}{2}\Gamma \nabla f\left(x_2^k\right)\right) \end{array}\right\rangle \\
=&\left\langle \begin{array}{l} u_1^{k+1} - u_2^{k+1}, M u_1^k + 2A\tilde{u}_1^{k+1} \\ +Ax_1^k - 2A\tilde{u}_1^k - M u_1^{k+1} \end{array}\right\rangle \\
&-\left\langle \begin{array}{l} u_1^{k+1} - u_2^{k+1}, M u_2^k + 2A\tilde{u}_2^{k+1} \\ +Ax_2^k - 2A\tilde{u}_2^k - M u_2^{k+1} \end{array}\right\rangle \\
=&\left\langle u_1^{k+1} - u_2^{k+1}, u_1^k - u_1^{k+1} - u_2^k + u_2^{k+1}\right\rangle_M \\
&+2\left\langle \begin{array}{l} A^\top\left(u_1^{k+1} - u_2^{k+1}\right), \frac{1}{2}x_1^k - \frac{1}{2}x_2^k \\ +\tilde{u}_1^{k+1} - \tilde{u}_1^k - \tilde{u}_2^{k+1} + \tilde{u}_2^k \end{array}\right\rangle.
\end{aligned} \tag{4.36}
$$

Obviously, with (4.26e), the second term has a similar equality:

$$
\begin{aligned}
&\left\langle s_1^{k+1}-s_2^{k+1}, q_{\delta_C^*}\left(s_1^{k+1}\right)-q_{\delta_C^*}\left(s_2^{k+1}\right)\right\rangle \\
=&2\left\langle N^\top\left(s_1^{k+1}-s_2^{k+1}\right), \frac{1}{2}x_1^k-\frac{1}{2}x_2^k+\tilde{s}_1^{k+1}-\tilde{s}_1^k-\tilde{s}_2^{k+1}+\tilde{s}_2^k\right\rangle \\
&+\left\langle s_1^{k+1}-s_2^{k+1}, s_1^k-s_1^{k+1}-s_2^k+s_2^{k+1}\right\rangle_H .
\end{aligned} \tag{4.37}
$$

Then for the third term, with (4.26d) and (4.26e), we have

$$
\begin{aligned}
&\left\langle \mathrm{x}_1^k-\mathrm{x}_2^k, \mathrm{q}_g\left(\mathrm{x}_1^k\right)-\mathrm{q}_g\left(\mathrm{x}_2^k\right)+\nabla f\left(\mathrm{x}_1^k\right)-\nabla f\left(\mathrm{x}_2^k\right)\right\rangle \\
=&\left\langle \begin{matrix}\Gamma^{-1}\left(\mathrm{x}_1^k-\mathrm{x}_2^k\right), \tilde{\mathrm{u}}_1^k+\tilde{\mathrm{s}}_1^k-\tilde{\mathrm{u}}_2^k-\tilde{\mathrm{s}}_2^k \\ -\mathrm{x}_1^k+\mathrm{x}_2^k+\Gamma\nabla f\left(\mathrm{x}_1^k\right)-\Gamma\nabla f\left(\mathrm{x}_2^k\right)\end{matrix}\right\rangle \\
=&\left\langle \mathrm{x}_1^k-\mathrm{x}_2^k, \Gamma^{-1}\begin{pmatrix}\tilde{\mathrm{u}}_1^k+\tilde{\mathrm{s}}_1^k-\tilde{\mathrm{u}}_1^{k+1}-\tilde{\mathrm{s}}_1^{k+1} \\ -\Gamma A^\top\mathrm{u}_1^{k+1}-\Gamma N^\top\mathrm{s}_1^{k+1} \\ -\tilde{\mathrm{u}}_2^k-\tilde{\mathrm{s}}_2^k+\tilde{\mathrm{u}}_2^{k+1}+\tilde{\mathrm{s}}_2^{k+1} \\ +\Gamma A^\top\mathrm{u}_2^{k+1}+\Gamma N^\top\mathrm{s}_2^{k+1}\end{pmatrix}\right\rangle .
\end{aligned} \tag{4.38}
$$

Combining (4.36)–(4.38) results in

$$
\begin{aligned}
&\left\langle \mathrm{u}_1^{k+1}-\mathrm{u}_2^{k+1}, \mathrm{q}_{h^*}\left(\mathrm{u}_1^{k+1}\right)-\mathrm{q}_{h^*}\left(\mathrm{u}_2^{k+1}\right)\right\rangle \\
&+\left\langle \mathrm{s}_1^{k+1}-\mathrm{s}_2^{k+1}, \mathrm{q}_{\delta_C^*}\left(\mathrm{s}_1^{k+1}\right)-\mathrm{q}_{\delta_C^*}\left(\mathrm{s}_2^{k+1}\right)\right\rangle \\
&+\left\langle \mathrm{x}_1^k-\mathrm{x}_2^k, \mathrm{q}_g\left(\mathrm{x}_1^k\right)-\mathrm{q}_g\left(\mathrm{x}_2^k\right)+\nabla f\left(\mathrm{x}_1^k\right)-\nabla f\left(\mathrm{x}_2^k\right)\right\rangle \\
=&\left\langle \mathrm{u}_1^{k+1}-\mathrm{u}_2^{k+1}, \mathrm{u}_1^k-\mathrm{u}_1^{k+1}-\mathrm{u}_2^k+\mathrm{u}_2^{k+1}\right\rangle_M \\
&+\left\langle \mathrm{s}_1^{k+1}-\mathrm{s}_2^{k+1}, \mathrm{s}_1^k-\mathrm{s}_1^{k+1}-\mathrm{s}_2^k+\mathrm{s}_2^{k+1}\right\rangle_H \\
&+\left\langle \begin{matrix}\mathrm{x}_1^k-\mathrm{x}_2^k-2\Gamma A^\top\left(\mathrm{u}_1^{k+1}-\mathrm{u}_2^{k+1}\right), \\ \Gamma^{-1}\left(\tilde{\mathrm{u}}_1^k-\tilde{\mathrm{u}}_1^{k+1}-\tilde{\mathrm{u}}_2^k+\tilde{\mathrm{u}}_2^{k+1}\right)\end{matrix}\right\rangle \\
&+\left\langle \begin{matrix}\mathrm{x}_1^k-\mathrm{x}_2^k-2\Gamma N^\top\left(\mathrm{s}_1^{k+1}-\mathrm{s}_2^{k+1}\right), \\ \Gamma^{-1}\left(\tilde{\mathrm{s}}_1^k-\tilde{\mathrm{s}}_1^{k+1}-\tilde{\mathrm{s}}_2^k+\tilde{\mathrm{s}}_2^{k+1}\right)\end{matrix}\right\rangle .
\end{aligned} \tag{4.39}
$$

Note that (4.26d) and (4.26e) can be substituted into (4.39). It follows that

$$
\left\langle \mathrm{u}_1^{k+1}-\mathrm{u}_2^{k+1}, \mathrm{q}_{h^*}\left(\mathrm{u}_1^{k+1}\right)-\mathrm{q}_{h^*}\left(\mathrm{u}_2^{k+1}\right)\right\rangle
$$

$$
\begin{aligned}
&+\left\langle \mathrm{s}_1^{k+1}-\mathrm{s}_2^{k+1}, \mathrm{q}_{\delta_C^*}\left(\mathrm{s}_1^{k+1}\right)-\mathrm{q}_{\delta_C^*}\left(\mathrm{s}_2^{k+1}\right)\right\rangle \\
&+\left\langle \mathrm{x}_1^k-\mathrm{x}_2^k, \mathrm{q}_g\left(\mathrm{x}_1^k\right)-\mathrm{q}_g\left(\mathrm{x}_2^k\right)+\nabla f\left(\mathrm{x}_1^k\right)-\nabla f\left(\mathrm{x}_2^k\right)\right\rangle \\
=&\frac{1}{2}\left\|\mathrm{z}_1^k-\mathrm{z}_2^k\right\|_D^2-\frac{1}{2}\left\|\mathrm{z}_1^{k+1}-\mathrm{z}_2^{k+1}\right\|_D^2 \\
&-\frac{1}{2}\left\|\mathrm{z}_1^k-\mathrm{z}_1^{k+1}-\mathrm{z}_2^k+\mathrm{z}_2^{k+1}\right\|_D^2 \\
&+\left\langle \nabla f\left(\mathrm{x}_1^k\right)-\nabla f\left(\mathrm{x}_2^k\right), \tilde{\mathrm{u}}_1^k-\tilde{\mathrm{u}}_1^{k+1}-\tilde{\mathrm{u}}_2^k+\tilde{\mathrm{u}}_2^{k+1}\right\rangle \\
&+\left\langle \nabla f\left(\mathrm{x}_1^k\right)-\nabla f\left(\mathrm{x}_2^k\right), \tilde{\mathrm{s}}_1^k-\tilde{\mathrm{s}}_1^{k+1}-\tilde{\mathrm{s}}_2^k+\tilde{\mathrm{s}}_2^{k+1}\right\rangle,
\end{aligned}
\tag{4.40}
$$

where the last equality holds by using the fact that $2\langle a, b\rangle=\|a+b\|^2-\|a\|^2-\|b\|^2$ for two arbitrary vectors a and b with the same dimension. ■

Note that the left-hand side of the equality (4.35) has a similar structure with the definition inequalities of convex property and smooth property. From the assumptions for problem (4.2), the following lemma holds.

Lemma 4.7 *Under Assumption 4.1, the following inequality holds for the two inputs* z_1, z_2, *and* $\mathrm{q}_{\cdot}(\cdot)$*:*

$$
\begin{aligned}
0 \leq&\left\langle \mathrm{x}_1^k-\mathrm{x}_2^k, \mathrm{q}_g\left(\mathrm{x}_1^k\right)-\mathrm{q}_g\left(\mathrm{x}_2^k\right)\right\rangle \\
&+\left\langle \mathrm{u}_1^{k+1}-\mathrm{u}_2^{k+1}, \mathrm{q}_{h^*}\left(\mathrm{u}_1^{k+1}\right)-\mathrm{q}_{h^*}\left(\mathrm{u}_2^{k+1}\right)\right\rangle \\
&+\left\langle \mathrm{s}_1^{k+1}-\mathrm{s}_2^{k+1}, \mathrm{q}_{\delta_C^*}\left(\mathrm{s}_1^{k+1}\right)-\mathrm{q}_{\delta_C^*}\left(\mathrm{s}_2^{k+1}\right)\right\rangle .
\end{aligned}
\tag{4.41}
$$

In addition, for the convex function $f_i\left(x_i\right)$ *with* $1/\beta_i$*–Lipschitz continuous gradients, it holds that*

$$
\left\langle \mathrm{x}_1-\mathrm{x}_2, \nabla f\left(\mathrm{x}_1\right)-\nabla f\left(\mathrm{x}_2\right)\right\rangle \geq\left\|\nabla f\left(\mathrm{x}_1\right)-\nabla f\left(\mathrm{x}_2\right)\right\|_{\mathrm{B}}^2, \tag{4.42}
$$

where the definition of B *is presented in (4.25).*

Proof For an arbitrary convex function $V(x)$, we have

$$
V(y) \geq V(x)+(\partial V(x))^{\top}(y-x) . \tag{4.43}
$$

Note that if we swap the roles of x and y in (4.43), the new obtained inequality still holds. Then, combining (4.43) and the new inequality, we have

$$
(\partial V(x)-\partial V(y))^{\top}(x-y) \geq 0. \tag{4.44}
$$

Hence, with the convexity of g, h^*, and δ_C^*, it follows that

$$\begin{aligned} 0 \leq & \left\langle \mathrm{x}_1^k - \mathrm{x}_2^k, \mathrm{q}_g\left(\mathrm{x}_1^k\right) - \mathrm{q}_g\left(\mathrm{x}_2^k\right)\right\rangle \\ & + \left\langle \mathrm{u}_1^{k+1} - \mathrm{u}_2^{k+1}, \mathrm{q}_{h^*}\left(\mathrm{u}_1^{k+1}\right) - \mathrm{q}_{h^*}\left(\mathrm{u}_2^{k+1}\right)\right\rangle \\ & + \left\langle \mathrm{s}_1^{k+1} - \mathrm{s}_2^{k+1}, \mathrm{q}_{\delta_C^*}\left(\mathrm{s}_1^{k+1}\right) - \mathrm{q}_{\delta_C^*}\left(\mathrm{s}_2^{k+1}\right)\right\rangle. \end{aligned} \tag{4.45}$$

Besides, summing up (4.3) over i from 1 to m, we have

$$\langle \mathrm{x}_1 - \mathrm{x}_2, \nabla f(\mathrm{x}_1) - \nabla f(\mathrm{x}_2)\rangle \geq \|\nabla f(\mathrm{x}_1) - \nabla f(\mathrm{x}_2)\|_{\mathrm{B}}^2. \tag{4.46}$$

The proof is completed. ■

Combining the inequalities in Lemma 4.7 with (4.35), Lemma 4.8 supplies the fundamental inequality for the convergence analysis of the proposed algorithm.

Lemma 4.8 *If Assumption 4.1 is satisfied, considering the two inputs* z_1^k *and* z_2^k*, it holds that*

$$\left\|\mathrm{z}_1^{k+1} - \mathrm{z}_2^{k+1}\right\|_D^2 - \left\|\mathrm{z}_1^k - \mathrm{z}_2^k\right\|_D^2 \leq - \left\|\mathrm{z}_1^k - \mathrm{z}_1^{k+1} - \mathrm{z}_2^k + \mathrm{z}_2^{k+1}\right\|_{\tilde{D}}^2, \tag{4.47}$$

where $\tilde{D}$ *is given in (4.27).*

Proof By (4.41) in Lemma 4.7, the equality (4.35) gives

$$\begin{aligned} & \left\|\mathrm{z}_1^{k+1} - \mathrm{z}_2^{k+1}\right\|_D^2 - \left\|\mathrm{z}_1^k - \mathrm{z}_2^k\right\|_D^2 \\ \leq & - \left\|\mathrm{z}_1^k - \mathrm{z}_1^{k+1} - \mathrm{z}_2^k + \mathrm{z}_2^{k+1}\right\|_D^2 \\ & + 2\left\langle \nabla f\left(\mathrm{x}_1^k\right) - \nabla f\left(\mathrm{x}_2^k\right), \tilde{\mathrm{u}}_1^k - \tilde{\mathrm{u}}_1^{k+1} - \tilde{\mathrm{u}}_2^k + \tilde{\mathrm{u}}_2^{k+1}\right\rangle \\ & + 2\left\langle \nabla f\left(\mathrm{x}_1^k\right) - \nabla f\left(\mathrm{x}_2^k\right), \tilde{\mathrm{s}}_1^k - \tilde{\mathrm{s}}_1^{k+1} - \tilde{\mathrm{s}}_2^k + \tilde{\mathrm{s}}_2^{k+1}\right\rangle \\ & - 2\left\langle \mathrm{x}_1^k - \mathrm{x}_2^k, \nabla f\left(\mathrm{x}_1^k\right) - \nabla f\left(\mathrm{x}_2^k\right)\right\rangle. \end{aligned} \tag{4.48}$$

In the following analysis, we first discuss the last three terms on the right side of (4.48). Letting θ_i be a positive constant and $\Theta = \mathrm{blkdiag}\left\{\theta_i I_{n_i}\right\}$ for $i \in \mathcal{V}$ be a diagonal positive definite matrix, we have

$$\begin{aligned} & - 2\left\langle \mathrm{x}_1^k - \mathrm{x}_2^k, \nabla f\left(\mathrm{x}_1^k\right) - \nabla f\left(\mathrm{x}_2^k\right)\right\rangle \\ & + 2\left\langle \nabla f\left(\mathrm{x}_1^k\right) - \nabla f\left(\mathrm{x}_2^k\right), \tilde{\mathrm{u}}_1^k - \tilde{\mathrm{u}}_1^{k+1} - \tilde{\mathrm{u}}_2^k + \tilde{\mathrm{u}}_2^{k+1}\right\rangle \end{aligned}$$

$$\begin{aligned}
&+2\left\langle \nabla f\left(\mathrm{x}_1^k\right)-\nabla f\left(\mathrm{x}_2^k\right), \tilde{\mathrm{s}}_1^k-\tilde{\mathrm{s}}_1^{k+1}-\tilde{\mathrm{s}}_2^k+\tilde{\mathrm{s}}_2^{k+1}\right\rangle \\
&\leq 2\left\|\tilde{\mathrm{u}}_1^k-\tilde{\mathrm{u}}_1^{k+1}-\tilde{\mathrm{u}}_2^k+\tilde{\mathrm{u}}_2^{k+1}\right\|_{\Theta\Gamma^{-1}}^2 \\
&\quad+2\left\|\tilde{\mathrm{s}}_1^k-\tilde{\mathrm{s}}_1^{k+1}-\tilde{\mathrm{s}}_2^k+\tilde{\mathrm{s}}_2^{k+1}\right\|_{\Theta\Gamma^{-1}}^2 \\
&\quad-2\left\|\nabla f\left(\mathrm{x}_1^k\right)-\nabla f\left(\mathrm{x}_2^k\right)\right\|_{\mathrm{B}}^2+\left\|\nabla f\left(\mathrm{x}_1^k\right)-\nabla f\left(\mathrm{x}_2^k\right)\right\|_{\Theta^{-1}\Gamma}^2 \\
&=\left\|\nabla f\left(\mathrm{x}_1^k\right)-\nabla f\left(\mathrm{x}_2^k\right)\right\|_{\Theta^{-1}\Gamma-2\mathrm{B}}^2 \\
&\quad+\left\|\tilde{\mathrm{u}}_1^k-\tilde{\mathrm{u}}_1^{k+1}-\tilde{\mathrm{u}}_2^k+\tilde{\mathrm{u}}_2^{k+1}\right\|_{2\Theta\Gamma^{-1}}^2 \\
&\quad+\left\|\tilde{\mathrm{s}}_1^k-\tilde{\mathrm{s}}_1^{k+1}-\tilde{\mathrm{s}}_2^k+\tilde{\mathrm{s}}_2^{k+1}\right\|_{2\Theta\Gamma^{-1}}^2,
\end{aligned} \tag{4.49}$$

where the inequality holds owing to (4.42) and $(1/2)\,\|a\|_{\Theta^{-1}\Gamma}^2 + 2\,\|b\|_{\Theta\Gamma^{-1}}^2 \geq 2\,\langle a, b\rangle$ for any vectors a and b as well as positive definite diagonal matrices Γ and Θ. Substituting (4.49) into (4.48), we obtain the following inequality:

$$\begin{aligned}
&\left\|\mathrm{z}_1^{k+1}-\mathrm{z}_2^{k+1}\right\|_D^2-\left\|\mathrm{z}_1^k-\mathrm{z}_2^k\right\|_D^2 \\
&\leq-\left\|\mathrm{u}_1^k-\mathrm{u}_1^{k+1}-\mathrm{u}_2^k+\mathrm{u}_2^{k+1}\right\|_M^2-\left\|\mathrm{s}_1^k-\mathrm{s}_1^{k+1}-\mathrm{s}_2^k+\mathrm{s}_2^{k+1}\right\|_H^2 \\
&\quad-\left\|\tilde{\mathrm{u}}_1^k-\tilde{\mathrm{u}}_1^{k+1}-\tilde{\mathrm{u}}_2^k+\tilde{\mathrm{u}}_2^{k+1}\right\|_{2(I-\Theta)\Gamma^{-1}}^2-\left\|\tilde{\mathrm{s}}_1^k-\tilde{\mathrm{s}}_1^{k+1}-\tilde{\mathrm{s}}_2^k+\tilde{\mathrm{s}}_2^{k+1}\right\|_{2(I-\Theta)\Gamma^{-1}}^2 \\
&\quad+\left\|\nabla f\left(\mathrm{x}_1^k\right)-\nabla f\left(\mathrm{x}_2^k\right)\right\|_{\Theta^{-1}\Gamma-2\mathrm{B}}^2.
\end{aligned} \tag{4.50}$$

Notice that when $\theta_i = \gamma_i/(2\beta_i)$ for $i \in \mathcal{V}$, the diagonal matrix $\Theta^{-1}\Gamma - 2\mathrm{B}$ in (4.50) becomes a null matrix where all elements are zero. Thus, letting $\Theta = (1/2)\,\Gamma\mathrm{B}^{-1}$, and then we have

$$\left\|\mathrm{z}_1^{k+1}-\mathrm{z}_2^{k+1}\right\|_D^2-\left\|\mathrm{z}_1^k-\mathrm{z}_2^k\right\|_D^2 \leq-\left\|\mathrm{z}_1^k-\mathrm{z}_1^{k+1}-\mathrm{z}_2^k+\mathrm{z}_2^{k+1}\right\|_{\tilde{D}}^2, \tag{4.51}$$

which is the desired result. ■

Remark 4.9 If there exists $\|\mathrm{T}a - \mathrm{T}b\| - \|a - b\| \leq 0$ for any two vectors a and b, then T is called a nonexpansive operator. Meanwhile, if there exists

$$\|\mathrm{T}a-\mathrm{T}b\|^2+\frac{1-\alpha}{\alpha}\|(I-\mathrm{T})\,a-(I-\mathrm{T})\,b\|^2 \leq\|a-b\|^2, \tag{4.52}$$

for a constant $\alpha \in (0, 1]$, the operator T is α-averaged. Noting that in (4.47), when $\gamma_i < 2\beta_i$ for $i \in \mathcal{V}$, the block diagonal matrix $\tilde{D}$ is positive definite so that T is a nonexpansive operator. Moreover, (4.47) also gives an inequality as

$$\begin{aligned} &\left\| T\mathrm{z}_1^k - T\mathrm{z}_2^k \right\|_D^2 - \left\| \mathrm{z}_1^k - \mathrm{z}_2^k \right\|_D^2 \\ \leq &- \left(\min_{i \in \mathcal{V}} \frac{2\beta_i - \gamma_i}{2\beta_i} \right) \left\| \mathrm{z}_1^k - T\mathrm{z}_1^k - \mathrm{z}_2^k + T\mathrm{z}_2^k \right\|_D^2, \end{aligned} \tag{4.53}$$

which means that T is $1/\left(1 + \min_{i \in \mathcal{V}} \left((2\beta_i - \gamma_i)/2\beta_i\right)\right)$-averaged.

In fact, Assumption 4.2 comes from the positive definite property of the block diagonal matrices $\tilde{D}$ defined in (4.27). Noticing that M and $2\Gamma^{-1} - \mathrm{B}^{-1}$ are decomposable with regard to $i \in \mathcal{V}$, we can compute $\sigma_i^{-1} I_{n_i} - 2\gamma_i A_i A_i^\top > 0$ and $2/\gamma_i - 1/\beta_i > 0$ instead of $M > 0$ and $2\Gamma^{-1} - \mathrm{B}^{-1} > 0$. However, $H = \mathrm{P}^{-1}\left(I - 2\mathrm{P}N\Gamma N^\top\right)$ is not a block diagonal matrix to be divided. Hence, we introduce the Schur complement to P^{-1} and $(1/2)\,\Gamma^{-1}$ respectively, which makes the following inequality equivalent:

$$\begin{aligned} \mathrm{P}^{-1} - 2N\Gamma N^\top > 0 \Leftrightarrow &\begin{bmatrix} \mathrm{P}^{-1} & N \\ N^\top & \frac{1}{2}\Gamma^{-1} \end{bmatrix} > 0 \\ \Leftrightarrow &\frac{1}{2}\Gamma^{-1} - N^\top \mathrm{P} N > 0. \end{aligned} \tag{4.54}$$

Here, $N^\top \mathrm{P} N$ is a block diagonal matrix such that the last inequality is able to be split as $1/(2\gamma_i) - \sum_{j \in \mathcal{N}_i} \rho_{(i,j)} \omega_{ij}^\top \omega_{ij} > 0$ for $i \in \mathcal{V}$. Summarize the above results as Assumption 4.2, and then we provide the convergence of Algorithm 5 in the following theorem.

Theorem 4.10 *Under Assumptions 4.1 and 4.2, for the sequence* $(\mathrm{u}^k, \mathrm{s}^k, \tilde{\mathrm{u}}^k, \tilde{\mathrm{s}}^k)_{k \geq 0}$ *generated by* T*, the following statements hold:*

(i) The sequence $\left(\|\mathrm{z}^k - \mathrm{z}^*\|_D\right)_{k \geq 0}$ *is monotonically decreasing and converges to zero;*
(ii) (Sublinear convergence rate) The sequence $\left(\|T\mathrm{z}^k - \mathrm{z}^k\|_{\tilde{D}}\right)_{k \geq 0}$ *is monotonically nonincreasing and converges to zero at the convergence rate of* $o(1/k)$*;*
(iii) $\left(\mathrm{x}^k\right)_{k \geq 0}$ *converges to an optimal solution* $\mathrm{x}^* \in \mathcal{S}$ *to the optimization problem (4.2).*

Proof

(i) With two inputs $\mathrm{z}^k = \left(\mathrm{u}^k, \mathrm{s}^k, \tilde{\mathrm{u}}^k, \tilde{\mathrm{s}}^k\right)$ and $\mathrm{z}^* = (\mathrm{u}^*, \mathrm{s}^*, \tilde{\mathrm{u}}^*, \tilde{\mathrm{s}}^*)$, the inequality (4.47) becomes

$$\left\| T\mathrm{z}^k - \mathrm{z}^* \right\|_D^2 - \left\| \mathrm{z}^k - \mathrm{z}^* \right\|_D^2 \leq - \left\| T\mathrm{z}^k - \mathrm{z}^k \right\|_{\tilde{D}}^2, \tag{4.55}$$

where the sequence $\left(\|z^k - z^*\|_D\right)_{k\geq 0}$ is monotonically decreasing. Then, there exists a weaker inequality condition:

$$\left\|Tz^k - z^*\right\|_D^2 - \left\|z^k - z^*\right\|_D^2 \leq 0. \tag{4.56}$$

Sum it up over k from 0 to ∞ such that $\|Tz^k - z^*\|_D^2$ has a constant upper bound, i.e.,

$$\left\|Tz^k - z^*\right\|_D^2 \leq \left\|z^0 - z^*\right\|_D^2, \tag{4.57}$$

demonstrating the convergence property of sequence $\left(\|z^k - z^*\|_D\right)_{k\geq 0}$.

(ii) Exchanging the positions on both sides of (4.55) and summing them up over k from 0 to ∞, we obtain

$$\sum_{k=0}^{\infty} \left\|Tz^k - z^k\right\|_{\tilde{D}}^2 \leq \left\|z^0 - z^*\right\|_D^2, \tag{4.58}$$

which indicates that the sequence $\left(\|Tz^k - z^k\|_{\tilde{D}}\right)_{k\geq 0}$ converges to zero. Since T is a nonexpansive operator, we have

$$\begin{aligned} \left\|Tz^{k+1} - z^{k+1}\right\|_{\tilde{D}} &= \left\|Tz^{k+1} - Tz^k\right\|_{\tilde{D}} \\ &\leq \left\|z^{k+1} - z^k\right\|_{\tilde{D}} = \left\|Tz^k - z^k\right\|_{\tilde{D}}, \end{aligned} \tag{4.59}$$

therefore, $\left(\|Tz^k - z^k\|_{\tilde{D}}\right)_{k\geq 0}$ is a monotonically nonincreasing sequence. Similarly, referring to [104, Theorem 1] and (4.58), we also have

$$\left\|Tz^k - z^k\right\|_{\tilde{D}}^2 \leq \frac{1}{k+1}\sum_{n=0}^{k} \|Tz^n - z^n\|_{\tilde{D}}^2 \leq \frac{1}{k+1}\left\|z^0 - z^*\right\|_D^2, \tag{4.60}$$

which meets the requirements of [54, Proposition 1] such that the non-ergodic convergence rate is $o(1/k)$.

(iii) Referring to the Krasnosel'skii-Mann theorem in [22, Theorem 5.14] with the result in Theorem 4.10(i), the sequence $\left(z^k\right)_{k\geq 0}$ converges to a fixed point of operator T. Then from Lemma 4.5, this statement holds.

■

Since z^k contains the components $\tilde{u}^k$ and $\tilde{s}^k$ which determine x^k, the convergence rate of $\left(x^k\right)_{k\geq 0}$ is $o(1/k)$. Thus, we establish the sublinear convergence rate for TPUS in terms of the first-order optimality residual in a non-ergodic sense. It is a slightly faster rate than the ergodic convergence rate $O(1/k)$. Notice that the concepts and conclusions on the ergodic and non-ergodic rates of convergence have been supplied in [18, 22, 54], so we will not specifically discuss them in this chapter. Readers interested in these can review the above references for more details.

4.5 Numerical Examples

In this section, we verify the effectiveness of TPUS through numerical experiments.

4.5.1 Constrained Quadratic Programming Problem

Consider a classical distributed quadratic programming problem with both equality constraints and inequality constraints as follows:

$$\begin{aligned}
\min_{x_1,\cdots,x_m\in\mathbb{R}} \quad & \sum_{i=1}^{m} f_i(x_i) = \sum_{i=1}^{m} x_i^{\top} V_i x_i + v_i^{\top} x_i, \\
\text{s.t.} \quad & K_i x_i = q_i, \quad i \in \mathcal{V}, \\
& M_i x_i \leq w_i, \quad i \in \mathcal{V}, \\
& x_i - x_j = 0, \; i \in \mathcal{V}, \; j \in \mathcal{N}_i.
\end{aligned} \tag{4.61}$$

Here, $V_i \in \mathbb{R}^{n_i \times n_i}$ is a positive definite diagonal matrix and v_i is a column vector. For agent $i \in \mathcal{V}$, $K_i \in \mathbb{R}^{r_i \times n_i}$ and $M_i \in \mathbb{R}^{p_i \times n_i}$ are two matrices while $q_i \in \mathbb{R}^{r_i}$ and $w_i \in \mathbb{R}^{p_i}$ are two column vectors. To begin with, we adopt the logarithmic barrier method in [105] to approximate the inequality constraints. Define an indicator function $\delta_{X_i^n}(x_i)$ where $X_i^n = \{x_i | M_i^n x_i - w_i^n \leq 0\}$. Here, $M_i^n x_i - w_i^n$ denotes the component in each row n of $M_i x_i - w_i$. Let $\delta_{X_i}(x_i) = \sum_{n=1}^{p_i} \delta_{X_i^n}(x_i^n)$ and we can contain the inequality constraints in $\delta_{X_i}(M_i x_i - w_i)$. Then, we use the approximate function of indicator function which is differentiable and convex by rewriting $\delta_{X_i}(M_i x_i - w_i)$ as $-(1/t)log(-(M_i x_i - w_i))$. Here, $log(y)$ is an operator representing the sum $\sum_{i=1}^{n} \log(y^i)$ for $y = [y^1, \ldots, y^n]^{\top} \in \mathbb{R}^n$, and t is a sufficiently large parameter. In the following experiments, we take $t = 2k$, where k is the number of iterations. Besides, we introduce another indicator function $\delta_{\mathcal{C}_i}(K_i x_i)$, where the set $\mathcal{C}_i = \{q_i\}$ converts the equality constraints into a function $\delta_{\mathcal{C}_i}(K_i x_i)$. Thus, problem (4.61) can be rewritten as

$$\begin{aligned}
\min_{x_1,\cdots,x_m} \quad & \sum_{i=1}^{m} \begin{bmatrix} f_i(x_i) - (1/t)log(-(M_i x_i - w_i)) \\ +\delta_{\mathcal{C}_i}(K_i x_i) \end{bmatrix}, \\
\text{s.t.} \quad & x_i - x_j = 0, \; (i, j) \in \mathcal{E},
\end{aligned} \tag{4.62}$$

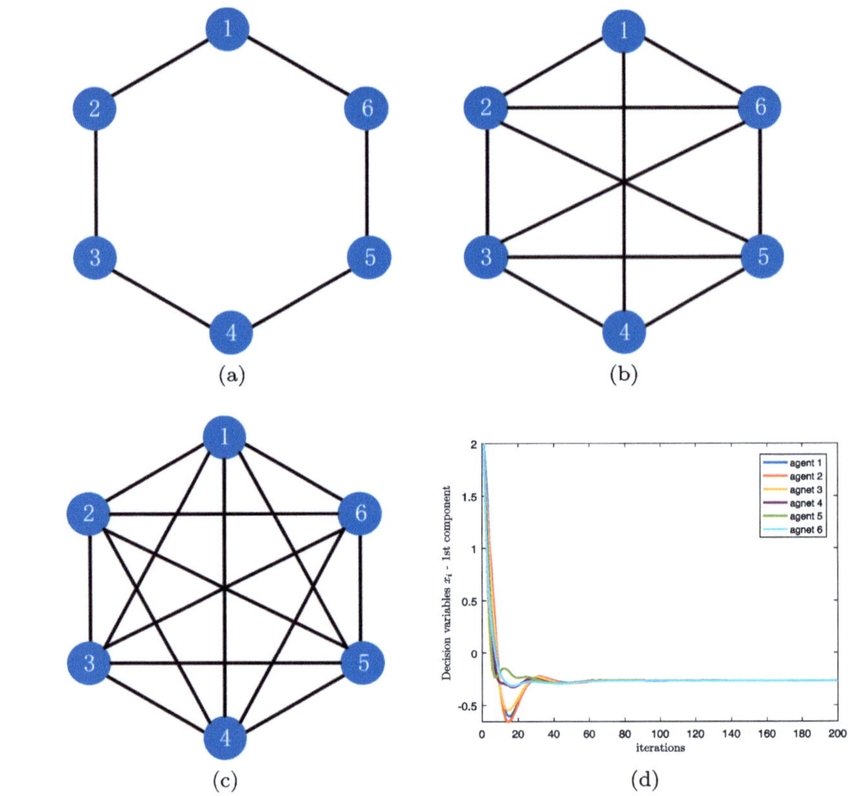

Fig. 4.1 The communication network and convergence of variable x_i. (**a**) The circle network. (**b**) The mesh network. (**c**) The full connected network. (**d**) Convergence of variable x_i (the first component)

which can be solved by TPUS. To compute the proximal operators in the algorithm, we set the differentiable part in problem (4.62) as $\tilde{f}_i(x_i)$ and let $g_i(x_i) = 0$. Then, due to the feasible scope $\mathcal{C}_i$, q_i can be directly used as the result of the proximal operator for $\delta_{\mathcal{C}_i}(K_i x_i)$.

Let $n_i = 20$, $r_i = 2$, and $p_i = 2$. Diagonal elements of V_i are randomly distributed in [1, 2] while all elements of K_i, M_i, v_i and q_i are randomly distributed in $[-1, 1]$. w_i takes the data from the interval [5, 6]. The communication networks are given in Fig. 4.1a–c. We first set the step sizes $\gamma_i = 0.05$, $\sigma_i = 0.5$, and $\rho_{(i,j)} = 5$. Based on Fig. 4.1a–d shows the convergence process of variable x_i for $i \in \mathcal{V}$. Figure 4.2 displays the performance of TPUS with the different network sparsity, where denser networks can lead to faster convergence. We also compare TPUS with another distributed algorithm for the nonsmooth composite optimization problem, TriPD-Dist [17]. Both of them adopt the step sizes above and perform over Fig. 4.1a. From Fig. 4.3, one can see that TPUS converges faster. Then, we study the

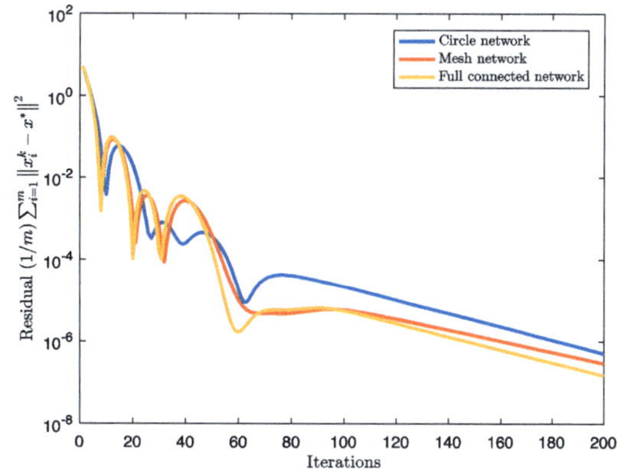

Fig. 4.2 Evolution of residuals with different networks

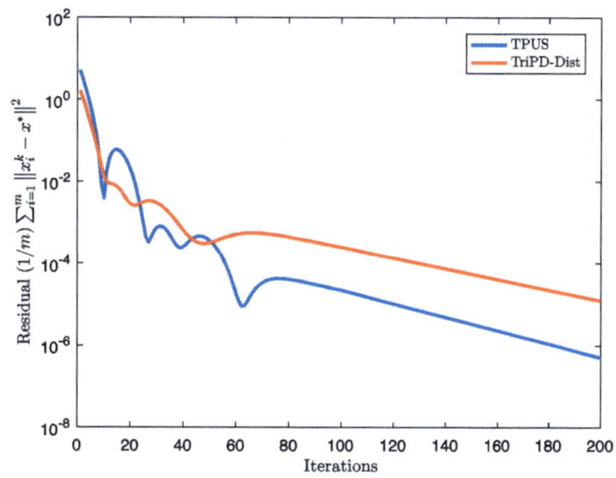

Fig. 4.3 Comparison across TPUS and TriPD-Dist

effect of the step sizes on the convergence performance. The residual is taken at iteration 200 and the step sizes above are taken as the default setting. When one step size is studied, the other two step sizes remain constant. Figure 4.4 shows the change of convergence rates with different step sizes.

4.5.2 Optimal Load Sharing Problem

Consider the optimal load sharing problem described in the motivating scenarios. Each bus is assumed to have both a generator to provide power and a local load demand to be met, which is thought as an agent. The experiment is performed over the network shown in Fig. 4.5. The arrows indicate the supposed reference direction of the power flows on the transmission lines. If the flow direction in the optimal dispatch scheme is the same as the reference direction, the result will be a positive

Fig. 4.4 Effect of the step sizes on the performance of TPUS. (**a**) Residuals at the 200th iteration with different γ_i. (**b**) Residuals at the 200th iteration with different σ_i. (**c**) Residuals at the 200th iteration with different $\rho_{(i,j)}$

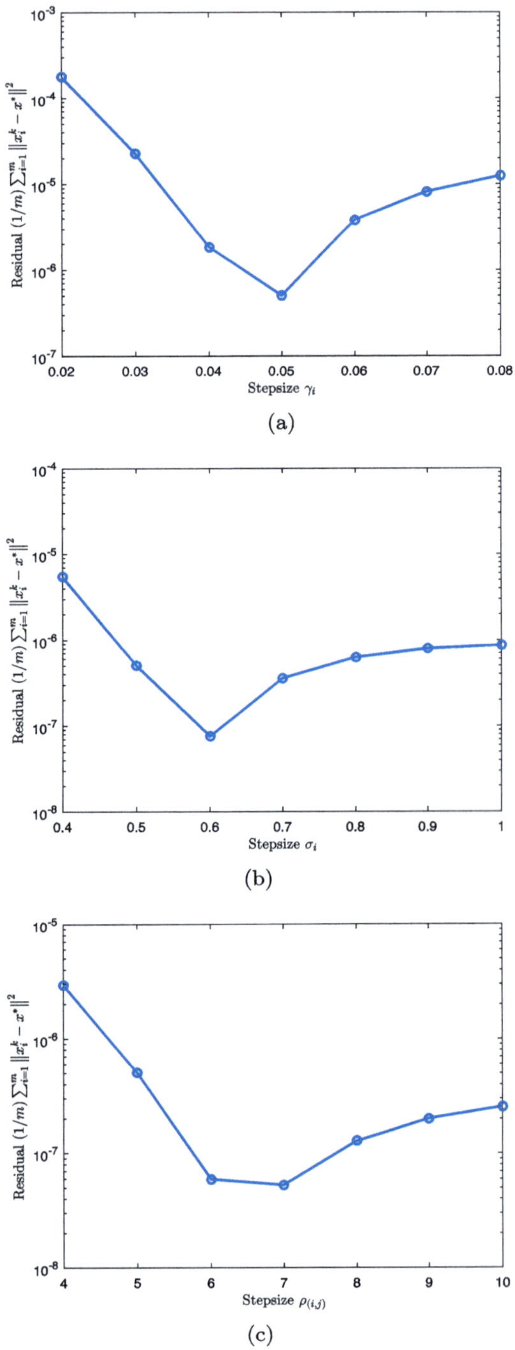

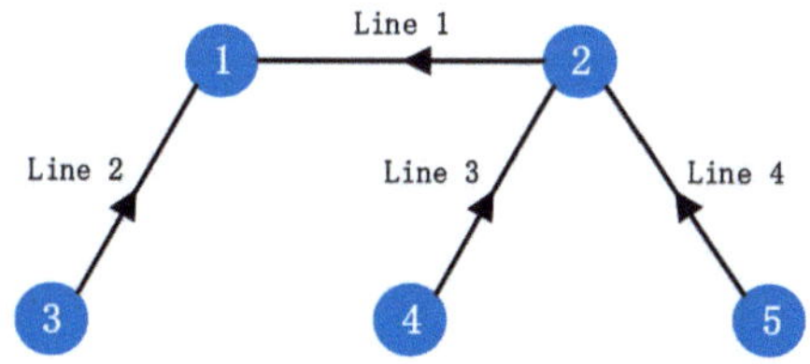

Fig. 4.5 The network for optimal load sharing problem

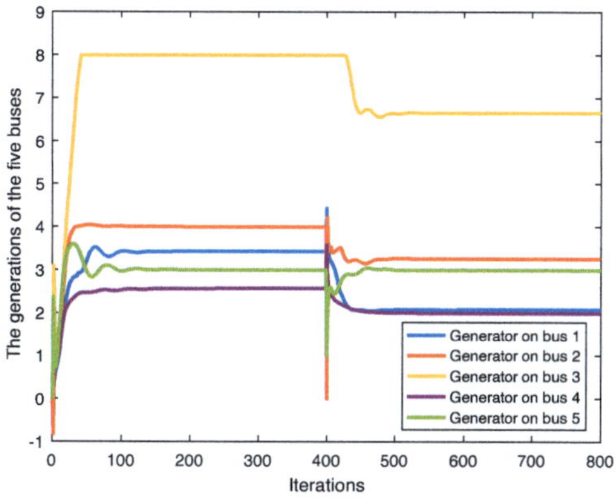

Fig. 4.6 The trajectories of generator output

value, otherwise it will be negative. The cost functions of generators on the buses are as follows:

$$C_1(p_1) = 3p_1^2 + p_1, \quad C_2(p_2) = 2p_2^2 + 3p_2,$$
$$C_3(p_3) = {p_3}^2 + 2p_3, \ C_4(p_4) = 3{p_4}^2 + 4p_4,$$
$$C_5(p_5) = 2{p_5}^2 + 2p_5.$$

The initial demand on the five buses is $D = [2\ 6\ 4\ 5\ 4]$. For each generator, the lowest power output is 0 while the maximum generating capacities are $p^{\max} = [6\ 4\ 8\ 12\ 3]$, respectively. The limits of power flows on the transmission lines are $v_1 \in [-8, 8]$, $v_2 \in [-4, 4]$, $v_3 \in [-4, 4]$, $v_4 \in [-6, 6]$. We perform the proposed algorithm with all variables starting at 0, and the step sizes are set as $\gamma_i = 0.1$, $\sigma_i = 0.5$, and $\rho_{(i,j)} = 0.5$. Figure 4.6 gives the dispatching scheme of all generators on the five buses and Fig. 4.7 shows the trajectories of power flow estimations. Between the 200-th iteration and 400-th iteration, the estimations of the same power flow on different buses have reached the consensus. During this time, generators on bus 2, 3, and 5 output their maximum power and the power flow on line 2 reaches its limit. From the 400-th iteration, the demands become $D = [3\ 2\ 4\ 6\ 2]$. The power outputs in Fig. 4.6, and the estimations of flows in Fig. 4.7 make corresponding changes and converge again, which demonstrates the dynamic adaptability of the proposed algorithm to demand changes.

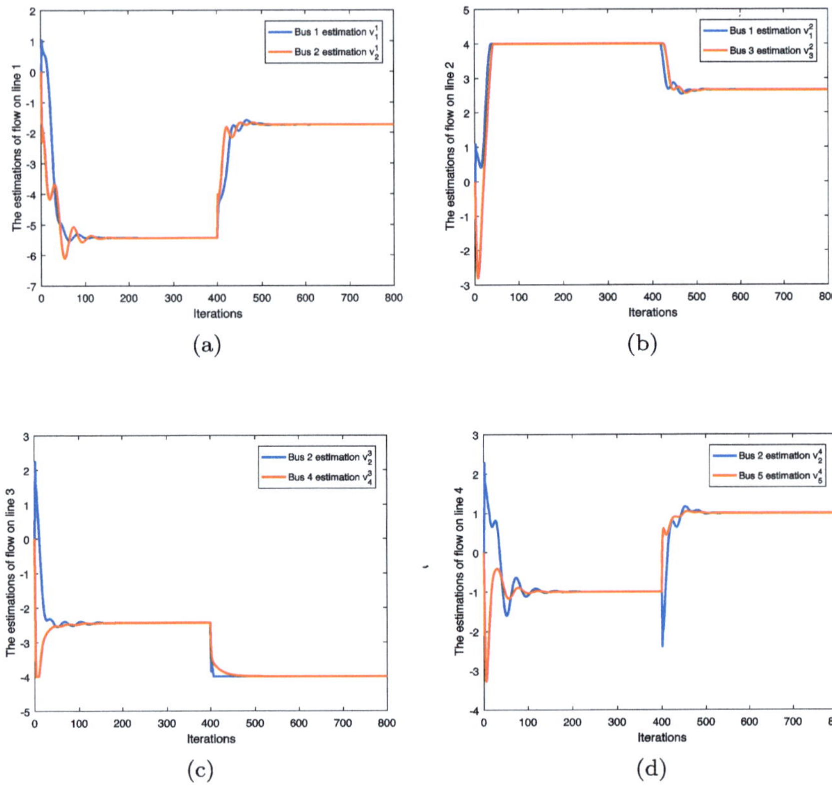

Fig. 4.7 The trajectories of power flow estimations. (**a**) The trajectories of estimations of flow on line 1. (**b**) The trajectories of estimations of flow on line 2. (**c**) The trajectories of estimations of flow on line 3. (**d**) The trajectories of estimations of flow on line 4

4.6 Conclusion

This chapter has proposed a novel distributed algorithm to solve the nonsmooth composite optimization problem where agents collectively minimize the sum of a smooth function and two nonsmooth convex functions containing a bounded linear operator. The main idea is to convert the constraint of edges into a penalty term and introduce three proximal operators to deal with the nonsmooth terms correspondingly. Moreover, the design of uncoordinated step sizes allows agents to employ independent parameters with independent acceptance ranges to solve the problem without exchanging any information of global graph and local objective functions.

Chapter 5
Distributed Dual Operator Splitting Algorithm for Nonsmooth Composite Optimization

Abstract Inspired by the advantages of the distributed network structure in large-scale data processing and system robustness, this chapter considers a fully distributed computation strategy for a nonsmooth composite optimization problem. The goal is to solve the problem only by resorting to local computation and local communications. Here, the local objective function is composed of two possibly nonsmooth functions where one is strongly convex and the other is proper closed convex (not necessarily strongly convex). Through associating variables with the agents and edges of the network, a distributed synchronous algorithm is developed based on the dual operator splitting method. The asynchronous version of the proposed algorithm is further developed based on the randomized block coordinate descent technique, where each agent performs the algorithm only under its independent activation. Then the convergence analysis is provided depending on the fixed point iterations and the property of strong duality. Simulations on regularized problems demonstrate the effectiveness of the proposed distributed algorithm.

Keywords Distributed optimization · Multi-agent system · Nonsmooth problem · Asynchronous algorithm · Randomized block coordinate · Uncoordinated step size

5.1 Introduction

With the rapid growth of data size, the centralized optimization algorithms that rely on a single machine to process information have been restricted by the computing and storage capacities of hardware. Therefore, this chapter considers a distributed computational model which combines multiple computing agents over a communication network to solve a common optimization problem cooperatively. The network is connected and undirected such that each agent can reach any other agent over the network via one or more edges. For each agent, the cost function is private and the information of local variables can only be exchanged with neighbors.

H. Li et al., *Network-System Research and Distributed Composite Algorithm Design*, Computational Intelligence Methods and Applications,
https://doi.org/10.1007/978-981-95-0911-9_5

Such a distributed structure is beneficial to the scalability of the whole network and protecting the privacy of agents, and shows great potential in many fields, such as model predictive control [64], formation control [106], resource allocation problem [73, 74, 107] and machine learning [103, 108, 109]. Recently, some successful works have been reported, see [9, 17, 49, 82, 95, 110–115], where multi-agent systems are applied to manage distributed optimization. Gradient-based algorithms are widely studied, e.g., the first-order [49, 115] and second-order [110] algorithms. Randomized gradient-free technology has also been applied, see [111, 112]. In addition, note that requiring all agents to participate in each iteration may not keep the network robust when some agents are inactivated. Asynchronous algorithms [17, 113] are proposed to address this issue.

This chapter focuses on the optimization problem formed by two groups of objective functions separated into m subfunctions as $\sum_{i=1}^{m} f_i(x) + g_i(x)$. Such a composite structure instead of a single group of generic functions is considered because f_i and g_i with inconsistent properties arise in a large number of signal processing [116], statistical inference [117] and operational research [118, 119], etc. For these problems, some successful algorithms were proposed. Shi et al. [54] develop PG-EXTRA and then Li et al. [18] improved it into NIDS with the independent step sizes. Aybat et al. [120] proposed DPDA-D for the time-varying networks. However, all of them required a partially smooth term in the nonsmooth objective function. In other words, traditional composite optimization problems should have a smooth + nonsmooth structure. In this chapter, we consider the problem composed of two possible nonsmooth functions, which do not depend on smooth assumptions. Note that for composite optimization problems, operator splitting is an efficient method [22]. But so far, relevant achievements are mainly concentrated on centralized forms [4–6, 8, 123]. Among them, Combettes and Pesquet [4] adopted a forward-backward-forward scheme. Then, a primal-dual algorithm Condat-Vũ was proposed in [5] and [99] with a restrictive range of acceptable parameters. Chen et al. [123] proposed Primal-Dual Fixed-Point algorithm (PDFP) with a larger range of acceptable parameters than Condat-Vũ. The Asymmetric Forward-Backward-Adjoint splitting algorithm (AFBA) was proposed in [6], which takes Condat-Vũ as a special case. Yan [8] developed an algorithm called Primal-Dual Three-Operator splitting (PD3O) which has the same regions of acceptable parameters as PDFP and the same per-iteration complexity as Condat-Vũ and AFBA. Then, a few distributed results appear. Notarnicola et al. [124] considered two nonsmooth functions and propose Distributed Dual Proximal Gradient algorithm (DDPG). For a more complex problem called Single-Smooth plus Double-Nonsmooth (SSDN) consisting of a smooth convex function and two nonsmooth convex functions, a continuous-time algorithm was presented in [98]. Discrete-time algorithm TriPD-Dist and its asynchronous version for SSDN were developed in [17].

The proposed algorithm is compared to the distributed discrete literature in the following way. The works [9, 49, 82, 95, 110–115] discussed the general single-function model, which cannot be applied to composite optimization problems and investigate special properties of local terms in composite structures (such as partially strongly convex). The works [17, 18, 54, 120] focused on nonsmooth composite optimization, but still require at least one local smooth term in problem formulation. Besides, algorithms in [18, 54, 120] were synchronous which depend on the global clock to control the communication and iteration for all agents. The contributions of this work are summarized as follows:

(i) We consider a composite optimization problem with two possible nonsmooth cost functions, which is different from the common smooth + nonsmooth problem [14, 17, 108, 114, 121, 122]. From the dual-domain of the objective problem, a novel distributed algorithm based on the operator splitting method is developed.
(ii) The proposed algorithm adopts uncoordinated step sizes, which do not require the multiple communication steps to achieve global consensus step sizes. The step sizes related to agents can be decided locally, while those related to edges only need to be consistent at two adjacent agents. Moreover, explicit ranges for parameter selections are provided.
(iii) Profiting from the distributed topology structure, the randomized block coordinate descent strategy is introduced to design an asynchronous version of the proposed algorithm. Each agent is allowed to possess an independent activation probability and no longer be controlled by a global iteration clock. In this situation, the algorithm can keep iteration running without implementing uniform computation at each agent.
(iv) Based on the fixed point theory and the property of strong duality, the convergence analysis is presented for the proposed algorithms. It is shown that in the asynchronous mode, although the agents do not always participate in the computation instantaneously, their optimal estimates converge to the optimal solution to the global optimization problem.

5.2 Preliminaries

In this section, we define some necessary notations and then introduce the distributed network structure and the optimization problem with necessary assumptions.

5.2.1 Notation

Throughout this chapter, without other specific statements, lowercase letters indicate column vectors and uppercase letters indicate matrices. For a matrix Q, $Q \in \mathbb{R}^{m \times n}$ means that the dimension is m rows and n columns. For arbitrary vectors x_i, $i = 1, \ldots, m$, we use $col(\cdot)$ to denote the collection vector. For arbitrary matrices Q_i, $i = 1, \ldots, m$, blkdiag$\{Q_i\}$ is the block diagonal matrix stacked by

Q_i. $Q^\top$ is the transposition of Q. I denotes the identity matrix and for notation simplicity, we do not specify its dimensions when it is clear from the context. For a symmetric matrix Q, let $\langle x, y\rangle_Q = \langle x, Qy\rangle$ and the induced norm for vector x is $\|x\|_Q = \sqrt{\langle x, x\rangle_Q}$. When $Q = I$, the induced norm becomes the 2-norm and we simply denote it by $\|\cdot\|$. $\|\cdot\|_1$ represents the 1-norm for vectors which is the sum of absolute values of components. $\mathbb{E} \circ (\cdot)$ indicates the mathematical expectation. For any two vectors x and y, the conjugate function for function $f(x)$ is defined as $f^*(y) = \sup_{x\in\mathbb{R}^n}\{\langle y, x\rangle - f(x)\}$. The proximal operator for a symmetric positive definite matrix Q is $\mathrm{prox}_f^Q(x) = (I + Q^{-1}\partial f)^{-1}(x) = \arg\min_y \left\{f(y) + (1/2)\|x - y\|_Q^2\right\}$, while that for constant λ is $\mathrm{prox}_{\lambda f}(x) = (I + \lambda\partial f)^{-1}(x) = \arg\min_y \left\{f(y) + (1/2\lambda)\|y - x\|^2\right\}$. For three arbitrary vectors x, y, z and a proper closed convex and smooth function f, ∂f is the sub-differential of f given by $\partial f(x) = \{y|\forall z \in \mathbb{R}^n, f(x) + \langle y, z - x\rangle \le f(z)\}$.

5.2.2 *Model of Optimization Problem*

In this chapter, we focus on an optimization problem which can be split as the sum of a series of subfunctions as follows:

$$\min_x \sum_{i=1}^m f_i(x) + g_i(x), \tag{5.1}$$

where $f_i : \mathbb{R}^n \to \mathbb{R}\cup\{+\infty\}$ and $g_i : \mathbb{R}^n \to \mathbb{R}\cup\{+\infty\}$ are two local cost functions that can only be obtained by agent i. The goal is to cooperatively solve optimization problem (5.1) through local computation and communication over graph $\mathcal{G}$. In order to realize the distributed processing at each agent, we introduce the consensus constraint to rewrite problem (5.1) as the following distributed form:

$$\min_x \sum_{i=1}^m f_i(x_i) + g_i(x_i), \quad \text{s.t.} \quad x_i - x_j = 0, \quad (i, j) \in \mathcal{E}. \tag{5.2}$$

Here, $x_i \in \mathbb{R}^n$, $i \in \mathcal{V}$, is the component split from $x \in \mathbb{R}^{mn}$ according to the number of agents, i.e., $x = col(x_1, x_2, \cdots, x_m)$. Thus, x_i becomes the local decision variable maintained by agent i and $f_i(x_i) + g_i(x_i)$ is only relevant to the local information, so that agents can solve the optimization problem in a distributed manner.

To specify the problem discussed in this chapter, we make the following assumptions for optimization problem (5.2) and the communication network.

Assumption 5.1 (Strong Convexity and Slater's Condition)

(i) For any $i \in \mathcal{V}$, the local objective function f_i is β_i-strongly convex with $\beta_i > 0$, i.e.,

$$f_i(y) - f_i(x) \geq \langle \partial f_i(x), y - x \rangle + \frac{\beta_i}{2} \|y - x\|^2, \tag{5.3}$$

for arbitrary vectors $x \in \mathbb{R}^n$ and $y \in \mathbb{R}^n$, and the local function g_i is a proper closed convex function;

(ii) There exists a global optimal solution to problem (5.2);

(iii) The undirected graph $\mathcal{G}$ is connected.

Remark 5.1 The conditions for cost functions in Assumption 5.1 are common in related literature [17, 54, 121, 124]. More conclusions upon the property of convex and strongly convex are provided in [22].

Note that we do not assume any smooth property for functions f_i and g_i, $i \in \mathcal{V}$, which is different from the smooth + nonsmooth structure requiring partially smooth property. Thus, problem (5.2) is a distributed nonsmooth composite optimization problem. In addition, problems satisfying Slater's condition are sufficient condition for strong duality. It ensures that when the dual problem achieves the optimal solution, the primal problem also obtains its optimal solution. It is a critical condition for the dual problem set up in the next section.

5.2.3 Communication Network

Consider an undirected network with m agents connected by l edges over the network. Each agent has a local memory and a local calculator, and only can exchange information with its neighbors. Let graph $\mathcal{G} = (\mathcal{V}, \mathcal{E})$ denote the network where $\mathcal{V}$ is the set of agents and $\mathcal{E}$ is the set of edges. The edge between agent i and agent j is denoted by an unordered pair $(i, j) \in \mathcal{E}$. Since the graph is undirected, information with regard to the same edge should be consistent, i.e., $x_{(i,j)} = x_{(j,i)}$. It is worth noting that pairs ij and ji are ordered, so x_{ij} and x_{ji} represent two unrelated pieces of information, respectively. Besides, we employ $\mathcal{N}_i$ to denote the set of neighbor agents of agent i.

5.2.4 Motivating Scenarios

Nonsmooth composite optimization problem (5.1) exists naturally or is not difficult to find in many fields. Using a composite structure instead of the generalized model $\min_x \sum_{i=1}^{m} f_i(x)$ also makes it possible to exploit the properties of local terms. In this subsection, we provide some practical examples for this structure.

5.2.4.1 Constrained Optimization

Consider a separable constrained optimization problem which has the following formulation:

$$\min_x \sum_{i=1}^{m} f_i(x), \text{ s.t. } x \in \bigcap_{i=1}^{m} X_i \subseteq \mathbb{R}^n, \tag{5.4}$$

where for $i \in \mathcal{V}$, X_i is a closed and convex set and f_i is strongly convex but not necessarily smooth. Problem (5.4) is a general formulation widely investigated in many scenarios. For example, when a quadratic cost is taken for the objective function and the demand balance constraint is adopted, problem (5.4) becomes a common problem in resource allocation [73, 74, 107]. Meanwhile, we introduce the indicator function:

$$\delta_D(x) = \begin{cases} 0, & x \in D, \\ +\infty, & \text{otherwise}. \end{cases} \tag{5.5}$$

For $i = 1, \ldots, m$, let D become the scope of constraint X_i such that (5.4) can be transformed as:

$$\min_x \sum_{i=1}^{m} f_i(x) + \delta_{X_i}(x), \tag{5.6}$$

where X_i is a convex set so $\delta_{X_i}(x)$ is a convex function. Thus, using $g_i(x)$ to replace the indicator function $\delta_{X_i}(x)$, problem (5.1) can finally cover the constrained optimization problem (5.4). In fact, it is also reasonable to include the constraint into f_i. However, we just employ this case as an example for problem (5.1) and do not supply more further discussion here. One can refer to [124] for more details.

5.2.4.2 Regularized Optimization

As an effective technique, regularization is widely applied in machine learning [103, 108, 109], signal processing [116], etc. In these problems, the loss function indicates the mismatch between the prediction of the theoretical model and the real data. Here, we consider the most widespread method, least square, which is constructed as:

$$\min_x \sum_{i=1}^{m} \|b_i - Y_i x\|^2, \tag{5.7}$$

where Y_i represents the matrix of the data and b_i denotes the label or observation. Note that the over-fitting phenomena for standard algorithms is not uncommon. In order to avoid this problem, the 1-norm is often added, which results in the well-known LASSO problem as follows:

$$\min_{x} \sum_{i=1}^{m} \|b_i - Y_i x\|^2 + \mu \|x\|_1, \tag{5.8}$$

where the positive parameter μ determines the sparsity of the solution. Since the ℓ_1-norm is a nonsmooth term, the LASSO problem can be viewed as the form of problem (5.1).

5.3 Algorithm Development

5.3.1 Dual Problem Setup

To obtain the desired separable structure of the dual problem, we establish the following equivalent form of problem (5.2) with another three variables $z_{ij} \in \mathbb{R}^n$, $z_{ji} \in \mathbb{R}^n$ and $y_i \in \mathbb{R}^n$ as:

$$\min_{x,y} \sum_{i=1}^{m} \left(f_i(x_i) + g_i(y_i)\right), \text{ s.t. } \begin{cases} x_i = z_{ij}, & x_j = z_{ji}, \\ x_i = y_i, & z_{ij} = z_{ji}, \\ i \in \mathcal{V}, & j \in \mathcal{N}_i. \end{cases} \tag{5.9}$$

Here, we let $y = col\,(y_1, y_2, \ldots, y_m)$ for notation simplicity. The introduction of y_i lets f_i and g_i be associated with different variables, making it possible to establish the needed dual problem later. z_{ij} and z_{ji} are two auxiliary variables related to edge (i, j), which convert the agent-based variables in the consensus constraint to the edge-based ones. Therefore, we call them bridge variables, and thus both the edge-based and agent-based variables can be employed to establish the dual problem. For each $(i, j) \in \mathcal{E}$, we define $z_{(i,j)} = \left(z_{ij}^\top, z_{ji}^\top\right)^\top \in \mathbb{R}^{2n}$ such that the two auxiliary variables can be considered as a whole in terms of edge (i, j). Then, define two linear matrix operators $A_{(i,j)} \in \mathbb{R}^{2n \times mn}$ and $P_{(i,j)} \in \mathbb{R}^{2n \times mn}$ for $(i, j) \in \mathcal{E}$ to transform the conditions of z_{ij} and z_{ji} in (5.9) into conditions of $z_{(i,j)}$. $A_{(i,j)}$ is the mapping from agents to edges, i.e.,

$$A_{(i,j)} : x \mapsto \left(x_i^\top, x_j^\top\right)^\top. \tag{5.10}$$

$P_{(i,j)}$ is a permutation matrix swapping the position of $z_{(i,j)}$ with $z_{(j,i)}$, i.e.,

$$P_{(i,j)} : z_{(i,j)} \mapsto \left(z_{ji}^\top, z_{ij}^\top\right)^\top. \tag{5.11}$$

Thus, problem (5.9) can be rewritten as the following problem with variables of edges:

$$\begin{aligned} \min_{x,y} & \sum_{i=1}^{m} \left[f_i(x_i) + g_i(y_i) \right], \\ \text{s.t.} \;\; & A_{(i,j)}x = z_{(i,j)}, \quad (I - P_{(i,j)})z_{(i,j)} = 0, \\ & x_i = y_i, \qquad\qquad \forall i \in \mathcal{V},\ (i,j) \in \mathcal{E}. \end{aligned} \tag{5.12}$$

Besides, define an indicator function $\delta_{D_{(i,j)}}\left(z_{(i,j)}\right)$ for $(i,j) \in \mathcal{E}$ with the set $D_{(i,j)} = \left\{z_{(i,j)} | \left(I - P_{(i,j)}\right) z_{(i,j)} = 0\right\}$ that returns 0 if $z_{(i,j)} \in D_{(i,j)}$, and $+\infty$, otherwise. Letting $\delta_{D_{(i,j)}}\left(z_{(i,j)}\right)$ as a penalty function to transfer the equality constraints in terms of $z_{(i,j)}$ to the objective optimization function, we obtain the final formulation of the problem as follows:

$$\begin{aligned} \min_{x,y,z} & \sum_{i=1}^{m} \left[f_i(x_i) + g_i(y_i) \right] + \sum_{(i,j)\in\mathcal{E}} \delta_{D_{(i,j)}}(z_{(i,j)}), \\ \text{s.t.} \;\; & A_{(i,j)}x = z_{(i,j)},\ x_i = y_i, \quad \forall i \in \mathcal{V},\ (i,j) \in \mathcal{E}. \end{aligned} \tag{5.13}$$

where $z \in \mathbb{R}^{2ln}$ is a column vector stacked by $z_{(i,j)}$ for all $(i,j) \in \mathcal{E}$.

The Lagrangian function of problem (5.13) is given as

$$\begin{aligned} \mathcal{L}(x,y,z,u,s) = & \sum_{i=1}^{m} \left[f_i(x_i) + g_i(y_i) + u_i^\top (x_i - y_i) \right] \\ & + \sum_{(i,j)\in\mathcal{E}} \left[\delta_{D_{(i,j)}}(z_{(i,j)}) + s_{(i,j)}^\top (A_{(i,j)}x - z_{(i,j)}) \right], \end{aligned} \tag{5.14}$$

where $s_{(i,j)} \in \mathbb{R}^{2n}$ and $u_i \in \mathbb{R}^n$ are two dual variables for the constraints in problem (5.13). $s \in \mathbb{R}^{2ln}$ is stacked by $s_{(i,j)}$, and $u = col\,(u_1, \ldots, u_m)$. Notice that there is a global variable x in (5.14) which prevents the Lagrangian function from possessing a completely distributed formulation. To address this, we consider splitting $s_{(i,j)}$ like $z_{(i,j)}$ since it is the variable for edge (i,j). Letting $s_{(i,j)} = \left(s_{ij}^\top, s_{ji}^\top\right)^\top$ for $i \in \mathcal{V}$ and $j \in \mathcal{N}_i$ we have

$$\sum_{(i,j)\in\mathcal{E}} s_{(i,j)}^\top A_{(i,j)}x = \sum_{i=1}^{m} \sum_{j\in\mathcal{N}_i} x_i^\top s_{ij}. \tag{5.15}$$

Therefore, the dual problem is

$$\begin{aligned}
&\max_{u,s}\min_{x,y,z}\mathcal{L}(x, y, z, u, s)\\
&=\max_{u,s}\left[\begin{array}{l}\min_{x}\sum_{i=1}^{m}\sum_{j\in\mathcal{N}_i}\left(f_i(x_i)+x_i^{\top}\left(u_i+s_{ij}\right)\right)\\
+\min_{y}\sum_{i=1}^{m}\left(g_i(y_i)-y_i^{\top}u_i\right)\\
+\min_{z}\sum_{(i,j)\in\mathcal{E}}\left(\delta_{D_{(i,j)}}\left(z_{(i,j)}\right)-z_{(i,j)}^{\top}s_{(i,j)}\right)\end{array}\right]\\
&=\max_{u,s}\left[\begin{array}{l}-\sum_{i=1}^{m}\sum_{j\in\mathcal{N}_i}f_i^{*}\left(-\left(u_i+s_{ij}\right)\right)\\
-\sum_{i=1}^{m}g_i^{*}(u_i)-\sum_{(i,j)\in\mathcal{E}}\delta_{D_{(i,j)}}\left(s_{(i,j)}\right)\end{array}\right],
\end{aligned}\tag{5.16}$$

where f_i^*, g_i^* and $\delta^*_{D_{(i,j)}}$ are the conjugate functions of f_i, g_i and $\delta_{D_{(i,j)}}$, respectively. Note that the goal is to obtain the optimal u and s. The results of (5.16) are also the solution to the following problem:

$$\min_{u,s}\sum_{i=1}^{m}\sum_{j\in\mathcal{N}_i}\left[f_i^{*}\left(-\left(u_i+s_{ij}\right)\right)+g_i^{*}(u_i)\right]+\sum_{(i,j)\in\mathcal{E}}\delta^{*}_{D_{(i,j)}}\left(s_{(i,j)}\right).\tag{5.17}$$

Under the Slater's condition in Assumption 5.1, there is zero duality gap between the primal problem (5.13) and the dual problem (5.16), which provides the theoretical guarantee to develop a distributed algorithm from the perspective of duality.

5.3.2 Synchronous Distributed Algorithm Development

Recall that in (5.14), for $i\in\mathcal{V}$, $j\in\mathcal{N}_i$, x_i is the decision variable and $s_{(i,j)}$ and u_i are two dual variables related to edges and agents, respectively. Based on [22, Proposition 19.18], the Lagrangian function of problem (5.17) is

$$\begin{aligned}
\widetilde{\mathcal{L}}=&\sum_{i=1}^{m}\left[f_i^{*}\left(-\left(u_i+\sum_{j\in\mathcal{N}_i}s_{ij}\right)\right)+g_i^{*}(u_i)\right]\\
&+\sum_{(i,j)\in\mathcal{E}}\left[v_{(i,j)}{}^{\top}s_{(i,j)}-\delta^{*}_{D_{(i,j)}}\left(v_{(i,j)}\right)\right],
\end{aligned}\tag{5.18}$$

where $v_{(i,j)} = \left(v_{ij}^\top, v_{ji}^\top\right)^\top$ is the dual variable for $s_{(i,j)}$ and also with respect to edges. From [105], as the conjugate function of a strongly convex function, f_i^* is differentiable. Taking partial derivatives on (5.18) with u_i, s_{ij} and $v_{(i,j)}$ for $i \in \mathcal{V}$, $j \in \mathcal{N}_i$ and applying the operator splitting method in [8], the iteration steps for solving problem (5.17) are

$$
\begin{aligned}
u_i^k &= \operatorname{prox}_{\gamma_i g_i^*}\left(\tilde{u}_i^k\right), \\
v_{(i,j)}^{k+1} &= \operatorname{prox}_{\sigma_{(i,j)}\delta_{D_{(i,j)}}}\left(\begin{pmatrix} \left(1-\sigma_{(i,j)}\rho_{(i,j)}\right) v_{(i,j)}^k + \sigma_{(i,j)} \times \\ \begin{pmatrix} s_{(i,j)}^k - \rho_{(i,j)} \times \\ \partial_{s_{(i,j)}} \begin{bmatrix} f_i^*\left(-\left(u_i^k + \sum_{j\in\mathcal{N}_i} s_{ij}^k\right)\right) \\ +f_j^*\left(-\left(u_j^k + \sum_{t\in\mathcal{N}_j} s_{jt}^k\right)\right) \end{bmatrix} \end{pmatrix} \end{pmatrix}\right), \\
\tilde{u}_i^{k+1} &= u_i^k - \gamma_i \partial_{u_i} f_i^*\left(-\left(u_i^k + \sum_{t\in\mathcal{N}_i} s_{it}^k\right)\right), \\
s_{ij}^{k+1} &= s_{ij}^k - \rho_{(i,j)} \partial_{s_{ij}} f_i^*\left(-\left(u_i^k + \sum_{t\in\mathcal{N}_i} s_{it}^k\right)\right) - \rho_{(i,j)} v_{ij}^{k+1},
\end{aligned} \tag{5.19}
$$

where $\tilde{u}_i \in \mathbb{R}^n$ generated by the operator splitting method is the auxiliary variable for u_i and the partial derivatives can be computed by

$$
\begin{aligned}
\partial_{u_i} f_i^*\left(-\left(u_i + \sum_{t\in\mathcal{N}_i} s_{it}\right)\right) &= \partial_{s_{ij}} f_i^*\left(-\left(u_i + \sum_{t\in\mathcal{N}_i} s_{it}\right)\right) \\
&= -\operatorname*{argmin}_{x_i}\left\{f_i(x_i) + x_i^\top\left(u_i + \sum_{t\in\mathcal{N}_i} s_{it}\right)\right\}.
\end{aligned} \tag{5.20}
$$

Combine (5.19) and (5.20) with introducing the Moreau decomposition in [22] for the proximal operators in (5.19). Thus, based on the dual problem (5.16), we put forward a novel distributed algorithm for the nonsmooth composite optimization problem (5.2) in Algorithm 6. For $i \in \mathcal{V}$ and $j \in \mathcal{N}_i$, the variables s_{ij} and v_{ij} are only maintained by agent i while their data still can participate in communication exchange over the network at each iteration k. The acceptable ranges of the step sizes are supplied in Assumption 5.2.

Algorithm 6 The synchronous distributed algorithm

Initialization : For each agent $i \in \mathcal{V}$ and all $j \in \mathcal{N}_i$, let $u_i^0 \in \mathbb{R}^n$, $\tilde{u}_i^0 \in \mathbb{R}^n$, $v_{ij}^0 \in \mathbb{R}^n$, $s_{ij}^0 \in \mathbb{R}^n$ and perform

$$x_i^0 = \underset{x_i}{\operatorname{argmin}} \left\{ f_i(x_i) + (x_i)^\top \left(u_i^0 + \sum\nolimits_{j \in \mathcal{N}_i} s_{ij}^0 \right) \right\}.$$

For $k = 1, 2, \cdots$ **do**

$$\begin{aligned}
u_i^k &= \tilde{u}_i^k - \gamma_i \operatorname{prox}_{\gamma_i^{-1} g_i} \left(\gamma_i^{-1} \tilde{u}_i^k \right), \\
v_{ij}^{k+1} &= \frac{1 - \sigma_{(i,j)} \rho_{(i,j)}}{2} \left(v_{ij}^k + v_{ji}^k \right) + \frac{\sigma_{(i,j)}}{2} \left(s_{ij}^k + s_{ji}^k + \rho_{(i,j)} x_i^k + \rho_{(i,j)} x_j^k \right), \\
\tilde{u}_i^{k+1} &= u_i^k + \gamma_i x_i^k, \\
s_{ij}^{k+1} &= s_{ij}^k + \rho_{(i,j)} x_i^k - \rho_{(i,j)} v_{ij}^{k+1}, \\
x_i^{k+1} &= \underset{x_i}{\operatorname{argmin}} \left\{ f_i(x_i) + (x_i)^\top \left(u_i^k + \sum\nolimits_{j \in \mathcal{N}_i} s_{ij}^k \right) \right\}.
\end{aligned}$$

Agent i sends v_{ij}^{k+1}, s_{ij}^{k+1} and x_i^{k+1} to all of its neighbors.
End
Output : The sequence $\left(x_i^k\right)_{k=1}^{\infty}$ to estimate the i-th component of an optimal solution.

Assumption 5.2 (Step Sizes Conditions) *For three positive constants γ_i, $\sigma_{(i,j)}$ and $\rho_{(i,j)}$ for $i \in \mathcal{V}$ and $(i, j) \in \mathcal{E}$, the following inequalities should be satisfied:*

$$\gamma_i < \frac{2\beta_i}{\sqrt{1+\omega_i}}, \quad \sigma_{i,j} < \frac{1}{\rho_{i,j}}, \quad \rho_{i,j} < \min \left(\frac{2\beta_i}{\sqrt{1+\omega_i}}, \frac{2\beta_j}{\sqrt{1+\omega_j}} \right), \tag{5.21}$$

where β_i is the strong convexity parameter of local cost function f_i, and ω_i is the number of the neighbors of agent i.

Note that in Algorithm 6, the step size γ_i for $i \in \mathcal{V}$ is related to the specific agent i, which allows uncoordinated step size settings for different agents. Similarly, $\rho_{(i,j)}$ and $\sigma_{(i,j)}$ for $(i, j) \in \mathcal{E}$ can be considered as the parameters for a specific communication link (i, j) and set differently. However, it is difficult to require consistent parameter ranges of each agent and communication link due to the complexity of network structure in reality. A compromised method is to adopt the global uniform step sizes according to the lower limit of local performance, but may lead to inadequate exploitation of the potential of the distributed network. Hence, these uncoordinated step sizes can avoid the restriction of global step sizes at each local agent, enlarge the acceptable range of local parameters and enhance the flexibility of the network.

When Algorithm 6 is executed, a global clock is required to control all variables update and ensure that all agents send and receive information at the same iteration

k. However, consider that some agents may sleep and not always be able to participate in updates immediately. This motivates us to develop an asynchronous version of Algorithm 6.

5.3.3 *Asynchronous Distributed Algorithm Development*

Algorithm 7 The asynchronous distributed algorithm

Initialization : For each agent $i \in \mathcal{V}$ and all $j \in \mathcal{N}_i$, let $u_i^0 \in \mathbb{R}^n$, $\tilde{u}_i^0 \in \mathbb{R}^n$, $v_{ij}^0 \in \mathbb{R}^n$, $s_{ij}^0 \in \mathbb{R}^n$ and perform

$$x_i^0 = \underset{x_i}{\operatorname{argmin}} \left\{ f_i(x_i) + (x_i)^\top \left(u_i^0 + \sum\nolimits_{j \in \mathcal{N}_i} s_{ij}^0 \right) \right\}.$$

Local Update : Each agent $i \in \mathcal{V}$ is awakened independently with the probability p_i. Each active agent executes the update flow in Algorithm 3 while inactive ones remain the latest data unchanged.

Output : The sequence $\left(x_i^k\right)_{k=1}^{\infty}$ to estimate the ith component of an optimal solution.

Regarding all variable data stored by agent i for $i \in \mathcal{V}$ as a single data block, we introduce the randomized block coordinate to improve the synchronous distributed algorithm. The agents at iteration k are divided into active and inactive states, which are determined by independent and random activation probabilities. When an agent is awakened, the update flow in Algorithm 6 is performed, otherwise the data of the previous iteration keeps unchanged. We use $U_i \in \mathbb{R}^{5mn \times 5mn}$ to denote the activation matrix selecting coordinate blocks to update. At iteration k, let $\eta^k \in \mathbb{R}^m$ be the 0–1 activation indicator vector indicating the states of agents. Concretely, for $i \in \mathcal{V}$, $\eta_i^k = 1$ means the i-th coordinate block is active at iteration k. Then, we give the setup to the update coordinate blocks in the following assumption.

Assumption 5.3 (Activated Settings)

(i) The sequence $\left(\eta^k\right)_{k \geq 0}$ *is independent with respect to iteration k with random* 0-1 *vector* η^k, *and the definition of the activation probability* p_i *is*

$$p_i = \mathbb{P}\left(\eta_i^k = 1\right) > 0, \; k \geq 0, \; i \in \mathcal{V}. \tag{5.22}$$

(ii) $\{U_i\}_{i=1}^m$ *are* 0-1 *diagonal matrices and* $\sum_{i=1}^m U_i = I$.

The asynchronous algorithm is shown in Algorithm 7 which has the same step size conditions as Algorithm 6. More discussions on the randomized block coordinate can be found in [17]. In the following subsections, we analyze the convergence of the proposed synchronous and asynchronous algorithms. To make the description clearer, we first establish a compact form of the proposed algorithms.

5.3.4 Compact Construction of Algorithm

Note that the variables u, s and the linear operators $A_{(i,j)}$, $P_{(i,j)}$ have been presented in Sect. 3.1. Let $\tilde{u} = col\left(\tilde{u}_1, \ldots, \tilde{u}_m\right)$ and v is stacked by $\left(v_{ij}^{\top}, v_{ji}^{\top}\right)^{\top}$ for $i = 1, \ldots, m$ with all $j \in \mathcal{N}_i$, where no duplicate variables are included. $\Gamma_1 = \text{blkdiag}\left\{\gamma_i I_n\right\}$ for all $i \in \mathcal{V}$, $\Gamma_2 = \text{blkdiag}\left\{\rho_{(i,j)} I_{2n}\right\}$ and $\Sigma = \text{blkdiag}\left\{\sigma_{(i,j)} I_{2n}\right\}$ for all $(i, j) \in \mathcal{E}$ are the step size matrices. Define the linear matrix operator $A : x \mapsto \left(A_{(i,j)} x\right)_{(i,j)\in\mathcal{E}}$, and the extended permutation matrix $P = \text{blkdiag}\left\{P_{(i,j)}\right\}$ for $(i, j) \in \mathcal{E}$ is stacked by $P_{(i,j)}$. For the cost functions, let $f(x) = \sum_{i=1}^{m} f_i(x_i)$ and $g(x) = \sum_{i=1}^{m} g_i(x_i)$. Moreover, with Moreau decomposition [22], the first step of the update flow in Algorithm 6 is equivalent to

$$u_i^k = \text{prox}_{\gamma_i g_i^*}\left(\tilde{u}_i^k\right).$$

Thus, we can obtain the compact form of the update flow in Algorithm 6 as follows:

$$\begin{cases} u^k = \text{prox}_{g^*}^{\Gamma_1^{-1}}\left(\tilde{u}^k\right), \\ v^{k+1} = \frac{1}{2}(I + P)\left((I - \Sigma\Gamma_2) v^k + \Sigma\left(s^k + \Gamma_2 A x^k\right)\right), \\ \tilde{u}^{k+1} = u^k + \Gamma_1 x^k, \\ s^{k+1} = s^k + \Gamma_2 A x^k - \Gamma_2 v^{k+1}, \\ x^{k+1} = \arg\min_x \left\{f(x) + x^{\top}\left(u^k + A^{\top} s^{k+1}\right)\right\}. \end{cases} \tag{5.23}$$

Meanwhile, the dual problem (5.16) can be rewritten as

$$\min_{u,s} f^*\left(-\left(u + A^{\top} s\right)\right) + g^*(u) + h^*(s), \tag{5.24}$$

where $h(s) = \sum_{(i,j)\in\mathcal{E}} \delta_{D_{(i,j)}}$ and f^*, g^*, h^* are the conjugate functions for f, g, h, respectively. Let $q = \left(u^{\top}, s^{\top}\right)^{\top}$, $\mathcal{A} = \left[I \ A^{\top}\right]$, $B_1 = [I \ 0]$ and $B_2 = [0 \ I]$ such that $\mathcal{A}q = u + A^{\top}s$, $B_1 q = u$ and $B_2 q = s$. We further transform problem (5.24) into

$$\min_q F^*(q) + G^*(q) + h^*(B_2 q), \tag{5.25}$$

where $F^*(q) = f^*(-\mathcal{A}q)$, $G^*(q) = g^*(B_1 q)$. Here, based on problem (5.25) and inspired by the operator splitting method in [8], we give an equivalent formulation of (5.23):

$$q^k = \text{prox}_{G^*}^{\Gamma^{-1}}\left(w^k\right), \tag{5.26a}$$

$$v^{k+1} = \mathrm{prox}_h^{\Sigma^{-1}} \begin{pmatrix} \left(I - \Sigma B_2 \Gamma B_2^\top\right) v^k \\ + \Sigma B_2 \left(2q^k - w^k - \Gamma \nabla F^* \left(q^k\right)\right) \end{pmatrix}, \tag{5.26b}$$

$$w^{k+1} = q^k - \Gamma \nabla F^* \left(q^k\right) - \Gamma B_2^\top v^{k+1}, \tag{5.26c}$$

where $\Gamma = \mathrm{blkdiag}\{\Gamma_1, \Gamma_2\}$ is an extended step size matrix and $w = \left(\tilde{u}^\top, \tilde{s}^\top\right)^\top$ consists of two auxiliary variables $\tilde{u} \in \mathbb{R}^{mn}$ and $\tilde{s} \in \mathbb{R}^{ln}$.

Remark 5.2 The compact formulation (5.26) recovers a similar structure with the centralized algorithm PD3O [8]. However, due to the use of uncoordinated step sizes, we employ the step size matrices instead of the constant step sizes in PD3O. In addition, PD3O requires that objective function contains a partially smooth term, while the problem discussed in this chapter does not need this assumption.

The transition process from (5.23) to (5.26) is supplied below. From (5.26a), we have

$$\begin{bmatrix} u^k \\ s^k \end{bmatrix} = \begin{bmatrix} \arg\min\limits_u \left\{g^*(u) + \frac{1}{2}\left\|u - \tilde{u}^k\right\|_{\Gamma_1^{-1}}^2\right\} \\ \arg\min\limits_s \left\{\frac{1}{2}\left\|s - \tilde{s}^k\right\|_{\Gamma_2^{-1}}^2\right\} \end{bmatrix} = \begin{bmatrix} \mathrm{prox}_{g^*}^{\Gamma_1^{-1}}\left(\tilde{u}^k\right) \\ \tilde{s}^k \end{bmatrix}, \tag{5.27}$$

where both the first and last steps are valid owing to the definition of the proximal operator. It is worth noting that we obtain an equality $s = \tilde{s}$ in (5.27) and then only s will be used in the remaining content of this chapter.

Next, we aim to unfold (5.26c). However, u and s are coupled in the gradient term $\nabla F^*(q)$. Therefore, we deduce an explicit expression of $\nabla F^*(q)$ before splitting (5.26c). According to the Danskin's theorem [125] and [126], where the latter gives the gradient of conjugate function f^* as $\nabla f^*(x) = \arg\max_y \left\{x^\top y - f(y)\right\}$, there exist the following equalities:

$$\begin{aligned} \nabla_u F^*(q) &= -\arg\max_x \left\{-f(x) - x^\top \left(u + A^\top s\right)\right\} \\ &= \arg\min_x \left\{f(x) + x^\top \left(u + A^\top s\right)\right\}, \end{aligned} \tag{5.28a}$$

$$\nabla_s F^*(q) = -A \arg\min_x \left\{f(x) + x^\top \left(u + A^\top s\right)\right\}. \tag{5.28b}$$

At each iteration k, we employ x to estimate the gradient term, i.e.,

$$x = \operatorname*{argmin}_x \left\{f(x) + x^\top \left(u + A^\top s\right)\right\}, \tag{5.29}$$

such that $\nabla F^*(q)$ has a computational formulation $\nabla F^*(q) = -\mathcal{A}^\top x$. Then, from (5.26c), we have

$$\begin{aligned}\begin{bmatrix}\tilde{u}^{k+1}\\ s^{k+1}\end{bmatrix} &= \begin{bmatrix}u^k\\ s^k\end{bmatrix} - \begin{bmatrix}\Gamma_1 & 0\\ 0 & \Gamma_2\end{bmatrix}\begin{bmatrix}-x^k\\ -Ax^k\end{bmatrix} - \begin{bmatrix}\Gamma_1 & 0\\ 0 & \Gamma_2\end{bmatrix}\begin{bmatrix}0\\ v^{k+1}\end{bmatrix}\\ &= \begin{bmatrix}u^k + \Gamma_1 x^k\\ s^k + \Gamma_2 A x^k - \Gamma_2 v^{k+1}\end{bmatrix}.\end{aligned} \tag{5.30}$$

For simplicity, let $K = (I - \Sigma B_2 \Gamma B_2^\top)v^k + \Sigma B_2(2q^k - w^k - \Gamma\nabla F^*(q^k))$. Thus, (5.26b) can be abbreviated as $v^{k+1} = \operatorname{prox}_h^{\Sigma^{-1}}(K)$ and there exists

$$\begin{aligned}\operatorname{prox}_h^{\Sigma^{-1}}(K) &= \arg\min_z \left\{h(z) + \frac{1}{2}\|z - K\|_{\Sigma^{-1}}^2\right\}\\ &= \arg\min_{z\in\{z|Pz=z\}} \left\{\frac{1}{2}\|z - K\|_{\Sigma^{-1}}^2\right\},\end{aligned} \tag{5.31}$$

where z is the bridge variable. Therefore, the variable v in (5.26c) is equivalent to the bridge variable. Note that the last term above can be considered as an optimization problem with an equality constraint, i.e.,

$$\min_z \frac{1}{2}\|z - K\|_{\Sigma^{-1}}^2, \quad \text{s.t. } Pz - z = 0. \tag{5.32}$$

Its Lagrangian function is

$$\hat{\mathcal{L}}(z, \lambda) = \frac{1}{2}\|z - K\|_{\Sigma^{-1}}^2 + \lambda^\top(Pz - z), \tag{5.33}$$

and the KKT conditions are

$$\begin{cases}\partial_z \hat{\mathcal{L}}(z, \lambda) = \Sigma^{-1}z - \Sigma^{-1}K + P^\top\lambda - \lambda = 0,\\ \partial_\lambda \hat{\mathcal{L}}(z, \lambda) = Pz - z = 0,\end{cases} \tag{5.34}$$

which result in

$$\begin{cases}z = \Sigma\left(\Sigma^{-1}K - P^\top\lambda + \lambda\right),\\ z = Pz.\end{cases} \tag{5.35}$$

Notice that the first equality in (5.35) can be substituted into the second one. Thus, we have

$$\begin{aligned}z &= PK - P\Sigma P^\top\lambda + P\Sigma\lambda\\ &= PK - \Sigma(I - P)\lambda.\end{aligned} \tag{5.36}$$

Since Σ and P are two block diagonal matrices with all submatrices having the same dimension, they are allowed to switch places under the multiplication rule. Then, through adjusting the positions in (5.36) and multiplying the permutation matrix P, the following equalities hold:

$$\begin{aligned} z = PK - \Sigma(I-P)\lambda &\Leftrightarrow P\Sigma^{-1}z - P^2\Sigma^{-1}K = P^2\lambda - P\lambda \\ &\Leftrightarrow (I-P)\lambda = \Sigma^{-1}(z - K). \end{aligned} \tag{5.37}$$

Substituting (5.37) into (5.36), we obtain

$$z = (P + I)\, K - z, \tag{5.38}$$

which can be rewritten as

$$z = \frac{1}{2}\,(P + I)\, K. \tag{5.39}$$

Note that z is the optimal solution to problem (5.32). Therefore, we set up the update formulation for v as

$$\begin{aligned} v^{k+1} &= \frac{1}{2}\,(P+I)\begin{pmatrix} \left(I - \Sigma[0\ I]\begin{bmatrix}\Gamma_1 & \\ & \Gamma_2\end{bmatrix}\begin{bmatrix}0\\ I\end{bmatrix}\right)v^k \\ +\Sigma\,[0\ I]\begin{pmatrix} 2\begin{bmatrix}u^k\\ s^k\end{bmatrix} - \begin{bmatrix}\tilde{u}^k\\ s^k\end{bmatrix}^k \\ -\begin{bmatrix}\Gamma_1 & \\ & \Gamma_2\end{bmatrix}\begin{bmatrix}x^k\\ Ax^k\end{bmatrix}\end{pmatrix}\end{pmatrix} \\ &= \frac{1}{2}\,(P+I)\left((I - \Sigma\Gamma_2)\,v^k + \Sigma\left(2s^k - \tilde{s}^k + \Gamma_2 Ax^k\right)\right). \end{aligned} \tag{5.40}$$

Combining the formulations (5.27)–(5.30) and (5.40), the update flow (5.23) is finally recovered by the update flow (5.26).

5.4 Convergence Analysis

5.4.1 Analysis of the Synchronous Algorithm

In this subsection, we provide the convergence analysis of Algorithm 6 based on the compact formulation (5.26). To begin with, define an iteration by (5.26) as an operator T and $c = col\,(v, w)$. Notice that in (5.26a), q^k depends on w^k such that we can abbreviate (5.26) as $c^{k+1} = Tc^k$. Considering the proximal operator

$\mathrm{prox}_f^{\Gamma}(\cdot) = \left(I + \Gamma^{-1}\partial f\right)^{-1}$, from (5.26a) and (5.26b), let

$$\begin{aligned} \mathrm{d}_h(\mathbf{v}^{k+1}) =& B_2\big(2\mathbf{q}^k - \mathbf{w}^k - \Gamma\nabla F^*(\mathbf{q}^k)\big) \\ &+ M\mathbf{v}^k - \Sigma^{-1}\mathbf{v}^{k+1} \in \partial h^*(\mathbf{v}^{k+1}), \end{aligned} \tag{5.41}$$

$$\mathrm{d}_{G^*}(\mathbf{q}^k) = \Gamma^{-1}(\mathbf{w}^k - \mathbf{q}^k) \in \partial G^*(\mathbf{q}^k). \tag{5.42}$$

where $M = \Sigma^{-1}\left(I - \Sigma B_2 \Gamma B_2^\top\right)$ is a block diagonal matrix. In the subsequent analysis, M needs to be a positive definite matrix, which leads to the step size condition between $\sigma_{(i,j)}$ and $\rho_{(i,j)}$. Then in terms of two inputs $\mathbf{c}_1 = (\mathbf{v}_1, \mathbf{w}_1)$ and $\mathbf{c}_2 = (\mathbf{v}_2, \mathbf{w}_2)$, the following lemmas hold.

Lemma 5.3 (Fundamental Equality) *If Assumptions 5.1 and 5.2 are satisfied, we have the following equality:*

$$\begin{aligned} &\left\langle \mathbf{v}_1^{k+1} - \mathbf{v}_2^{k+1}, \mathrm{d}_h\left(\mathbf{v}_1^{k+1}\right) - \mathrm{d}_h\left(\mathbf{v}_2^{k+1}\right)\right\rangle \\ &+\left\langle \mathbf{q}_1^k - \mathbf{q}_2^k, \mathrm{d}_{G^*}\left(\mathbf{q}_1^k\right) - \mathrm{d}_{G^*}\left(\mathbf{q}_2^k\right) + \nabla F^*\left(\mathbf{q}_1^k\right) - \nabla F^*\left(\mathbf{q}_2^k\right)\right\rangle \\ =& \frac{1}{2}\left\|\mathbf{c}_1^k - \mathbf{c}_2^k\right\|_{\tilde{M}}^2 - \frac{1}{2}\left\|\mathbf{c}_1^{k+1} - \mathbf{c}_2^{k+1}\right\|_{\tilde{M}}^2 \\ &- \frac{1}{2}\left\|\mathbf{v}_1^k - \mathbf{v}_1^{k+1} - \mathbf{v}_2^k + \mathbf{v}_2^{k+1}\right\|_M^2 \\ &- \frac{1}{2}\left\|\mathbf{w}_1^k - \mathbf{w}_1^{k+1} - \mathbf{w}_2^k + \mathbf{w}_2^{k+1}\right\|_{\Gamma^{-1}}^2 \\ &+\left\langle \nabla F^*\left(\mathbf{q}_1^k\right) - \nabla F^*\left(\mathbf{q}_2^k\right), \mathbf{w}_1^k - \mathbf{w}_1^{k+1} - \mathbf{w}_2^k + \mathbf{w}_2^{k+1}\right\rangle, \end{aligned} \tag{5.43}$$

where the block diagonal matrix $\tilde{M} = \mathrm{blkdiag}\{M, \Gamma^{-1}\}$ *is positive definite.*

Proof Adjusting the position of the terms in (5.26c), we have the following two equalities:

$$\mathbf{w}^{k+1} + \Gamma B_2^\top \mathbf{v}^{k+1} = \mathbf{q}^k - \Gamma\nabla F^*(\mathbf{q}^k), \tag{5.44a}$$

$$\mathbf{w}^{k+1} + \Gamma\nabla F^*(\mathbf{q}^k) = \mathbf{q}^k - \Gamma B_2^\top \mathbf{v}^{k+1}. \tag{5.44b}$$

With (5.44a) and the definition of $\mathrm{d}_h\left(\mathbf{v}^{k+1}\right)$, it holds that

$$\begin{aligned} &\left\langle \mathbf{v}_1^{k+1} - \mathbf{v}_2^{k+1}, \mathrm{d}_h\left(\mathbf{v}_1^{k+1}\right) - \mathrm{d}_h\left(\mathbf{v}_2^{k+1}\right)\right\rangle \\ =&\left\langle \mathbf{v}_1^{k+1} - \mathbf{v}_2^{k+1}, \mathbf{v}_1^k - \mathbf{v}_1^{k+1} - \mathbf{v}_2^k + \mathbf{v}_2^{k+1}\right\rangle_M \end{aligned}$$

$$+\left\langle \begin{array}{l} \mathbf{v}_1^{k+1} - \mathbf{v}_2^{k+1}, B_2\mathbf{q}_1^k - B_2\mathbf{w}_1^k + B_2\mathbf{w}_1^{k+1} \\ -B_2\mathbf{q}_2^k + B_2\mathbf{w}_2^k - B_2\mathbf{w}_2^{k+1} \end{array} \right\rangle. \tag{5.45}$$

Similarly, with (5.44a) and the definition of $\mathrm{d}_{G^*}\left(\mathbf{q}^k\right)$, there holds

$$\begin{aligned} &\left\langle \mathbf{q}_1^k - \mathbf{q}_2^k, \mathrm{d}_{G^*}\left(\mathbf{q}_1^k\right) - \mathrm{d}_{G^*}\left(\mathbf{q}_2^k\right) + \nabla F^*\left(\mathbf{q}_1^k\right) - \nabla F^*\left(\mathbf{q}_2^k\right) \right\rangle \\ =& \left\langle \begin{array}{l} \mathbf{q}_1^k - \mathbf{q}_2^k, \mathbf{w}_1^k - \mathbf{w}_2^k - \mathbf{w}_1^{k+1} + \mathbf{w}_2^{k+1} \\ -\Gamma B_2^\top \mathbf{v}_1^{k+1} + \Gamma B_2^\top \mathbf{v}_2^{k+1} \end{array} \right\rangle_{\Gamma^{-1}}. \end{aligned} \tag{5.46}$$

Summing up (5.45) and (5.46), we have

$$\begin{aligned} &\left\langle \mathbf{v}_1^{k+1} - \mathbf{v}_2^{k+1}, \mathrm{d}_h\left(\mathbf{v}_1^{k+1}\right) - \mathrm{d}_h\left(\mathbf{v}_2^{k+1}\right) \right\rangle \\ &+ \left\langle \mathbf{q}_1^k - \mathbf{q}_2^k, \mathrm{d}_{G^*}\left(\mathbf{q}_1^k\right) - \mathrm{d}_{G^*}\left(\mathbf{q}_2^k\right) + \nabla F^*\left(\mathbf{q}_1^k\right) - \nabla F^*\left(\mathbf{q}_2^k\right) \right\rangle \\ =& \left\langle \mathbf{v}_1^{k+1} - \mathbf{v}_2^{k+1}, \mathbf{v}_1^k - \mathbf{v}_1^{k+1} - \mathbf{v}_2^k + \mathbf{v}_2^{k+1} \right\rangle_M \\ &+ \left\langle \begin{array}{l} \mathbf{q}_1^k - \mathbf{q}_2^k - \Gamma B_2^\top \mathbf{v}_1^{k+1} + \Gamma B_2^\top \mathbf{v}_2^{k+1}, \\ \mathbf{w}_1^k - \mathbf{w}_1^{k+1} - \mathbf{w}_2^k + \mathbf{w}_2^{k+1} \end{array} \right\rangle_{\Gamma^{-1}}. \end{aligned} \tag{5.47}$$

Then, with (5.44b), we further rewrite (5.47) as

$$\begin{aligned} &\left\langle \mathbf{v}_1^{k+1} - \mathbf{v}_2^{k+1}, \mathrm{d}_h\left(\mathbf{v}_1^{k+1}\right) - \mathrm{d}_h\left(\mathbf{v}_2^{k+1}\right) \right\rangle \\ &+ \left\langle \mathbf{q}_1^k - \mathbf{q}_2^k, \mathrm{d}_{G^*}\left(\mathbf{q}_1^k\right) - \mathrm{d}_{G^*}\left(\mathbf{q}_2^k\right) + \nabla F^*\left(\mathbf{q}_1^k\right) - \nabla F^*\left(\mathbf{q}_2^k\right) \right\rangle \\ =& \frac{1}{2}\left\| \mathbf{c}_1^k - \mathbf{c}_2^k \right\|_{\tilde{M}}^2 - \frac{1}{2}\left\| \mathbf{c}_1^{k+1} - \mathbf{c}_2^{k+1} \right\|_{\tilde{M}}^2 \\ &- \frac{1}{2}\left\| \mathbf{v}_1^k - \mathbf{v}_1^{k+1} - \mathbf{v}_2^k + \mathbf{v}_2^{k+1} \right\|_M^2 \\ &- \frac{1}{2}\left\| \mathbf{w}_1^k - \mathbf{w}_1^{k+1} - \mathbf{w}_2^k + \mathbf{w}_2^{k+1} \right\|_{\Gamma^{-1}}^2 \\ &+ \left\langle \nabla F^*\left(\mathbf{q}_1^k\right) - \nabla F^*\left(\mathbf{q}_2^k\right), \mathbf{w}_1^k - \mathbf{w}_1^{k+1} - \mathbf{w}_2^k + \mathbf{w}_2^{k+1} \right\rangle, \end{aligned} \tag{5.48}$$

where the last step holds because $2\langle a, b\rangle = \|a+b\|^2 - \|a\|^2 - \|b\|^2$ for any vectors a and b. The proof is completed. ■

Lemma 5.4 *Under Assumptions 5.1 and 5.2, for the two inputs* $\mathbf{c}_1$ *and* $\mathbf{c}_2$*, we have the following inequality:*

$$\left\| \mathbf{c}_1^{k+1} - \mathbf{c}_2^{k+1} \right\|_{\tilde{M}}^2 - \left\| \mathbf{c}_1^k - \mathbf{c}_2^k \right\|_{\tilde{M}}^2 \leq - \left\| \mathbf{c}_1^k - \mathbf{c}_1^{k+1} - \mathbf{c}_2^k + \mathbf{c}_2^{k+1} \right\|_{\breve{M}}^2, \tag{5.49}$$

where $\breve{M} = \text{blkdiag}\{M\left(I - \frac{1}{2}\Gamma L^{-1}\right), \Gamma^{-1}\}$. *L is the block diagonal parameter matrix with elements* $\sqrt{1+\omega_i/\beta_i}$, $i \in \mathcal{V}$.

Proof Consider a convex function $V(x)$, and through the convex property, we have

$$V(y) \geq V(x) + \partial V(x)^\top (y - x). \tag{5.50}$$

In fact, we can also write (5.50) as

$$V(x) \geq V(y) + \partial V(y)^\top (x - y). \tag{5.51}$$

Combining (5.50) and (5.51), we obtain

$$(\partial V(x) - \partial V(y))^\top (x - y) \geq 0. \tag{5.52}$$

Recalling the definitions of $\mathrm{d}_h\left(\mathbf{v}^{k+1}\right)$ and $\mathrm{d}_{G^*}\left(\mathbf{q}^k\right)$ which are belong to the subdifferential of h and G^* respectively, it holds

$$\begin{aligned}0 \leq &\left\langle \mathbf{v}_1^{k+1} - \mathbf{v}_2^{k+1}, \mathrm{d}_h\left(\mathbf{v}_1^{k+1}\right) - \mathrm{d}_h\left(\mathbf{v}_2^{k+1}\right)\right\rangle \\ &+ \left\langle \mathbf{q}_1^k - \mathbf{q}_2^k, \mathrm{d}_{G^*}\left(\mathbf{q}_1^k\right) - \mathrm{d}_{G^*}\left(\mathbf{q}_2^k\right)\right\rangle.\end{aligned} \tag{5.53}$$

Change the positions of the terms in (5.49) by substituting (5.53), which results in

$$\begin{aligned}&\left\|\mathbf{c}_1^{k+1} - \mathbf{c}_2^{k+1}\right\|_{\tilde{M}}^2 - \left\|\mathbf{c}_1^k - \mathbf{c}_2^k\right\|_{\tilde{M}}^2 \\ \leq &- \left\|\mathbf{v}_1^k - \mathbf{v}_1^{k+1} - \mathbf{v}_2^k + \mathbf{v}_2^{k+1}\right\|_M^2 \\ &- \left\|\mathbf{w}_1^k - \mathbf{w}_1^{k+1} - \mathbf{w}_2^k + \mathbf{w}_2^{k+1}\right\|_{\Gamma^{-1}}^2 \\ &- 2\left\langle \mathbf{q}_1^k - \mathbf{q}_2^k, \nabla F^*\left(\mathbf{q}_1^k\right) - \nabla F^*\left(\mathbf{q}_2^k\right)\right\rangle \\ &+ 2\left\langle \nabla F^*\left(\mathbf{q}_1^k\right) - \nabla F^*\left(\mathbf{q}_2^k\right), \mathbf{w}_1^k - \mathbf{w}_1^{k+1} - \mathbf{w}_2^k + \mathbf{w}_2^{k+1}\right\rangle.\end{aligned} \tag{5.54}$$

Then, we focus on discussing the upper bound of the inequality (5.54). Since f_i for $i \in \mathcal{V}$ is β_i-strongly convex, its conjugate function f_i^* is $1/\beta_i$-smooth. Referring to [124, Lemma V.8], $\nabla_i F^*(q)$ is $\sqrt{1+\omega_i/\beta_i}$ Lipschitz continuous such that for arbitrary x_1 and x_2, from [22, Theorem 18.15] we have

$$\langle x_1 - x_2, \nabla F^*(x_1) - \nabla F^*(x_2)\rangle \geq \left\|\nabla F^*(x_1) - \nabla F^*(x_2)\right\|_L^2, \tag{5.55}$$

where L is the Lipschitz parameter matrix. Thus, for the last two terms in (5.54), we have

$$\begin{aligned}
&-2\left\langle \mathbf{q}_1^k - \mathbf{q}_2^k, \nabla F^*\left(\mathbf{q}_1^k\right) - \nabla F^*\left(\mathbf{q}_2^k\right)\right\rangle \\
&+2\left\langle \nabla F^*\left(\mathbf{q}_1^k\right) - \nabla F^*\left(\mathbf{q}_2^k\right), \mathbf{w}_1^k - \mathbf{w}_1^{k+1} - \mathbf{w}_2^k + \mathbf{w}_2^{k+1}\right\rangle \\
\leq &\left\| \nabla F^*\left(\mathbf{q}_1^k\right) - \nabla F^*\left(\mathbf{q}_2^k\right)\right\|_{\Theta^{-1}\Gamma - 2L}^2 \\
&+ \left\| \mathbf{w}_1^k - \mathbf{w}_1^{k+1} - \mathbf{w}_2^k + \mathbf{w}_2^{k+1}\right\|_{\Theta\Gamma^{-1}}^2,
\end{aligned} \tag{5.56}$$

where Θ is a diagonal positive definite matrix such that $\|a\|_{\Theta^{-1}\Gamma}^2 + \|b\|_{\Theta\Gamma^{-1}}^2 \geq 2\langle a, b\rangle$. Through (5.56), (5.54) can be rewritten as

$$\begin{aligned}
&\left\| \mathbf{c}_1^{k+1} - \mathbf{c}_2^{k+1}\right\|_{\tilde{M}}^2 - \left\| \mathbf{c}_1^k - \mathbf{c}_2^k\right\|_{\tilde{M}}^2 \\
\leq &- \left\| \mathbf{v}_1^k - \mathbf{v}_1^{k+1} - \mathbf{v}_2^k + \mathbf{v}_2^{k+1}\right\|_{M}^2 \\
&+ \left\| \mathbf{w}_1^k - \mathbf{w}_1^{k+1} - \mathbf{w}_2^k + \mathbf{w}_2^{k+1}\right\|_{(\Theta - I)\Gamma^{-1}}^2 \\
&+ \left\| \nabla F^*\left(\mathbf{q}_1^k\right) - \nabla F^*\left(\mathbf{q}_2^k\right)\right\|_{\Theta^{-1}\Gamma - 2L}^2 .
\end{aligned} \tag{5.57}$$

When $\Theta^{-1}\Gamma - 2L$ in (5.57) becomes a null matrix, we finally obtain the inequality (5.49), which finishes the proof. ■

The goal is to prove the convergence of the proposed algorithm through the fixed point theory. Hence, we provide the equivalence between the optimal solution and the fixed point before giving the convergence theorem.

Lemma 5.5 *If Assumptions 5.1 and 5.2 hold, T is a nonexpansive operator. Let $(\mathbf{q}^*, \mathbf{v}^*, \mathbf{w}^*)$ represent the fixed point for the operator T. x^* is equivalent to the optimal solution to the nonsmooth composite optimization problem.*

Proof Given that for any vectors a and b, an operator $\mathbf{T}$ is nonexpansive if $\|\mathbf{T}a - \mathbf{T}b\| \leq \|a - b\|$. When the parameters satisfy the step size conditions in Assumption 5.2, $\breve{M}$ is a positive definite matrix. Thus, the inequality (5.49) leads to

$$\left\| \mathbf{c}_1^{k+1} - \mathbf{c}_2^{k+1}\right\|_{\tilde{M}}^2 \leq \left\| \mathbf{c}_1^k - \mathbf{c}_2^k\right\|_{\tilde{M}}^2, \tag{5.58}$$

so T is nonexpansive. Substituting the fixed point into (5.26), we have

$$\mathbf{q}^* = \mathrm{prox}_{G^*}^{\Gamma^{-1}}\left(\mathbf{w}^*\right), \tag{5.59a}$$

$$\mathbf{v}^* = \operatorname{prox}_h^{\Sigma^{-1}} \begin{pmatrix} \left(I - \Sigma B_2 \Gamma B_2^\top\right) \mathbf{v}^* \\ +\Sigma B_2 \left(2\mathbf{q}^* - \mathbf{w}^* - \Gamma \nabla F^* \left(\mathbf{q}^*\right)\right) \end{pmatrix}, \tag{5.59b}$$

$$\mathbf{w}^* = \mathbf{q}^* - \Gamma \nabla F^* \left(\mathbf{q}^*\right) - \Gamma B_2^\top \mathbf{v}^*. \tag{5.59c}$$

From (5.59a), it holds that

$$\mathbf{q}^* = \operatorname{prox}_{G^*}^{\Gamma^{-1}} \left(\mathbf{w}^*\right) \Leftrightarrow \mathbf{w}^* - \mathbf{q}^* \in \Gamma \partial G^* \left(\mathbf{q}^*\right), \tag{5.60}$$

which leads to

$$\begin{aligned} \mathbf{w}^* &= \mathbf{q}^* - \Gamma \nabla F^*(\mathbf{q}^*) - \Gamma B_2^\top \mathbf{v}^* \\ &\Leftrightarrow \partial G^*(\mathbf{q}^*) + \nabla F^*(\mathbf{q}^*) + B_2^\top \mathbf{v}^* = 0. \end{aligned} \tag{5.61}$$

Then, for (5.59c), we similarly have

$$\begin{aligned} &\left(I - \Sigma B_2 \Gamma B_2^\top\right) \mathbf{v}^* + \Sigma B_2 \left(2\mathbf{q}^* - \mathbf{w}^* - \Gamma \nabla F^* \left(\mathbf{q}^*\right)\right) - \mathbf{v}^* \\ &= -\Sigma B_2 \Gamma B_2^\top \mathbf{v}^* + \Sigma B_2 \left(\mathbf{q}^* - \mathbf{w}^* + \mathbf{w}^* + \Gamma B_2^\top \mathbf{v}^*\right) \in \Sigma \partial h \left(\mathbf{v}^*\right) \\ &\Leftrightarrow B_2 \mathbf{q}^* \in \partial h \left(\mathbf{v}^*\right). \end{aligned} \tag{5.62}$$

Note that (5.61) and (5.62) satisfy the KKT conditions of problem (5.25) such that the fixed point for T is the optimal solution to the dual problem. Meanwhile, recalling Slater's condition in Assumption 5.1, when the dual problem reaches optimality, the primal problem obtains its optimal solution. The proof is completed. ■

Theorem 5.6 *Consider the fixed point* $\mathbf{c}^*$ *for the operator* T. *Under Assumptions 5.1 and 5.2, for the sequence* $\left(\mathbf{c}^k\right)_{k \geq 0}$ *generated by Algorithm 6, we have the statements below:*

(i) The sequence $\left(\left\|\mathbf{c}^k - \mathbf{c}^*\right\|_{\tilde{M}}\right)_{k \geq 0}$ *is monotonically decreasing;*
(ii) The sequence $\left(\left\|T\mathbf{c}^k - \mathbf{c}^k\right\|_{\tilde{M}}\right)_{k \geq 0}$ *is monotonically nonincreasing and converges to 0 at the non-ergodic convergence rate of* $o(1/k)$;
(iii) The sequence $\left(\mathbf{c}^k\right)_{k \geq 0}$ *converges to the fixed point* $\mathbf{c}^*$ *and the sequence* $\left(x^k\right)_{k \geq 0}$ *converges to the optimal solution* x^* *to the nonsmooth composite optimization problem (5.2).*

Proof

(i) Letting the two inputs $\mathbf{c}_1 = \mathbf{c}$ and $\mathbf{c}_2 = \mathbf{c}^*$, with Lemma 5.4, there holds that

$$\left\|T\mathbf{c}^k - \mathbf{c}^*\right\|_{\tilde{M}}^2 - \left\|\mathbf{c}^k - \mathbf{c}^*\right\|_{\tilde{M}}^2 \leq - \left\|T\mathbf{c}^k - \mathbf{c}^k\right\|_{\breve{M}}^2. \tag{5.63}$$

Note that when the step sizes satisfy the step size conditions in Assumption 5.2, $\breve{M}$ is a positive definite matrix. Hence, $\left(\|\mathbf{c}^k - \mathbf{c}^*\|_{\tilde{M}}\right)_{k\geq 0}$ is a monotonically decreasing sequence.

(ii) Summing up (5.63) from $k = 0$ to ∞ and adjusting the positions, we have

$$\sum_{k=0}^{\infty} \left\| T\mathbf{c}^k - \mathbf{c}^k \right\|_{\breve{M}}^2 \leq \left\| \mathbf{c}^0 - \mathbf{c}^* \right\|_{\tilde{M}}^2, \tag{5.64}$$

such that $\left(\|T\mathbf{c}^k - \mathbf{c}^k\|_{\tilde{M}}\right)_{k\geq 0}$ is a sequence that can converge to 0. Meanwhile, there holds that

$$\begin{aligned} \left\| T\mathbf{c}^{k+1} - \mathbf{c}^{k+1} \right\|_{\breve{M}}^2 &= \left\| T\mathbf{c}^{k+1} - T\mathbf{c}^k \right\|_{\breve{M}}^2 \\ &\leq \left\| \mathbf{c}^{k+1} - \mathbf{c}^k \right\|_{\breve{M}}^2 = \left\| T\mathbf{c}^{k+1} - \mathbf{c}^k \right\|_{\breve{M}}^2, \end{aligned} \tag{5.65}$$

resulting in the property of monotone non-incrementing of the sequence $\left(\|T\mathbf{c}^k - \mathbf{c}^k\|_{\tilde{M}}\right)_{k\geq 0}$. Furthermore, from [104, Theorem 1] and (5.64), it holds that

$$\left\| T\mathbf{c}^k - \mathbf{c}^k \right\|_{\breve{M}}^2 \leq \frac{1}{k+1} \sum_{t=0}^{k} \|T\mathbf{c}^t - \mathbf{c}^t\|_{\breve{M}}^2 \leq \frac{1}{k+1} \left\| \mathbf{c}^0 - \mathbf{c}^* \right\|_{\tilde{M}}^2, \tag{5.66}$$

which meets the requirements of [54, Proposition 1] leading to the non-ergodic convergence rate of $o(1/k)$.

(iii) According to the Krasnosel'skii-Mann Theorem [22, Theorem 5.14] and Theorem 4.10(i), the sequence $\left(\mathbf{c}^k\right)_{k\geq 0}$ converges to the fixed point of the operator T. Then under Lemma 5.5, the statement holds. □

5.4.2 *Analysis of the Asynchronous Algorithm*

Recall the setup of the randomized block-coordinate. We define the activation probability matrix for all agents as $\Pi = \sum_{i=1}^m p_i U_i$ and the activation indicator matrix as $E_k = \sum_{i=1}^m \eta_i^k U_i$. Meanwhile, we abbreviate the conditional expectation $\mathbb{E}[\cdot|\mathcal{F}_k]$ as $\mathbb{E}_k[\cdot]$, where $\mathcal{F}$ is the filtration generated by the sequence $\left(\eta^k\right)_{k\geq 0}$. Let $\tilde{\mathbf{c}} = \left(\tilde{\mathbf{v}}, \tilde{\mathbf{w}}\right)$ denote the data processed by the operator T for $\mathbf{c} = (\mathbf{v}, \mathbf{w})$ when all of the agents are active. Thus, we can establish the compact formulation of the proposed distributed asynchronous algorithm as follows:

$$\begin{cases} \tilde{\mathbf{c}}^{k+1} = T\mathbf{c}^k, \\ \mathbf{c}^{k+1} = \mathbf{c}^k + E_{k+1}\left(\tilde{\mathbf{c}}^{k+1} - \mathbf{c}^k\right). \end{cases} \tag{5.67}$$

Lemma 5.7 *Under Assumption 5.3, we have the following two properties for the activation indicator matrix E_k:*

(i) E_k is an idempotent matrix, i.e., $(E_k)^t = E_k$ for the positive integer t;
(ii) For the expectation of E_{k+1}, there exists $\mathbb{E}_k \circ (E_{k+1}) = \Pi$.

Proof

(i) Noting that U_i is a diagonal matrix consisting of 0 and 1, for $i, j \in \mathcal{V}$, we have

$$\begin{cases} U_i U_j = 0, & i \neq j, \\ U_i U_j = U_i, & i = j. \end{cases} \tag{5.68}$$

Then, it holds that

$$E_k^2 = \left(\sum_{i=1}^{m} \eta_i^k U_i \right)^2 = \sum_{i=1, i \neq j}^{m} \eta_i^k \eta_j^k U_i U_j + \sum_{i=1}^{m} \left(\eta_i^k U_i \right)^2 = E_k, \tag{5.69}$$

where we obtain the property of idempotent by generalizing this equality.

(ii) The statement holds because

$$\begin{aligned} \mathbb{E}_k \circ (E_{k+1}) &= \sum_{\varepsilon \in \varphi} \mathbb{P} \left(\eta^{k+1} = \varepsilon \right) \sum_{i=1}^{m} \eta_i^{k+1} U_i \\ &= \sum_{i=1}^{m} \sum_{\varepsilon=1} \mathbb{P} \left(\eta^{k+1} = \varepsilon \right) U_i \\ &= \sum_{i=1}^{m} p_i U_i = \Pi, \end{aligned} \tag{5.70}$$

where $\varphi = \{0, 1\}^m$ represents the set of binary strings of length m.

■

Theorem 5.8 *Supposing Assumptions 5.1–5.3 hold, for the fixed point $\mathbf{c}^*$ and the sequence $\left(\mathbf{c}^k\right)_{k \geq 0}$ generated by Algorithm 7, we have*

$$\mathbb{E} \left[\left\| \mathbf{c}^{k+1} - \mathbf{c}^* \right\|_{\Pi^{-1} \tilde{M}}^2 \right] \leq \left\| \mathbf{c}^k - \mathbf{c}^* \right\|_{\Pi^{-1} \tilde{M}}^2 - \left\| \mathbf{c}^k - \tilde{\mathbf{c}}^{k+1} \right\|_{\breve{M}}^2 . \tag{5.71}$$

Consequently, under the randomized block coordinate, the sequence $\left(x^k\right)_{k \geq 0}$ converges to the optimal solution to the nonsmooth composite optimization problem (5.2).

Proof Similar to the analysis of Theorem 4.10(i), for two inputs $\mathbf{c}_1 = \mathbf{c}$ and $\mathbf{c}_2 = \mathbf{c}^*$, (5.67) leads to the following inequality:

$$\left\|\tilde{\mathbf{c}}^{k+1} - \mathbf{c}^*\right\|_{\tilde{M}}^2 - \left\|\mathbf{c}^k - \mathbf{c}^*\right\|_{\tilde{M}}^2 \leq - \left\|\tilde{\mathbf{c}}^{k+1} - \mathbf{c}^k\right\|_{\breve{M}}^2 . \tag{5.72}$$

Then, for the expectation of the optimal residual, we have

$$\begin{aligned}
&\mathbb{E}\left[\left\|\mathbf{c}^{k+1} - \mathrm{c}^*\right\|_{\Pi^{-1}\tilde{M}}^2\right] \\
&= \mathbb{E}\left[\begin{array}{l} \left\|\mathbf{c}^k - \mathrm{c}^*\right\|_{\Pi^{-1}\tilde{M}}^2 + \left\|E_{k+1}\left(\tilde{\mathbf{c}}^{k+1} - \mathbf{c}^k\right)\right\|_{\Pi^{-1}\tilde{M}}^2 \\ +2\left(\mathbf{c}^k - \mathbf{c}^*\right)^\top \Pi^{-1}\tilde{M}\left(E_{k+1}\left(\tilde{\mathbf{c}}^{k+1} - \mathbf{c}^k\right)\right) \end{array}\right] \\
&= \left\|\mathbf{c}^k - \mathbf{c}^*\right\|_{\Pi^{-1}\tilde{M}}^2 + \mathbb{E}\left[\left\|\tilde{\mathbf{c}}^{k+1} - \mathbf{c}^k\right\|_{E_{k+1}\Pi^{-1}\tilde{M}E_{k+1}}^2\right] \\
&\quad + \mathbb{E}\left[2\left(\mathbf{c}^k - \mathbf{c}^*\right)^\top \Pi^{-1}\tilde{M}\left(E_{k+1}\left(\tilde{\mathbf{c}}^{k+1} - \mathbf{c}^k\right)\right)\right] \\
&= \left\|\mathbf{c}^k - \mathbf{c}^*\right\|_{\Pi^{-1}\tilde{M}}^2 + \left\|\tilde{\mathbf{c}}^{k+1} - \mathbf{c}^k\right\|_{\tilde{M}}^2 + 2\left(\mathbf{c}^k - \mathbf{c}^*\right)^\top \tilde{M}\left(\tilde{\mathbf{c}}^{k+1} - \mathbf{c}^k\right),
\end{aligned} \tag{5.73}$$

where we use the results in Lemma 5.7 at the last step. Noting that for the last two terms in (5.73), there exists an upper bound from (5.72):

$$\begin{aligned}
&\left\|\tilde{\mathbf{c}}^{k+1} - \mathbf{c}^k\right\|_{\tilde{M}}^2 + 2\left(\mathbf{c}^k - \mathbf{c}^*\right)^\top \tilde{M}\left(\mathbf{c}^{k+1} - \mathbf{c}^k\right) \\
&= \left\|\tilde{\mathbf{c}}^{k+1} - \mathbf{c}^*\right\|_{\tilde{M}}^2 - \left\|\mathbf{c}^k - \mathbf{c}^*\right\|_{\tilde{M}}^2 \\
&\leq - \left\|\tilde{\mathbf{c}}^{k+1} - \mathbf{c}^k\right\|_{\breve{M}}^2 .
\end{aligned} \tag{5.74}$$

Substituting (5.74) into (5.73), we obtain the inequality in Theorem 5.8 such that $\left(\mathbf{c}^k\right)_{k\geq 0}$ converges to the fixed point $\mathbf{c}^*$. Finally, with Lemma 5.5, the proof is completed. ■

5.5 Numerical Experiments

In this section, we perform Algorithms 6 and 7 on machine learning problems to verify the theoretical analysis.

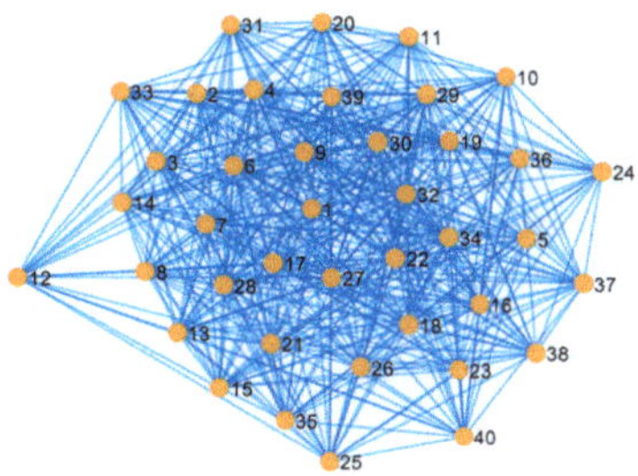

Fig. 5.1 The communication network with 40 agents

5.5.1 *Constrained Regularized Optimization*

In this case study, we use the proposed algorithms to solve a constrained LASSO problem. The networks are randomly generated with the network sparsity p_e. When $p_e = 0$ there is no edge, and when $p_e = 1$ the network is fully connected. We conduct experiments on the network shown in Fig. 5.1 with 40 agents and $p_e = 0.6$. The optimization problem is

$$\min_{x \in \mathcal{X}} \frac{1}{2} \sum_{i=1}^{m} \|x - p_i\|^2 + \lambda m \|x\|_1, \tag{5.75}$$

where p_i is the label private to agent i and the constraint is $\mathcal{X} = \{x | \, \|x\| \leq 1\}$. The parameters set for this problem comes from [103], where $\lambda = 0.1$ and p_i is randomly generated over $[-1, 1] \times [-1] \in \mathbb{R}^2$. Employing the Lagrangian method in Sect. 5.3.1, the optimization problem is equivalent to

$$\min \frac{1}{2} \sum_{i=1}^{m} \|x - p_i\|^2 + \lambda m \|x\|_1 + m\delta_{\mathcal{X}}(x). \tag{5.76}$$

Let the cost functions $f_i(x_i) = \|x_i - p_i\|^2 + \lambda \|x_i\|_1$ and $g_i(x_i) = \delta_{\mathcal{X}_i}(x_i)$ for $i \in \mathcal{V}$ such that both of them are nonsmooth functions. To verify the effectiveness of the uncoordinated step sizes, we take them as $\gamma_i \in [0.3, 0.4]$, $\sigma_{(i,j)} \in [0.3, 0.4]$ and $\rho_{(i,j)} \in [0.03, 0.04]$.

We show the convergence of the proposed distributed synchronous and asynchronous algorithms with the first components of the decision variables in Fig. 5.2. Here, p_i is set as 0.8. Figure 5.3 shows the residual $(1/m) \sum_{i=1}^{m} \left\|x_i^k - x^*\right\|^2$ of both the synchronous and asynchronous versions of the proposed algorithm. One can see that the synchronous version is faster than the asynchronous version and the convergence rate of the asynchronous algorithm becomes slow with the agent activation probabilities decreasing. In Figs. 5.4, 5.5, and 5.6, we study the effect of changing the step sizes on the convergence. The residual is taken at the iteration 800

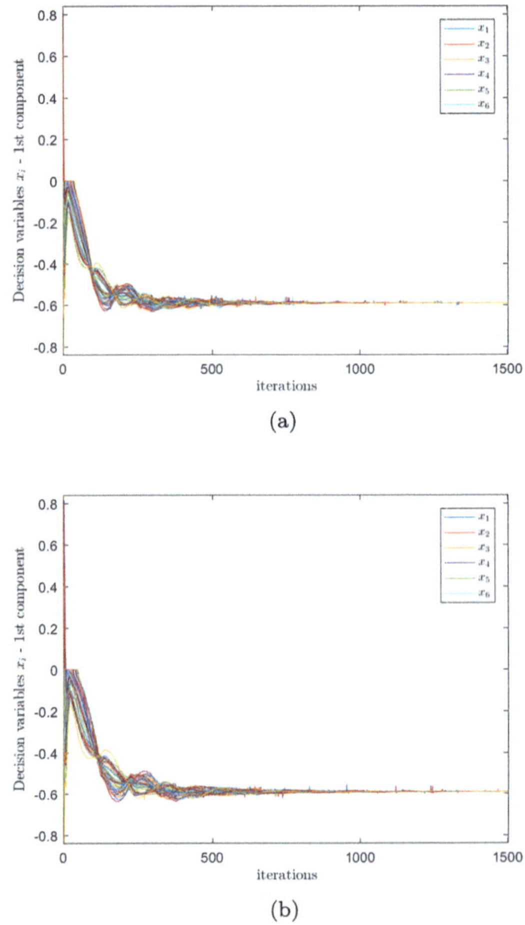

Fig. 5.2 Convergence of the variable x_i. (**a**) The result of the distributed synchronous algorithm. (**b**) The result of the distributed asynchronous algorithm

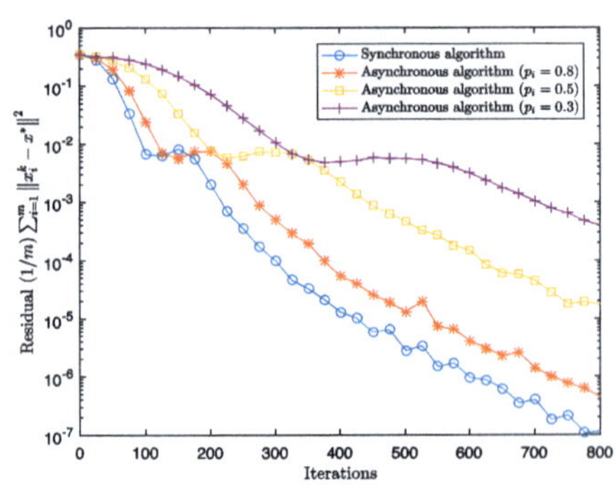

Fig. 5.3 Residuals of the distributed synchronous and asynchronous algorithms

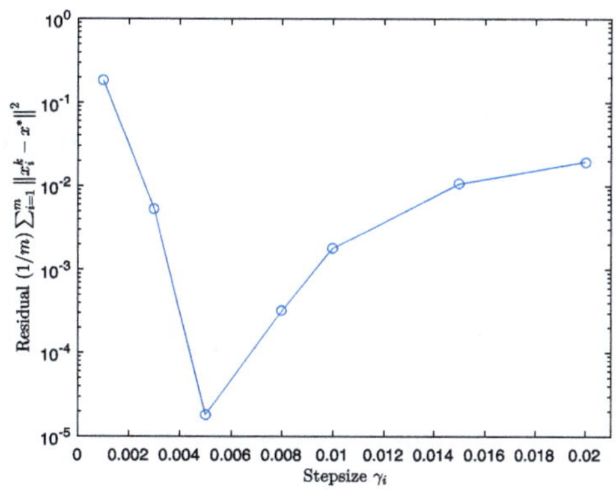

Fig. 5.4 Residuals at the 800-th iteration with different γ_i

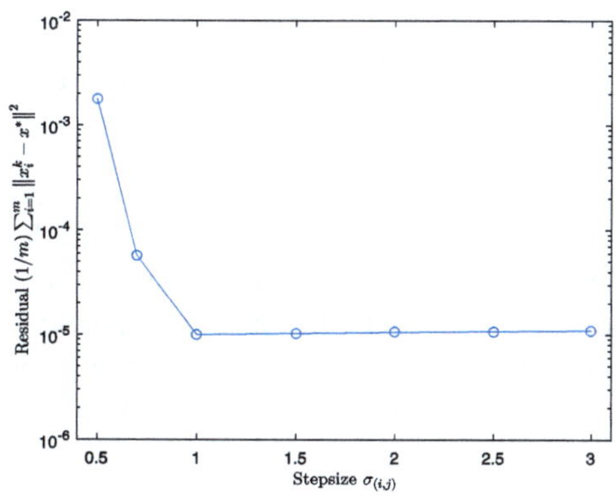

Fig. 5.5 Residuals at the 800-th iteration with different $\sigma_{(i,j)}$

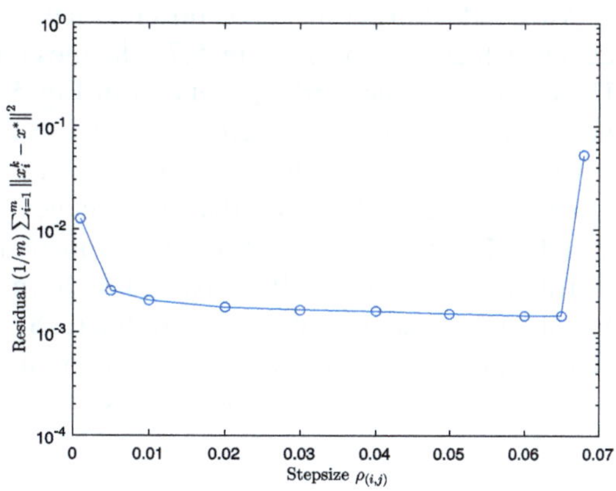

Fig. 5.6 Residuals at the 800-th iteration with different $\rho_{(i,j)}$

and the step sizes are set as $\gamma_i = 0.01$, $\sigma_{(i,j)} = 0.5$ and $\rho_{(i,j)} = 0.01$ by default. When one step size is studied, the other two step sizes remain constant. Under these conditions, γ_i has a good effect around 0.005. $\sigma_{(i,j)}$ around 1 leads to faster convergence, but the influence caused by the continuous increase is not obvious. $\rho_{(i,j)}$ has a better range around 0.065 but enjoys good results in $[0.005, 0.065]$.

5.5.2 Sparse-Group LASSO Problem

In this case study, we consider the sparse-group LASSO problem with m response vectors $b_i \in \mathbb{R}^{n_b}$ and m matrices of the features $Y_i \in \mathbb{R}^{n_b \times n}$ for $i = 1, \ldots, m$. The formulation is given as

$$\min_x \frac{1}{2n_b} \sum_{i=1}^{m} \|b_i - Y_i x\|^2 + (1-\alpha)\, \mu m \sqrt{n} \|x\|_2 + \alpha \mu m \|x\|_1, \tag{5.77}$$

where the parameter $\alpha \in [0, 1]$ is the penalty coefficient of the convex combination of the LASSO and group-LASSO, and the parameter μ determines the sparsity of the solution. Set the scale of data as $n = 30$ and $n_b = 120$. The parameter α is generated randomly in its acceptable range and μ is taken as $1/m$. Elements of matrices Y_i for $i = 1, \ldots, m$ are randomly selected in $[0, 1]$ and those of response vectors b_i are randomly selected in $[-0.5, 0.5]$. In the experiments, let the local objective functions $f_i(x_i) = (1/2n_b)\|b_i - Y_i x_i\|^2$ and $g_i(x_i) = (1-\alpha)\,\mu\sqrt{n}\|x_i\|_2 + \alpha\mu\|x_i\|_1$ for each agent i. The step sizes are $\gamma_i = 0.005$, $\sigma_{(i,j)} = 0.5$ and $\rho_{(i,j)} = 1$.

We conduct experiments on different network sparsity over networks with eight agents, which are given in Fig. 5.7. The mesh network is generated with $p_e = 0.5$. Under the same network sparsity as in Fig. 5.7b, the influence of different agent numbers is also studied. Here, we increase the number of agents to 16 through letting the agent i and the agent $(i + 8)$ take half of the original i-th local cost function. Figure 5.8 shows that more edges and more agents can lead to faster speeds. Moreover, over Fig. 5.7a, we compare the proposed algorithms with another distributed algorithm TriPD-Dist and its asynchronous version [17] which is also based on the randomized block coordinate. Synchronous and asynchronous TriPD-Dist adopt the same step sizes as the proposed algorithms. Figure 5.9 shows that the proposed algorithms have better speeds.

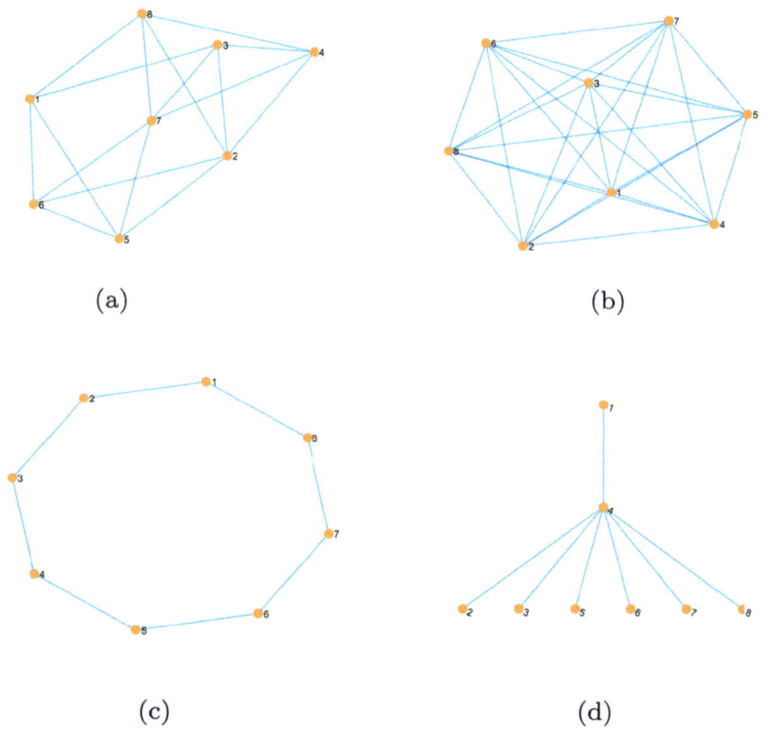

Fig. 5.7 The communication networks with eight agents. (**a**) The mesh network. (**b**) The full connected network. (**c**) The circle network. (**d**) The star network

Fig. 5.8 Evolution of residuals with different networks

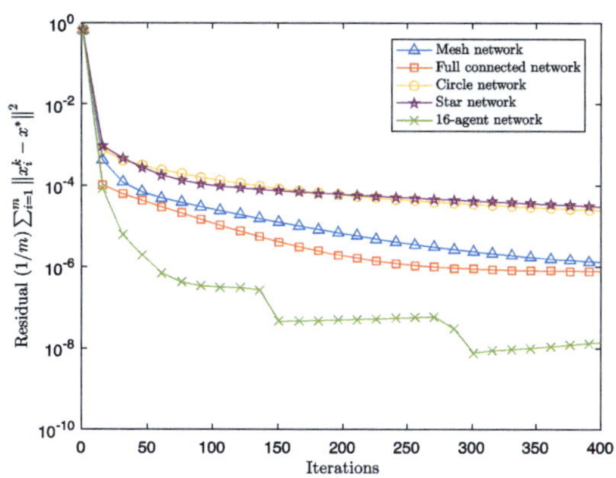

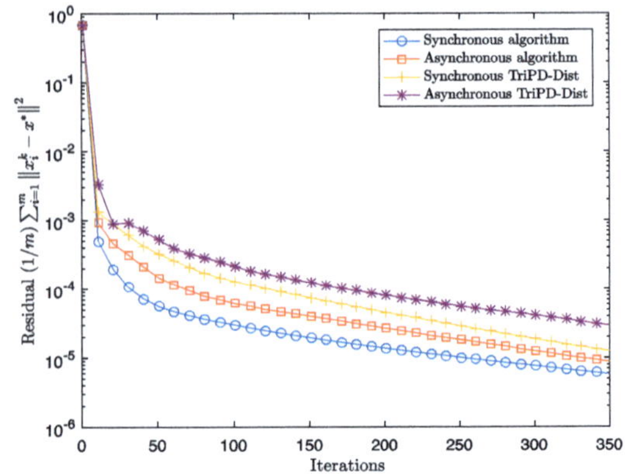

Fig. 5.9 Comparison across TriPD-Dist and the proposed distributed algorithms

5.6 Conclusion

This chapter has considered nonsmooth composite optimization problems over distributed networks. Based on the dual operator splitting method, we have proposed a novel distributed algorithm that can converge to the optimal solution to the primal problem. Further, relying on the randomized block coordinate descent technique, the asynchronous version of the algorithm has been developed where each agent can perform separate calculations under random and independent activation probabilities. Both the proposed algorithms have employed the uncoordinated step sizes related to agents or edges.

Chapter 6
Distributed Primal-Dual Forward-Backward Splitting Algorithm for Nonsmooth Composite Optimization

Abstract Motivated by modern large-scale information processing problems in engineering, this chapter concentrates on studying distributed constrained convex optimization problems over a connected undirected network. The problem involves a sum of a differentiable convex function with Lipschitz continuous gradient and two nonsmooth convex functions with a linear operator. To solve such a problem, we propose a novel distributed primal-dual forward-backward splitting algorithm, called D-PDFBS. Each agent locally computes the Lipschitz continuous gradient and two proximal operators, and exchanges information with its neighbors. D-PDFBS adopts non-identical step sizes, and we reveal the relationship between selection of step sizes and parameters of objective functions. The simulation results verify the feasibility of D-PDFBS and the correctness of theoretical findings.

Keywords Forward-backward splitting method · Distributed optimization · Primal-dual algorithm · Nonsmooth function

6.1 Introduction

The following general optimization problem that appears in machine learning [127–130] has attracted much attention in recent years:

$$\min_{x \in \mathbb{R}^n} \; F(x) + G(x) + H(Lx), \tag{6.1}$$

where F is convex, differentiable on $\mathbb{R}^n$ with Lipschitz continuous gradient, G and H are proper lower semicontinuous convex, possibly nonsmooth functions, and L is a bounded linear mapping.

The early algorithms mainly focus on problem (6.1) when $G(x) = 0$. Inspired by the proximity operator (FP^2O) [20], a primal-dual fixed point method was developed in [33], called PDFP^2O. The PDFP^2O was simplified to the generalized softthresholding method appeared in [131] with $F(x) = (1/2)\|Ax - b\|_2^2$. In recent decades, a growing number of approaches have been emerged to solve

H. Li et al., *Network-System Research and Distributed Composite Algorithm Design*, Computational Intelligence Methods and Applications,
https://doi.org/10.1007/978-981-95-0911-9_6

problem (6.1). A primal-dual splitting method was studied in [4], which calculates twice applications of F, L, L^{T} at each iteration. Based on [4], the Condat-Vũ algorithm [5, 99] only needs one application of F, L, L^{T} at each iteration. A significant merit of the Condat-Vũ algorithm is that it does not require any inverse operator or inner loop. The Condat-Vũ algorithm is simplified to [35] with $F = 0$. In particular, the work [39] utilized a quasi-Newton method to speed up the Condat-Vũ algorithm and took it as a special case. A preconditioned Condat-Vũ algorithm without the information of L was presented in [40], which expands the algorithm [41]. An asymmetric forward-backward-adjoint splitting algorithm was studied in [6], which contains the Condat-Vũ algorithm. The work [7] developed a new-style algorithm, called primal-dual fixed point (PDFP) algorithm, by combining PDFP^{2}O [33] with the preconditioned alternating projection algorithm (PAPA) [34]. Different from the above-mentioned algorithms, a novel primal-dual algorithm was designed by Yan [8], called primal-dual three-operator (PD^{3}O) algorithm, which can be respectively converted into [41], PDFP^{2}O [33], and [132] when $F = 0$, $G = 0$, and L is the identity operator. Inspired by Combettes and Wajs [133], Combettes and Yamada [134], and Zong et al. [135], several inner-outer iterative algorithms were presented in [136], which are related to some algorithms involving Condat-Vũ, PDFP, and PD^{3}O.

However, the above algorithms are centralized. Such a centralized structure does compromises their practicabilities to deal with large-scale optimization problems due to the bottleneck of communication and computation. For complex large-scale systems, distributed methods are more flexible, robust, and extensible than their centralized counterparts. Distributed optimization has been widely used in wireless communication, sensor network, smart grid, resource allocation, machine learning, and other scenarios [137–141].

In the framework of problem (6.1), we consider a set of m agents where each agent $i = 1, \cdots, m$ has its own private objective function with the form $F_i + G_i + H_i$. All agents are aimed to cooperatively deal with

$$\min_{x\in\mathbb{R}^n} \sum_{i=1}^{m} F_i(x) + G_i(x) + H_i(L_i x). \tag{6.2}$$

Let $G_i = 0$ and $H_i = 0$. Then, problem (6.2) turns to $\min_{x\in\mathbb{R}^n} F_i(x)$. A few notable distributed methods to solve this problem are gradient-based methods [9, 10, 49, 142]. For these algorithms, their main advantage is being intuitive and computationally simple. In the case that $H_i = 0$, problem (6.2) reduces to $\min_{x\in\mathbb{R}^n} F_i(x) + G_i(x)$. Based on the forward-backward splitting technique [5, 99], the early work [23] presented a distributed primal-dual algorithm to solve this problem. In [54], the authors employed the composite structure to propose an exact first-order method (PG-EXTRA) and presented good performance. In the case that $F_i = 0$, problem (6.2) is equivalent to $\min_{x\in\mathbb{R}^n} G_i(x) + H_i(L_i x)$. Based on the asymmetric forward-backward-adjoint splitting technique [6], a distributed primal-dual algorithm is obtained to deal with this problem by the authors in [16]. [143]

introduced a consensus constrain into this composite optimization problem, and proposed fully distributed synchronous and asynchronous primal-dual algorithms, which could be well applied to distributed model predictive control problems. For studying problem (6.2) with an equality constraint, the work [17] innovatively developed a distributed primal-dual method, which establishes an asymptotic linear convergence when all functions are piecewise linear-quadratic. However, few efforts have been made to investigate distributed variants of the Condat-Vũ algorithm to deal with problem (6.2). Meanwhile, compared with the existing literature that only consider F_i term [9, 10, 49, 142] or F_i+G_i terms [23, 54] or G_i+H_i terms [16, 143], the composite optimization problem (6.2) will be more general and could be suitable for a wider range of application scenarios[63–65]. Motivated by this, we introduce the idea of Latafat [17] into the Condat-Vũ algorithm and propose a new algorithm (D-PDFBS). This chapter possesses the following contributions:

(i) We propose a distributed extension of the Condat-Vũ algorithm [5, 99]. Such a distributed pattern has superiorities in flexibility, efficiency and security compared with its centralized counterparts. The complex problem is divided into each agent that locally updates a differentiable term and two nonsmooth terms, as well as exchanges information, by which to simplify the complex problem.
(ii) Compared with the Condat-Vũ algorithm [5, 99], our algorithm relies on the local Lipschitz constants to prevent a scalar constant from imprecisely expressing the Lipschitz continuity of a differentiable term. A characteristic of the above algorithm is that the step sizes are chosen to be inversely proportional to the coordinatewise Lipschitz constant of the smooth term rather than the global constant. This leads to a faster convergence by applying larger step sizes in directions with smaller Lipschitz constant.

6.2 Preliminaries

We present the distributed optimization problem and give the communication network in this section. Then, some necessary assumptions and definitions are provided.

6.2.1 *Notation*

Let $\mathbb{N}$ be the set of natural numbers. Define $\mathcal{H}$ as a real Euclidean space. The symbols $\langle \cdot, \cdot \rangle$ and $\|\cdot\|_2$ represent the scalar product and the Euclidean norm, respectively. Denote $\Gamma_0(\mathcal{H})$ the set of proper lower semicontinuous convex functions from $\mathcal{H}$ to $(-\infty, +\infty)$. The proximal operator of $f \in \Gamma_0(\mathcal{H})$ relative to $\|\cdot\|_V$ is represented by $\text{prox}_f^V(y) = \arg\min_{z\in\mathbb{R}^n}\{f(z) + (1/2)||y - z||_V^2\}$, where V

and Id are symmetric positive definite matrix and identity operator, respectively. For constant $\gamma > 0$, the proximity operator of f is denoted by $\text{prox}_{\gamma f}(y) = \arg\min_{z\in\mathbb{R}^n}\{f(z) + (1/2\lambda)||z - y||^2\}$. The domain of f is described by $\text{dom}(f) = \{y \in H : f(y) < +\infty\}$. The symbol $f^*(y) = \sup_{z\in\mathcal{H}} \langle y, z\rangle - f(z)$ represents the conjugate of f. The subdifferential of f is indicative of $\partial f : y \in \mathcal{H} \mapsto \{u \in \mathcal{H} | (\forall z \in \mathcal{H}) \langle z - y, u\rangle + f(y) \leq f(z)\}$. In addition, $\partial f(y) = \{\nabla f(y)\}$ is satisfied when f is differentiable. The symbol blkdiag $(\cdot)$ denotes the block diagonal matrix. Define $\lambda_{\max}(Q)$ as the largest eigenvalues of Q, where Q is a positive semi-definite matrix. The notation $\circ$ stands for the combination of functions or operators. The symbol ri C is called the relative interior of a set C. Define $M : \mathcal{H} \to \mathcal{H}$ as a set-valued operator. The graph of M and its inverse are represented by $\text{gra}(M) = \{(y, z) \in \mathcal{H}^2 : z \in \mathcal{H}y\}$ and M^{-1}, respectively. Let $\text{zer}(M) = \{y \in \mathcal{H} : 0 \in My\}$. M is monotone if $\forall (a, b) \in H^2, \forall (c, d) \in Ma \times Mb, \langle a - b, c - d\rangle \geq 0$. If its graph is not strictly included in the graph of any other monotone operator, then it is maximal monotone.

6.2.2 *Model of Optimization Problem*

We focus on studying the following optimization problem:

$$\min_{x_1,\ldots,x_m\in\mathbb{R}^n} U(\mathrm{x}) = \sum_{i=1}^{m} f_i(x_i) + g_i(x_i) + h_i(L_i x_i), \tag{6.3a}$$

$$\text{s.t. } E_{ij}x_i + E_{ji}x_j = b_{(i,j)}, \quad (i, j) \in \mathcal{E}, \tag{6.3b}$$

where $f_i : \mathbb{R}^{n_i} \to \mathbb{R}$ is convex, continuously differentiable, $g_i : \mathbb{R}^{n_i} \to \bar{\mathbb{R}}$ and $h_i : \mathbb{R}^{r_i} \to \bar{\mathbb{R}}$ are proper closed convex functions, $L_i : \mathbb{R}^{n_i} \to \mathbb{R}^{r_i}$ is a linear mapping, $E_{ij} \in \mathbb{R}^{l_{(i,j)}\times n_i}$, $x_i \in \mathbb{R}^{n_i}$, $b_{(i,j)} \in \mathbb{R}^{l_{(i,j)}}$, each function f_i, g_i, and $h_i \circ L_i$ are known only to agent i.

6.2.3 *Communication Network*

We consider m agents communicating through an undirected graph $\mathcal{G} = (\mathcal{V}, \mathcal{E})$, where $\mathcal{V} = \{1, \ldots, m\}$ is regarded as the vertex collection of m agents and $\mathcal{E} \subseteq \mathcal{V} \times \mathcal{V}$ is utilized to represent the edge set. The symbol $\mathcal{N}_i$ denotes the set consisting of neighbors of the agent i.

Assumption 6.1 *The gradient of f_i is β_i-Lipschitz, that is,*

$$\|\nabla f_i(y) - \nabla f_i(z)\| \leq \beta_i \|y - z\|, \quad y, z \in \mathbb{R}^{n_i}. \tag{6.4}$$

Assumption 6.2 *The solution set of problem (6.3) is nonempty, and there exists* $x_i \in \mathrm{r_i}\ \mathrm{dom}\ g_i$ *such that* $L_i x_i \in \mathrm{r_i}\ \mathrm{dom}\ h_i$*, and* $E_{ij}x_i + E_{ji}x_j = b_{(i,j)}$ *for all* $(i, j) \in \mathcal{E}$.

Assumption 6.3 *The undirected graph* $\mathcal{G}$ *is connected.*

Definition 6.1 Define the indicator function of the closed convex set K as

$$\delta_K(z) = \begin{cases} 0, & \text{if } z \in K, \\ \infty, & \text{if } z \notin K. \end{cases} \tag{6.5}$$

Definition 6.2 $T : \mathcal{H} \to \mathcal{H}$ is nonexpansive if

$$\|Ta - Td\| \leq \|a - d\|, \ \forall (a, d) \in \mathcal{H}^2. \tag{6.6}$$

T is firmly nonexpansive if $2T - Id$ is nonexpansive. Letting $\alpha \in (0, 1]$, T is α-averaged if there exists a nonexpansive operator J such that $T = \alpha J + (1 - \alpha) Id$. The collection of α-averaged operators is denoted by $\mathcal{A}(\mathcal{H}, \alpha)$. Especially, $\mathcal{A}(\mathcal{H}, 1)$ and $\mathcal{A}\left(\mathcal{H}, 1/2\right)$ are defined by nonexpansive operators set and firmly nonexpansive operators set, respectively. Define $\mathrm{fix}\,(T) = \{y \in \mathcal{H},\ y = Ty\}$.

Definition 6.3 ([22]) Let D be a nonempty subset of $\mathcal{H}$, $T : D \to \mathcal{H}$, and $\gamma \in (0, +\infty)$. Then T is γ-cocoercive if γT is firmly nonexpansive,

$$\gamma \|Ta - Tb\|^2 \leq \langle a - b, Ta - Tb \rangle, \ \forall (a, b) \in D^2. \tag{6.7}$$

6.3 Algorithm Development

In this chapter, *X*, *Y*, and *W* are three real Euclidean spaces. Condat [5] designed an algorithm to solve problem (1). Choose $(x_0, y_0) \in X \times Y$, proximal step sizes $\tau > 0, \sigma > 0$, and positive relaxation parameters $(\rho_k)_{k\in\mathbb{N}}$. For $k = 0, 1, 2, \ldots$, the sequences $(x_k)_{k\in\mathbb{N}}$ and $(y_k)_{k\in\mathbb{N}}$ are as follows:

$$\begin{aligned} \tilde{x}_{k+1} &= \mathrm{prox}_{\tau G}\left(x_k - \tau\left(\nabla F\left(x_k\right)\right) - \tau L^{\mathrm{T}} y_k\right), \\ \tilde{y}_{k+1} &= \mathrm{prox}_{\sigma H^*}\left(y_k + \sigma L\left(2\tilde{x}_{k+1} - x_k\right)\right), \\ (x_{k+1}, y_{k+1}) &= \rho_k\left(\tilde{x}_{k+1}, \tilde{y}_{k+1}\right) + (1 - \rho_k)\left(x_k, y_k\right). \end{aligned} \tag{6.8}$$

Based on (6.8), we devise a distribute algorithm called D-PDFBS to solve problem (6.3). The implementation of algorithm is only based on local computation and communication among m agents over graph G.

In the process of transforming the multi-agent optimization problem (6.3) into a structural optimization problem (6.1), we describe how to derive the D-PDFBS algorithm. Let

$$
\begin{aligned}
Q &= \text{blkdiag}\left(\left(\omega_{(i,j)} I_{2l_{(i,j)}}\right)_{(i,j)\in\mathcal{E}}\right),\\
\Sigma &= \text{blkdiag}\left(\sigma_1 I_{r_1}, \ldots, \sigma_m I_{r_m}\right),\\
\Gamma &= \text{blkdiag}\left(\tau_1 I_{n_1}, \ldots, \tau_m I_{n_m}\right),\\
B &= \text{blkdiag}\left(\beta_1 I_{n_1}, \ldots, \beta_m I_{n_m}\right),
\end{aligned}
\tag{6.9}
$$

where I represents the identity matrix. Define $\mathrm{x} = \text{col}\left\{x_i^k\right\}_{i=1}^m$ and $\tilde{x} = \text{col}\left\{\tilde{x}_i^k\right\}_{i=1}^m$, the linear operators $S_{(i.j)} : \mathrm{x} \to \left(E_{ij}x_i,\ E_{ji}x_j\right) \in \mathbb{R}^{2l_{(i,j)}\times\sum_{i=1}^m n_i}$ and S : $\mathrm{x} \to \left(S_{(i,j)}\mathrm{x}\right)_{(i,j)\in\mathcal{E}} \in \mathbb{R}^{\sum_{(i,j)\in\mathcal{E}} 2l_{(i,j)}\times\sum_{i=1}^m n_i}$. The transpose of S is S^{T} : $\left(w_{(i,j)}\right)_{(i,j)\in\mathcal{E}} \mapsto \tilde{\mathrm{x}} = \sum_{(i,j)\in\mathcal{E}} S_{(i,j)}^{\mathrm{T}} w_{(i,j)}$ with $\tilde{x}_i = \sum_{j\in\mathcal{N}_i} E_{ij}^{\mathrm{T}} w_{(i,j),i}$. Let $w_{(i,j)} = \left(w_{(i,j),i}, w_{(i,j),j}\right)$. For each edge, consider the collection:

$$
C_{(i,j)} = \left\{(a_1, a_2) \in \mathbb{R}^{l_{(i,j)}} \times \mathbb{R}^{l_{(i,j)}} | a_1 + a_2 = b_{(i,j)}\right\}. \tag{6.10}
$$

Define the equality constraint $E_{ij}x_i + E_{ji}x_j = b_{(i,\ j)}$ in the set C. Problem (6.3) can be rewritten as

$$
\min_{x_1,\ldots,x_m} \sum_{i=1}^m f_i\left(x_i\right) + g_i\left(x_i\right) + h_i\left(L_i x_i\right) + \sum_{i=1}^m \sum_{(i,j)\in\mathcal{E}} \delta_{C_{(i,j)}}\left(S_{(i,j)}\mathrm{x}\right). \tag{6.11}
$$

Reformulate (6.11) as

$$
\min_{\mathrm{x}}\ F\left(\mathrm{x}\right) + G\left(\mathrm{x}\right) + H\left(L\mathrm{x}\right) + \delta_C\left(S\mathrm{x}\right), \tag{6.12}
$$

where $C = \times_{(i,j)\in\mathcal{E}} C_{(i,j)}$, $L = \text{blkdiag}\left(L_1, \ldots, L_m\right)$, $F\left(\mathrm{x}\right) = \sum_{i=1}^m f_i\left(x_i\right)$, $G\left(\mathrm{x}\right) = \sum_{i=1}^m g_i\left(x_i\right)$, $H\left(L\mathrm{x}\right) = \sum_{i=1}^m \left(L_i x_i\right)$, $\delta_C\left(S\mathrm{x}\right) = \sum_{i=1}^m \sum_{(i,j)\in\mathcal{E}} \delta_{C_{(i,j)}} \left(S_{(i,j)}\mathrm{x}\right)$.

We define the Lagrangian function of problem (6.12) as

$$
\begin{aligned}
\Phi\left(\mathrm{x}, y, w\right) =& F\left(\mathrm{x}\right) + G\left(\mathrm{x}\right) + y^{\mathrm{T}}\left(L\mathrm{x}\right) - H^*\left(y\right)\\
&+ w^{\mathrm{T}}\left(S\mathrm{x}\right) - \delta_C^*\left(w\right).
\end{aligned}
\tag{6.13}
$$

The primal-dual optimality conditions are

$$
\begin{pmatrix} 0\\ 0\\ 0 \end{pmatrix} \in \begin{pmatrix} \nabla F\left(\hat{x}\right) + \partial G\left(\hat{x}\right) + L^{\mathrm{T}}\hat{y} + S^{\mathrm{T}}\hat{w}\\ \partial H^*\left(\hat{y}\right) - L\hat{x}\\ \partial\delta_C^*\left(\hat{w}\right) - S\hat{x} \end{pmatrix}, \tag{6.14}
$$

where the pair $(\hat{x}, \hat{y}, \hat{w})$ is the optimal solution to problem (6.13). According to (6.8), one has

$$
\begin{aligned}
\tilde{x}_i^{k+1} &= \text{prox}_{\tau_i G_i}(x_i^k - \tau_i \nabla F_i(x_i^k) - \tau_i L_i^{\mathrm{T}} y_i^k - \tau_i (S^{\mathrm{T}} w)_i),\\
\tilde{y}_i^{k+1} &= \text{prox}_{\sigma_i H_i^*}(y_i^k + \sigma_i L_i (2\tilde{x}_i^{k+1} - x_i^k)),\\
\tilde{w}_{(i,j)}^{k+1} &= \text{prox}_{\omega_{(i,j)}\delta^*_{C_{(i,j)}}}(w_{(i,j)}^k + \omega_{(i,j)} S_{(i,j)}(2\tilde{\mathrm{x}}^{k+1} - \mathrm{x}^k)),\\
(x_i^{k+1}, y_i^{k+1}, w_{(i,j)}^{k+1}) &= \rho_k(\tilde{x}_i^{k+1}, \tilde{y}_i^{k+1}, \tilde{w}_{(i,j)}^{k+1}) + (1-\rho_k)(x_i^k, y_i^k, w_{(i,j)}^k).
\end{aligned}
\tag{6.15}
$$

From Moreau decomposition [22]:

$$
\text{prox}_{\xi f}(u) + \xi \text{prox}_{\frac{1}{\xi} f^*}\left(\frac{1}{\xi} u\right) = u, \tag{6.16}
$$

we have

$$
\begin{aligned}
&\text{prox}_{\omega_{(i,j)}^{-1}\delta_{C_{(i,j)}}}\left(\omega_{(i,j)}^{-1} w_{(i,j)}^k + S_{(i,j)}\left(2\tilde{\mathrm{x}}^{k+1} - \mathrm{x}^k\right)\right)\\
&= P_{C_{(i,j)}}\left(\omega_{(i,j)}^{-1} w_{(i,j)}^k + S_{(i,j)}\left(2\tilde{\mathrm{x}}^{k+1} - \mathrm{x}^k\right)\right),
\end{aligned}
\tag{6.17}
$$

and the projection of $\varphi_1, \varphi_2 \in \mathbb{R}^{l_{(i,j)}}$ on $C_{(i,j)}$ can be set as

$$
\mathcal{P}_{C_{(i,j)}}(\varphi_1, \varphi_2) = \frac{1}{2}\left(\varphi_1 - \varphi_2 + b_{(i,j)}, -\varphi_1 + \varphi_2 + b_{(i,j)}\right). \tag{6.18}
$$

Thus, we have

$$
\begin{aligned}
&\text{prox}_{\omega_{(i,j)}^{-1}\delta_{C_{(i,j)}}}\left(\omega_{(i,j)}^{-1} w_{(i,j)}^k + S_{(i,j)}\left(2\tilde{\mathrm{x}}^{k+1} - \mathrm{x}^k\right)\right)\\
&= \frac{1}{2}\begin{pmatrix}
\left(\omega_{(i,j)}^{-1} w_{(i,j),i}^k + E_{ij}\left(2\tilde{x}_i^{k+1} - {x_i}^k\right)\right)\\
-\left(\omega_{(i,j)}^{-1} w_{(i,j),j}^k + E_{ji}\left(2\tilde{x}_j^{k+1} - {x_j}^k\right)\right) + b_{(i,j)},\\
\left(\omega_{(i,j)}^{-1} w_{(i,j),j}^k + E_{ji}\left(2\tilde{x}_j^{k+1} - {x_j}^k\right)\right)\\
-\left(\omega_{(i,j)}^{-1} w_{(i,j),i}^k + E_{ij}\left(2\tilde{x}_i^{k+1} - {x_i}^k\right)\right) + b_{(i,j)}
\end{pmatrix}.
\end{aligned}
\tag{6.19}
$$

Then, we present the D-PDFBS algorithm, see Algorithm 8.

Algorithm 8 Distributed primal-dual forward-backward splitting algorithm (D-PDFBS)

Initialization : Given arbitrary $x_i^0 \in \mathbb{R}^{n_i}$, $y_i^0 \in \mathbb{R}^{r_i}$, $w_{(i,j),i}^0 \in \mathbb{R}^{l(i,j)}$, $\tau_i > 0$, $\sigma_i > 0$, and $\omega_{(i,j)} > 0$.
For $k = 0, 1, \ldots, i \in \mathcal{V}$ and $j \in \mathcal{N}_i$ **do:**

$$\tilde{x}_i^{k+1} = \text{prox}_{\tau_i G_i}\left(x_i^k - \tau_i \nabla F_i(x_i^k) - \tau_i L_i^{\text{T}} y_i^k - \tau_i \sum_{j \in \mathcal{N}_i} E_{ij}^{\text{T}} w_{(i,j),i}^k\right),$$

$$\tilde{y}_i^{k+1} = \text{prox}_{\sigma_i H_i^*}\left(y_i^k + \sigma_i L_i(2\tilde{x}_i^{k+1} - x_i^k)\right),$$

$$\tilde{w}_{(i,j),i}^{k+1} = \frac{1}{2}\left(w_{(i,j),i}^k + w_{(i,j),j}^k\right) + \frac{\omega_{(i,j)}}{2}\left(E_{ij}(2\tilde{x}_i^{k+1} - x_i^k)\right.$$
$$\left. + E_{ji}(2\tilde{x}_j^{k+1} - x_j^k) + b_{(i,j)}\right),$$

$$(x_i^{k+1}, y_i^{k+1}, w_{(i,j),i}^{k+1}) = \rho_k\left(\tilde{x}_i^{k+1}, \tilde{y}_i^{k+1}, \tilde{w}_{(i,j),i}^{k+1}\right) + (1 - \rho_k)\left(x_i^k, y_i^k, w_{(i,j),i}^k\right).$$

6.4 Convergence Analysis

In this section, we first present some crucial lemmas. Then, the convergence of D-PDFBS is rigorously proved based on these lemmas. The first lemma shows krasnosel'skii-mann iteration, which is important for convergence analysis.

Lemma 6.4 ([144]) *Suppose that* $(\rho_k)_{k\in\mathbb{N}}$ *is a sequence in* $(0, 1)$ *and* $(e_k)_{k\in\mathbb{N}}$ *is a sequence in* $\mathcal{H}$. *Denote* fix $(T) \neq \emptyset$, $\sum_{k\in\mathbb{N}} \rho_k (1 - \rho_k) = +\infty$, *and* $\sum_{k\in\mathbb{N}} \rho_k \|e_k\| < +\infty$. *Let* $b_0 \in \mathcal{H}$ *and set*

$$b_{k+1} = b_k + \rho_k (T(b_k) + e_k - b_k), \ k \in \mathbb{N}, \tag{6.20}$$

where operator $T : \mathcal{H} \to \mathcal{H}$ *is nonexpansive. Then, the sequence* $(b_k)_{k\in\mathbb{N}}$ *converges to* $\hat{b} \in$ fix (T). *When* $e_k = 0$, *we have* $b_{k+1} = b_k + \rho_k (T(b_k) - b_k)$, *and then* $(b_k)_{k\in\mathbb{N}}$ *converges to* $\hat{b} \in$ fix (T).

The following result implies that the composition of average operators is average.

Lemma 6.5 ([145]) *Let* $T_1 \in \mathcal{A}(\mathcal{H}, \alpha_1)$ *and* $T_2 \in \mathcal{A}(\mathcal{H}, \alpha_2)$, *for some* $\alpha_1 \in (0, 1)$ *and* $\alpha_2 \in (0, 1]$. *Then,* $T_1 \circ T_2 \in \mathcal{A}(\mathcal{H}, \alpha')$, *where*

$$\alpha' = \frac{\alpha_1 + \alpha_2 - 2\alpha_1\alpha_2}{1 - \alpha_1\alpha_2} \in [0, 1). \tag{6.21}$$

In what follows, the forward-backward iteration is presented.

Lemma 6.6 ([5]) *Let* M_1 *be maximally monotone and* M_2 *be* θ*-cocoercive, where* $\theta \in (0, +\infty)$, *i.e.,* $\theta M_2 \in \mathcal{A}(\mathcal{H}, 1/2)$. *Assume that* zer $(M_1 + M_2) \neq \emptyset$, $\gamma \in (0, 2\theta]$ *and* $\varpi = 2 - \gamma/2\theta$. *Moreover, suppose that* $(\rho_k)_{k\in\mathbb{N}}$ *is a sequence in* $(0, \varpi)$

such that $\sum_{k\in\mathbb{N}} \rho_k (\varpi - \rho_k) = +\infty$, *and* $(e_{1,k})_{k\in\mathbb{N}}$ *and* $(e_{2,k})_{k\in\mathbb{N}}$ *are sequences in* $\mathcal{H}$ *such that* $\sum_{k\in\mathbb{N}} \rho_k \|e_{1,k}\| < +\infty$ *and* $\sum_{k\in\mathbb{N}} \rho_k \|e_{2,k}\| < +\infty$, *respectively. Let* $s_0 \in \mathcal{H}$ *and set*

$$\begin{aligned} b_{k+1} =& \rho_k \left((Id + \gamma M_1)^{-1} \left(b_k - \gamma \left(M_2(b_k) + e_{2,k}\right)\right) + e_{1,k} \right) \\ &+ (1-\rho_k) b_k, \ k \in \mathbb{N}. \end{aligned} \tag{6.22}$$

Then, the sequence $(b_k)_{k\in\mathbb{N}}$ *converges to* $\hat{b} \in \operatorname{zer}(M_1 + M_2)$. *When* $e_{1,k} = 0$ *and* $e_{2,k} = 0$, *we have* $b_{k+1} = \rho_k \left((Id + \gamma M_1)^{-1} (b_k - \gamma M_2(b_k))\right) + (1-\rho_k) b_k$, *and then* $(b_k)_{k\in\mathbb{N}}$ *converges to* $\hat{b} \in \operatorname{zer}(M_1 + M_2)$.

Next, the baillon-haddad theorem is provided.

Lemma 6.7 ([22]) *Let* $J : \mathcal{H} \to \mathbb{R}$ *be convex, differentiable on* $\mathcal{H}$ *such that* $\theta \nabla J$ *is nonexpansive, for some* $\theta \in (0, +\infty)$. *Then* ∇J *is* θ*-cocoercive, i.e.,* $\theta \nabla J$ *is firmly nonexpansive.*

Now, we study the convergence result of Algorithm 8.

Theorem 6.8 *Suppose that* $\beta_i > 0$, $\forall i \in \mathcal{V}$,

(i) $\tau_i^{-1} - ||\sigma_i L_i^{\mathrm{T}} L_i + \sum\limits_{j\in\mathcal{N}_i} E_{ij}^{\mathrm{T}} \omega_{(i,j)} E_{ij}|| \geq \frac{\beta_i}{2}$;

(ii) $\forall k \in \mathbb{N}$, $\rho_k \in (0, \varpi)$, *where*

$$\varpi = \min_{i\in\mathcal{V}} \{2 - \frac{\beta_i}{2} (\tau_i^{-1} - ||\sigma_i L_i^{\mathrm{T}} L_i + \sum_{j\in\mathcal{N}_i} E_{ij}^{\mathrm{T}} \omega_{(i,j)} E_{ij}||)^{-1}\} \in [1, 2);$$

(iii) $\sum\limits_{k\in\mathbb{N}} (\varpi - \rho_k) = +\infty$.

Then, the sequences $(x_k)_{k\in\mathbb{N}}$, $(y_k)_{k\in\mathbb{N}}$, *and* $(w_k)_{k\in\mathbb{N}}$ *generated by D-PDFBS converge to* $\hat{x}$, $\hat{y}$, *and* $\hat{w}$, *respectively.*

Proof We prove that D-PDFBS has the forward-backward iteration structure, when expressed by a nonexpansive operator on $V = X \times Y \times W$. Define the inner product $\langle \cdot, \cdot \rangle_I$ in $\mathcal{H}$ as follows:

$$\langle v, v' \rangle_I = \langle x, x' \rangle + \langle y, y' \rangle + \langle w, w' \rangle, \ \langle v, v' \rangle \in V^2, \tag{6.23}$$

where $v = \langle x, y, w \rangle$ and $v' = \langle x', y', w' \rangle \in V$. By assigning this inner product to V, the Euclidean space V_I is obtained. We introduce a bounded and self-adjoint linear operator P on V as

$$P : \begin{pmatrix} x \\ y \\ w \end{pmatrix} \mapsto \begin{pmatrix} \Gamma^{-1} & -L^{\mathrm{T}} & -S^{\mathrm{T}} \\ -L & \Sigma^{-1} & 0 \\ -S & 0 & Q^{-1} \end{pmatrix} \begin{pmatrix} x \\ y \\ w \end{pmatrix}. \tag{6.24}$$

When the condition (i) is satisfied, we can obtain $\tau_i < 1/||\sigma_i(L_i)^{\mathrm{T}}L_i + \sum_{j\in\mathcal{N}_i}\omega_{(i,j)}E_{ij}^{\mathrm{T}}E_{ij}||$. Therefore, P is positive. Define $\langle\cdot,\cdot\rangle_P$ and norm $\|\cdot\|_P = \langle\cdot,\cdot\rangle_P^{1/2}$ by

$$\left\langle v, v'\right\rangle_P = \left\langle v, Pv'\right\rangle_I,\ \left\langle v, v'\right\rangle \in V^2. \tag{6.25}$$

By assigning this inner product to V, the Euclidean space V_P is obtained. The concepts of convergence in V_P and in V_I are equivalent due to the fact that P and L are bounded. The following inclusion is established by $\tilde{v}_{k+1} = (\tilde{x}_{k+1}, \tilde{y}_{k+1}, \tilde{w}_{k+1})$ computed by D-PDFBS, for any $k \in \mathbb{N}$:

$$-\underbrace{\begin{pmatrix}\nabla F(x_k)\\ 0\\ 0\end{pmatrix}}_{K(v_k)} \in \underbrace{\begin{pmatrix}\partial G(\tilde{x}_{k+1}) + L^\top \tilde{y}_{k+1} + S^\top \tilde{w}_{k+1}\\ -L\tilde{x}_{k+1} + \partial H^*(\tilde{y}_{k+1})\\ -S\tilde{x}_{k+1} + \partial\delta_C^*(\tilde{w}_{k+1})\end{pmatrix}}_{D(\tilde{v}_{k+1})} + \underbrace{\begin{pmatrix}\Gamma^{-1} & -L^\top & -S^\top\\ -L & \Sigma^{-1} & 0\\ -S & 0 & Q^{-1}\end{pmatrix}}_{P}\underbrace{\begin{pmatrix}\tilde{x}_{k+1} - x_k\\ \tilde{y}_{k+1} - y_k\\ \tilde{w}_{k+1} - w_k\end{pmatrix}}_{(\tilde{v}_{k+1}-v_k)}, \tag{6.26}$$

or

$$\tilde{v}_{k+1} = \left(Id + P^{-1}\circ D\right)^{-1}\circ\left(Id - P^{-1}\circ K\right)(v_k). \tag{6.27}$$

Considering the relaxation step, we get

$$v_{k+1} = \rho_k\left(\left(Id + P^{-1}\circ D\right)^{-1}\left(v_k - P^{-1}\circ K\left(v_k\right)\right)\right) + (1-\rho_k)\, v_k. \tag{6.28}$$

Obviously, we can observe that formula (6.28) satisfies the forward-backward iteration structure. Therefore, by verifying the application condition of Lemma 6.6, the convergence result of Theorem 6.8 can be sufficient. Let $M_1 = P^{-1}\circ D$. The operator $(x, y, w) \mapsto \partial G \times \partial H^* \times \partial\delta_C^*$ is maximally monotone in V_I [22, Proposition 23.16]. Further, the skew operator

$$\begin{pmatrix}x\\ y\\ w\end{pmatrix} \mapsto \begin{pmatrix}0 & L^{\mathrm{T}} & S^{\mathrm{T}}\\ -L & 0 & 0\\ -S & 0 & 0\end{pmatrix}\begin{pmatrix}x\\ y\\ w\end{pmatrix}, \tag{6.29}$$

is maximally monotone in V_I by Example 20.30 of [22] and has a full domain. According to Corollary 24.4 (i) of [22], we can obtain D is maximally monotone. Therefore, M_1 is monotone in V_P, and it is maximally monotone due to the injectivity of P. Define $M_2 = P^{-1} \circ K$ and $\theta = \min_{i\in\mathcal{V}}\{\tau_i^{-1} - ||\sigma_i L_i^{\mathrm{T}} L_i + \sum_{j\in\mathcal{N}_i} \omega_{(i,j)} E_{ij}^{\mathrm{T}} E_{ij}||/\beta_i\}$. Noting that $K(v) = ((\nabla F(x))^{\mathrm{T}}, 0, 0)^{\mathrm{T}}$ in (6.26), the cocoercivity of M_2 is shown as follows:

$$
\begin{aligned}
&\left\| M_2(v) - M_2\left(v'\right) \right\|_P^2 \\
=&\left\langle P^{-1} \circ K(v) - P^{-1} \circ K\left(v'\right), K(v) - K\left(v'\right) \right\rangle_I \\
\le& \sum_{i=1}^{m} \beta_i^2 \left(\tau_i^{-1} - \left\| \sum_{j\in\mathcal{N}_i} E_{ij}^{\mathrm{T}} \omega_{(i,j)} E_{ij} + L_i^{\mathrm{T}} \sigma_i L_i \right\| \right)^{-1} \left\| x_i - x_i' \right\|^2 .
\end{aligned} \tag{6.30}
$$

Then, we set

$$
\lambda_{\max} = \max_{i\in\mathcal{V}} \left\{ \beta_i^2 \left(\tau_i^{-1} - \left\| \sigma_i L_i^{\mathrm{T}} L_i + \sum_{j\in\mathcal{N}_i} \omega_{(i,j)} E_{ij}^{\mathrm{T}} E_{ij} \right\| \right)^{-1} \right\}. \tag{6.31}
$$

Therefore, we obtain

$$
\left\| M_2(v) - M_2\left(v'\right) \right\|_P^2 \le \lambda_{\max} \left\| x - x' \right\|^2 . \tag{6.32}
$$

Let $R(x, y, w) \to (x, 0, 0)$ be a linear operator. Further, since $P - \max_{i\in\mathcal{V}}(\beta_i)\,\theta R$ is positive definite, we get

$$
\begin{aligned}
&\theta^2 \left\| M_2(v) - M_2\left(v'\right) \right\|_P^2 \\
\le& \max_{i\in\mathcal{V}} (\beta_i)\,\theta \left\| x - x' \right\|^2 \\
=& \max_{i\in\mathcal{V}} (\beta_i)\,\theta \left\langle \left(v - v'\right), R\left(v - v'\right) \right\rangle_I \\
=& \left\langle \left(v - v'\right), \max_{i\in\mathcal{V}} (\beta_i)\,\theta R\left(v - v'\right) \right\rangle_I \\
\le& \left\langle \left(v - v'\right), P\left(v - v'\right) \right\rangle_I \\
=& \left\| v - v' \right\|_P^2 .
\end{aligned} \tag{6.33}
$$

We can further get $\theta \left\| M_2(v) - M_2\left(v'\right) \right\|_P \le \left\| v - v' \right\|_P$, i.e., θM_2 is nonexpansive. Therefore, according to Lemma 6.7, we can conclude that θM_2 is firmly nonexpansive, that is, $M_2 = P^{-1} \circ K$ is θ-cocoercive. Then, based on Lemma 6.6, setting $\gamma = 1$, we can obtain $b_{k+1} = b_k + \rho_k (T(b_k) - b_k)$, where $T = (Id + M_1)^{-1}(Id - M_2)$. Finally, convergence results can be obtained via employing Lemma 6.4. ■

Remark 6.9 Lemma 6.4 gives the krasnosel'skii-mann iteration, which is the key to the convergence analysis. The conclusion of the forward-backward iteration of Lemma 6.6 is derived based on Lemmas 6.4 and 6.5, for which please refer to [5]. The convergence analysis results of Theorem 6.8 are obtained based on the forward-backward iteration of Lemma 6.6 and the baillon-haddad theorem of Lemma 6.7. First we observe that (6.28) has a forward-backward iterative structure. Therefore, the convergence result of Theorem 6.8 can be obtained by satisfying the application conditions of Lemma 6.6. In the convergence analysis process, we apply Lemma 6.7 to obtain that θM_2 is firmly nonexpansive.

6.5 Numerical Experiments

We provide numerical simulations to validate the performance of D-PDFBS in this section.

6.5.1 *Case Study I*

We consider six agents moving in a 2-D space with first-order dynamics over an undirected network [98], where $x_i = \left[x_i^1, x_i^2\right]^{\mathrm{T}} \in \mathbb{R}^2$, $i \in \{1, 2, 3, 4, 5, 6\}$. The adjacency matrix is shown by

$$A = \begin{bmatrix} 0\ 1\ 1\ 0\ 1\ 1 \\ 1\ 0\ 1\ 0\ 0\ 0 \\ 1\ 1\ 0\ 1\ 0\ 0 \\ 0\ 0\ 1\ 0\ 1\ 0 \\ 1\ 0\ 0\ 1\ 0\ 1 \\ 1\ 0\ 0\ 0\ 1\ 0 \end{bmatrix}. \tag{6.34}$$

The local function consists of the following:

$$f_i\left(x_i\right) = \|x_i - p_i\|^2,\ g_i\left(x_i\right) = \|x_i - q_i\|_1,\ h_i\left(L_i x_i\right) = \begin{cases} 0, & \text{if} x_i \in \Lambda_i, \\ \infty, & \text{if} x_i \notin \Lambda_i, \end{cases} \tag{6.35}$$

where $p_i = \left[p_i^1, p_i^2\right]^{\mathrm{T}} = [i - 3.5, 0]^{\mathrm{T}}$, $\Lambda_i = \left\{\varsigma \in \mathbb{R}^2 \ \middle|\ \|\varsigma - x_i^0\|^2 \le 64\right\}$, $q_i = \left[q_i^1, q_i^2\right]^{\mathrm{T}} = [0, i - 3.5]^{\mathrm{T}}$. The initial values of the six agents, respectively, are set $x_1^0 = [-4, 5.5]^{\mathrm{T}}$, $x_2^0 = [0, 7]^{\mathrm{T}}$, $x_3^0 = [6, 5]^{\mathrm{T}}$, $x_4^0 = [5, -3.5]^{\mathrm{T}}$, $x_5^0 = [0, -7]^{\mathrm{T}}$, $x_6^0 = [-5, -5]^{\mathrm{T}}$. Then, we employ the proposed algorithm and the algorithm (TriPD-Dist (synch))[17] to deal with this problem for comparison.

The parameters of Algorithm 8 are set as $\tau_1 = 0.07$, $\tau_2 = 0.13$, $\tau_3 = 0.09$, $\tau_4 = 0.13$, $\tau_5 = 0.09$, $\tau_6 = 0.13$, $\sigma_i = 0.5$, $\omega_{(i,j)} = 3$, $\rho_k = 1.1$, which are obtained by using $\tau_i^{-1} - ||\sigma_i L_i^{\mathrm{T}} L_i + \sum_{j\in\mathcal{N}_i} E_{ij}^{\mathrm{T}} \omega_{(i,j)} E_{ij}|| \geq \beta_i/2$ and $\varpi = \min_{i\in\mathcal{V}}\{2-(\beta_i/2)(\tau_i^{-1} - ||\sigma_i L_i^{\mathrm{T}} L_i + \sum_{j\in\mathcal{N}_i} E_{ij}^{\mathrm{T}} \omega_{(i,j)} E_{ij}||)^{-1}\} \in [1, 2)$. The step sizes of TriPD-Dist (synch) [17] are the same with that of Algorithm 8. The residual is defined as $\log_{10}\left(\left(1/m\right)\sum_{i=1}^{m}\left\|x_i^k - x^*\right\|\right)$.

The experiment results are described in Figs. 6.1 and 6.2. Figure 6.1a, b reflect the trajectories of x_i^k, $i \in \{1, 2, 3, 4, 5, 6\}$, where all agents converge to $(0, 0)$ as the iterations increase. Figure 6.1c shows that the summation of the local functions reaches the minimum. Figure 6.1d depicts the evolution of the whole system over iterations, where p_i and q_i, $i \in \{1, 2, 3, 4, 5, 6\}$ are defined by red and blue stars, respectively. Moreover, the proposed algorithm performs better than TriDP-Dist (synch), which is shown in Fig. 6.2. These experiment results verify the correctness of our algorithm.

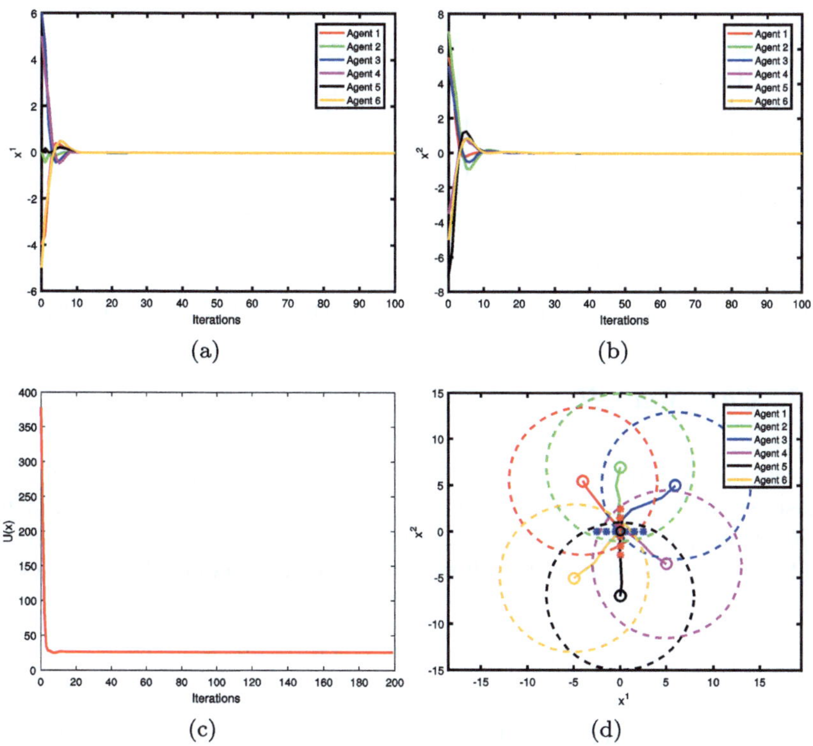

Fig. 6.1 The simulation results of Algorithm 8. (**a**) Evolutions of x_i^k. (**b**) Evolutions of x_i^k. (**c**) Evolutions of $U(x)$. (**d**) Motions of all agents

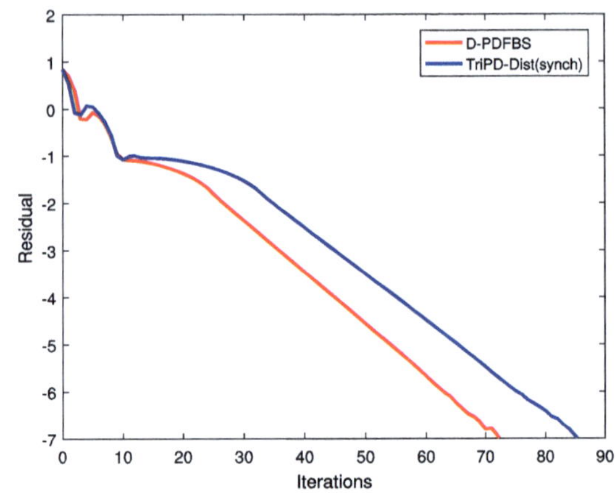

Fig. 6.2 Evolutions of residual with iterations

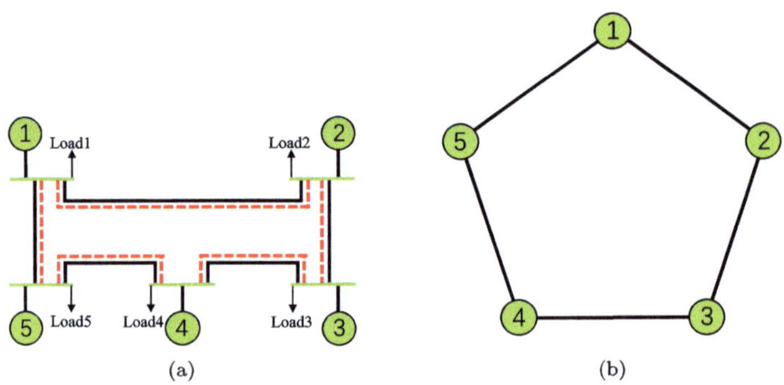

Fig. 6.3 The microgrid test system. (**a**) Simplified illustration. (**b**) Communication topology

6.5.2 *Case Study II*

This test is based on a microgrid system given in [140]. The microgrid system consists of five buses and each bus has a load and a generator. The symbol $C_i(p_i)$ denotes the cost function where p_i is the power generation of generator i, $i \in \{1, \ldots, m\}$. We consider the following distributed economic dispatch problem:

$$\min_{p_i \in \mathbb{R}^m} \sum_{i=1}^{m} C_i(p_i), \quad p_i^{\max} \leq p_i \leq p_i^{\min}, \quad \text{s.t.} \quad \sum_{i=1}^{m} p_i = \sum_{i=1}^{m} D_i, \tag{6.36}$$

where D_i represents the power demand of load i, $p_i^{\max}$ and $p_i^{\min}$ are the lower and upper bounds of the generator's power generation.

The cost function C_i is defined as $C_i(p_i) = \phi_i + \varepsilon_i p_i + \zeta_i p_i^2$, where ϕ_i, ε_i, and ζ_i are cost coefficients. As shown in Fig. 6.3, we depict the test system diagram and communication topology of the microgrid. The power demands for each load are set as follows: $D_1 = 35KW$, $D_2 = 20KW$, $D_3 = 25KW$, $D_4 = 30KW$, $D_5 =$

Table 6.1 Parameters of five generators

G_i	ϕ_i	ε_i	ζ_i	$p_i^{\min}(KW)$	$p_i^{\max}(KW)$
1	51	1.22	0.094	10	80
2	31	3.41	0.078	8	60
3	78	2.53	0.105	3.8	40
4	42	4.02	0.082	5.4	45
5	62	3.17	0.074	4.2	18

$10KW$. The cost coefficients and the generation capacities are given in Table 6.1. By direct calculation, the optimal generations are $p_1^* = 32.81KW$, $p_2^* = 25.51KW$, $p_3^* = 23.14KW$, $p_4^* = 20.54KW$, $p_5^* = 18.00KW$, and the optimal incremental cost is $7.39\$/KW$.

Define the set $K_i = \{y | p_i^{\min} \leq y \leq p_i^{\max}\}$ and the indicator function $\delta_{K_i}(p_i)$. We consider the following Lagrangian function:

$$f(p, x) = \sum_{i=1}^{m} C_i(p_i) + x \sum_{i=1}^{m} (D_i - p_i), \tag{6.37}$$

where $p \in [p_1, \cdots, p_m]^{\mathrm{T}}$ and x is the Lagrangian multiplier. The related Lagrangian dual problem of (6.36) is $\max_{x\in\mathbb{R}} \min_{p\in\mathbb{R}^m} f(p, x)$, and we convert it into

$$\min_{x\in\mathbb{R}} f(x) \triangleq \sum_{i=1}^{m} f_i(x), \tag{6.38}$$

where $f_i(x) = \max_{p\in\mathbb{R}^m} \{x p_i - C_i(p_i) - \delta_{K_i}(p_i)\} - x D_i$. Then, problem (6.38) is rewritten as

$$\min_{x_i\in\mathbb{R}} \sum_{i=1}^{m} f_i(x_i), \text{ s.t. } E_{ij}x_i + E_{ji}x_j = 0, \quad (i, j) \in \mathcal{E}, \tag{6.39}$$

where $E_{ij} = 1$ if $i < j$ and $E_{ij} = -1$ if $i > j$.

In this simulation, it can be seen that $g_i(x_i) = 0$ and $h_i(L_i x_i) = 0$. Then, we set the relevant parameters as follows: $\tau_i \in (0.079, 0.089)$, $\omega_{(i,j)} \in (2.9, 3.0)$, $\rho_k = 0.5$. As described in Fig. 6.4, the generators achieve the optimal generations, the total generation converges to the total demand, and x_i, $i \in \{1, \cdots, m\}$ converge to x^*. These results prove the effectiveness of the proposed algorithm.

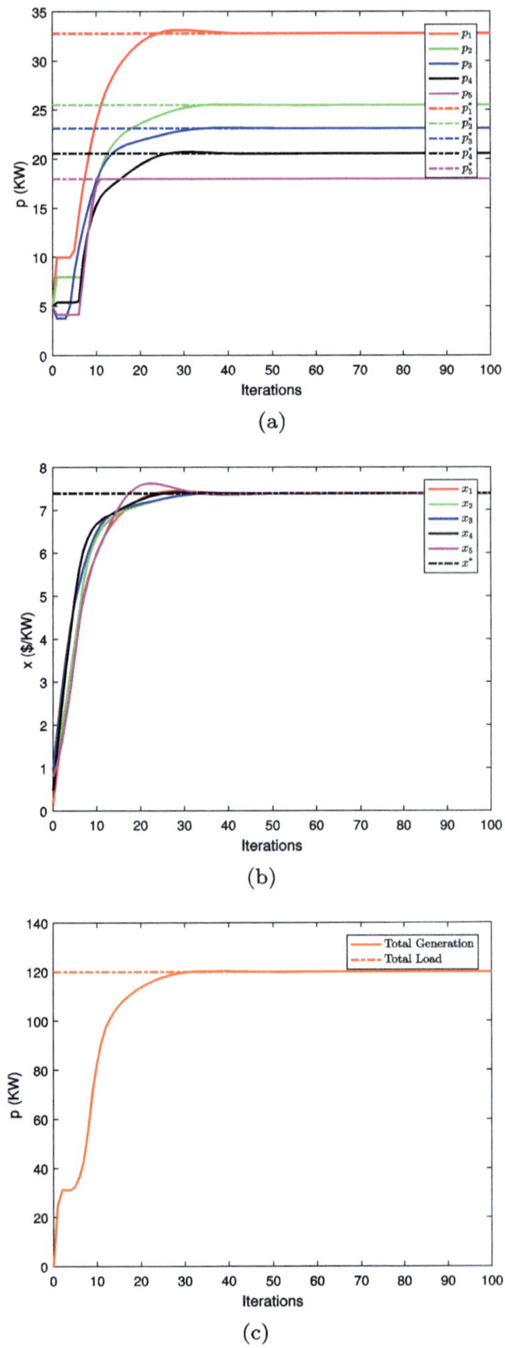

Fig. 6.4 The simulation results of Algorithm 8. (**a**) Power generation. (**b**) Incremental cost. (**c**) Power balance

6.6 Conclusion

We have designed a distributed algorithm (D-PDFBS) for solving problem (6.3) in this chapter. We have utilized the local Lipschitz constant for avoiding the slower convergence rate caused by the traditional step size. In the future, we will focus on establishing an explicit convergence rate and potential accelerations. In addition, it would be also worthy of extending D-PDFBS to deal with a host of problems, involving directed and time-varying networks, as well as communication delays. Besides, more complex, i.e., stochastic noises, asynchronous interaction, etc. optimization problems are also valuable to be studied.

Chapter 7
Distributed Algorithm for Constrained Optimization with Asynchrony and Delays

Abstract This chapter investigates the distributed composite optimization problem over an undirected network with equality constraints. The optimization problem includes a smooth term and two possibly nonsmooth terms. Most existing results are devoted to developing distributed algorithms in a synchronous setting with a global clock, where the agents cannot move to the next iteration until the slowest agent completes its update. A new asynchronous distributed primal-dual forward-backward splitting algorithm (AD-PDFBS) is presented to solve this problem. Each agent can compute and communicate independently at different times, with the information it has even if the latest information from its neighbors is not yet available. The proposed algorithm is characterized by its ability to reduce synchronization wait and alleviate communication bottleneck. The convergence of AD-PDFBS is proved by transforming the asynchronous algorithm into a fixed-point problem utilizing the operator splitting scheme under bounded delay assumption. Experimental results confirm the effectiveness of AD-PDFBS.

Keywords Asynchronous algorithm · Primal-dual algorithm · Forward-backward splitting method · Nonsmooth function · Delay

7.1 Introduction

This chapter considers a network of n agents, each of which has its own private function. All agents cooperatively deal with the composite optimization problem:

$$\min_{x \in \mathbb{R}^n} \sum_{i=1}^{m} g_i(x) + u_i(x) + h_i(N_i x), \tag{7.1}$$

where N_i is a bounded linear mapping, u_i and h_i are proper lower semicontinuous convex, possibly nonsmooth functions, and g_i is convex, differentiable with Lipschitz-continuous gradient.

H. Li et al., *Network-System Research and Distributed Composite Algorithm Design*, Computational Intelligence Methods and Applications,
https://doi.org/10.1007/978-981-95-0911-9_7

In recent years, the synchronous distributed methods to solve problems similar to (7.1) have been well developed. When problem (7.1) reduces to $\min_{x\in\mathbb{R}^n}\sum_{i=1}^{n} g_i(x)$, a class of methods to deal with this problem are the gradient-based methods [9, 10, 49, 142]. These methods are featured by their intuitiveness and computational convenience. When $h_i = 0$, problem (7.1) turns to $\min_{x\in\mathbb{R}^n}\sum_{i=1}^{n} g_i(x) + u_i(x)$. Shi et al. [54] presented a proximal gradient exact first-order algorithm (PG-EXTRA) to address this problem. In [54], a difference structure was employed to deal with the steady-state error in gradient descent step, which developed the algorithm EXTRA [49]. For problem (7.1) with an equality constraint, Li et al. [146] designed a new distributed primal-dual algorithm (D-PDFBS) based on forward-backward splitting mechanism, which extends the Condat-Vũ algorithm [5, 99] to a distributed fashion. D-PDFBS has strong robustness and can reduce the computational burden of a single machine in large-scale networks. However, the algorithm execution efficiency is limited by the processing speed of the slowest agent, thus we propose an asynchronous version of D-PDFBS to improve the algorithm execution efficiency.

To solve the problems similar to (7.1), the existing distributed algorithms are divided into two categories according to the communication methods: synchronous algorithms and asynchronous algorithms. In the synchronous setting, all agents cannot proceed to the next iteration until the slowest agent has completed its update. Such a distributed computation may be inefficient or impractical owing to the running and communication delays. Moreover, a clock coordinator is essential for synchronization, and in large scale decentralized networks, maintaining a clock coordinator is costly and demanding. Synchronous algorithms are not suitable for realistic domains with large-scale networks [147]. Therefore, we are motivated to study asynchronous algorithm mechanisms, where the agents do not need to iterate simultaneously. To enable agents to compute and communicate at different moments and different durations, we introduce the delayed information in the algorithm, i.e., the agents' updates can depend on delayed information received from its neighbors. The information may be outdated several times. The asynchronous algorithm runs continuously with little idle time, reducing communication and memory access blocking and making it more tolerant of computational errors and communication failures. Several reasons may cause delays. The first one is resulted from communication latency. The next is computation, since each agent completes the entire iteration independently, an agent may update its information while its neighbors are still using its old information for the current iteration [157].

1. Asynchronous Activations without Delays Link failures often occur in the network that communication among agents cannot be ensured, especially in large scale networks. Nedic [50] designed an asynchronous algorithm based on random (one-way) broadcasts [148] that allows for random link failures in agents' communications. Bianchi et al. [23] proposed a randomized primal-dual algorithm based on the stochastic coordinate descent of the average operator. The algorithm establishes a variant of the Condat-Vũ algorithm, and treats the alternating-direction method of multipliers (ADMM) [149] as a special case. Based on [19, 150, 151], a novel algorithm with distributed gradient tracking mechanism was proposed in [51]. Recently, an innovative asynchronous algorithm for solving composite constrained optimization problems was proposed in [17] based on a randomized coordinate activation mechanism. By establishing the stochastic monotonicity of the generated sequence, Latafat et al. [17] achieved the convergence analysis. The above algorithms are activated, update, and communicate with their neighbors; between two activations, the agents are presumed to be in idle mode. But, no delay is considered. Each agent must execute its local update using the latest information from its neighbors. This implies that all operations performed by an agent in an activation must be completed before a new activation occurs, which requires some kind of coordination among the agents. The above are asynchronous distributed algorithms without delays.

2. Asynchronous Activations with Delays Based on ADMM [152], Chang et al. [153] developed an asynchronous distributed algorithm that effectively enhances the time efficiency of synchronous distributed ADMM. An asynchronous parallel algorithmic framework, ARock, was presented to find a fixed-point of a nonexpansive operator in [154]. An agent updates a randomly selected coordinate based on possibly outdated information at each iteration. It is proved that ARock converges to a fixed-point of the nonexpansive operator. In the framework of ARock, Yi et al. [155] developed a new asynchronous algorithm to seek generalized Nash equilibria, and by introducing the partial primal-dual gradient algorithm, a distributed voltage control approach was proposed in [156]. In addition, Wu et al. [157] proposed an asynchronous distributed algorithm for solving consensus optimization problems and proved convergence under bounded or unbounded delay assumptions.

Inspired by the limitations of the synchronous algorithm [146], we design an asynchronous distributed algorithm (AD-PDFBS) within the framework of ARock [154]. AD-PDFBS are considered as forward-backward splitting algorithm for finding zeros of a sum of monotone operators, [146] as well. The main contributions of this chapter are presented as follows:

1. A new asynchronous distributed primal-dual forward-backward splitting algorithm (AD-PDFBS) is proposed and analyzed in this chapter for a composite constrained optimization problem. However, compared with [9, 10, 49, 54, 142, 146], the proposed algorithm does not require a global clock, makes full use of local computational resources, and eliminates the idle time of waiting for the slowest agent, thus effectively improving the computational efficiency of the algorithm.
2. In contrasted to [17, 23, 50, 51], we propose an asynchronous distributed algorithm with bounded delays that each agent performs asynchronous iteration only using private data and possible delayed information from neighbors. This allows the proposed algorithm to be well applied to some real scenarios such as communication loss or packet loss.

7.2 Preliminaries

In this section, the distributed optimization problem, some preliminary definitions in the communication network, and some essential assumptions are presented.

7.2.1 Notation

Let $\mathcal{H}$ denote a real Euclidean space. Define $\mathbb{N}$ as the set of natural numbers. The notations $\langle \cdot, \cdot \rangle$ and $\|\cdot\|_2$ indicate the scalar product and the norm it induces, respectively. Define $\mathbf{1}_N = (1, \ldots, 1)^{\mathrm{T}} \in \mathcal{H}^N$. The block diagonal matrix is denoted by blkdiag $(\cdot)$. The symbols Id denotes the identity operator. For $i = 1, \ldots, N$, the symbol $\Pi_{i=1}^N C_i$ represents the Cartesian product. Define $\Gamma_0(\mathcal{H})$ as the set of proper lower semicontinuous convex functions from $\mathcal{H}$ to $(-\infty, +\infty)$. Let $f \in \Gamma_0(\mathcal{H})$, and its proximal operator associated with the symmetric positive definite matrix P is defined as $\mathrm{prox}_f^P(w) = \arg\min_{v \in \mathbb{R}^n}\{f(v) + (1/2)||w - v||_P^2\}$. For index $\lambda > 0$, its proximity operator is defined by $\mathrm{prox}_{\gamma f}(w) = \arg\min_{v \in \mathbb{R}^n}\{f(v) + (1/2\lambda)||v - w||^2\}$ and its conjugate by $f^*(w) = \sup_{v \in \mathcal{H}} \langle w, v \rangle - f(v)$. The symbol $\circ$ represents the combination of functions or operators. Let $M : \mathcal{H} \to \mathcal{H}$ be a set-valued operator. Its graph is defined as $\mathrm{gra}(M) = \{(w, v) \in \mathcal{H}^2 : v \in \mathcal{H}w\}$. M is monotone if $\forall (w, v) \in \mathcal{H}^2, \forall (y, z) \in Mw \times Mv, \langle w - v, y - z \rangle \geq 0$. It is maximal monotone if its graph is not strictly contained in the graph of any other monotone operator. Define $\mathrm{zer}(M) = \{w \in \mathcal{H} : 0 \in Mw\}$. Define ri K as the relative interior of a set K.

7.2.2 Model of Optimization Problem

Consider the composite constrained convex optimization problem as follows:

$$\begin{aligned} &\min_x \sum_{i=1}^n g_i(x_i) + u_i(x_i) + h_i(N_i x_i), \\ &\text{s.t. } K_{ij}x_i + K_{ji}x_j = b_{(i,j)}, \quad (i, j) \in \mathcal{E}, \end{aligned} \tag{7.2}$$

where $N_i : \mathbb{R}^{m_i} \to \mathbb{R}^{r_i}$ is a linear mapping, $u_i : \mathbb{R}^{m_i} \to \bar{\mathbb{R}}$ and $h_i : \mathbb{R}^{r_i} \to \bar{\mathbb{R}}$ are proper closed convex functions, $g_i : \mathbb{R}^{m_i} \to \mathbb{R}$ is convex, continuously differentiable, $K_{ij} \in \mathbb{R}^{l(i,j) \times m_i}$, $x_i \in \mathbb{R}^{m_i}$, $b_{(i,j)} \in \mathbb{R}^{l(i,j)}$, functions g_i, u_i, and $h_i \circ N_i$ are known only by agent i.

7.2.3 *Communication Network*

The interactions among agents are represented by an undirected and connected network $\mathcal{G} = \{\mathcal{V}, \mathcal{E}\}$, where $\mathcal{V} = \{1, \ldots, n\}$ denotes the vertex collection and $\mathcal{E} \subseteq \mathcal{V} \times \mathcal{V}$ is used to denote the set of interaction links. $(i, j) \in \mathcal{E}$ indicates that agent i can pass the information directly to agent j. The notation $\mathcal{N}_i$ represents the neighbor set of agent i.

Assumption 7.1 *The solution set to problem (7.2) is nonempty, and there exists* $x_i \in \mathrm{r_i\ dom}\ u_i$ *such that* $L_i x_i \in \mathrm{r_i\ dom}\ h_i$, $i \in \mathcal{V}$, *and* $K_{ij}x_i + K_{ji}x_j = b_{(i,j)}$ *for all* $(i, j) \in \mathcal{E}$.

Assumption 7.2 *The function* g_i *is* Λ_i*-Lipschitz continuous, i.e., for some* $\Lambda_i > 0$,

$$\|g_i(w) - g_i(v)\| \leq \Lambda_i \|w - v\|, \ w, v \in \mathbb{R}^{m_i}. \tag{7.3}$$

7.3 Algorithm Development

This section presents a novel asynchronous distributed algorithm (AD-PDFBS) to deal with problem (7.2). First, its synchronous version is derived from [146]. Define $\mathrm{x} = \mathrm{col}\{x_i\}_{i=1}^n$ and $\widetilde{\mathrm{x}} = \mathrm{col}\{\tilde{x}_i\}_{i=1}^n$, the linear operators $D_{(i,j)} : \mathrm{x} \to \left(K_{ij}x_i, K_{ji}x_j\right) \in \mathbb{R}^{2l_{(i,j)} \times \sum_{i=1}^n m_i}$ and $D : \mathrm{x} \to \left(D_{(i,j)}\mathrm{x}\right)_{(i,j)\in\mathcal{E}} \in \mathbb{R}^{\sum_{(i,j)\in\mathcal{E}} 2l_{(i,j)} \times \sum_{i=1}^n m_i}$. The transpose of D is $D^{\mathrm{T}} : \left(w_{(i,j)}\right)_{(i,j)\in\mathcal{E}} \mapsto \tilde{\mathrm{x}} = \sum_{(i,j)\in\mathcal{E}} D_{(i,j)}^{\mathrm{T}} w_{(i,j)}$ with $\tilde{\mathrm{x}}_i = \sum_{j\in\mathcal{N}_i} K_{ij}^{\mathrm{T}} w_{(i,j),i}$. Let $w_{(i,j)} = \left(w_{(i,j),i}, w_{(i,j),j}\right)$. Let $\Omega = \mathrm{blkdiag}\left(\left(\omega_{(i,j)} I_{2l_{(i,j)}}\right)_{(i,j)\in\mathcal{E}}\right)$, $\Xi = \mathrm{blkdiag}\left(\xi_1 I_{r_1}, \ldots, \xi_n I_{r_n}\right)$, $\Sigma = \mathrm{blkdiag}\left(\sigma_1 I_{m_1}, \ldots, \sigma_n I_{m_n}\right)$, $B = \mathrm{blkdiag}\left(\beta_1 I_{m_1}, \ldots, \beta_n I_{m_n}\right)$, and $N = \mathrm{blkdiag}$ $(N_1, \ldots, N_n)$, where I denotes the identity matrix.

From [146], by introducing an equality constraint $K_{ij}x_i + K_{ji}x_j = b_{(i,j)}$ in the set C, problem (7.2) can be written as

$$\min_{\mathrm{x}} \ G(\mathrm{x}) + U(\mathrm{x}) + H(N\mathrm{x}) + \delta_C(D\mathrm{x}), \tag{7.4}$$

where $C = \Pi_{(i,j)\in\mathcal{E}} C_{(i,j)}$. The Lagrangian of (7.4) is

$$\begin{aligned}\Lambda(\mathrm{x}, y, w) =& G(\mathrm{x}) + U(\mathrm{x}) + y^{\mathrm{T}}(N\mathrm{x}) - H^*(y) \\ &+ w^{\mathrm{T}}(D\mathrm{x}) - \delta_C^*(w),\end{aligned} \tag{7.5}$$

and its KKT condition is

$$\begin{pmatrix} 0 \\ 0 \\ 0 \end{pmatrix} \in \begin{pmatrix} \nabla G\left(\hat{x}\right) + \partial U\left(\hat{x}\right) + N^{\mathrm{T}}\hat{y} + D^{\mathrm{T}}\hat{w} \\ \partial H^{*}\left(\hat{y}\right) - N\hat{x} \\ \partial \delta_{C}^{*}\left(\hat{w}\right) - D\hat{x} \end{pmatrix}, \tag{7.6}$$

where $\hat{v} = \left(\hat{x}, \hat{y}, \hat{w}\right)$ is the optimal solution to (7.5). Furthermore, we can obtain the following iteration (For details, please see [146]):

$$\begin{aligned} \tilde{x}^{k} &= \mathrm{prox}_{U}^{\Sigma}\left(x^{k} - \Sigma\nabla G(x^{k}) - \Sigma N^{\mathrm{T}} y^{k} - \Sigma(D^{\mathrm{T}}w)\right), \\ \tilde{y}^{k} &= \mathrm{prox}_{H^{*}}^{\Xi}\left(y^{k} + \Xi N(2\tilde{x}^{k+1} - x^{k})\right), \\ \tilde{w}^{k} &= \mathrm{prox}_{\delta_{C}^{*}}^{\Omega}\left(w^{k} + \Omega D(2\tilde{x}^{k+1} - x^{k})\right), \\ x^{k+1} &= (1-\rho^{k})x^{k} + \rho^{k}\tilde{x}^{k}, \\ y^{k+1} &= (1-\rho^{k})y^{k} + \rho^{k}\tilde{y}^{k}, \\ w^{k+1} &= (1-\rho^{k})w^{k} + \rho^{k}\tilde{w}^{k}. \end{aligned} \tag{7.7}$$

In addition, (7.7) can be rewritten as a krasnosel'skii-mann iteration:

$$v^{k+1} = v^{k} + \rho^{k}\left(Tv^{k} - v^{k}\right), \tag{7.8}$$

where $v^{k} = \left(x^{k}, y^{k}, w^{k}\right)$, $T = \left(Id + P^{-1} \circ S\right)^{-1} \circ \left(Id - P^{-1} \circ Q\right)$ with

$$P = \begin{pmatrix} \Sigma^{-1} & -N^{\mathrm{T}} & -D^{\mathrm{T}} \\ -N & \Xi^{-1} & 0 \\ -D & 0 & \Omega^{-1} \end{pmatrix}, \tag{7.9}$$

$$S = \begin{pmatrix} \partial U\left(x\right) + N^{\mathrm{T}}y + D^{\mathrm{T}}w \\ -Nx + \partial H^{*}\left(y\right) \\ -Dx + \partial \delta_{C}^{*}\left(w\right) \end{pmatrix}, Q = \begin{pmatrix} \nabla G\left(x\right) \\ 0 \\ 0 \end{pmatrix}. \tag{7.10}$$

Assume that the matrix P is positive definite by setting proper step sizes ([146], Theorem 1). We further show that for any fixed-point of T in (7.8) coincides with the solution to $0 \in (S + Q)$, since the following holds:

$$\begin{aligned} v \in \mathrm{fix}\left(T\right) &\Leftrightarrow v = Tv \\ &\Leftrightarrow v = \left(Id + P^{-1} \circ S\right)^{-1} \circ \left(Id - P^{-1} \circ Q\right)v \end{aligned}$$

$$\Leftrightarrow Pv - Qv \in Pv + Sv$$
$$\Leftrightarrow 0 \in (S + Q)\,. \tag{7.11}$$

Therefore, one has $\mathrm{fix}\,(T) = \mathrm{zer}\,(S + Q)$. The following proposition characterizes $0 \in (S + Q)$.

Proposition 7.1 *For any* $\mathrm{col}\,(\hat{x}, \hat{y}, \hat{w}) \in \mathrm{zer}\,(S + Q)$ *in* (7.10), *one has that* $\hat{x}$, $\hat{y}$ *and* $\hat{w}$ *satisfy the KKT condition* (7.6) *and* $\hat{x}$ *is the optimal solution to problem* (7.2).

Proof Assume that $\mathrm{col}\,(\hat{x}, \hat{y}, \hat{w}) \in \mathrm{zer}\,(S + Q)$. Based on the definitions of S and Q in (7.10), one gets

$$\begin{pmatrix} \partial U & N^{\mathrm{T}} & D^{\mathrm{T}} \\ -N & \partial H^{*} & 0 \\ -D & 0 & \partial \delta_C^{*} \end{pmatrix} \begin{pmatrix} \hat{x} \\ \hat{y} \\ \hat{w} \end{pmatrix} + \begin{pmatrix} \nabla G\,(\hat{x}) \\ 0 \\ 0 \end{pmatrix} = \begin{pmatrix} 0 \\ 0 \\ 0 \end{pmatrix}. \tag{7.12}$$

Comparing (7.12) with (7.6), we have that $\hat{x}$, $\hat{y}$ and $\hat{w}$ satisfy the KKT condition (7.6) and $\hat{x}$ is the optimal solution to problem (7.2). ■

Algorithm 9 AD-PDFBS

Input : $x_i^0 \in \mathbb{R}^{m_i}$, $y_i^0 \in \mathbb{R}^{r_i}$, $w_{(i,j),i}^0 \in \mathbb{R}^{l(i,j)}$, $\sigma_i > 0$, $\tau_i > 0$, and $\omega_{(i,j)} > 0$, $j \in \mathcal{N}_i$.
Iterations : Agent i_k is activated at time k and the local variables are updated as follows:

$$\begin{aligned}
\tilde{x}_{i_k}^k =& \mathrm{prox}_{\sigma_{i_k} U_{i_k}}(x_{i_k}^{k-\iota_{i_k}^k} - \sigma_{i_k} \nabla G_{i_k}(x_{i_k}^{k-\iota_{i_k}^k}) - \sigma_{i_k} N_{i_k}^{\mathrm{T}} y_{i_k}^{k-\iota_{i_k}^k} \\
& - \sigma_{i_k} \sum_{j \in \mathcal{N}_{i_k}} K_{i_k j}^{\mathrm{T}} w_{(i_k,j),i_k}^{k-\iota_{i_k}^k}), \\
\tilde{y}_{i_k}^k =& \mathrm{prox}_{\xi_{i_k} H_{i_k}^*}(y_{i_k}^{k-\iota_{i_k}^k} + \xi_{i_k} N_{i_k}(2\tilde{x}_{i_k}^k - x_{i_k}^{k-\iota_{i_k}^k})), \\
\tilde{w}_{(i_n,j),i_k}^k =& \frac{1}{2}(w_{(i_k,j),i_k}^{k-\iota_{i_k}^k} + w_{(i_k,j),j}^{k-\iota_j^k}) + \frac{\omega(i_k,j)}{2}(K_{i_k j}(2\tilde{x}_{i_k}^k - x_{i_k}^{k-\iota_{i_k}^k}) \\
& + K_{j i_k}(2\tilde{x}_j^k - x_j^{k-\iota_j^k}) + b_{(i_k,j)}), \\
x_{i_k}^{k+1} =& x_{i_k}^{k-\iota_{i_k}^k} + \rho^k(\tilde{x}_{i_k}^k - x_{i_k}^{k-\iota_{i_k}^k}), \\
y_{i_k}^{k+1} =& x_{i_k}^{k-\iota_{i_k}^k} + \rho^k(\tilde{x}_{i_k}^k - x_{i_k}^{k-\iota_{i_k}^k}), \\
w_{(i_k,j),i_k}^{k+1} =& w_{(i_k,j),i_k}^{k-\iota_{i_k}^k} + \rho^k(\tilde{w}_{(i_k,j),i_k}^k - w_{(i_k,j),i_k}^{k-\iota_{i_k}^k}).
\end{aligned}$$

Transfer $x_{i_k}^{k+1}$, $y_{i_k}^{k+1}$, and $w_{(i_k,j),i_k}^{k+1}$ to its neighbors.

For the synchronous algorithm, the next update will be performed only if all agents complete the current iteration. Therefore, the slowest updated agent may bring the system down. In the proposed algorithm (AD-PDFBS), each agent performs local computation and communicates with its neighbors independently without any clock coordination, making full use of local computational resources and eliminating the idle time of waiting for the slowest agent. Whenever any agent ends its variable update, the iteration counter is added by one. In the next section, we detail the development of the proposed asynchronous algorithm. For a concrete form of the asynchronous algorithm, see Algorithm 9.

7.4 Convergence Analysis

This section describes the convergence of AD-PDFBS. First, we proved that T is the average operator. Then, the AD-PDFBS can be transformed into a fixed-point iteration employing the averaging operator T. In addition, a nonexpansive operator is constructed, which lays the foundation for the convergence of AD-PDFBS. Finally, the results in [154] can be employed.

We can obtain the result of the following lemma by using [146].

Lemma 7.2 ([146]) *$P^{-1} \circ S$ is a maximally monotone operator, $P^{-1} \circ Q$ is θ-cocoercive.*

Next, T is proved to be an average operator.

Lemma 7.3 ([145], Theorem 3) $T_1 = \left(Id + P^{-1} \circ S\right)^{-1} \in \mathcal{A}\left(\frac{1}{2}\right)$, $T_2 = Id - P^{-1} \circ Q \in A\left(1/2\theta\right)$ *([22], Corollary 23.8, Proposition 4.33). Hence,* $T = T_1 \circ T_2 \in 2\theta/(4\theta - 1)$ *is an averaged operator.*

The asynchronous iteration mechanism is similar to (7.8), except that at each iteration, one randomly activated agent i updates its local variables x_i, y_i, and w_i. To clarify this concept mathematically, we introduce a diagonal matrix $\aleph_i$ with 0–1 diagonal elements. When the j-th term of $v = \mathrm{col}\,(x, y, w)$ is a term of $\mathrm{col}\,(x_i, y_i, w_i)$, $[\aleph_i]_{jj} = 1$ and 0 otherwise. We call $\aleph_i$ the activation matrix, which is utilized to select the coordinates to be updated. We assume that each agent performs the update is determined by an i.i.d. random variable ζ^k, taking values in $\aleph = \{\aleph_i\}_{i \in \mathcal{N}}$. Let $P\left(\zeta^k = \aleph_i\right) = 1/n$, $i = 1, \ldots, n$ obey a uniform distribution. Then, iteration (7.8) can be converted to a randomized block-coordinate fixed-point iteration as follows:

$$v^{k+1} = v^k + \rho^k \zeta^k \left(T v^k - v^k\right). \tag{7.13}$$

The delay information is not considered in equality (7.13). It requires that the computation and communication are almost instantaneous at each iteration. Agents can only wait at the end of the current iteration before proceeding to the next iteration. To avoid this situation, we introduce delayed information in evaluating T. Denote ι_i^k as the delays of agent i at iteration k. Then, the asynchronous iteration of (7.13) ends up in the following form:

$$v^{k+1} = v^k + \rho^k \zeta^k \left(T\hat{v}^k - v^k\right). \tag{7.14}$$

Assumption 7.3 *The maximum delay per iteration is bounded, i.e.,*

$$\sup_k \max_{i\in\mathcal{N}} \left\{\iota_i^k\right\} \le \varphi.$$

Based on Assumption 7.3, the convergence of Algorithm 1 is shown as follows.

Theorem 7.4 *Suppose that Assumption 7.3 holds. Let* $0 < \rho^k < (4\theta - 1)/2\theta(1 + 2\varphi\sqrt{n})$*. Then, the sequence* $(v_k)_{k\in\mathbb{N}}$ *generated by Algorithm 9 converges to* $\hat{v}$.

Proof Combining Lemma 7.2 and the definition of the averaged operator, one has

$$T = \left(1 - \frac{2\theta}{4\theta - 1}\right) Id + \frac{2\theta}{4\theta - 1}\tilde{T}, \tag{7.15}$$

where $\tilde{T}$ is a nonexpansive operator and $\operatorname{fix}(T) = \operatorname{fix}(\tilde{T})$. Then using equality (7.14), we get

$$\begin{aligned} v^{k+1} &= v^k + \rho^k \zeta^k \left(T\hat{v}^k - v^k\right) \\ &= v^k + \rho^k \zeta^k \left(\left(\left(1 - \frac{2\theta}{4\theta - 1}\right)\hat{v}^k + \frac{2\theta}{4\theta - 1}\tilde{T}\hat{v}^k\right) - v^k\right) \\ &= v^k + \rho^k \zeta^k \left(\frac{2\theta}{4\theta - 1}\left(\tilde{T}\hat{v}^k - \hat{v}^k\right) + \hat{v}^k - v^k\right). \end{aligned} \tag{7.16}$$

Note that $x_{i_k}^{k-\iota_{i_k}^k} = x_{i_k}^{k-\iota_{i_k}^k+1} = \cdots = x_{i_k}^k$ and the similar relations for $y_{i_k}^{k+1}$ and $w_{(i_k,j),i_k}^{k+1}$. We have $\zeta^k\left(\hat{v}^k - v^k\right) = 0$. Thus, equality (7.16) is rewritten as

$$v^{k+1} = v^k + \frac{2\theta}{4\theta - 1}\rho^k \zeta^k \left(\tilde{T}\hat{v}^k - \hat{v}^k\right). \tag{7.17}$$

Notice that iteration (7.17) conforms to the algorithmic framework proposed by [154]. Based on Lemma 13 and Theorem 14 in [154], it can be shown that v^k generated by (7.17) is bounded and v^k converges to a random variable $\hat{v}$ that gets its value in the fixed-points of $\tilde{T}$ if $0 < \rho^k < (4\theta - 1)/2\theta\left(1 + 2\varphi\sqrt{n}\right)$. In addition, we have $\operatorname{fix}(\tilde{T}) = \operatorname{fix}(T) = \operatorname{zer}(S + Q)$. Therefore, $\hat{v}$ satisfies the KKT condition (7.6) by using Proposition 7.1. ■

7.5 Numerical Experiments

Experimental results are given in this section to elucidate the effectiveness of the proposed asynchronous distributed algorithm (AD-PDFBS).

We consider the problem of formation control of a group of robots [62, 63]. Each robot has its own states $x_i = \left(q_{x_i}, q_{y_i}, u_{x_i}, u_{y_i}\right)$, where $\left(q_{x_i}, q_{y_i}\right)$ and $\left(u_{x_i}, u_{y_i}\right)$ represent the position and the velocity vectors, respectively. For each system, the input is $v_i = \left(u^v_{x_i}, u^v_{y_i}\right)$ and the discrete-time LTI model is shown as follows:

$$x_i\left(k+1\right) = \Theta_i x_i\left(k\right) + \Psi_i v_i\left(k\right), \quad k = 0, 1, \ldots.$$

The state and input transition matrices Θ_i and Ψ_i are as follows:

$$\Theta_i = \begin{pmatrix} I & 0 & X_1 & 0 \\ 0 & I & 0 & X_1 \\ 0 & 0 & X_2 & 0 \\ 0 & 0 & 0 & X_2 \end{pmatrix}, \quad \Psi_i = \begin{pmatrix} X_3 & 0 \\ 0 & X_3 \\ X_1 & 0 \\ 0 & X_1 \end{pmatrix}, \tag{7.18}$$

where $X_1 = -t_d\left(e^{-1/t_d} - 1\right)$, $X_2 = e^{-1/t_d}$ and $X_3 = t_d^2\left(e^{-1/t_d} - 1 + 1/t_d\right)$ with time constant $t_d = 5\,(s)$.

Define N as the horizon length. The optimization problem is illustrated as:

$$\begin{aligned} \min_{\mathbf{x}_i, \mathbf{v}_i} r & \sum_{i=1}^{m} \frac{1}{2}\|\Delta_i \mathbf{x}_i - q_i\|^2 + \sum_{i=1}^{m} \frac{1}{2}\|\Phi_i \mathbf{v}_i - t_i\|^2 \\ & + \sum_{i=1}^{m} \sum_{j\in\mathcal{N}_i} \frac{\gamma_i}{2}\left\|\mathcal{L}\left(\mathbf{x}_i - \mathbf{x}_j\right) - d_{ij}\right\|^2, \\ \text{s.t.} \quad & \mathcal{K}_i \mathbf{x}_i + \mathcal{A}_i \mathbf{v}_i = b_i, \ \mathbf{x}_i \in \mathcal{X}_i, \ \mathbf{v}_i \in \mathcal{V}_i, \quad i = 1, \ldots, m, \end{aligned} \tag{7.19}$$

where $\mathbf{x}_i = \left(x_i\left(1\right), \ldots, x_i\left(N\right)\right) \in \mathbb{R}^{4N}$, $\mathbf{v}_i = \left(v_i\left(0\right), \ldots, v_i\left(N-1\right)\right) \in \mathbb{R}^{2N}$, Δ_i and Φ_i are input and state cost matrices, $\mathcal{K}_i \mathbf{x}_i + \mathcal{A}_i \mathbf{v}_i = b_i$ denotes the dynamics of each agent, the relative desired distance between an agent i and its neighbor j is denoted by d_{ij}, $\mathcal{L}$ is a proper linear mapping, and γ_i is the scalar weight.

We use the local variable $\mathbf{x}_{ij}$ to denote the estimate of agent i for $\mathbf{x}_j$, $j \in \mathcal{N}_i$. Redefine $\mathbf{x}_i$ and $\mathbf{v}_i$ as $\mathbf{x}_{ii}$ and $\mathbf{v}_{ii}$, respectively. Denote the stacked vector $z_{\mathcal{N}_i} = \left((\mathbf{x}_{ij})_{j\in\mathcal{N}_i\cup\{i\}}, \mathbf{v}_{ii}\right) \in \mathbb{R}^{n_i}$, where $n_i = 4N\left(|\mathcal{N}_i| + 1\right) + 2N$. Let $E_i z_{\mathcal{N}_i} = \mathcal{K}_i \mathbf{x}_{ii} + \mathcal{A}_i \mathbf{v}_{ii}$ in the set $\mathcal{D}_i$, where E_i is a linear mapping. Denote $L_i z_{\mathcal{N}_i} = (\mathbf{x}_{ii}, \mathbf{v}_{ii})$, $\mathcal{Z}_i = \mathcal{X}_i \times \mathcal{V}_i$, and

$$g_i\left(z_{\mathcal{N}_i}\right) = \frac{1}{2}\|\Delta_i \mathbf{x}_{ii} - q_i\|^2 + \frac{1}{2}\|\Phi_i \mathbf{v}_{ii} - t_i\|^2 + \frac{\gamma_i}{2} \sum_{j\in\mathcal{N}_i} \left\|\mathcal{L}\left(\mathbf{x}_{ii} - \mathbf{x}_{ij}\right) - d_{ij}\right\|^2.$$

We have

$$\min_{z_{\mathcal{N}_i}} \sum_{i=1}^{m} g_i\left(z_{\mathcal{N}_i}\right) + \delta_{D_i}\left(z_{\mathcal{N}_i}\right) + \delta_{Z_i}\left(L_i z_{\mathcal{N}_i}\right),$$
$$\text{s.t.}\quad R_{ij} z_{\mathcal{N}_i} + R_{ji} z_{\mathcal{N}_j} = 0\ (i,\ j) \in \mathcal{E}, \tag{7.20}$$

where $R_{ij} z_{\mathcal{N}_i} = \left(x_{ii}, -x_{ij}\right)$ for $i < j$ and $R_{ij} z_{\mathcal{N}_i} = (-x_{ii}, x_{ij})$, otherwise. Therefore, we apply Algorithm 9 to solve this problem in an asynchronous manner. In our experiment, $m = 4$, $N = 4$, $q_i, t_i = 0$, $\gamma_i = 10$, $p_{x_i} = p_{y_i} \in [0, 20]$, $v_{x_i}, v_{y_i} \in [0, 15]$, $\Delta_i = 0.1I$, $\Phi_i = I$ for $i = 1, 2$ and $\Phi_i = 2I$, otherwise. The step sizes are set as $\omega_{(i,j)} = 3$, $\xi_i = 0.1$, $\sigma_i = 0.99/(\beta_i/2 + \xi_i + \sum_{j \in \mathcal{N}_i} \omega_{(i,j)})$. Figure 7.1 exhibits the trajectory of the robots, where four robots are reorganized from a line to a shape of 8. Figure 7.2 depicts the better performance of asynchronous over synchronous counterpart.

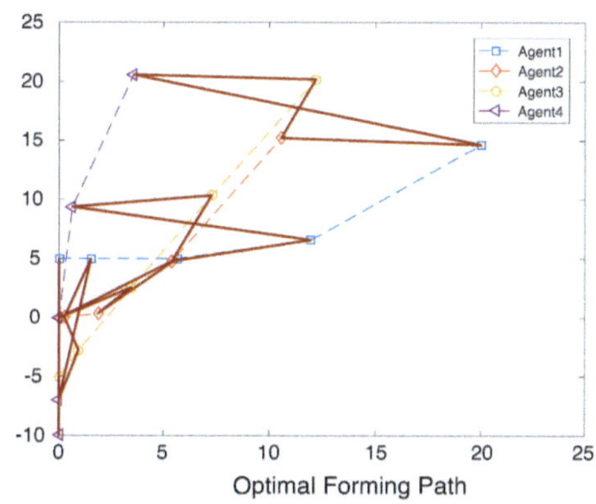

Fig. 7.1 Robot formation trajectory

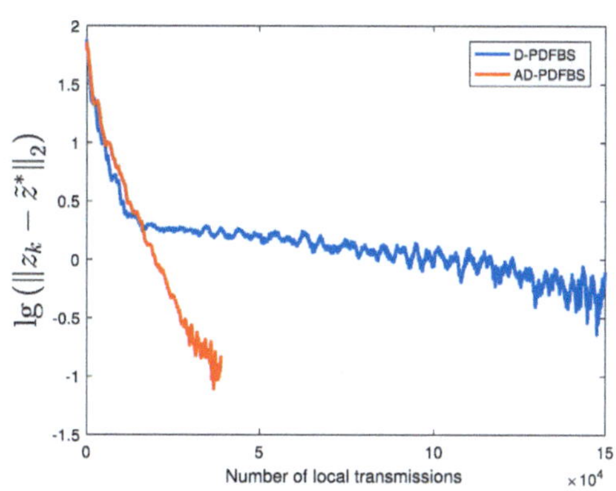

Fig. 7.2 Evolutions of residual with number of local transmissions

7.6 Conclusion

A new asynchronous distributed algorithm has been presented to solve composite constrained convex optimization problems. The agents could work asynchronously with each other without a central coordinator, i.e., they could compute and communicate uncoordinatedly. Their updates depend on outdated information from their neighbors. Further, we have proven the convergence of AD-PDFBS using the theory of randomized fixed-point iteration of nonexpansive operators with delayed information. Finally, experimental results have verified the performance and convergence of AD-PDFBS.

Chapter 8
Distributed Model Predictive Control Algorithm for Optimal Output Consensus of High-Order Multi-agent Systems

Abstract Considering the extensive applications of the model predictive control (MPC), this chapter investigates the MPC problem with an application to the optimal output consensus of high-order multi-agent systems. A synchronous distributed optimization algorithm for the MPC problem is proposed, and we further devise its asynchronous version. The algorithm allows agents to choose the uncoordinate step sizes depending on local information, which improves the flexibility of multi-agent systems. The convergence of the proposed algorithm is guaranteed if the positive uncoordinate step sizes satisfy the explicit conditions. Compared with the synchronous version that needs a global clock to control all agents for communication and update, the asynchronous algorithm does not require each agent in the multi-agent systems to update and communicate simultaneously, and also converges to the optimal global solution to the problem. The numerical simulations demonstrate the availability of the proposed algorithm and the validity of the theoretical results.

Keywords Distributed optimization · Model predictive control · Optimal control · Output consensus · Multi-agent systems

8.1 Introduction

In the past decades, model predictive control (MPC) has played an essential role in many application areas, including optimal dynamic resource allocation [158], cost-optimal operation [159], fuel cost minimization [160], unmanned aerial vehicle formation flight, and aerospace applications. The earliest theory and application of MPC can be traced back to a series of works that arose in the 1970s [161, 162]. MPC refers to a type of control algorithms that employs a given process model to predict a system's future behavior [163, 164]. As a closed-loop approach, one advantage of MPC is that MPC achieves better performance during a relatively long period when interferences possibly occur [165]. In the background of MPC, the control problem is usually formulated as a dynamic optimization problem [166]. Therefore, some optimization algorithms can solve the MPC problem [85, 167, 168].

H. Li et al., *Network-System Research and Distributed Composite Algorithm Design*, Computational Intelligence Methods and Applications,
https://doi.org/10.1007/978-981-95-0911-9_8

Considering that distributed optimization has received the attention of numerous scholars and has been successfully applied in various scientific fields [17, 102, 151, 152, 169–175], a natural idea is to use distributed optimization algorithms to solve the distributed MPC problem. In the distributed situation, multiple agents collaboratively solve the distributed MPC problem, which is modeled as a group of local objective functions. However, not all of the distributed optimization algorithms can solve the distributed MPC problem. The main challenge lies in guaranteeing exactly satisfying global coupled constraints in a distributed manner. To address this problem, the algorithms proposed in [92, 115, 176, 177] are supposed to access the complete information of the global system, which is unrealistic in the distributed MPC problem. In [85], Mota et al. investigated the distributed optimization problem and proposed an algorithm for the distributed MPC problem and the network flow problem, where the convergence was guaranteed if the network was bipartite or the objective functions are strongly convex. A non-iterative distributed MPC scheme for spatially interconnected systems was presented in [178] by investigating the cost function switching strategy. With cost-switching, the stability of the global system was confirmed by the terminal decoupled MPC law that did not require compatibility constraints. Trodden et al. [179] developed a tube-based distributed MPC algorithm, where the rationale of the approach lied in the optimization of the input and state constraint sets to minimize the joint disturbances between subsystems. By constructing auxiliary predictive inputs of neighbors for each agent at update time, a distributed MPC algorithm is developed for a group of nonlinear second-order systems to track a dynamic reference system [180], and then the literature [181] extended the results to an event-triggered mechanism. Moreover, Shi et al. [64] put forward a two-stage optimization method for the distributed MPC problem to achieve an output consensus at equilibrium points for each agent.

It should be noted that the above algorithms for the MPC problem are synchronous, which means that there needs to be a global clock to control the multi-agent system so that all agents can communicate and update at the same time. The global clock only issues new communication and update instructions after all agents have completed their tasks. This makes the agent that completes the task first will spend unnecessary time waiting for the agent with poor performance. Thus, this chapter will provide a distributed asynchronous algorithm for MPC problems. In addition, we propose an idea to utilize the penalty function to convert the model predictive control problem with multiple complex constraints into a distributed optimization problem which can be solved by the distributed algorithms. This will provide new ideas for the distributed solution of model predictive control.

Therefore, a distributed MPC algorithm is proposed and applied to the distributed optimal output consensus problem of the high-order multi-agent system in this chapter. The main contributions are summarized as follows:

(i) We present an analysis method to transform the general distributed MPC problem into a special optimization problem, which is made up of a convex function with Lipschitz-continuous and two closed and convex functions (possibly nonsmooth).

(ii) We propose a synchronous distributed optimization algorithm and further devise its asynchronous version to solve the MPC problem. Comparing with the synchronous version that needs a global clock to control all agents to communicate and update simultaneously, the asynchronous algorithm allows each agent to update the variables and communicate among its neighbor agents with a positive probability in the current time instant, which immensely improves the robustness of the multi-agent system.

(iii) We give the ranges of uncoordinated step sizes, which ensure the convergence of the proposed algorithm and improve the flexibility of all agents. This releases the limitation that all networked agents need to the same step sizes.

8.2 Preliminaries

8.2.1 Notation

All vectors are viewed as column vectors. We apply $\|\cdot\|$ for both vectors and matrices, in the former case, $\|\cdot\|$ represents the Euclidean norm, whereas in the latter case, it is the spectral norm. We write x^{T} and A^{T} to indicate the transpose of a vector x and a matrix A. We write blkdiag(A, B) to denote a block-diagonal matrix with diagonal elements given by matrices A and B. Let $\otimes$ denote the Kronecker product. The notation $\mathbf{1}_n$ indicates the n-dimensional vector of ones. I and $\mathbf{0}$ represent the identity matrix and zero matrix with proper dimensions. $g^*(\cdot)$ is utilized to indicate the Fenchel conjugate of function $g(\cdot)$, i.e., $g^*(a) := \sup_b \{\langle a, b\rangle - f(b)\}$. Proximal mapping of f relative to $\|\cdot\|_V$ is defined as $\mathrm{prox}_f^V(x) := \arg\min_{z\in\mathbb{R}^n} \left\{ f(z) + \frac{1}{2}\|x - z\|_V^2 \right\}$. The distance from a nonempty closed convex set, X, is denoted by $d(\cdot, X)$.

8.2.2 Model of Optimization Problem

For all $l \geq 0$, each agent i has a discrete-time dynamic given by

$$x^i(l+1) = A_i x^i(l) + B_i u^i(l), \, i \in \mathcal{V} \tag{8.1}$$

where $x^i(l) \in \mathbb{R}^{n_i}$ is the state, $u^i(l) \in \mathbb{R}^{m_i}$ is the control input, $A_i \in \mathbb{R}^{n_i\times n_i}$ is the state matrices, and $B_i \in \mathbb{R}^{n_i\times m_i}$ is the input matrices which is assumed to have full column rank with $n_i \geq m_i$, respectively. Defining $x = \left[(x^1)^{\mathrm{T}}, \cdots, (x^m)^{\mathrm{T}}\right]^{\mathrm{T}}$ with $x^i = \left[(x^i(0|t))^{\mathrm{T}}, \cdots, (x^i(T|t))^{\mathrm{T}}\right]^{\mathrm{T}}$ and $u = \left[(u^1)^{\mathrm{T}}, \cdots, (u^m)^{\mathrm{T}}\right]^{\mathrm{T}}$ with $u^i =$

$\left[\left(u^i(0|t)\right)^{\mathrm{T}}, \cdots, \left(u^i(T-1|t)\right)^{\mathrm{T}}\right]^{\mathrm{T}}$, the aim of the distributed MPC is to predict the future behavior of the system and determine proper control inputs to optimize a performance index over a finite horizon as follows:

$$
\begin{aligned}
\min_{x,u} \quad & \sum_{i=1}^{m}\sum_{l=0}^{T-1} \tilde{F}_i\left(x^i(l|t), u^i(l|t)\right) + \sum_{i=1}^{m} F_i\left(x^i(T|t)\right), \\
\text{s.t.} \quad & x^i(l+1|t) = A_i x^i(l|t) + B_i u^i(l|t), \quad i \in \mathcal{V}, \\
& x^i(l|t) \in \mathcal{X}_i, \quad i \in \mathcal{V}, \\
& u^i(l|t) \in \mathcal{U}_i, \quad i \in \mathcal{V},
\end{aligned}
\tag{8.2}
$$

where T represents the predictive horizon, $x^i(l|t)$ and $u^i(l|t)$ are the state and control input of agent i at time instant l after time t, $|t$ will be omitted if no confusion arises, and $\mathcal{X}^i$ and $\mathcal{U}^i$ are the convex constraint sets for local state and control inputs, $\tilde{F}_i(\cdot)$ is the convex stage cost function, and $F_i(\cdot)$ is the terminal cost function, respectively.

8.2.3 Communication Network

Consider an undirected graph $\mathcal{G} = (\mathcal{V}, \mathcal{E})$ consisting of a nonempty finite agent set $\mathcal{V} = \{v_1, v_2, \cdots, v_m\}$ and an edge set $\mathcal{E} \subseteq \mathcal{V} \times \mathcal{V}$. We employ (i, j) to denote the unordered pair of agents i and j. Agent i can communicate with agent j if and only if $(i, j) \in \mathcal{E}$.

Assumption 8.1 *The undirected graph $\mathcal{G} = (\mathcal{V}, \mathcal{E})$ is connected.*

8.2.4 High-Order Multi-agent System

Motivated by Ren et al. [182], He and Cao [183], Xin and Cheng [184], Olfati-Saber et al. [185], the literature [186] proposed a high-order multi-agent system as follows:

$$
\begin{aligned}
x^{i,0}(l+1) &= x^{i,0}(l) + \eta_i x^{i,1}(l), \\
&\vdots \\
x^{i,s_i-2}(l+1) &= x^{i,s_i-2}(l) + \eta_i x^{i,s_i-1}(l), \\
x^{i,s_i-1}(l+1) &= x^{i,s_i-1}(l) + \zeta_i u^i(l),
\end{aligned}
\tag{8.3}
$$

where $i \in \mathcal{V}$, $\eta_i > 0$ and $\zeta_i > 0$ are step sizes, $x^{i,\rho}(l) \in \mathbb{R}^{\gamma_i}$, $\rho = 0, \cdots, s_i - 1$, are the ρ-th order states of agent i. Defining $x^i(l) = [(x^{i,0}(l))^{\mathrm{T}}, \cdots, (x^{i,s_i-1}(l))^{\mathrm{T}}]^{\mathrm{T}}$, we can rewrite (8.3) in a compact form as $x^i(l+1) = A_i x^i(l) + B_i u^i(l)$, where $i \in \mathcal{V}$,

$$A_i = \left(I + \begin{bmatrix} 0 & \eta_i & 0 & 0 \\ 0 & 0 & \ddots & 0 \\ 0 & 0 & 0 & \eta_i \\ 0 & 0 & 0 & 0 \end{bmatrix} \right) \otimes I \text{ and } B_i = \begin{bmatrix} 0 \\ \vdots \\ 0 \\ \zeta_i \end{bmatrix} \otimes I \tag{8.4}$$

Remark 8.1 Early consensus methods mainly focus on first-order agent systems. However, there is a broad class of systems that cannot be expressed by first-order models [185, 187, 188]. For example, when the control inputs of agents are forces or torques, it is necessary to consider second-order dynamics [189–191]. Moreover, there are many systems and vehicles such as unmanned helicopters and car-like mobile robots whose input-output relationship should be described as the high-order agent systems [192, 193]. To make the results of this chapter applicable to model predictive control problems in more situations, we study the high-order multi-agent system which has been widely studied in [194–201]. For example, a single link flexible joint manipulator is well modeled by a fourth-order nonlinear system [201]. Besides, the jerk (i.e., derivative of acceleration) systems, described by third order differential equations, are of particular interest in mechanical engineering. (These systems can be regarded as special cases of the high-order agent system (8.3).) Due to the high-order system (8.3) generalizing numerous applications of interest [200–205], we use the high-order system (8.3) to model multi-agent systems.

8.2.5 Optimal Output Consensus

Considering an output, $y^i(l) = C_i x^i(l)$, $i \in \mathcal{V}$, of the dynamic (8.1), we get a high-order multi-agent system containing a group of agents with heterogeneous dynamics described by

$$\begin{aligned} x^i(l+1) &= A_i x^i(l) + B_i u^i(l), i \in \mathcal{V}, \\ y^i(l) &= C_i x^i(l), \quad i \in \mathcal{V}, \end{aligned} \tag{8.5}$$

where $C_i \in \mathbb{R}^{r \times n_i}$. The goal of distributed output consensus is employing local communication among each agent i with its neighbor agents, $\mathcal{N}_i$, to design proper control input, $u^i(l)$, $l \geq 0$, such that $\lim_{l \to \infty} \left\| y^i(l) - y^j(l) \right\| = 0$, $\forall i, j \in \mathcal{V}$. We define the set of all possible outputs of (8.5) at state and control equilibrium pairs as follows:

$$\begin{aligned}\Theta := \Big\{ \hat{y} \in \mathbb{R}^r \,|\, \exists \hat{x}^i \in \mathcal{X}_i, \hat{u}^i \in \mathcal{U}_i, \text{ such that} \\ \hat{x}^i = A_i \hat{x}^i + B_i \hat{u}^i, C_i \hat{x}^i = \hat{y}, i \in \mathcal{V} \Big\},\end{aligned} \tag{8.6}$$

where $\hat{x}^i$, $\hat{u}^i$, and $\hat{y}^i$ are the state, the control input, and the control output of the equilibrium points.

For the multi-agent system, the aim of output consensus is to make the output, y^i, of each agent i converge to $\hat{y}$. Denoting $\left[\left(\hat{x}^1\right)^{\mathrm{T}}, \cdots, \left(\hat{x}^m\right)^{\mathrm{T}}\right]^{\mathrm{T}}$ by $\hat{x}$, we will get the optimal output consensus point y^* by solving the distributed MPC problem as follows:

$$\begin{aligned}
\min_{\hat{x},x,u} \quad & \sum_{i=1}^{m} \sum_{l=0}^{T-1} \tilde{F}_i \left(\tilde{x}^i (l|t), \tilde{u}^i (l|t)\right) + \sum_{i=1}^{m} F_i \left(\tilde{x}^i (T|t)\right), \\
\text{s.t.} \quad & x^i (l+1|t) = A_i x^i (l|t) + B_i u^i (l|t), i \in \mathcal{V} \\
& \tilde{x}^i (l|t) = x^i (l|t) - \hat{x}^i, i \in \mathcal{V}, \\
& \tilde{u}^i (l|t) = u^i (l|t) - \hat{u}^i, i \in \mathcal{V}, \\
& \tilde{x}^i (l|t) \in \tilde{\mathcal{X}}_i, i \in \mathcal{V}, \\
& x^i (l|t) \in \mathcal{X}_i, i \in \mathcal{V}, \\
& u^i (l|t) \in \mathcal{U}_i, i \in \mathcal{V}, \\
& x^i (0|t) = x^i (t), i \in \mathcal{V}, \\
& \hat{x}^i = A_i \hat{x}^i + B_i \hat{u}^i \in \hat{\mathcal{X}}_i, i \in \mathcal{V}, \\
& \hat{u}^i \in \hat{\mathcal{U}}_i, i \in \mathcal{V}, \\
& C_i \hat{x}^i = \hat{y} \in \Theta, i \in \mathcal{V}.
\end{aligned} \tag{8.7}$$

Define the notations, $\hat{x}^*$, x^*, and u^*, as the optimal solution to problem (8.7). The convex stage cost function and the terminal cost function for agent i at $l \geq 0$ are defined as:

$$\tilde{F}_i \left(\tilde{x}^i (l), \tilde{u}^i (l)\right) = \tilde{x}^i (l)^{\mathrm{T}} \mathcal{Q}_i \tilde{x}^i (l) + \tilde{u}^i (l)^{\mathrm{T}} \mathcal{R}_i \tilde{u}^i (l), \tag{8.8}$$

and

$$F_i \left(\tilde{x}^i (T)\right) = \tilde{x}^i (T)^{\mathrm{T}} \mathcal{P}_i \tilde{x}^i (T), \tag{8.9}$$

where $i \in \mathcal{V}$, $\mathbf{0} < \mathcal{Q}_i \in \mathbb{R}^{n_i \times n_i}$, $\mathbf{0} < \mathcal{R}_i \in \mathbb{R}^{m_i \times m_i}$, and $\mathcal{P}_i$ is the solution of the equation $\mathcal{P}_i = A_i^{\mathrm{T}} \mathcal{P}_i A_i + \mathcal{Q}_i - A_i^{\mathrm{T}} \mathcal{P}_i B_i \left(\mathcal{R}_i + B_i^{\mathrm{T}} \mathcal{P}_i B_i\right)^{-1} B_i^{\mathrm{T}} \mathcal{P}_i A_i$ [64].

8.3 Algorithm Development

8.3.1 Distributed Optimization Algorithm

Recalling that $x^i(l+1) = A_i x^i(l) + B_i u^i(l)$ and $\hat{x}^i = A_i \hat{x}^i + B_i \hat{u}^i$, for all $l > 0$ and $i \in \mathcal{V}$, one has that

$$A_i^{-l} x^i(l) - \sum_{\varepsilon=0}^{l-1} A_i^{-(\varepsilon+1)} B_i u^i(\varepsilon) = x^i(0), \tag{8.10}$$

and

$$\left(B_i^{\mathrm{T}} B_i\right)^{-1} B_i^{\mathrm{T}} (I - A_i) \hat{x}^i = \hat{u}^i. \tag{8.11}$$

Based on Eqs. (8.10) and (8.11), we define a matrix $D_i = I - A_i - B_i \Omega_i$, $i = 1, \cdots, m$, where $\Omega_i = \left(B_i^{\mathrm{T}} B_i\right)^{-1} B_i^{\mathrm{T}} (I - A_i)$, and

$$\Lambda_i = \begin{bmatrix} I & \mathbf{0} & \mathbf{0} & \mathbf{0} & \mathbf{0} & \mathbf{0} & \mathbf{0} \\ \mathbf{0} & A_i^{-1} & \mathbf{0} & \mathbf{0} & -A_i^{-1} B_i & \mathbf{0} & \mathbf{0} \\ \mathbf{0} & \mathbf{0} & \ddots & \mathbf{0} & \vdots & \ddots & \mathbf{0} \\ \mathbf{0} & \mathbf{0} & \mathbf{0} & A_i^{-T} & -A_i^{-1} B_i & \cdots & -A_i^{-T} B_i \end{bmatrix}, \tag{8.12}$$

such that $D_i \hat{x}^i = \mathbf{0}$ and $\Lambda_i \left[\left(x^i\right)^{\mathrm{T}}, \left(u^i\right)^{\mathrm{T}}\right]^{\mathrm{T}} = \mathbf{1}_{T+1} \otimes x^i(0) := b_i \in \mathbb{R}^{(T+1)n_i}$, $i \in \mathcal{V}$, respectively. Define several parameters as follows:

$$\nabla f_{i,k}^{x} = \mathrm{blkdiag}\left(I \otimes \left(\mathcal{Q}_i^{\mathrm{T}} + \mathcal{Q}_i\right), \mathcal{P}_i^{\mathrm{T}} + \mathcal{P}_i\right) \tilde{x}^i, \tag{8.13a}$$

$$\nabla f_{i,k}^{u} = \left(I \otimes \left(\mathcal{R}_i^{\mathrm{T}} + \mathcal{R}_i\right)\right) \tilde{u}^i, \tag{8.13b}$$

$$\nabla f_{i,k}^{\hat{x}} = -\left(1_{T+1}^{\mathrm{T}} \otimes I\right) \mathrm{blkdiag}\left(I \otimes \left(\mathcal{Q}_i^{\mathrm{T}} + \mathcal{Q}_i\right), \mathcal{P}_i^{\mathrm{T}} + \mathcal{P}_i\right) \tilde{x}^i. \tag{8.13c}$$

For arbitrary vectors $a \in \mathbb{R}^{n_i}$ and $c \in \mathbb{R}^{(T+1)n_i + Tm_i}$, the indicator functions $h_i^1(\cdot)$ and $h_i^2(\cdot)$ are defined as

$$h_i^1(a) = \begin{cases} 0, & \text{if } D_i a = \mathbf{0}, \\ \infty, & \text{if } D_i a \neq \mathbf{0}, \end{cases}$$

and

$$h_i^2(c) = \begin{cases} 0, & \text{if } \Lambda_i c = b_i, \\ \infty, & \text{if } \Lambda_i c \neq b_i. \end{cases}$$

Then the distributed synchronous optimization algorithm for the problem (8.7) is proposed in Algorithm 10, and the distributed asynchronous algorithm is put forward in Algorithm 11, where the subscript k denotes the time instant k.

Algorithm 10 Synchronous version of distributed optimization algorithm for MPC

1: Each agent $i \in \mathcal{V}$ sets $x_0^i \in \mathbb{R}^{(T+1)n_i}$ according to the initial state of itself, $u_0^i \in \mathbb{R}^{Tm_i}$, $\hat{x}_0^i \in \mathbb{R}^{n_i}$, $\hat{v}_0^i \in \mathbb{R}^{n_i}$, $\tilde{v}_0^i \in \mathbb{R}^{Tm_i}$, $\bar{v}_0^i \in \mathbb{R}^{(T+1)n_i}$ and $w_0^{i,j} \in \mathbb{R}^r$, and chooses proper positive step sizes $\kappa_{i,j}$, σ_i, and τ_i.

2: Set $k = 0$.

3: Each agent $i \in \mathcal{V}$ computes

$$\bar{w}_k^{i,j} = \frac{\kappa_{i,j}}{2}\left(c_{ij}\hat{x}_k^i + c_{ji}\hat{x}_k^j\right) + \frac{1}{2}\left(w_k^{i,j} + w_k^{j,i}\right), \ j \in \mathcal{N}_i, \tag{8.14}$$

$$\hat{\lambda}_k^i = \hat{v}_k^i + \sigma_i \hat{x}_k^i - \sigma_i P_{\hat{\mathcal{X}}_i}\left(\sigma_i^{-1}\hat{v}_k^i + \hat{x}_k^i\right), \tag{8.15}$$

$$\tilde{\lambda}_k^i = \tilde{v}_k^i + \sigma_i u_k^i - \sigma_i P_{\mathcal{U}_i}\left(\sigma_i^{-1}\tilde{v}_k^i + u_k^i\right), \tag{8.16}$$

$$\bar{\lambda}_k^i = \bar{v}_k^i + \sigma_i x_k^i - \sigma_i P_{\mathcal{X}_i}\left(\sigma_i^{-1}\bar{v}_k^i + x_k^i\right), \tag{8.17}$$

$$\hat{x}_{k+1}^i = \operatorname{prox}_{\tau_i h_i^1}\left(\hat{x}_k^i - \tau_i\hat{\lambda}_k^i - \tau_i \nabla f_{i,k}^{\hat{x}} - \tau_i \sum_{j\in\mathcal{N}_i} c_{ij}\bar{w}_k^{i,j}\right), \tag{8.18}$$

$$\begin{bmatrix} x_{k+1}^i \\ u_{k+1}^i \end{bmatrix} = \operatorname{prox}_{\tau_i h_i^2}\begin{bmatrix} x_k^i - \tau_i\bar{\lambda}_k^i - \tau_i\nabla f_{i,k}^x \\ u_k^i - \tau_i\tilde{\lambda}_k^i - \tau_i\nabla f_{i,k}^u \end{bmatrix}, \tag{8.19}$$

$$\hat{v}_{k+1}^i = \hat{\lambda}_k^i + \sigma_i\left(\hat{x}_{k+1}^i - \hat{x}_k^i\right), \tag{8.20}$$

$$\tilde{v}_{k+1}^i = \tilde{\lambda}_k^i + \sigma_i\left(u_{k+1}^i - u_k^i\right), \tag{8.21}$$

$$\bar{v}_{k+1}^i = \bar{\lambda}_k^i + \sigma_i\left(x_{k+1}^i - x_k^i\right), \tag{8.22}$$

$$w_{k+1}^{i,j} = \bar{w}_k^{i,j} + \kappa_{i,j}c_{ij}\left(\hat{x}_{k+1}^i - \hat{x}_k^i\right), \ j \in \mathcal{N}_i, \tag{8.23}$$

where $c_{ij} = [1, \ \mathbf{0}]$ if $i > j$ and $c_{ij} = [-1, \ \mathbf{0}]$ if $i < j$.

4: Each agent $i \in \mathcal{V}$ sends information $\hat{x}_{k+1}^i$ and $w_{k+1}^{i,j}$ to neighbor agents $j \in \mathcal{N}_i$.

5: Go to Step 3 and set $k = k + 1$ until a certain end condition is satisfied, e.g., $\|x_k - x_{k+1}\| \leq \vartheta$ where ϑ is a predefined threshold.

Assumption 8.2 *For agent $i \in \mathcal{V}$, the positive step sizes τ_i, σ_i and $\kappa_{i,j}$, satisfy the following condition:*

$$\tau_i < \left(\frac{\beta_i}{2} + \sigma_i + \sum_{j \in \mathcal{N}_i} \kappa_{i,j} \right)^{-1}, \tag{8.24}$$

where β_i is the largest eigenvalue of $E_i^{\mathrm{T}} (I \otimes \mathcal{Q}_i) E_i + H_i^{\mathrm{T}} (I \otimes \mathcal{R}_i) H_i + L_i^{\mathrm{T}} \mathcal{P}_i L_i$.

Algorithm 11 Asynchronous version of distributed optimization algorithm for MPC

1: Each agent $i \in \mathcal{V}$ sets $x_0^i \in \mathbb{R}^{(T+1)n_i}$ according to the initial state of itself, $u_0^i \in \mathbb{R}^{Tm_i}$, $\hat{x}_0^i \in \mathbb{R}^{n_i}$, $\hat{v}_0^i \in \mathbb{R}^{n_i}$, $\tilde{v}_0^i \in \mathbb{R}^{Tm_i}$, $\bar{v}_0^i \in \mathbb{R}^{(T+1)n_i}$ and $w_0^{i,j} \in \mathbb{R}^r$, and chooses proper positive step sizes $\kappa_{i,j}$, σ_i, and τ_i.
2: Set $k = 0$.
3: Each agent $i \in \mathcal{V}$ is activated independently with probability $0 < p_i < 1$.
4: Each active agent i updates local variables according to Eqs. (8.14)–(8.23).
5: Each active agent i sends information $\hat{x}_{k+1}^i$ and $w_{k+1}^{i,j}$ to neighbor agents $j \in \mathcal{N}_i$.
6: Go to Step 3 and set $k = k+1$ until a certain end condition is satisfied, e.g., $\|x_k - x_{k+1}\| \le \vartheta$ where ϑ is a predefined threshold.

Remark 8.2 From the formal point of view, Algorithms 10 and 11 seem to be the same. The most important thing is to note that one is a synchronous algorithm, and the other is an asynchronous algorithm. In Algorithm 10, all agents need to communicate and update simultaneously, which means that there needs to be a global clock to control the agents. The global clock only issues new communication and updates instructions when all agents complete the previous tasks. As a result, agents with good performance will waste much time waiting for agents with poor performance. However, in Algorithm 11, the control of the global clock is unnecessary. That is, each agent can decide the update and communication time independently, without waiting for other agents. This feature improves the robustness of the system and makes full use of the computing resources of each agent.

8.3.2 Problem Reformulation

Defining variables $z = \left[(z^1)^{\mathrm{T}}, \cdots, (z^m)^{\mathrm{T}} \right]^{\mathrm{T}}$ with $z^i = \left[(x^i)^{\mathrm{T}}, (u^i)^{\mathrm{T}}, (\hat{x}^i)^{\mathrm{T}} \right]^{\mathrm{T}} \in \mathbb{R}^{d_i}$, we can set $E_i = [I \ \ \mathbf{0} \ \ -1_T \otimes I]$ and $H_i = [\mathbf{0} \ \ I \ \ -1_T \otimes \Omega_i]$ such that $E_i z^i = x^i(0 : T-1) - 1_T \otimes \hat{x}^i$ and $H_i z^i = u^i - 1_T \otimes \hat{u}^i$ with $x^i(0 : T-1) = \left[\left(x^i(0)\right)^{\mathrm{T}}, \cdots, \left(x^i(T-1)\right)^{\mathrm{T}} \right]^{\mathrm{T}}$, respectively. Then, the summation over l from 0 to $T-1$ of Eq. (8.8) is equal to

$$\tilde{\mathcal{F}}_i\left(z^i\right)=\left(z^i\right)^{\mathrm{T}}\left(E_i^{\mathrm{T}}\left(I\otimes\mathcal{Q}_i\right)E_i+H_i^{\mathrm{T}}\left(I\otimes\mathcal{R}_i\right)H_i\right)z^i. \tag{8.25}$$

We equivalently rewrite the terminal cost function (8.9) as:

$$\tilde{F}_i\left(z^i\right)=\left(z^i\right)^{\mathrm{T}}L_i^{\mathrm{T}}\mathcal{P}_iL_iz^i, \tag{8.26}$$

where $L_iz^i=x^i(T)-\hat{x}^i$.

Then, we reformulate problem (8.7) as follows:

$$\begin{aligned}\min_z\ &\sum_{i=1}^m f_i\left(z^i\right),\\ \text{s.t.}\ &\Lambda_iz^i=b_i,\ i\in\mathcal{V},\\ &z^i\in\mathcal{Z}_i,\ i\in\mathcal{V},\\ &C_{ij}z^i+C_{ji}z^j=\mathbf{0},\ (i,j)\in\mathcal{E},\end{aligned} \tag{8.27}$$

where $f_i\left(z^i\right)=\tilde{\mathcal{F}}_i\left(z^i\right)+\tilde{F}_i\left(z^i\right)$ and C_{ij} are a linear mapping such that $C_{ij}z^i=\hat{x}^i$ if $i>j$ and $C_{ij}z^i=-\hat{x}^i$ if $i<j$. Employing the indicator functions $g_i(\cdot)$ and $h_i(\cdot)$, which are defined as

$$g_i\left(z^i\right)=\begin{cases}0, & \text{if } z^i\in\mathcal{Z}_i,\\ \infty, & \text{if } z^i\notin\mathcal{Z}_i,\end{cases} \tag{8.28}$$

and

$$h_i\left(z^i\right)=\begin{cases}0, & \text{if } \tilde{\Lambda}_iz_i=b_i,\\ \infty, & \text{if } \tilde{\Lambda}_iz_i\neq b_i,\end{cases} \tag{8.29}$$

where $\tilde{\Lambda}_i=[\Lambda_i,0]$, problem (8.27) is consequently transformed into the following distributed optimization problem:

$$\begin{aligned}\min_z\ &\sum_{i=1}^m f_i\left(z^i\right)+g_i\left(z^i\right)+h_i\left(z^i\right),\\ \text{s.t.}\ &C_{ij}z^i+C_{ji}z^j=\mathbf{0},\ (i,j)\in\mathcal{E}.\end{aligned} \tag{8.30}$$

Define the notation z^* as the optimal solution to the problem (8.30).

Assumption 8.3 *For all $i \in \mathcal{V}$, each local function $f_i(\cdot)$ is convex and has β_f-Lipschitz continuous gradient, where $\beta_f > 0$ is the Lipschitz-constant such that*

$$\|\nabla f_i(a) - \nabla f_i(b)\| \leq \beta_f \|a - b\|.$$

Remark 8.3 According to the above analysis, we transform the original model predictive control problem into a distributed optimization problem with consensus constraint, as shown in Eq. (8.30). The purpose of the problem reformulation is to analyze the effectiveness of the proposed algorithm for the MPC problem conveniently. Different from the general distributed optimization problem, which is just a convex and smooth function, the objective function of (8.30) is a composite function that includes a convex function with Lipschitz-continuous and two closed and convex functions (possibly nonsmooth). Therefore, the general distributed optimization algorithms which are only suitable for convex and smooth objective functions cannot solve this problem. To analyze the convergence conveniently, we reconstruct the proposed algorithm next.

8.3.3 Algorithm Transformation

Applying the definition of z^i and the linear mapping C_{ij}, for all $i \in \mathcal{V}$ and $j \in \mathcal{N}_i$, the updates of $\bar{w}_k^{i,j}$ and $w_{k+1}^{i,j}$ can be rewritten as

$$\bar{w}_k^{i,j} = \frac{1}{2}\left(w_k^{i,j} + w_k^{j,i}\right) + \frac{\kappa_{i,j}}{2}\left(C_{ij} z_k^i + C_{ji} z_k^j\right), \tag{8.31}$$

and

$$w_{k+1}^{i,j} = \bar{w}_k^{i,j} + \kappa_{i,j} C_{ij}\left(z_{k+1}^i - z_k^i\right). \tag{8.32}$$

Denote the variables $\lambda_k^i = [(\bar{\lambda}_k^i)^{\mathrm{T}}, (\tilde{\lambda}_k^i)^{\mathrm{T}}, (\hat{\lambda}_k^i)^{\mathrm{T}}]^{\mathrm{T}}$ and $v_k^i = [(\bar{v}_k^i)^{\mathrm{T}}, (\tilde{v}_k^i)^{\mathrm{T}}, (\hat{v}_k^i)^{\mathrm{T}}]^{\mathrm{T}}$. Then, we obtain the forms of (8.15)–(8.17) and (8.20)–(8.22), which are represented respectively by

$$\lambda_k^i = v_k^i + \sigma_i z_k^i - \sigma_i P_{\mathcal{Z}_i}\left(\sigma_i^{-1} v_k^i + z_k^i\right), \tag{8.33}$$

and

$$v_{k+1}^i = \lambda_k^i + \sigma_i\left(z_{k+1}^i - z_k^i\right). \tag{8.34}$$

Recalling the indicator function $g_i(\cdot)$, $i \in \mathcal{V}$, and the definition of proximal mapping, Eq. (8.33) equals to

$$\lambda_k^i = \mathrm{prox}_{\sigma_i g_i^*}\left(v_k^i + \sigma_i z_k^i\right). \tag{8.35}$$

Similarly, we equivalently rewrite updates (8.18) and (8.19) as

$$z_{k+1}^i = \mathrm{prox}_{\tau_i h_i}\left(z_k^i - \tau_i \sum_{j\in\mathcal{N}_i} C_{ij}^{\mathrm{T}} \bar{w}_k^{i,j} - \tau_i \nabla f_i\left(z_k^i\right) - \tau_i \lambda_k^i\right). \tag{8.36}$$

8.4 Convergence Analysis

This section presents the convergence analysis of the proposed algorithm. Considering the constraint of (8.30), we can define an indicator function:

$$\delta_{\bar{C}_{i,j}}\left(C_{ij}z^i, C_{ji}z^j\right) = \begin{cases} 0, & \text{if } (C_{ij}z^i, C_{ji}z^j) \in \bar{C}_{i,j}, \\ \infty, & \text{if } (C_{ij}z^i, C_{ji}z^j) \notin \bar{C}_{i,j}, \end{cases} \tag{8.37}$$

with $\bar{C}_{i,j} = \left\{(a,b) \in \mathbb{R}^{d_i} \times \mathbb{R}^{d_i} | C_{ij}a + C_{ji}b = \mathbf{0}\right\}$. Let $C = \times_{(i,j)\in\mathcal{E}} \bar{C}_{i,j}$ and $\Phi z = (z, Nz)$ where N is an operator $N : z \to \left(N_{i,j}z\right)_{(i,j)\in\mathcal{E}}$ with $N_{i,j} : z \to \left[\left(C_{ij}z^i\right)^{\mathrm{T}}, \left(C_{ji}z^j\right)^{\mathrm{T}}\right]^{\mathrm{T}}$, and rewrite (8.30) in the following optimization problem, which can be distributed solved:

$$\min_z f(z) + h(z) + \tilde{g}(\Phi z), \tag{8.38}$$

where $f(z) = \sum_{i=1}^m f_i\left(z^i\right)$, $h(z) = \sum_{i=1}^m h_i\left(z^i\right)$ and $\tilde{g}(\Phi z) = g(z) + \delta_C(Nz) = \sum_{i=1}^m g_i\left(z^i\right) + \sum_{i=1}^m \sum_{j\in\mathcal{N}_i} \delta_{\bar{C}_{i,j}}\left(N_{i,j}z\right)$. Consider that problem (8.38) contains a convex function with Lipschitz-continuous and two closed and convex functions (possibly nonsmooth), which is a special form of optimal problem that general optimal algorithms are hard to solve this one. For problem (8.38), the literature [17] proposed the triangularly preconditioned primal-dual (TriPD) algorithm as follows:

$$\begin{cases} \mathcal{W}_k = \mathrm{prox}_{\tilde{g}^*}^{\Sigma^{-1}}\left(W_k + \Sigma\Phi z_k\right), \\ z_{k+1} = \mathrm{prox}_h^{\Gamma^{-1}}\left(z_k - \Gamma\nabla f(z_k) - \Gamma\Phi^{\mathrm{T}}\mathcal{W}_k\right), \\ W_{k+1} = \mathcal{W}_k + \Sigma\Phi\left(z_{k+1} - z_k\right), \end{cases} \tag{8.39}$$

where Σ and Γ are the symmetric positive definite dual step size matrix and primal step size matrix, respectively. Moreover, the step sizes satisfy $\Gamma^{-1} - \frac{\beta_f}{2} - \Sigma > 0$ where β_f is the Lipschitz constant of $\nabla f(\cdot)$. The literature [17] proved the convergence of the algorithm (8.39) under different assumptions.

8.4.1 Main Results

Defining the linear operator $W_k^{i,j} = [(w_k^{i,j})^{\mathrm{T}}, (w_k^{j,i})^{\mathrm{T}}]^{\mathrm{T}}$, it can be deduced that $\mathrm{prox}_{\kappa_{i,j}^{-1}\delta_{\bar{C}_{ij}}}(\Delta_{ij}) = \mathcal{P}_{\bar{C}_{i,j}}(\Delta_{ij})$ where $\Delta_{ij} = \kappa_{i,j}^{-1} W_k^{i,j} + N_{i,j} z_k$ and $\mathcal{P}_{\bar{C}_{i,j}}(a) = \frac{1}{2}(a_1 - a_2, a_2 - a_1)$ with $a = [a_1, a_2]^{\mathrm{T}}$. Letting $\mathcal{W}_k^{i,j} = \left(\bar{w}_k^{i,j}, \bar{w}_k^{j,i}\right)$, we then have

$$\mathcal{W}_k^{i,j} = W_k^{i,j} + \kappa_{i,j}\left(N_{i,j} z_k - \mathrm{prox}_{\kappa_{i,j}^{-1}\delta_{\bar{C}_{i,j}}}(\Delta_{ij})\right), \tag{8.40}$$

which means $\mathcal{W}_k^{i,j} = \mathrm{prox}_{\kappa_{i,j}\delta^*_{\bar{C}_{i,j}}}\left(W_k^{i,j} + \kappa_{i,j} N_{i,j} z_k\right)$. Constructing a new variable $s_k^i = \left[\left(\mathcal{W}_k^{i,j}\right)^{\mathrm{T}}_{j\in\mathcal{N}_i}, \left(\lambda_k^i\right)^{\mathrm{T}}\right]^{\mathrm{T}}$ and $\theta_k^i = \left[\left(W_k^{i,j}\right)^{\mathrm{T}}_{j\in\mathcal{N}_i}, \left(v_k^i\right)^{\mathrm{T}}\right]^{\mathrm{T}}$, the compact form of (8.31) and (8.33)–(8.36) can be rewritten as follows:

$$\begin{cases} s_k = \mathrm{prox}_{\tilde{g}^*}^{\Sigma^{-1}}(\theta_k + \Sigma\Phi z_k), \\ z_{k+1} = \mathrm{prox}_h^{\Gamma^{-1}}\left(z_k - \Gamma\Phi^{\mathrm{T}} s_k - \Gamma\nabla f(z_k)\right), \\ \theta_{k+1} = s_k + \Sigma\Phi(z_{k+1} - z_k), \end{cases} \tag{8.41}$$

where $\Sigma = \mathrm{blkdiag}(\sigma_1 I, \cdots, \sigma_m I, \mathcal{K})$ with $\mathcal{K} = \mathrm{blkdiag}\left(\left(\kappa_{i,j} I\right)_{(i,j)\in\mathcal{E}}\right)$ and $\Gamma = \mathrm{blkdiag}(\tau_1 I, \cdots, \tau_m I)$. Defining variables $V_k = \left[\theta_k^{\mathrm{T}}, z_k^{\mathrm{T}}\right]^{\mathrm{T}}$ and $V^* = \left[(\theta^*)^{\mathrm{T}}, (z^*)^{\mathrm{T}}\right]^{\mathrm{T}}$ where θ^* is the optimal solution to the dual problem $\min_\theta (f+h)^*\left(-\Phi^{\mathrm{T}}\theta\right) + \tilde{g}^*(\theta)$, and denoting an operator Ψ such that $\Psi z_k = (s_k + \Sigma\Phi(z_{k+1} - z_k), z_{k+1})$, one has $V_{k+1} = z_k + \Pi(\Psi z_k - z_k)$ where $\Pi < 2I$ is a positive definite matrix. Define $S = \mathrm{blkdiag}\left(\Sigma^{-1}, \Gamma^{-1}\right)$ and

$$\bar{P} = \begin{bmatrix} \Sigma^{-1} & -\frac{1}{2}I \\ -\frac{1}{2}I & \Gamma^{-1} - \frac{\beta_f}{4}D \end{bmatrix}, \tag{8.42}$$

with $D = \mathrm{blkdiag}(\beta_1 I, \cdots, \beta_m I)$.

Based on the above analysis, we transform the proposed algorithm for model predictive control into a distributed optimization algorithm from [17]. Then, we obtain the following results to prove the convergence of the proposed algorithm.

Theorem 8.4 ([17]) *Let Assumptions 8.1–8.3 hold. Considering the sequence* $\{V_k\}$ *generated by Algorithm 10, the following Fejér-type inequality holds:*

$$\|V_{k+1} - V^*\|_S^2 \leq \|V_k - V^*\|_S^2 - \|V_{k+1} - V_k\|_{2\bar{P}-S}^2. \tag{8.43}$$

Then, the sequence $\{u_k\}$ *generated by Algorithm 10 converges to the optimal solution* u^*.

Theorem 8.5 ([17]) *Let Assumptions 8.1–8.3 hold and* $\mathbb{F}_k$ *measure the history of the system up until time instant k. Considering the sequence* $\{V_k\}$ *generated by Algorithm 11 and defining a vector* $P = \left[P_1^{\mathrm{T}}, \cdots, P_m^{\mathrm{T}}\right]^{\mathrm{T}}$ *with* $P_i = p_i \mathbf{1}_{n_i+m_i}$, *the following Fejér-type inequality holds:*

$$\mathbb{E}\left[\| V_{k+1} - V^* \|_{\mathbb{P}S}^2 | \mathbb{F}_k\right] \leq \| V_k - V^* \|_{\mathbb{P}S}^2 - \| \Psi V_k - V_k \|_{2\bar{P}-S}^2, \tag{8.44}$$

where $\mathbb{P} = (\operatorname{diag}(P))^{-1}$. *Then, the sequence* $\{u_k\}$ *generated by Algorithm 11 converges almost surely to the optimal solution* u^*.

Remark 8.6 Under Assumptions 8.1–8.3, Theorems 8.4 and 8.5 show the convergence of synchronous and asynchronous algorithms, respectively. It should be noted that Assumption 8.3 only assumes that each local function $f_i(\cdot)$ is convex and has β_f-Lipschitz continuous gradient. However, in actual scenarios, the objective functions may have some special properties. When the objective functions are either piecewise linear quadratic, or when they satisfy a certain quadratic growth condition (which is weaker than strong convexity), the proposed algorithm can converge to the global optimal solution at a linear convergence rate [17].

Definition 8.7 A function $f : \mathbb{R}^n \to \mathbb{R}$ is called piecewise linear-quadratic (PLQ) if its domain can be represented as the union of finitely many polyhedral sets, and in each such set $f(x)$ is given by an expression of the form $\frac{1}{2}\langle x, Qx\rangle + \langle d, x\rangle + c$ some $c \in \mathbb{R}$, $d \in \mathbb{R}^n$, and symmetric matrix $Q \in \mathbb{R}^{n\times n}$.

Theorem 8.8 ([17]) *Consider the Algorithm 10 under Assumptions 8.1–8.3. Suppose that the functions* $f(\cdot)$, $g(\cdot)$ *and* $h(\cdot)$ *are PLQ. Then, the sequence* $\{u_k\}$ *generated by Algorithm 10 converges R-linearly to the optimal solution* u^*.

Theorem 8.9 ([17]) *Consider the Algorithm 11 under the Assumptions 8.1–8.3. Suppose that the functions* $f(\cdot)$, $g(\cdot)$ *and* $h(\cdot)$ *are PLQ. Then, the sequence* $\{u_k\}$ *generated by Algorithm 11 converges Q-linearly to the optimal solution* u^*.

8.5 Numerical Examples

8.5.1 *Case I*

In this subsection, an example with 4 agents is given to illustrate the theoretical results. Consider a high-order multi-agent system with $m = 4$ agents and the optimal output consensus problem defined in (8.27). Define that the state and input of agent i satisfy $\underline{x}_i \leq x_i \leq \bar{x}_i$ and $\underline{u}_i \leq u_i \leq \bar{u}_i$. We present the system parameters and step sizes in Table 8.1. As shown in Fig. 8.1, the evolutions of the outputs

Table 8.1 Parameters assigned in Case I

Agent	$i=1$	$i=2$	$i=3$	$i=4$
s_i	2	2	3	3
$x^{i,0}(0)$	−30	−20	10	50
$x^{i,0}(l), l \geq 1$	0	0	0	0
$\mathcal{Q}_i$	I_2	I_2	I_3	I_3
$\mathcal{R}_i$	0.1	0.1	0.1	0.1
η_i	1	1	1	1
ζ_i	1	1	1	1
$\bar{x}_i$	50	50	50	50
$\underline{x}_i$	−30	−30	−30	−30
$\bar{u}_i$	10	10	10	10
$\underline{u}_i$	−10	−10	−10	−10
β_i	16.2272	16.2272	31.9457	31.9457
τ_i	0.0164	0.0085	0.0085	0.0164
σ_i	2.75	5.25	5.25	2.75
$\kappa_{i,j}$ ($j \in \mathcal{N}_i$)	1	1	1	1

of agents generated by Algorithms 10 and 11 converge to the optimal consensus solution y^*. The trajectories of the states and the control inputs of agents generated by Algorithms 10 and 11 are illustrated in Figs. 8.2 and 8.3.

8.5.2 *Case II*

This case employs the asynchronous version of the proposed MPC algorithm to solve the optimal output control problem where the receding horizon is needed. Consider the multi-agent system with $m = 6$ agents where the initial states of agents are defined as $x^{1,0}(0) = -60$, $x^{2,0}(0) = -40$, $x^{3,0}(0) = -20$, $x^{4,0}(0) = 0$, $x^{5,0}(0) = 30$, $x^{6,0}(0) = 60$ and $x^{i,l}(0) = 0$, $i = 1, \cdots, m$, $l = 1, \cdots, s_i$. The bounds of all states are defined as $[-70, -30]^{\mathrm{T}} \leq x^1 \leq [50, 30]^{\mathrm{T}}$, $[-40, -20]^{\mathrm{T}} \leq x^2 \leq [80, 10]^{\mathrm{T}}$, $[-40, -20]^{\mathrm{T}} \leq x^3 \leq [80, 10]^{\mathrm{T}}$, $[-30, -13, -13]^{\mathrm{T}} \leq x^4 \leq [60, 13, 13]^{\mathrm{T}}$, $[-40, -10, -14]^{\mathrm{T}} \leq x^5 \leq [40, 10, 16]^{\mathrm{T}}$ and $[-5, -20, -20]^{\mathrm{T}} \leq x^6 \leq [70, 15, 10]^{\mathrm{T}}$. The bounds of all control inputs are defined as $-10 \leq u^1 \leq 15$, $-20 \leq u^2 \leq 20$, $-20 \leq u^3 \leq 20$, $-10 \leq u^4 \leq 15$, $-8 \leq u^5 \leq 30$ and $-18 \leq u^6 \leq 25$. For all $i \in \mathcal{V}$, we set the system parameters $Q_i = I_{s_i}$, $\mathcal{R}_i = 0.1$, $\eta_i = 1$, $\zeta_i = 1$ and choose the step sizes $\beta_1 = \beta_2 = \beta_3 = 11.0989$, $\beta_4 = \beta_5 = \beta_6 = 26.8225$, $\tau_1 = \tau_6 = 0.0164$, $\tau_2 = \tau_3 = \tau_4 = \tau_5 = 0.0085$, $\sigma_1 = \sigma_6 = 2.75$ and $\sigma_2 = \sigma_3 = \sigma_4 = \sigma_5 = 5.25$. Set the predictive horizon $T = 6$. In this case, each agent $i \in \mathcal{V}$ predicts the state and the control input of the next T steps at each step, and decides the control input according to the prediction result, i.e., $x^i(0|t+1) = x^i(1|t)$ and $u^i(0|t+1) = u^i(1|t)$. Figures 8.4 and 8.5 show the evolutions of the states and the control inputs of all

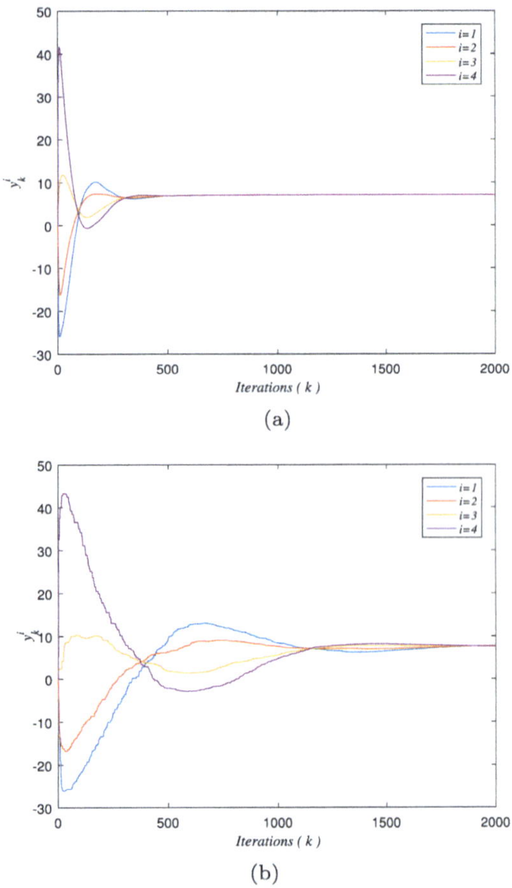

Fig. 8.1 The control outputs of agents. (**a**) Synchronous algorithm. (**b**) Asynchronous algorithm

agents, which demonstrate the effectiveness of the proposed algorithm for the MPC problem where the receding horizon is needed.

8.5.3 *Case III*

To illustrate the effectiveness of the proposed distributed algorithm for the MPC problem with a large-scale network, we consider a network with 100 second-order agents and show the network topology in Fig. 8.6. In this subsection, we randomly select the initial state $x^{i,0}(0)$, $i = 1, \cdots, 100$, from $[-50, 50]$. A part of simulation parameters for all agent $i = 1, \cdots, 100$ are shown in Table 8.2. We select the parameters β_i, τ_i and σ_i, according to Assumption 8.2. Due to the limitation of the space, the remaining parameters will not be stated in detail. From Figs. 8.7, 8.8 and 8.9, it can be found that the control outputs of all agents converge, which

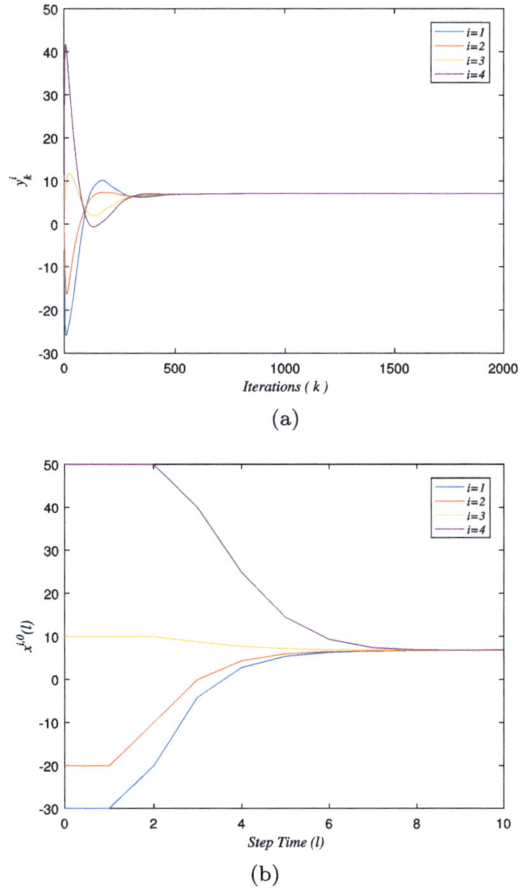

Fig. 8.2 The states of agents. (**a**) Synchronous algorithm. (**b**) Asynchronous algorithm

illustrate the effectiveness of the proposed algorithm for a large-scale multi-agent system and the correctness of the theorem analysis.

8.6 Conclusion

This chapter has studied the distributed MPC problem and proposed the distributed optimization algorithm to solve this problem. When each local cost function is smooth, and the uncoordinate step sizes satisfy the given conditions, the proposed algorithm converged by the synchronous or asynchronous update and communication. Finally, we have presented simulations to illustrate the effectiveness of the proposed algorithm. Developing distributed online algorithms for the MPC problem with receding horizon over directed communication networks will be the future research work.

Fig. 8.3 The control inputs of agents. (**a**) Synchronous algorithm. (**b**) Asynchronous algorithm

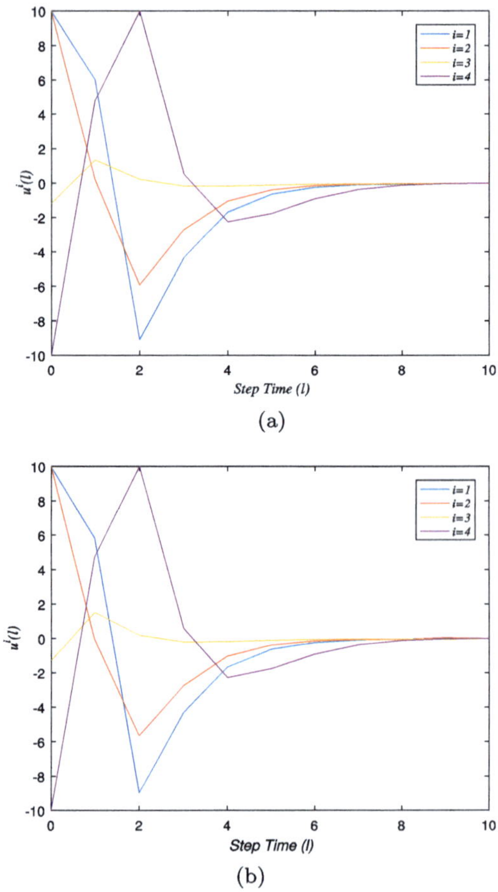

Fig. 8.4 The states of six agents

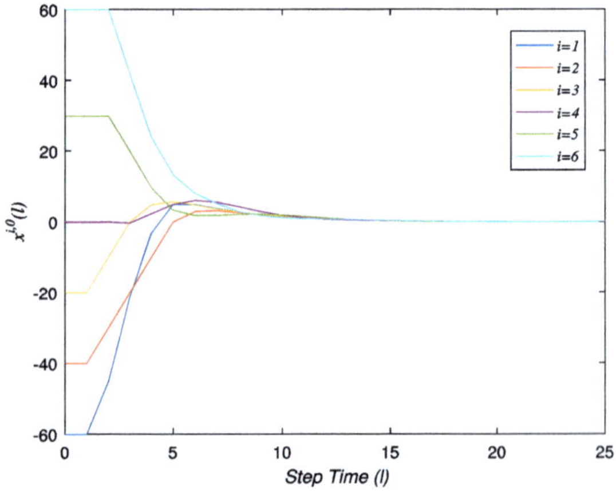

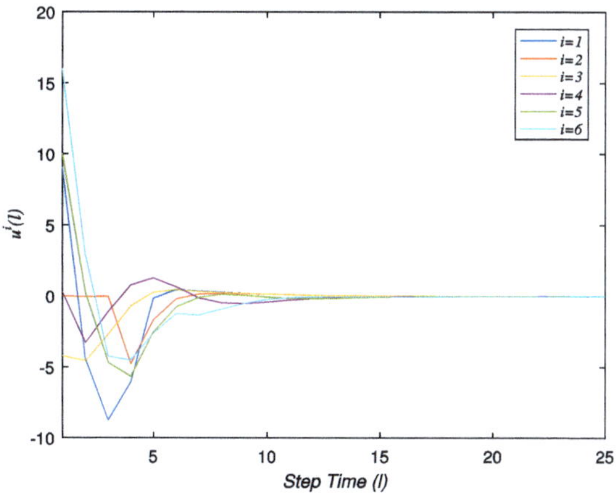

Fig. 8.5 The control inputs of six agents

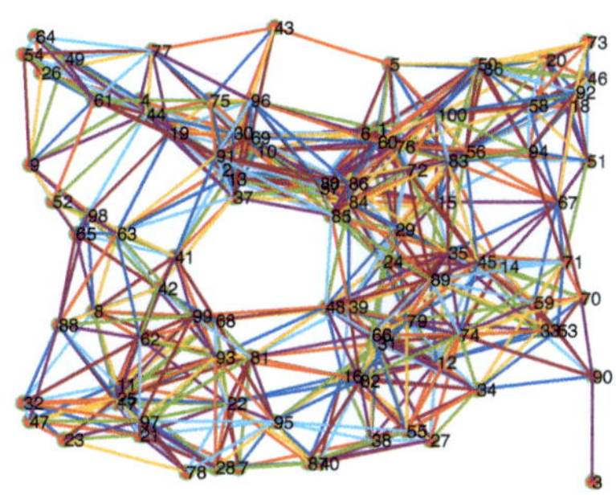

Fig. 8.6 The network topology

Table 8.2 Parameters assigned in Case III

s_i	$\mathcal{Q}_i$	$\mathcal{R}_i$	η_i	$x(l)^{i,0}, l \geq 1$	ζ_i
2	I	0.1	1	0	1
$\underline{x}_i$	$\bar{x}_i$	$\underline{u}_i$	$\bar{u}_i$	$\kappa_{i,j}$ $(j \in \mathcal{N}_i)$	
-50	50	-10	10	1	

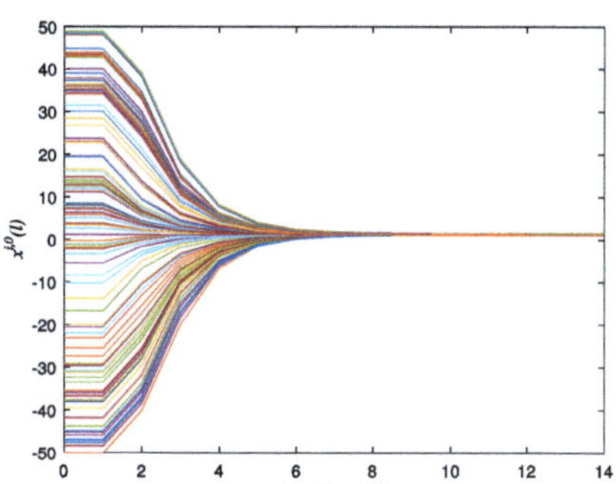

Fig. 8.7 The states of 100 agents

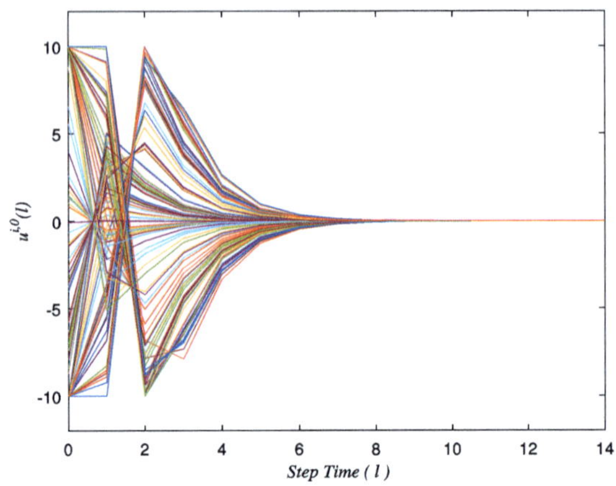

Fig. 8.8 The control inputs of 100 agents

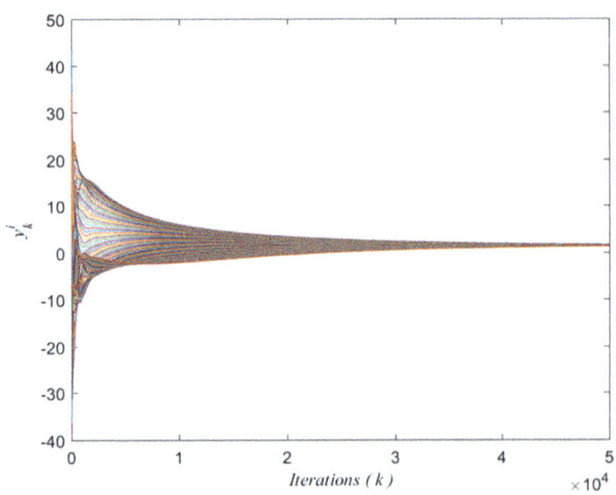

Fig. 8.9 The control outputs of 100 agents

Chapter 9
Distributed Dual Proximal Gradient Algorithms for Nonsmooth Constrained Composite Optimization

Abstract Distributed dual methods play significant roles in large-scale optimization, which effectively resolve many constrained optimization problems in machine learning and power systems. In this chapter, we focus on studying a class of totally nonsmooth constrained composite optimization problems over multi-agent systems, where the mutual goal of agents in the system is to optimize a sum of two separable nonsmooth functions consisting of a strongly-convex function and another convex (not necessarily strongly-convex) function. Agents in the system conduct parallel local computation and communication in the overall process without leaking their private information. In order to resolve the totally nonsmooth constrained composite optimization problem in a fully distributed manner, we devise a synchronous distributed dual proximal (SynDe-DuPro) gradient algorithm and its asynchronous version (AsynDe-DuPro) based on the randomized block-coordinate method. Both SynDe-DuPro and AsynDe-DuPro algorithms are theoretically proved to achieve the globally optimal solution to the totally nonsmooth constrained composite optimization problem relied on the quasi-Fejér monotone theorem. As a main result, AsynDe-DuPro algorithm attains the globally optimal solution without requiring all agents to be activated at each iteration and thus is more robust than most existing synchronous algorithms. The practicability of the proposed algorithms and correctness of the theoretical findings are demonstrated by the experiments on a constrained Distributed Sparse Logistic Regression (DSLR) problem in machine learning and a Distributed Energy Resources Coordination (DERC) problem in power systems.

Keywords Convex optimization · Synchronous and asynchronous distributed algorithms · Multi-agent systems · Nonsmooth constrained composite optimization problems · Distributed machine learning · DSLR problems · DERC problems

H. Li et al., *Network-System Research and Distributed Composite Algorithm Design*, Computational Intelligence Methods and Applications,
https://doi.org/10.1007/978-981-95-0911-9_9

9.1 Introduction

Recently, distributed optimization has been extensively studied owing to its significant applications in the fields of coordinated control [17], machine learning [108, 109, 122, 206], and power systems [207–209]. In comparison to the centralized optimization methods [210–213] that work in a master-worker network as shown in Fig. 9.1a, distributed optimization methods [15, 207, 214] have the advantages of alleviating the computational burden for the agents, high efficiency for the whole multi-agent system, and guaranteed privacy for each agent in the peer-to-peer network as shown in Fig. 9.1b. Notice that the dotted line in Fig. 9.1b indicates the possible existence of many agents. Specifically, the master-worker architectures require a sophisticated central agent to maintain all the update information to coordinate the communication and computation of the multi-agent system in optimization processes. On the contrary, the peer-to-peer architectures are ad hoc and contain no specialized agents [108]. This chapter considers a general nonsmooth constrained optimization model in a peer-to-peer network, which has many practical significance in various fields [124, 126, 215].

Distributed optimization has been well-developed in recent years with the emerging of big-data-driven large-scale industries, such as deep learning, Internet of Things, smart grids and power systems [67, 108, 207, 209, 216]. Some notable works, including EXTRA [49], Push-DIGing [217], and [218], studied single separable smooth and convex objective functions. The methods in [49, 217, 218] achieved linear convergence rates and reduced complexity. Then, NIDS [18] considered a relatively general objective function in the form of a smooth convex objective function plus a nonsmooth convex function and derives the network-independent range for the constant step size. More recently, an insightful work [15] proposed a general algorithmic framework and a unified analysis technique for the above mentioned smooth plus nonsmooth optimization problem models. The researchers in [17] and [219] studied a class of general frameworks of

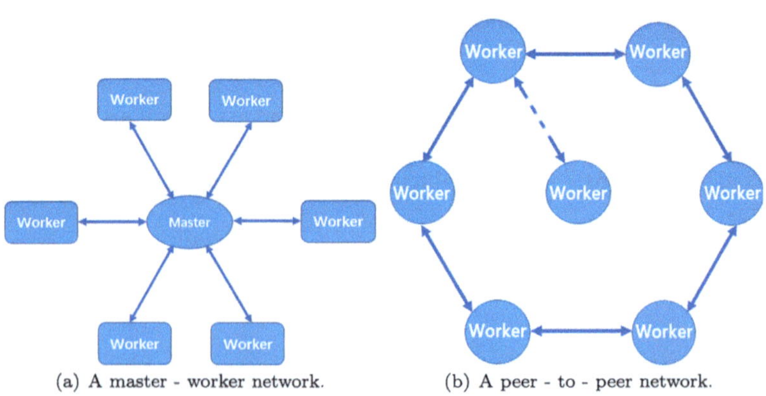

Fig. 9.1 Centralized network (**a**) vs distributed network (**b**)

smooth plus nonsmooth optimization problem models and devise both elegant synchronous and asynchronous distributed algorithms. Although aforementioned methods [15, 17, 49, 67, 108, 216–219] find various applications in the fields of signal processing and cooperative control, they could not be applied to tackling totally nonsmooth optimization problems which can be frequently found in machine learning, power systems, and smart grids. Moreover, the updates in [15, 18, 49, 67, 108, 122, 126, 206–209, 216–218] are all synchronous, which require all agents to engage in the updates at every iteration and thus are not robust to the situation of possible failure or non-activation of some agents. Therefore, the researchers in [124] constructed a separable nonsmooth objective function consisting of a strongly-convex objective function plus a convex objective function. However, the problem model studied in [124] did not consider any constraints (except the consensus constraint) that may be inevitable in many practical situations, for example, constrained machine learning problems [124, 220], DERC problems [207–209], economic dispatch problems [67, 221], and model predictive control problems [64]. Therefore, motivated by some practical applications in power systems [207–209], smart grid [67], and machine learning [124, 220], this chapter further investigates the problem model proposed in [124] by considering simultaneously the coupled local equality constraint and the local box constraints. Moreover, this chapter studies a class of non-consensus optimization problems which are assumed to be a general case of existing consensus problems [12, 15, 49, 67, 108, 113, 124, 126, 157, 214, 221], which can be demonstrated by Sect. 9.2.4.1 of this chapter. In fact, many energy coordination problems in power systems reach the optimal generation of Distributed Generators (DGs) or Energy Storages (ESs) when the participants are not in the consensus position. The main contributions of this chapter are summarized in the following:

(i) This chapter first proposes a more general model for a class of totally nonsmooth convex optimization problems in contrast to the existing works [14, 18, 102, 121, 124]. Then, aiming at resolving the totally nonsmooth constrained composite optimization problem in a fully distributed manner, a synchronous distributed algorithm named SynDe-DuPro based on the dual proximal gradient method is designed. Furthermore, to increase the robustness of SynDe-DuPro algorithm and eliminate the influence caused by possible failure or non-activation of some agents in the updates, we employ a randomized block-coordinate technique to devise an asynchronous distributed algorithm named AsynDe-DuPro. Both SynDe-DuPro and AsynDe-DuPro algorithms are proved to converge to the globally optimal solution as long as the local constant step sizes are chosen from specified ranges. Moreover, the asynchronous scheme adopted in this chapter allows arbitrary activated probabilities and the probabilities do not need to be same for different agents, which is less restrictive than the asynchronous scheme adopted in [23].

(ii) Compared with the insightful works [14, 17, 18, 121, 219] studying partly smooth problems, we consider a more general formulation of totally nonsmooth constrained composite optimization problems and devise two novel distributed algorithms SynDe-DuPro and AsynDe-DuPro. Both SynDe-DuPro and AsynDe-DuPro algorithms achieve exact convergence without any global information embedded, for example, the identically constant or decaying step sizes required by recent distributed algorithms [12, 15, 67, 108, 126, 157, 207–209, 217, 218, 221].

(iii) Owing to the fact that both SynDe-DuPro and AsynDe-DuPro algorithms can handle the totally nonsmooth composite optimization problems, we consider the nonsmooth operation costs of ESs, which include more general objective functions compared with [207–209]. Moreover, we further introduce the environmental cost/economic emission cost function [215] of the DGs into the total cost functions of DGs in simulations, which further advances the problem models proposed in [207–209]. Moreover, we design AsynDe-DuPro (asynchronous) to study the DERC problem in power systems.

(iv) We provide a unified convergence analysis for a class of structured optimization problems, which facilitates the convergence analysis for both SynDe-DuPro and AsynDe-DuPro algorithms. Furthermore, the convergent conditions of local constant step sizes in SynDe-DuPro and AsynDe-DuPro algorithms stay consistent, which simplifies the results in [12, 113, 157].

9.2 Preliminaries

In this section, we introduce some basic notations, formulate a structured optimization problem, provide two motivating examples corresponding to the optimization problem, and describe the communication network model.

9.2.1 Notation

We utilize $\mathbb{R}$, $\mathbb{R}^n$, $\mathbb{R}^{m\times n}$ and $\mathbb{N}$ to denote the set of real numbers, the set of n-dimensional column real vectors, the set of $m \times n$ real matrices, and the set of natural numbers, respectively. All vectors in this chapter are column vectors if not otherwise specified. The vectors and matrices with all-zero elements are denoted by 0 while the dimensions are clear from the context. The identity matrices are denoted as I while the dimensions are clear from the context. For arbitrary vectors $a_i \in \mathbb{R}^{n_i}$, $i = 1, \ldots, m$, we use $a = \mathbf{col}\{a_i\} \in \mathbb{R}^n$ to denote its collected column vector, where $n = \sum_{i=1}^{m} n_i$. For a given nonempty set $\mathcal{C}$, we denote its indicator function as $\delta_{\mathcal{C}}(a) = 0$ when $a \in \mathcal{C}$ and $\delta_{\mathcal{C}}(a) = +\infty$ otherwise. Besides, we use $\mathbf{ri}\ \mathcal{C}$ to denote the relative interior of nonempty set $\mathcal{C}$. The Euclidean norm for vectors and the spectral norm for matrices is denoted by $\|\cdot\|$ while $\|\cdot\|_1$ represents the ℓ_1-norm. For a positive (semi)definite matrix $X \in \mathbb{R}^{n\times n}$ and arbitrary two vectors $a, b \in \mathbb{R}^n$, we define the scalar product $\langle a, b\rangle_X = \langle a, Xb\rangle$ and let $\|a\|_X^2 = a^{\mathrm{T}} X a$ indicate the X-weighted norm of vector

a. For arbitrary two vectors $a, b \in \mathbb{R}^n$, the conjugate function $F^{\otimes} : \mathbb{R}^n \to \mathbb{R}$ corresponding to $F : \mathbb{R}^n \to \mathbb{R}$ is defined as $F^{\otimes}(a) = \max_b \left\{a^{\mathrm{T}} b - F(b)\right\}$. For arbitrary two matrices $X, Y \in \mathbb{R}^{n \times n}$, considering a closed, proper, convex function, $F : \mathbb{R}^n \to \mathbb{R}$, and a positive definite matrix Z, we denote the proximal operator as $\mathbf{prox}_F^Z\{X\} = \arg\min_Y\{F(Y) + \|Y - X\|_Z^2\}$ while for a positive scalar a, the proximal operator is defined as: $\mathrm{prox}_{aF}\{X\} = \arg\min_Y\{F(Y) + \frac{1}{2a}\|Y - X\|^2\}$. For arbitrary three vectors $a, b, c \in \mathbb{R}^n$, let ∂F denote the sub-differential of a proper, closed and convex function $F : \mathbb{R}^n \to \mathbb{R}$, where ∂F is given by

$$\partial F(a) = \left\{b \mid \forall c \in \mathbb{R}^n,\ F(a) + \langle b, c - a\rangle \le F(c)\right\}.$$

With a slight abuse of notation, we utilize $\partial_\theta F$ to represent the partial derivative of function F with respect to variable θ. For arbitrary positive matrix X, let $X \succ 0$ indicate that all the elements of X are positive. For an operator, $\mathcal{J} : \mathbb{R}^n \to \mathbb{R}^d$, we utilize $\mathbf{dom}\mathcal{J} = \{z \in \mathbb{R}^n | \mathcal{J}z \neq \emptyset\}$ to represent the domain of $\mathcal{J}$. Let $\prod_{i=1}^m \mathcal{C}_i$ denote the Cartesian product of $\mathcal{C}_1, \ldots, \mathcal{C}_m$. For vectors or matrices X and Y, the inequality $X \le Y$ means component-wise.

9.2.2 Model of Optimization Problem

Considering a multi-agent system consists of m agents which cooperatively resolve the following structured optimization problem:

$$\min_{x_1,\cdots,x_m} \sum_{i=1}^m f_i(x_i) + g_i(x_i), \tag{9.1a}$$

$$\text{s.t.} \sum_{i=1}^m A_i x_i = \sum_{i=1}^m b_i, \tag{9.1b}$$

$$x_i^{\min} \le x_i \le x_i^{\max}, i = 1, \ldots, m, \tag{9.1c}$$

where each agent i maintains the local decision variable, $x_i \in \mathbb{R}^{n_i}$. For $i = 1, \ldots, m$, the local objective functions (local tasks), $f_i : \mathbb{R}^{n_i} \to \mathbb{R}$ and $g_i : \mathbb{R}^{n_i} \to \mathbb{R}$, are privately known by agent i; the coupled local equality constraint is specified by matrices $A_i \in \mathbb{R}^{\tilde{r} \times n_i}$ and vectors $b_i \in \mathbb{R}^{\tilde{r}}$ while $x_i^{\min} \le x_i \le x_i^{\max}$ represent the local box constraints with component-wise. In order to specify the problems studied in this chapter, we make the following assumptions.

Assumption 9.1 (Strong Convexity and Slater's Condition)

(i) For $i = 1, \ldots, m$, the local objective functions f_i are proper, closed, and μ_i-strongly convex, i.e., for arbitrary vectors $x, y \in \mathbb{R}^n$, it holds that

$$f_i(x) - f_i(y) \geq \langle \partial f_i(y), x - y \rangle + \frac{\mu_i}{2} \|x - y\|^2, \tag{9.2}$$

with $\mu_i > 0$; the local objective functions g_i are proper, closed, and convex, i.e., $\mu_i = 0$ in (9.2);

(ii) There exists a set consisting of feasible points denoted as x_i^*, $i = 1, \ldots, m$, for (9.1a), which simultaneously meets coupled local equality constraint (9.1b), i.e., $\sum_{i=1}^m A_i x_i^* = \sum_{i=1}^m b_i$, and local box constraint (9.1c) with strict inequality, i.e., $x_i^{\min} < x_i^* < x_i^{\max}$.

Remark 9.1 Assumption 9.1 is not uncommon in recent literature [17, 54, 121, 124] and one can see [22, Section 10.2] for detailed discussions about the strongly convex and convex properties. Under Assumption 9.1, we know that the globally optimal solution to primal problem (9.1) exists uniquely. Notice that the differentiability of both f_i and g_i is not required in this chapter, which relaxes the conditions in many recent works, such as [15, 17, 108, 121, 122, 124, 214, 219].

9.2.3 Communication Network

The overall optimization process is assumed to be conducted in an undirected network which is featured by $\mathcal{G} = \{\mathcal{V}, \mathcal{E}\}$, where $\mathcal{V} = \{1, \ldots, m\}$ is the set of agents, and $\mathcal{E} \subseteq \mathcal{V} \times \mathcal{V}$ denotes the set of edges. The edge $(i, j) \in \mathcal{E}$ indicates that agent i can exchange information with agent j. For $\forall i \in \mathcal{V}$, the set of neighbors of agent i in $\mathcal{G}$ is denoted by $\mathcal{N}_i$. The network $\mathcal{G}$ is simple, which means that there are no self-loops and multiple links in the network.

Assumption 9.2 *The undirected network, $\mathcal{G}$, is connected.*

9.2.4 Motivating Examples

9.2.4.1 The Constrained DSLR Problem

A well-known example of problem (9.1) is the DSLR problem, which has important applications in machine learning [14, 102, 121]. Inspired by Notarnicola and Notarstefano [124], Xi and Khan [220], we also introduce local box constraints into the DSLR problem, the interest of which is to avoid some seriously deviated estimations in the process of optimization and restrict the optimal solution in a given box. In order to resolve the constrained DSLR problem in a distributed manner,

Table 9.1 Definitions for the constrained DSLR problem

Symbols	Definitions
m	The total number of agents in the system
x_i	The decision variable
Q_i	The number of samples allocated to agent i, $i \in \mathcal{V}$
c_{ij}	The j-th sample belongs to agent i, $i \in \mathcal{V}$
b_{ij}	The j-th label belongs to agent i, $i \in \mathcal{V}$
θ_1	The positive regularized constant of the regularized term aiming to prevent from the over-fitting situation in the process of classification
θ_2	The positive regularized constant of the regularized term aiming to attain a sparse optimal solution
θ_r	The ratio between the prevention of over-fitting situation and the requirement of a sparse solution, i.e., $\theta_r = \theta_1/\theta_2$
ub	The upper bound on the decision varible
lb	The lower bound on the decision varible

coupled local equality constraint (9.1b) should reduce to the consensus constraint. Therefore, the explicit formulation of the constrained DSLR problem can be written as:

$$\min_{x_1,\ldots,x_m} \frac{1}{m}\sum_{i=1}^{m} \tilde{f}_i\left(x_i\right) + \theta_1 \|x_i\|^2 + \theta_2 \|x_i\|_1, \tag{9.3a}$$

$$\text{s.t.} \quad x_i = x_j,\ (i, j) \in \mathcal{E}, \tag{9.3b}$$

$$lb \leq x_i \leq ub,\ i \in \mathcal{V}, \tag{9.3c}$$

where $\tilde{f}_i(x_i) = (1/Q_i)\sum_{j=1}^{Q_i} \log(1 + \exp(-b_{ij}c_{ij}^{\mathrm{T}}x_i))$, $x_i \in \mathbb{R}^n$, $c_{ij} \in \mathbb{R}^n$, $b_{ij} \in \mathbb{R}$, and the definitions of the symbols in (9.3) are given in Table 9.1 for a clear presentation. One can easily specialize problem (9.1) into the form of problem (9.3) by setting $f_i\left(x_i\right) = (1/m)\left(\tilde{f}_i\left(x_i\right) + \theta_1 \|x_i\|^2\right)$, $g_i\left(x_i\right) = (\theta_2/m)\|x_i\|_1$, A_i as the i-th column of the Laplacian matrix associated with the undirected network $\mathcal{G}$, $b_i = 0$, $x_i^{\min} = lb$, and $x_i^{\max} = ub$ for $\forall i \in \mathcal{V}$. The goal of solving problem (9.3) is to utilize the training set to obtain the discriminator/optimal solution $\tilde{x}^*$ that can, in turn, be used to identify the testing set. In Sect. 9.4.1, a large-scale real-world dataset will be used in the simulation to show the performance of the proposed algorithms on resolving the constrained DSLR problem.

9.2.4.2 The DERC Problem

Another notable example of problem formulation (9.1) comes from DERC problems in power systems. A properly designed coordination and control mechanism of the DGs and ESs plays an indispensable role in power systems [209], which can optimize the investment on infrastructures as well as guarantee an effective and efficient operation for the system. However, a more critical objective is to establish a general problem formulation considering practically physical constraints as much as possible for the costs on both DGs and ESs. Inspired by Yang et al. [207], Wu et al. [209], we set up the DERC problem as follows:

$$\min_{p_1,\ldots,p_m} \sum_{i=1}^{m} C_i\left(p_i\right)+\delta_{J_i}\left(p_i\right), \tag{9.4a}$$

$$\text{s.t.} \quad \sum_{i=1}^{m} p_i = D_m, \tag{9.4b}$$

$$p_i^{\min} \leq p_{i,t} \leq p_i^{\max}, i \in \mathcal{D} \cup \mathcal{S}, t \in \{1, \ldots, T\}, \tag{9.4c}$$

where the definitions of the symbols in (9.4) are given in Table 9.2 for a clear presentation. The charging or discharging losses are also considered in (9.4) through setting $p_{i,t}^{batt} = p_{i,t}^{+}/\eta_i^{+} - p_{i,t}^{-}\eta_i^{-}$ and $E_{i,t} = E_{i,t-1} - p_{i,t}^{batt}\Delta T$ with $E_{i,T} = E_{i,0}$ for $i \in \mathcal{S}$. Problem (9.4) can be transformed into problem (9.1) through setting $C_i = f_i$, $\delta_{J_i} = g_i$, $A_i = I$, and $D_m = \sum_{i=1}^{m} b_i$ with $b_i \in \mathbb{R}^T$ being the virtual local demand for $i \in \mathcal{D} \cup \mathcal{S}$. In this chapter, the environmental cost of the DGs is also considered, and this is different with the models developed in [207–209].

9.3 Algorithm Development

9.3.1 *Dual Problem Setup*

It is clear that the strong duality of primal problem (9.1) holds under Assumption 9.1, which allows us to resolve primal problem (9.1) via solving its dual problem. In this section, we focus on formulating the dual problem of primal problem (9.1). To begin with, we first introduce new variables z_i, $i \in \mathcal{V}$ into primal problem (9.1), which aims at obtaining the separable structure of the dual problem. Thus, an equivalent formulation of primal problem (9.1) is formulated as follows:

$$\min_{x_1,\cdots,x_m} \sum_{i=1}^{m} f_i\left(x_i\right)+g_i\left(z_i\right), \tag{9.5a}$$

$$\text{s.t.} \quad \sum_{i=1}^{m} A_i x_i = \sum_{i=1}^{m} b_i, \tag{9.5b}$$

Table 9.2 Definitions for the DERC problem

Symbols	Definitions
m	The total number of DGs and ESs in the system
$\mathcal{D}$	The set of DGs
$\mathcal{S}$	The set of ESs
DG_i	The i-th distributed generator, $i \in \mathcal{D}$
ES_i	The i-th energy storage, $i \in \mathcal{S}$
T	The coordination period
$p_{i,t}$	The power from DG_i or ES_i during period t
p_i	The collected power over coordination period T, i.e., $p_i = [p_{i,1}, p_{i,2}, ..., p_{i,T}]^{\text{T}} \in \mathbb{R}^T$
C_i	The operation cost function of DG_i, $i \in \mathcal{D}$ or the operation and environmental cost function of ES_i, $i \in \mathcal{S}$ during coordination period T
$J_i^{\mathcal{D}}$	$J_i^{\mathcal{D}} = \{p_i \mid \Delta \underline{p_i} \leq p_{i,t} - p_{i,t-1} \leq \Delta \bar{p}_i, t \in \{2, 3, \ldots, T\}\}$
$J_i^{\mathcal{S}}$	$J_i^{\mathcal{S}} = \left\{p_i = p_i^+ - p_i^- \,\middle|\, 0 \leq E_{i,t} \leq E_i^{\max}, t \in \{1, 2, \ldots, T\}\right\}$
J_i	$J_i = \left\{p_i \mid p_i \in J_i^{\mathcal{D}} \cup J_i^{\mathcal{S}}\right\}$
δ_{J_i}	The indicator function with respect to the set J_i
D_m	The required total demand
$p_{i,t}^{batt}$	The rate of change of energy stored in ES_i at period t
$p_{i,t}^+$	The discharged power from ES_i at period t
$p_{i,t}^-$	The charged power from ES_i at period t
η_i^+	The discharging efficiency of ES_i and $\eta_i^+ \in (0, 1)$
η_i^-	The charging efficiency of ES_i and $\eta_i^+ \in (0, 1)$
$E_{i,t}$	The energy stored in ES_i at period t
ΔT	The size of period T

$$x_i = z_i, i \in \mathcal{V}, \tag{9.5c}$$

$$x_i^{\min} \leq x_i \leq x_i^{\max}, i \in \mathcal{V}. \tag{9.5d}$$

Then, in order to cope with the constraints in (9.5), we derive the dual problem corresponding to (9.5) as follows:

$$\min_{\tilde{\lambda}, u} \sum_{i=1}^{m} f_i^{\otimes}(-(A_i^{\text{T}}\tilde{\lambda} + u_i)) + g_i^{\otimes}(u_i) + \tilde{\lambda}^{\text{T}} b_i, \tag{9.6}$$

where $\tilde{\lambda} \in \mathbb{R}^{\tilde{r}}$ and $u = \mathbf{col}\{u_i\} \in \mathbb{R}^n$ are the Lagrange multipliers corresponding to constraints (9.5b) and (9.5c), respectively; $f_i^{\otimes} : \mathbb{R}^{n_i} \to \mathbb{R}$ and $g_i^{\otimes} : \mathbb{R}^{n_i} \to \mathbb{R}$ are the conjugate functions corresponding to f_i and g_i, respectively. The details about deriving (9.6) are placed in Appendix A available in the online supplementary file to ensure the coherence of the chapter. To study the dual problem (9.6) in a distributed manner, we introduce copies of $\tilde{\lambda}$ and the corresponding consensus constraints such that optimization problem (9.6) can be equivalently rewritten as:

$$\min_{\lambda,u} \sum_{i=1}^{m} f_i^{\otimes}\left(-\left(A_i^{\mathrm{T}}\lambda_i + u_i\right)\right) + g_i^{\otimes}(u_i) + \lambda_i^{\mathrm{T}} b_i, \tag{9.7a}$$

$$\text{s.t. } \lambda_i = \lambda_j,\ (i,j) \in \mathcal{E}, \tag{9.7b}$$

where $\lambda_i \in \mathbb{R}^{\tilde{r}}$ and $\lambda = \mathbf{col}\{\lambda_i\} \in \mathbb{R}^r$, $r = m\tilde{r}$, $i \in \mathcal{V}$. To tackle the consensus constraint, defining $D_{ij} = \begin{cases} I, & i < j \\ -I, & i > j \end{cases}$, problem (9.7) can be rewritten as

$$\min_{\lambda,u} \sum_{i=1}^{m} f_i^{\otimes}\left(-\left(A_i^{\mathrm{T}}\lambda_i + u_i\right)\right) + g_i^{\otimes}(u_i) + \lambda_i^{\mathrm{T}} b_i, \tag{9.8a}$$

$$\text{s.t. } D_{ij}\lambda_i + D_{ji}\lambda_j = 0,\ (i,j) \in \mathcal{E}, \tag{9.8b}$$

where the local objective functions, $f_i^{\otimes}$, are convex, continuously differentiable, and $1/\mu_i$-Lipschitz smooth [124, Lemma V.8] [222, Theorem 4.2.1]; the local objective functions, $g_i^{\otimes}$, are proper, closed, and convex. Moreover, the local objective functions $f_i^{\otimes}$ and $g_i^{\otimes}$ are privately known by agent i, $i \in \mathcal{V}$, and (9.8b) represents a coupled edge constraint for $(i,j) \in \mathcal{E}$. Therefore, we define a linear operator as follows:

$$\mathcal{B}_{(i,j)} : \lambda \to \left[\left(D_{ij}\lambda_i\right)^{\mathrm{T}}, \left(D_{ji}\lambda_j\right)^{\mathrm{T}}\right]^{\mathrm{T}},\ (i,j) \in \mathcal{E}, \tag{9.9}$$

where $\mathcal{B}_{(i,j)} : \mathbb{R}^r \to \mathbb{R}^{\tilde{l}}$ and $\tilde{l} = 2\tilde{r}$. The stacked form of $\mathcal{B}_{(i,j)}$ is given by

$$\mathcal{B} : \lambda \to (\mathcal{B}_{(i,j)}\lambda)_{(i,j)\in\mathcal{E}}, \tag{9.10}$$

where $\mathcal{B} : \mathbb{R}^r \to \mathbb{R}^l$ and $l = 2\sum_{(i,j)\in\mathcal{E}} \tilde{r}$. Define a set

$$\mathcal{M}_{(i,j)} = \left\{[s_1^{\mathrm{T}}, s_2^{\mathrm{T}}]^{\mathrm{T}} \in \mathbb{R}^{\tilde{l}} | s_1 + s_2 = 0\right\}. \tag{9.11}$$

Thus, we obtain the desired formulation which is equivalent to optimization problem (9.8) as follows:

$$\min_{\lambda,u} \sum_{i=1}^{m} f_i^{\otimes}\left(-\left(A_i^{\mathrm{T}}\lambda_i + u_i\right)\right) + g_i^{\otimes}(u_i) + \lambda_i^{\mathrm{T}} b_i + \sum_{i=1}^{m} \sum_{(i,j)\in\mathcal{E}} \delta_{\mathcal{M}_{(i,j)}}(\mathcal{B}_{(i,j)}\lambda). \tag{9.12}$$

9.3.2 SynDe-DuPro and AsynDe-DuPro Algorithms Development

In this section, we develop SynDe-DuPro and AsynDe-DuPro algorithms to solve for the globally optimal solution to optimization problem (9.12). Based on [22, Proposition 19.18], we construct the Lagrangian function of (9.12) as follows:

$$
\begin{aligned}
\Phi(\lambda, u, w) &= \sum_{i=1}^{m} f_i^{\otimes}\left(-\left(A_i^{\mathrm{T}}\lambda_i + u_i\right)\right) + g_i^{\otimes}(u_i) + \lambda_i^{\mathrm{T}} b_i \\
&\quad + \sum_{i=1}^{m} \sum_{(i,j)\in\mathcal{E}} \left(\mathcal{B}_{(i,j)}\lambda\right)^{\mathrm{T}} w_{(i,j)} - \delta_{\mathcal{M}_{(i,j)}}^{\otimes}\left(w_{(i,j)}\right) \\
&= \sum_{i=1}^{m} f_i^{\otimes}\left(-\left(A_i^{\mathrm{T}}\lambda_i + u_i\right)\right) + g_i^{\otimes}(u_i) + \lambda_i^{\mathrm{T}} b_i \\
&\quad + \sum_{i=1}^{m} \sum_{j\in\mathcal{N}_i} \left(D_{ij}\lambda_i\right)^{\mathrm{T}} w_{(i,j),i} - \delta_{\mathcal{M}_{(i,j)}}^{\otimes}\left(w_{(i,j)}\right),
\end{aligned}
\tag{9.13}
$$

where $w_{(i,j)} = [(w_{(i,j),i})^{\mathrm{T}}, (w_{(i,j),j})^{\mathrm{T}}]^{\mathrm{T}} \in \mathbb{R}^{\tilde{l}}$, is the edge variable corresponding to coupled edge constraint (9.8b); $\lambda = \mathbf{col}\{\lambda_i\} \in \mathbb{R}^r$, $u = \mathbf{col}\{u_i\} \in \mathbb{R}^n$, $w = \mathbf{col}\{w_{(i,j)}\}_{(i,j)\in\mathcal{E}} \in \mathbb{R}^l$, and $\delta_{\mathcal{M}_{(i,j)}}^{\otimes}$ is the conjugate function of $\delta_{\mathcal{M}_{(i,j)}}$. Taking partial derivatives on (9.13) with respect to variables λ_i, u_i, $w_{(i,j)}$, $i, j \in \mathcal{V}$, and then applying the operator splitting method in [17], one can briefly describe updates to resolve (9.12) as follows:

$$
\bar{w}_{(i,j)}^{k} = \mathrm{prox}_{\kappa_{(i,j)}\delta_{\mathcal{M}_{(i,j)}}^{\otimes}} \left\{ w_{(i,j)}^{k} + \kappa_{(i,j)}(\mathcal{B}_{(i,j)}\lambda^k) \right\}, \tag{9.14a}
$$

$$
u_i^{k+1} = \mathrm{prox}_{\sigma_i g_i^{\otimes}} \left\{ u_i^k - \sigma_i \partial_{u_i} f_i^{\otimes}\left(-A_i^{\mathrm{T}}\lambda_i^k - u_i^k\right) \right\}, \tag{9.14b}
$$

$$
\lambda_i^{k+1} = \lambda_i^k - \tau_i \left(\partial_{\lambda_i} f_i^{\otimes}\left(-A_i^{\mathrm{T}}\lambda_i^k - u_i^k\right) + b_i + \sum_{j\in\mathcal{N}_i} D_{ij}^{\mathrm{T}} \bar{w}_{(i,j),i}^{k} \right), \tag{9.14c}
$$

$$
w_{(i,j),i}^{k+1} = \bar{w}_{(i,j),i}^{k} + \kappa_{(i,j)} D_{ij} \left(\lambda_i^{k+1} - \lambda_i^k\right), \tag{9.14d}
$$

where $\bar{w}_{(i,j)} = [(\bar{w}_{(i,j),i})^{\mathrm{T}}, (\bar{w}_{(i,j),j})^{\mathrm{T}}]^{\mathrm{T}} \in \mathbb{R}^{\tilde{l}}$, $j \in \mathcal{N}_i$ and the partial derivatives are calculated as follows:

$$
\partial_{u_i} f_i^{\otimes}\big(-(A_i^{\mathrm{T}}\lambda_i + u_i)\big) = -\arg\min_{x_i\in\mathcal{X}_i} \left\{ f_i(x_i) + x_i^{\mathrm{T}}(A_i^{\mathrm{T}}\lambda_i + u_i) \right\}, \tag{9.15a}
$$

$$
\partial_{\lambda_i} f_i^{\otimes}\big(-(A_i^{\mathrm{T}}\lambda_i + u_i)\big) = -A_i \arg\min_{x_i\in\mathcal{X}_i} \left\{ f_i(x_i) + x_i^{\mathrm{T}}(A_i^{\mathrm{T}}\lambda_i + u_i) \right\}. \tag{9.15b}
$$

Then, combining (9.14) with (9.15) and leveraging Moreau decomposition [22] on (9.14a)–(9.14b), we propose a synchronous algorithm named SynDe-DuPro and the detailed updates are described in Algorithm 12.

Algorithm 12 SynDe-DuPro algorithm

Initialization: For $j \in \mathcal{N}_i$, each agent $i, i \in \mathcal{V}$ initializes the dual variables $\lambda_i^0 \in \mathbb{R}^{\tilde{r}}$ and $u_i^0 \in \mathbb{R}^{n_i}$, the dual variable $w_{(i,j),i}^0 \in \mathbb{R}^{\tilde{r}}$ corresponding to the communication edge (i, j), and the primal variable

$$x_i^0 = \underset{x_i \in \mathcal{X}_i}{\arg\min} \left\{ f_i(x_i) + x_i^{\mathrm{T}} \left(A_i^{\mathrm{T}} \lambda_i^0 + u_i^0 \right) \right\}$$

with $\mathcal{X}_i = \left\{ x_i \in \mathbb{R}^{n_i} | x_i^{\min} \le x_i \le x_i^{\max} \right\}$. Then, for $j \in \mathcal{N}_i$, each agent $i, i \in \mathcal{V}$ chooses properly positive constant step sizes σ_i and τ_i, and the positive constant communication edge step size/weight $\kappa_{(i,j)}$.

For $k = 0, 1, \ldots,$ **do:**

For $j \in \mathcal{N}_i$, each agent i computes

1:

$$\bar{w}_{(i,j),i}^k = \frac{1}{2} \left(w_{(i,j),i}^k + w_{(i,j),j}^k \right) + \frac{\kappa_{(i,j)}}{2} \left(D_{ij} \lambda_i^k + D_{ji} \lambda_j^k \right), \tag{9.16}$$

$$u_i^{k+1} = u_i^k + \sigma_i x_i^k - \sigma_i \mathrm{prox}_{\sigma_i^{-1} g_i} \left(\sigma_i^{-1} u_i^k + x_i^k \right), \tag{9.17}$$

$$\lambda_i^{k+1} = \lambda_i^k - \tau_i \left(-A_i x_i^k + b_i + \sum_{j \in \mathcal{N}_i} D_{ij}^{\mathrm{T}} \bar{w}_{(i,j),i}^k \right), \tag{9.18}$$

$$w_{(i,j),i}^{k+1} = \bar{w}_{(i,j),i}^k + \kappa_{(i,j)} D_{ij} \left(\lambda_i^{k+1} - \lambda_i^k \right). \tag{9.19}$$

2: Agent i sends $D_{ij} \lambda_i^{k+1}$ and $w_{(i,j),i}^k$ to agent j, then computes

$$x_i^{k+1} = \underset{x_i \in \mathcal{X}_i}{\arg\min} \left\{ f_i(x_i) + x_i^{\mathrm{T}} \left(A_i^{\mathrm{T}} \lambda_i^{k+1} + u_i^{k+1} \right) \right\}. \tag{9.20}$$

End

Definition 9.2 Recalling the definitions of the variables u, λ, and w, we first partition these variables into m blocks of coordinates. Then, define diagonal activation matrices $\mathbb{A}_i \in \mathbb{R}^{(n+r+l) \times (n+r+l)}$, $i \in \mathcal{V}$, with 0–1 diagonal entries, and therein 1 represents the selected coordinates and 0 otherwise. Therefore, one can use $\mathbb{A}_i$ to choose the activated coordinate. Moreover, denote $\varphi = \{0, 1\}^m$ as the set of binary strings of length m, the elements of which are considered to compose an m-dimensional vector. Then, we define a φ-valued activation vector $v^k \in \mathbb{R}^m$, which is used to determine the updated blocks of coordinates at k-th iteration. That is to say, when $v_i^k = 1$, the i-th block is updated at the k-th iteration.

Assumption 9.3 (Activated Schemes)

(i) The activated matrices, $\mathbb{A}_i$*,* $i \in \mathcal{V}$*, are 0-1 diagonal matrices and* $\sum_{i=1}^{m} \mathbb{A}_i = I$*;*

(ii) The sequence, $\{v^k\}_{k \geq 0}$*, is a sequence of independent and identically distributed* m*-dimensional 0-1 vectors with probability*

$$P_i = \mathbb{P}(v_i^k = 1) > 0, \; k \geq 0, \; i \in \mathcal{V}.$$

Definition 9.3 Based on Definition 9.2 and Assumption 9.3, a coordinate probability matrix $\mathbb{M}$ can be naturally defined as:

$$\mathbb{M} = \sum_{i=1}^{m} P_i \mathbb{A}_i. \tag{9.21}$$

Then, we briefly denote the conditional expectation $\mathbb{E}[\cdot|\mathcal{F}_k]$ as $\mathbb{E}_k[\cdot]$, where $\mathcal{F}_k$ is the filtration yielded by the sequence, $(v^1 \dots v^k)$. We further define an operator, $E^k = \sum_{i=1}^{m} v_i^k \mathbb{A}_i$, which maps the elements of $(\mathbb{R}^{n+r}, \mathcal{F}_{k-1})$ to $(\mathbb{R}^{n+r}, \mathcal{F}_k)$.

Remark 9.4 Notice that the step sizes, σ_i and τ_i, are local constant step sizes maintained only by agent i. The edge step sizes/weights $\kappa_{(i,j)}$, $(i, j) \in \mathcal{E}$, can be considered as inherent parameters or step sizes of the communication link used to capture the quality of the communication and maintained by agent i and its neighbors $j \in \mathcal{N}_i$. As shown in Algorithm 12, each agent i, $i \in \mathcal{V}$ keeps privately local primal variable x_i^k and local dual variables u_i^k and λ_i^k while the edge variable, $w_{(i,j),i}^k$, should be shared with its neighbors $j \in \mathcal{N}_i$ at k-th iteration. Note that the variables x_i^k, $i \in \mathcal{V}$, serve as intermediate variables in the whole updates.

Remark 9.5 It is worth mentioning that similar with existing distributed methods [14, 15, 18, 54, 67, 121, 207, 214, 221], SynDe-DuPro algorithm requires all agents in the multi-agent system to engage in the updates at every iteration, which may be impractical in practice due to the possible failure or non-activation of some agents at typical iterations. Thus, we further develop an asynchronous algorithm named AsynDe-DuPro in Algorithm 13, which enhances the robustness to the situation of failure or non-activation of some agents and thus renders the whole multi-agent system more robust in some environments. Additionally, Algorithm 13 is based on a randomized block-coordinate model which captures many existing activation mechanisms, such as the single coordinate activation mechanism [223, 224] and the multiple coordinate activation mechanism [23, 100].

Definition 9.6 For each edge $(i, j) \in \mathcal{E}$, the edge step size/weight matrix is defined as follows:

$$\mathrm{K} = \mathbf{blkdiag}\{(\kappa_{(i,j)} I)_{(i,j) \in \mathcal{E}}\} \in \mathbb{R}^{l \times l}.$$

Algorithm 13 AsynDe-DuPro algorithm

Initialization: For $j \in \mathcal{N}_i$, each agent $i, i \in \mathcal{V}$ initializes $\lambda_i^0 \in \mathbb{R}^{\tilde{r}}$, $u_i^0 \in \mathbb{R}^{n_i}$, $w_{(i,j),i}^0 \in \mathbb{R}^{\tilde{r}}$ and

$$x_i^0 = \arg\min_{x_i \in \mathcal{X}_i} \left\{ f_i(x_i) + x_i^{\mathrm{T}} \left(A_i^{\mathrm{T}} \lambda_i^0 + u_i^0 \right) \right\},$$

then chooses properly positive step - sizes, σ_i, τ_i, and $\kappa_{(i,j)}$.

For $k = 0, 1, \ldots,$ **do**: For $\forall j \in \mathcal{N}_i$, each agent i, $i \in \mathcal{V}$ is activated independently with probability P_i and a group of activated agents compute the steps (you need to define these steps properly). The agents not activated at k-th iteration do not participate in the updates and rather keep the states unchanged.

End

Furthermore, for each agent i, $i \in \mathcal{V}$, we define positive step sizes, σ_i and τ_i, which are associated with dual variables u_i and λ_i, respectively. Moreover, we define

$$\begin{aligned}
\Sigma &= \mathbf{blkdiag}\{\sigma_1 I, \ldots, \sigma_m I\} \in \mathbb{R}^{n \times n}, \\
\bar{\Sigma} &= \mathbf{blkdiag}\{\sigma_1 I, \ldots, \sigma_m I, \mathrm{K}\} \in \mathbb{R}^{(n+l)\times(n+l)}, \\
\Gamma &= \mathbf{blkdiag}\{\tau_1 I, \ldots, \tau_m I\} \in \mathbb{R}^{r \times r}, \\
Q &= \mathbf{blkdiag}\{\beta_1 I, \ldots, \beta_m I\} \in \mathbb{R}^{(r+n)\times(r+n)},
\end{aligned}$$

where $\beta_i = \sqrt{1 + \|A_i\|^2 / \mu_i}$.

Assumption 9.4 (The Step Sizes of Algorithms 12–13) *The step sizes Σ, $\bar{\Sigma}$, and Γ as defined in Definition 9.6, are assumed to be symmetric positive definite and further satisfy the following condition:*

$$0 < \tau_i < \frac{1}{\frac{\sqrt{1+\|A_i\|}}{2\mu_i} + \sigma_i + \sum_{j \in \mathcal{N}_i} \kappa_{(i,j)}}, \tag{9.22}$$

where A_i is defined in (9.1b) and μ_i can be referred to Assumption 9.1. The descriptions of the local constant step sizes τ_i, σ_i and $\kappa_{(i,j)}$ can be referred to Remark 9.4.

Remark 9.7 The detailed analysis that demonstrates the convergence of both SynDe-DuPro and AsynDe-DuPro algorithms is placed in Appendix B available in the online supplementary file. It is worth mentioning that the key point in the convergence analysis is to establish a quasi-Fejér monotone sequence for Algorithm 12 and a stochastic quasi-Fejér monotone sequence for Algorithm 13 with the help of the convergence analysis on synchronous and asynchronous TriPD-Dist algorithms [17]. However, we need to emphasize that Algorithms 12–13 are not equivalent to synchronous and asynchronous TriPD-Dist algorithms [17] since the distributed forms of Algorithms 12–13 and synchronous and asynchronous TriPD-

Dist algorithms [17] are totally different owing to the different optimization problem model studied in this chapter.

9.4 Numerical Examples

In this section, two case studies in machine learning and power systems are provided to demonstrate the effectiveness and better performance of Algorithms 12–13. Throughout the simulations, we set the activated probability of agents in asynchronous algorithms equal to 0.6. All simulations are carried out in MATLAB on a Lenovo Laptop with 4.10 GHz, 4 Cores 8 Threads Intel i5-9300HF processor and 16 GB memory.

9.4.1 Case Study I: Constrained DSLR in Machine Learning

In the first case study, we revisit the example of the constrained DSLR problem introduced in Sect. 9.2.4.1. The performance of the proposed algorithms, PG-EXTRA [54] and synchronous and asynchronous TriPD-Dist algorithms [17] are compared by resolving constrained DSLR problem (9.3). The simulation is based on a benchmark Mushroom dataset provided in UCI Machine Learning Repository [225]. The common task of all the tested algorithms is to train a discriminator, and then use it to identify whether a mushroom is poisonous or edible according to its various features including cap-shape, cap-surface, cap-color, bruises, habitat, and so on. A total number of 8124 samples from the dataset are selected to conduct the simulation, from which $N = 6000$ samples are used to train the discriminator and the rest of samples are used for testing. Each agent maintains $Q_i = 200$ samples and a network of $m = 30$ agents communicate over a randomly generated undirected network with connectivity ratio $\tau_c = 0.5$ as depicted in Fig. 9.2. Each sample has $n = 112$ dimensions that consist of the total attributes of the sample.

We study the impact of ratio constant θ_r on the performance of all the tested algorithms via setting $\theta_r = 10{,}000$ in Figs. 9.3 and 9.4, $\theta_r = 1000$ in Figs. 9.5

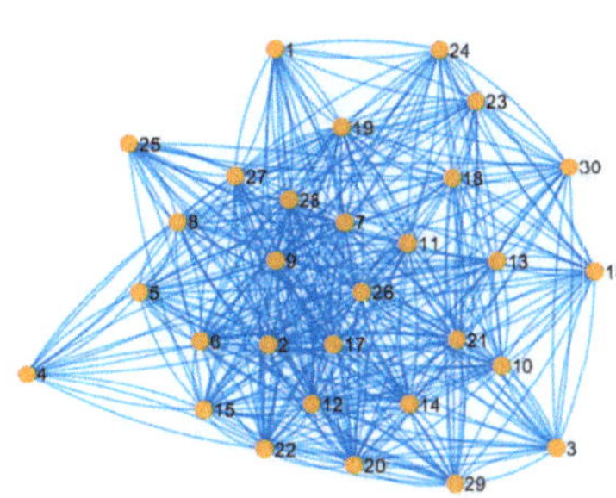

Fig. 9.2 An undirected network with $m = 30$ agents

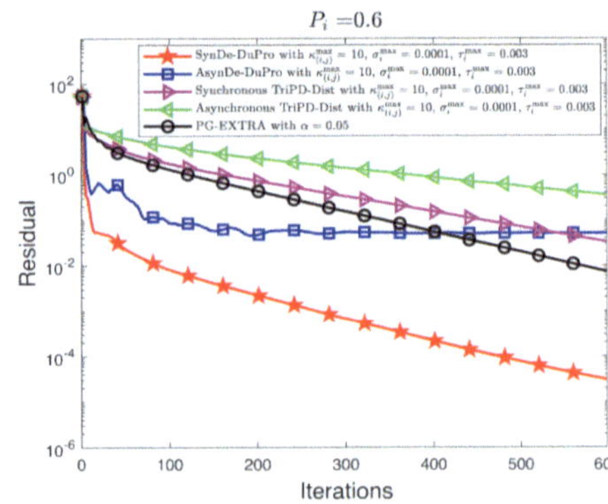

Fig. 9.3 Training performance with $\theta_r = 10{,}000$

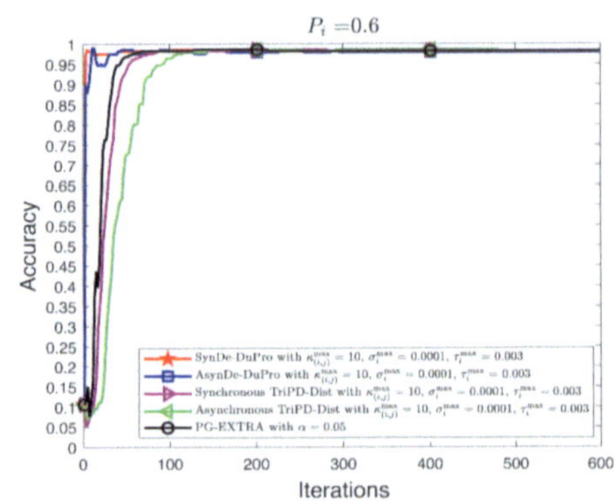

Fig. 9.4 Testing accuracy with $\theta_r = 10{,}000$

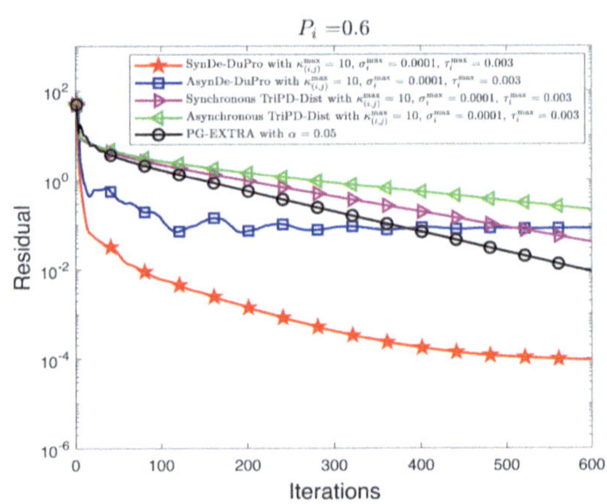

Fig. 9.5 Training performance with $\theta_r = 1000$

and 9.6, and $\theta_r = 100$ in Figs. 9.7 and 9.8, respectively. As stated in Sect. 9.2.4.1, we set A_i as the i-th column of the Laplacian matrix associated with Fig. 9.2, $lb = [-1, \ldots, -1]^{\mathrm{T}} \in \mathbb{R}^n$, and $ub = [1, \ldots, 1]^{\mathrm{T}} \in \mathbb{R}^n$. In Figs. 9.3, 9.4, 9.5, 9.6, 9.7, and 9.8, the projected method [115] are equipped with PG-EXTRA and synchronous and asynchronous TriPD-Dist algorithms to address local box

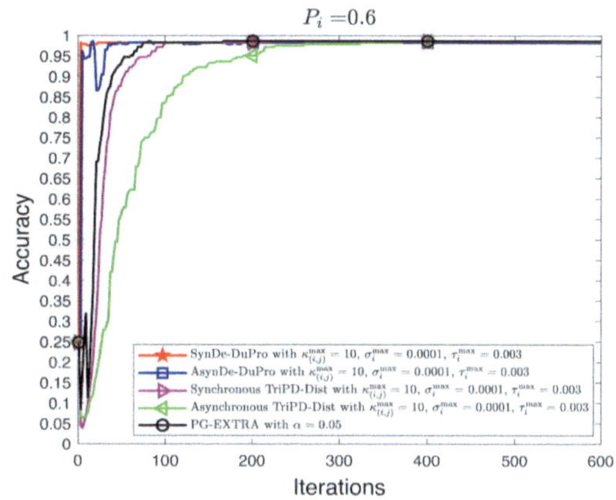

Fig. 9.6 Testing accuracy with $\theta_r = 1000$

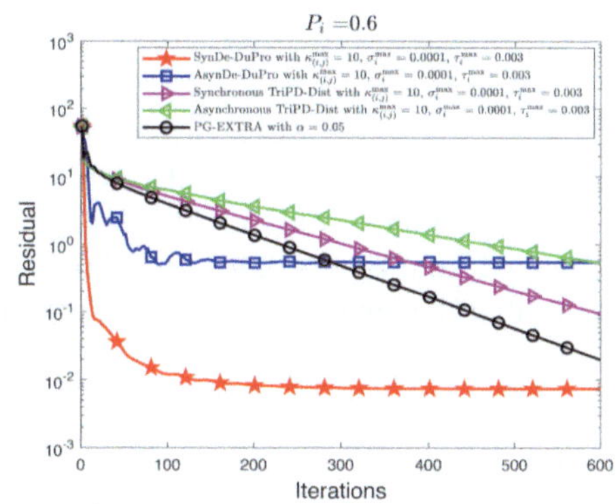

Fig. 9.7 Training performance with $\theta_r = 100$

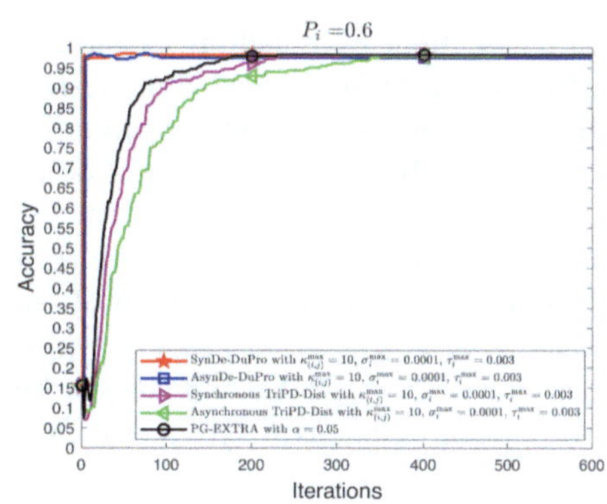

Fig. 9.8 Testing accuracy with $\theta_r = 100$

constraint (9.3c). The residual used in vertical axes of Figs. 9.3, 9.5, and 9.7, is defined as $(1/m)\sum_{i=1}^{m}\left\|x_i^k - \tilde{x}^*\right\|^2$, where $\tilde{x}^*$ is the optimal solution to (9.3) generated by the projected PG-EXTRA algorithm. The accuracy used in vertical axes of Figs. 9.4, 9.6, and 9.8, is denoted as the ratio between the number of correct prediction and the total number of the testing set. One can clearly see

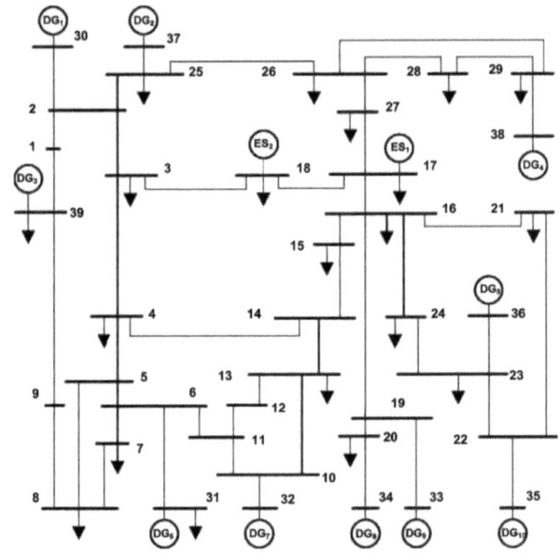

Fig. 9.9 A modified IEEE 39-bus system

that SynDe-DuPro and AsynDe-DuPro algorithms converge faster than the other tested algorithms from Figs. 9.3, 9.4, 9.5, 9.6, 9.7, and 9.8. Moreover, it can also be observed from Figs. 9.3, 9.4, 9.5, 9.6, 9.7, and 9.8 show that the performance tested algorithms becomes better when θ_r becomes larger.

9.4.2 *Case Study II: DERC in Power Systems*

In this section, we recall the example of DERC in Sect. 9.2.4.2. The performance of both SynDe-DuPro and AsynDe-DuPro algorithms is exploited on a modified IEEE 39-bus system originated from [226], which is shown in Fig. 9.9. As shown in Fig. 9.9, the sets of DGs and ESs are denoted by $\mathcal{D} = \{i \mid i = 1, \ldots, 10\}$ and $\mathcal{S} = \{i \mid i = 1, 2\}$, respectively. The communication among the DGs and ESs is undirected and the communication network is assumed to be connected. The cost functions of DGs are specified by strongly-convex functions $C_i\left(p_{i,t}\right) = a_i^2 p_{i,t} + b_i p_{i,t} + c_i + 10^{-2}(\alpha_i + \chi_i p_{i,t} + \gamma_i p_{i,t}^2) + \xi_i \exp\left(\rho_i p_{i,t}\right)$ for DGs $i = 30, \ldots, 39$ and $t \in \{1, 2, \ldots, 24\}$ while the cost functions of ESs are specified by convex but nonsmooth functions $C_i(p_{i,t}) = d_i \left|p_{i,t}\right|$ for ES_i, $i \in \mathcal{S}$, and $t \in \{1, 2, \ldots, 24\}$. Please note that a_i, b_i, c_i, α_i, χ_i, γ_i, ξ_i, and ρ_i are cost coefficients of DG_i, $i \in \mathcal{D}$ while d_i is the cost coefficient of ES_i, $i \in \mathcal{S}$. Different with the problem models devised in [207–209], we further consider the environmental cost $10^{-2}(\alpha_i + \chi_i p_{i,t} + \gamma_i p_{i,t}^2) + \xi_i \exp\left(\rho_i p_{i,t}\right)$ for DGs, $i \in \mathcal{D}$ and the costs for ES_i, $i \in \mathcal{S}$ are convex but nonsmooth. The parameters of DGs' cost functions and ESs' cost functions are presented in Tables 9.3 and 9.4, respectively. The ramping up/down values of each DG are equal to 10 kW.

Table 9.3 Parameters of DGs

Bus	a_i	b_i	c_i	α_i	χ_i	γ_i	ξ_i	ρ_i	$[p_i^{\min}, p_i^{\max}]$
30	2.4×10^{-4}	2.67×10^{-2}	3.8×10^{-1}	2×10^{-4}	−3.8	4.8	2×10^{-4}	3.8×10^{-2}	[30, 60]
31	1.99×10^{-4}	1.16×10^{-2}	4.969×10^{-1}	5×10^{-4}	−4.969	2.7	2×10^{-4}	7.7×10^{-2}	[110, 500]
32	2.8×10^{-4}	1.95×10^{-2}	3.2×10^{-1}	3.8×10^{-4}	−3.25	5.2	5×10^{-4}	6.2×10^{-2}	[40, 250]
33	4.2×10^{-4}	1.85×10^{-2}	4×10^{-1}	4.2×10^{-4}	−45	2.5	5×10^{-4}	3.5×10^{-2}	[50, 200]
34	2.8×10^{-4}	1.95×10^{-2}	3.2×10^{-1}	1.8×10^{-4}	−42.5	6.1	1×10^{-4}	5.1×10^{-2}	[40, 250]
35	3.1×10^{-4}	2.94×10^{-2}	3×10^{-1}	3×10^{-4}	−35	1.2	2×10^{-4}	5.4×10^{-2}	[20, 140]
36	2.48×10^{-4}	1.56×10^{-2}	3.312×10^{-1}	2×10^{-4}	−3.3	1.4	1×10^{-4}	2.4×10^{-2}	[30, 300]
37	5.28×10^{-4}	1.52×10^{-2}	6.5×10^{-1}	5×10^{-4}	−6.5	4.5	5×10^{-4}	6.5×10^{-2}	[20, 60]
38	3.1×10^{-4}	2.97×10^{-2}	3×10^{-1}	3×10^{-4}	−3	2.8	2×10^{-4}	4.8×10^{-2}	[20, 140]
39	4.2×10^{-4}	1.85×10^{-2}	4×10^{-1}	4×10^{-4}	−4	5.5	5×10^{-4}	3.5×10^{-2}	[50, 200]

Note: Units for $a_i, b_i, c_i, \alpha_i, \chi_i, \gamma_i, \xi_i, \rho_i$ are $\$/(kW^2h)$, $\$/(kWh)$, $\$/h$, $\$/h$, $\$/(kWh)$, $\$/(kW^2h)$, $\$/h$, $\$/kWh$ respectively

Table 9.4 Parameters of ESs

Bus	d_i (\$/kWh)	$E_{i,0}$(kWh)	$E_i^{\max}$(kWh)	$\left[p_i^{\min}, p_i^{\max}\right]$	η_i^+	η_i^-
17	1×10^{-4}	250	500	$[-50, 50]$	0.8	0.8
18	1×10^{-4}	100	400	$[-40, 40]$	0.88	0.88

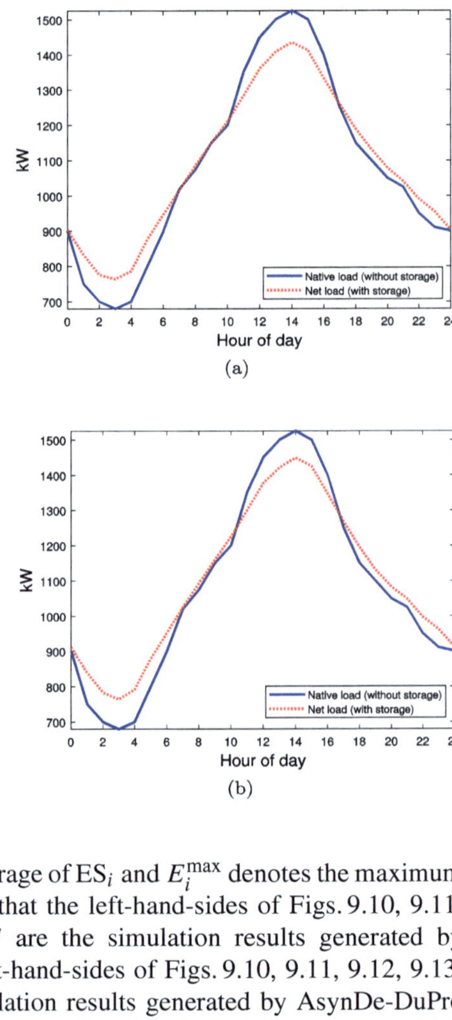

Fig. 9.10 Cut the peak and fill the valley. (**a**) SynDe-DuPro. (**b**) AsynDe-DuPro

Notice that $E_{i,0}$ denotes the initial storage of ES_i and $E_i^{\max}$ denotes the maximum storage of ES_i. It is worth mentioning that the left-hand-sides of Figs. 9.10, 9.11, 9.12, 9.13, 9.14, 9.15, 9.16, and 9.17 are the simulation results generated by SynDe-DuPro algorithm while the right-hand-sides of Figs. 9.10, 9.11, 9.12, 9.13, 9.14, 9.15, 9.16, and 9.17 are the simulation results generated by AsynDe-DuPro algorithm. Figure 9.10 shows the desired effect for the whole system, which indicates that the ESs discharge at the peak hours, for example, Hours 12–16 of the horizontal axis in Fig. 9.10, and charge at the off-peak hours, for example, Hours 2–4 of the horizontal axis in Fig. 9.10. In Fig. 9.11, the total generation generated by the whole system can better meet the total demand at Hour 12 after approximate 2500 iterations for SynDe-DuPro and 5500 iterations for AsynDe-DuPro, i.e., $D_{12}^{\text{emand}} = 1347.3061$ kW. The transient behaviors of DGs and ESs during the 24 hours coordination period are depicted in Fig. 9.12. Figures 9.13

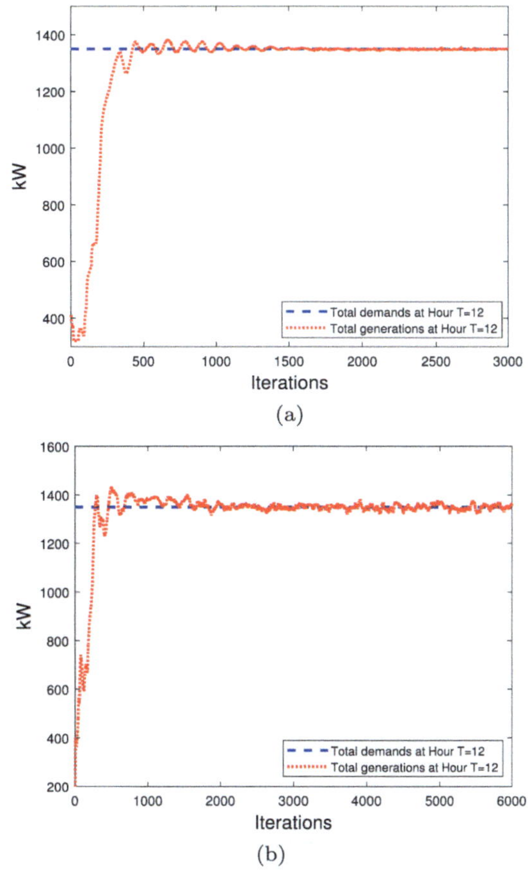

Fig. 9.11 Total demands and total generations. (**a**) SynDe-DuPro. (**b**) AsynDe-DuPro

and 9.14 show respectively the power output and state of charge (SOC) for two ESs, where the SOC of ESs is its available capacity expressed as a percentage of its rated capacity. Moreover, the charging power of ESs is denoted to be a negative value while the discharging power of ESs is denoted to be a positive value. Notice that the total charging energy is more than the total discharging energy because of the charging and discharging losses, and SOC at Hour 24 returns to the starting point for each ES. The transient behaviors of dual variables, λ_i^k and u_i^k, $i \in \mathcal{D} \cup \mathcal{S}$, at Hour 12 are depicted in Figs. 9.15 and 9.16, from which we can see that the optimal incremental costs of both SynDe-DuPro and AsynDe-DuPro algorithms approach roughly to $-\lambda_{12}^* = 0.0981\,\$/\text{kWh}$ and the other virtual optimal incremental costs of both SynDe-DuPro and AsynDe-DuPro algorithms approach roughly to $u_{12}^* = 7.6868 \times 10^{-7}\,\$/\text{kWh}$. The transient behaviors of selected primal variables (or generations of the selected DGs and ESs), p_i^k, $i \in \mathcal{D} \cup \mathcal{S}$, are depicted in Fig. 9.17. Notice that the residual used in vertical axis of Fig. 9.18 is defined as $(1/m)\sum_{i=1}^{m} \left\| p_i^k - p_i^* \right\|^2$, where p_i^* denotes the optimal solution of DG$_i$ or ES$_i$

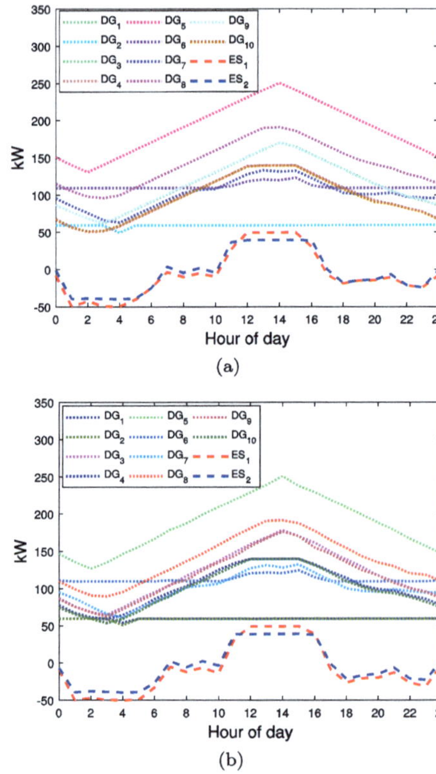

Fig. 9.12 Optimal power generations for DGs and ESs over 24 hours. (**a**) SynDe-DuPro. (**b**) AsynDe-DuPro

to problem (9.4). The results in Fig. 9.18 show that SynDe-DuPro converges faster than AsynDe-DuPro in terms of iterations and slower than AsynDe-DuPro in terms of communication costs.

9.5 Conclusion

In this chapter, we propose two fully distributed algorithms named SynDe-DuPro and AsynDe-DuPro, respectively. Theoretically, via building convergent quasi-Fejér monotone sequences, we establish a unified convergence analysis method for a class of structured optimization problems to nicely conduct the convergence analysis of our proposed two algorithms in this chapter. In simulations, the first case study compares the performance of SynDe-DuPro and AsynDe-DuPro algorithms with existing notable distributed algorithms via resolving a large-scale machine learning problem based on a real-world dataset. Then, the second case study considers the environmental cost/economic emission cost of DGs of DERC in power systems, and the formulation of the cost functions can include some functions reflecting the physical constraints of power systems thanks to the generic nonsmooth problem

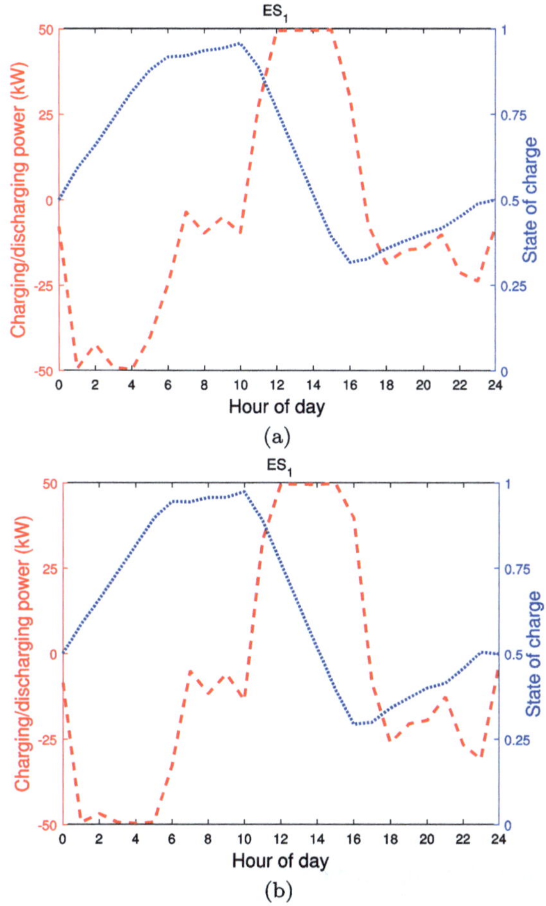

Fig. 9.13 Charging (negative) and discharging (positive) power (red dotted line) and state of charge (blue dash-and-dot line). (**a**) SynDe-DuPro. (**b**) AsynDe-DuPro

model studied in this chapter. Unfortunately, the linear convergence rates of both SynDe-DuPro and AsynDe-DuPro algorithms are not established due to the totally nonsmooth property of the primal problems.

Appendix

Appendix A: The Derivation of Dual Problem (9.6)

In this section, the details about the derivation of (9.6) are given. Recalling the definition of the indicator function and defining a set, $\mathcal{X}_i = \{x_i \in \mathbb{R}^{n_i} | x_i^{\min} \leq x_i \leq x_i^{\max}\}$, $i \in \mathcal{V}$, we can rewrite (9.5) into the following

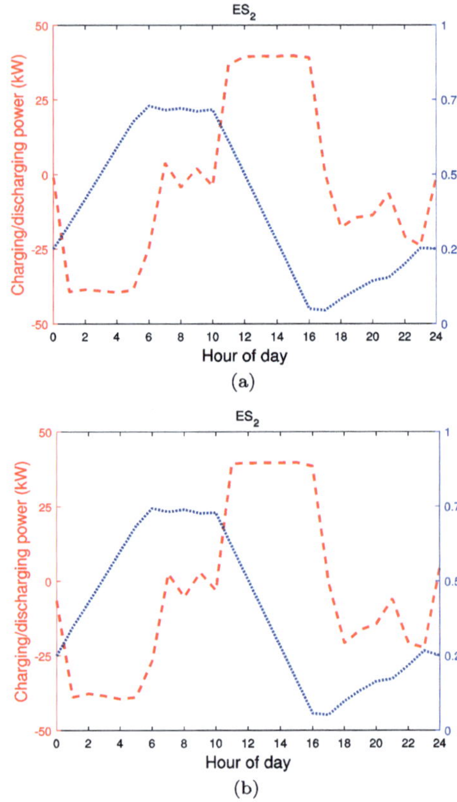

Fig. 9.14 Charging (negative) and discharging (positive) power (red dotted line) and state of charge (blue dash-and-dot line). (**a**) SynDe-DuPro. (**b**) AsynDe-DuPro

equivalent formulation:

$$\min_{x_1,\cdots,x_m} \sum_{i=1}^{m} f_i(x_i) + g_i(z_i) + \delta_{\mathcal{X}_i}(x_i), \tag{9.23a}$$

$$\text{s.t.} \sum_{i=1}^{m} A_i x_i = \sum_{i=1}^{m} b_i, \tag{9.23b}$$

$$x_i = z_i, \quad i \in \mathcal{V}. \tag{9.23c}$$

Then, through setting $x = \mathbf{col}\{x_i\} \in \mathbb{R}^n$ and $z = \mathbf{col}\{z_i\} \in \mathbb{R}^n$ with $n = \sum_{i=1}^{m} n_i$, we construct the Lagrangian function of (9.23) as follows:

$$\begin{aligned}\mathcal{L}\left(x, z, \tilde{\lambda}, u\right) = & \sum_{i=1}^{m} f_i(x_i) + g_i(z_i) + \delta_{\mathcal{X}_i}(x_i) + \sum_{i=1}^{m} \tilde{\lambda}^{\mathrm{T}}(A_i x_i - b_i) \\ & + u_i^{\mathrm{T}}(x_i - z_i),\end{aligned} \tag{9.24}$$

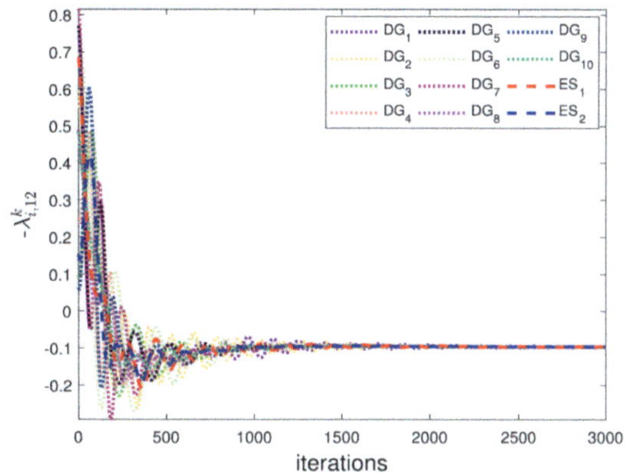

(a)

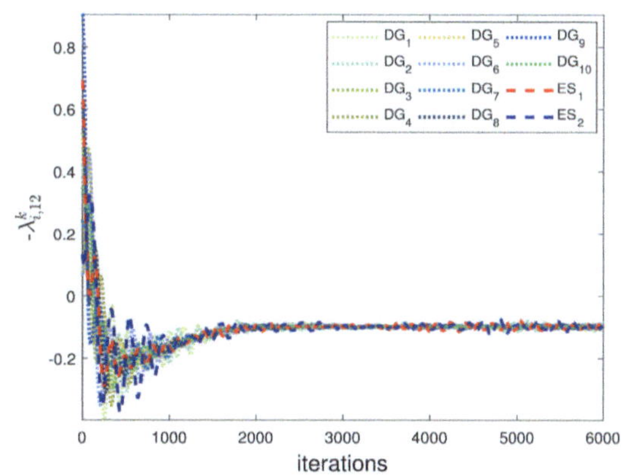

(b)

Fig. 9.15 Transient behaviors of dual variables λ_i^k at $T = 12$. (**a**) SynDe-DuPro. (**b**) AsynDe-DuPro

where $\tilde{\lambda} \in \mathbb{R}^{\tilde{r}}$ and $u = \mathbf{col}\{u_i\} \in \mathbb{R}^n$ are Lagrange multipliers corresponding to constraints (9.23b) and (9.23c), respectively. To proceed, the dual problem of primal problem (9.1) is given as follows:

$$\max_{\tilde{\lambda},u} \min_{x,z} \mathcal{L}(x, z, \tilde{\lambda}, u). \tag{9.25}$$

Based on dual problem (9.25), we define the dual function as follows:

$$d(\tilde{\lambda}, u) = \min_{x,z} \mathcal{L}(x, z, \tilde{\lambda}, u). \tag{9.26}$$

Fig. 9.16 Transient behaviors of dual variables u_i^k at $T = 12$. (**a**) SynDe-DuPro. (**b**) AsynDe-DuPro

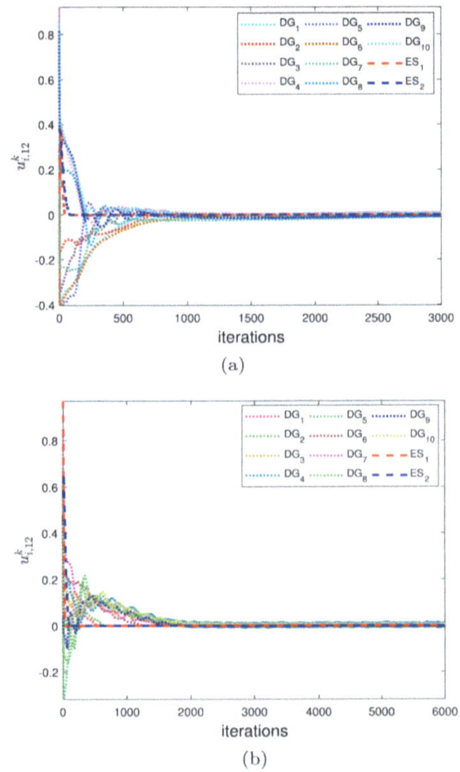

Applying the separable property of the Lagrangian function with respect to x_i and z_i, we obtain

$$
\begin{aligned}
d(\tilde{\lambda}, u) &= \sum_{i=1}^{m} \min_{x_i \in \mathcal{X}_i} \left(f_i(x_i) - x_i^{\mathrm{T}} \left(- \left(A_i^{\mathrm{T}} \tilde{\lambda} + u_i \right) \right) \right) \\
&\quad + \sum_{i=1}^{m} \min_{z_i} \left(g_i(z_i) - z_i^{\mathrm{T}} u_i \right) - \sum_{i=1}^{m} \tilde{\lambda}^{\mathrm{T}} b_i \\
&= \sum_{i=1}^{m} - f_i^{\otimes} \left(- \left(A_i^{\mathrm{T}} \tilde{\lambda} + u_i \right) \right) - g_i^{\otimes}(u_i) - \sum_{i=1}^{m} \tilde{\lambda}^{\mathrm{T}} b_i,
\end{aligned}
\tag{9.27}
$$

where $f_i^{\otimes} : \mathbb{R}^{n_i} \to \mathbb{R}$ and $g_i^{\otimes} : \mathbb{R}^{n_i} \to \mathbb{R}$ are the conjugate functions corresponding to f_i and g_i, respectively. According to the strong duality of primal problem (9.1), seeking the globally optimal solution to primal problem (9.1) is equivalent to solving

Fig. 9.17 Transient behaviors of primal variables p_i^k at $T = 12$. (**a**) SynDe-DuPro. (**b**) AsynDe-DuPro

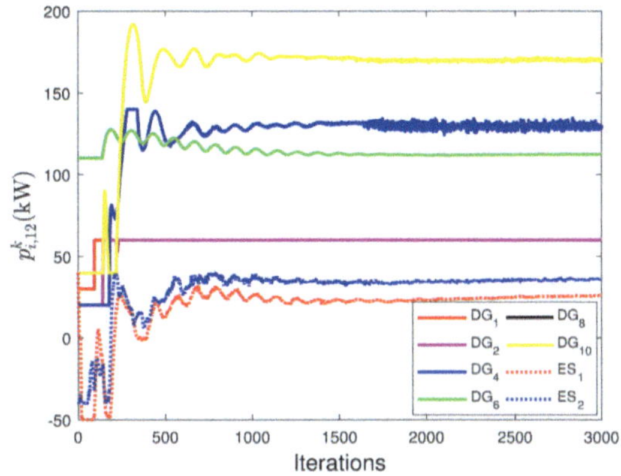

(a)

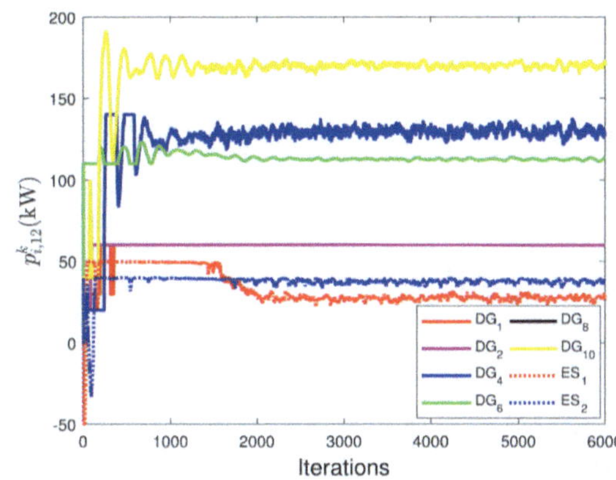

(b)

for the optimal solution to the following dual problem:

$$\begin{aligned}\max_{\tilde{\lambda},u} d(\tilde{\lambda}, u) &= \max_{\tilde{\lambda},u} \sum_{i=1}^{m} -f_i^{\otimes}\left(-\left(A_i^{\mathrm{T}}\tilde{\lambda} + u_i\right)\right) - g_i^{\otimes}(u_i) - \sum_{i=1}^{m} \tilde{\lambda}^{\mathrm{T}} b_i \\ &= -\min_{\tilde{\lambda},u} \sum_{i=1}^{m} f_i^{\otimes}\left(-\left(A_i^{\mathrm{T}}\tilde{\lambda} + u_i\right)\right) + g_i^{\otimes}(u_i) + \tilde{\lambda}^{\mathrm{T}} b_i.\end{aligned} \tag{9.28}$$

Appendix B: The Convergence Analysis of Algorithms 12–13

In this section, the convergence results of SynDe-DuPro and AsynDe-DuPro algorithms are presented.

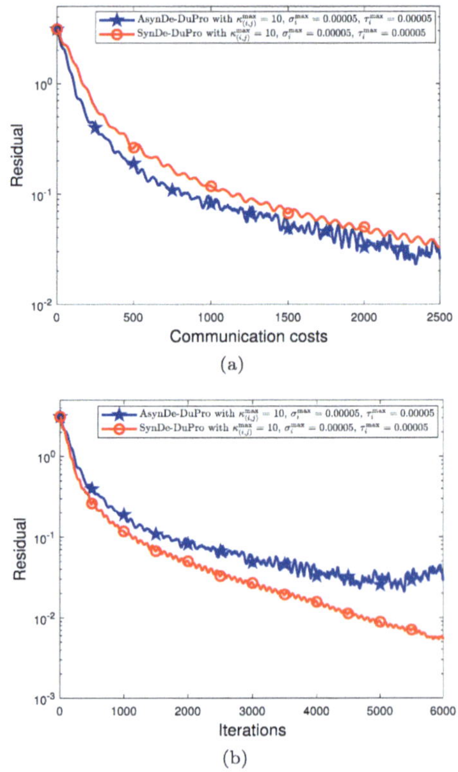

Fig. 9.18 Performance comparison between SynDe-DuPro and AsynDe-DuPro. (**a**) Performance comparison across communication costs. (**b**) Performance Comparison across iterations

Auxiliary Results

We first present some unified analysis results on a general problem formulation, $\min F + G + H$. Borrowed from [17, 225], we set a general optimization problem with a structured form as follows:

$$\min_x F(x) + G(x) + H(\mathbf{L}x), \tag{9.29}$$

where $\mathbf{L} : \mathbb{R}^n \to \mathbb{R}^{(r+l)}$, is an aggregated linear operator, i.e., $\mathbf{L}x = [(Lx)^{\mathrm{T}}, (\tilde{N}x)^{\mathrm{T}}]^{\mathrm{T}}$ where $L : \mathbb{R}^n \to \mathbb{R}^l$ and $\tilde{N} : \mathbb{R}^n \to \mathbb{R}^r$ are linear operators. In addition, problem (9.29) satisfies the following assumption.

Assumption 9.5 (Convexity, Smoothness and Feasibility)

(i) Function $F : \mathbb{R}^n \to \mathbb{R}$ is separable and can be decomposed as: $F = \sum_{i=1}^m f_i$, $i \in \mathcal{V}$, where $f_i : \mathbb{R}^{n_i} \to \mathbb{R}$ is convex, continuously differentiable and $\tilde{\beta}_i$-Lipschitz continuous corresponding to the metric induced by $\tilde{Q}_i$, i.e., for some

$\tilde{\beta}_i \in [0\,,\,+\infty)$, we have

$$\|\nabla f_i\,(a) - \nabla f_i\,(b)\|_{\tilde{Q}_i^{-1}} \leq \tilde{\beta}_i \|a - b\|_{\tilde{Q}_i}, \tag{9.30}$$

where $a, b \in \mathbb{R}^{n_i}$ and $\tilde{Q}_i \succ 0$;

(ii) Function $G : \mathbb{R}^n \to \mathbb{R}$ and aggregated function $H : \mathbb{R}^{r+l} \to \mathbb{R}$ are separable and can be decomposed as: $G = \sum_{i=1}^{m} g_i$ and $H = \sum_{i=1}^{m} h_i$, respectively. Moreover $g_i : \mathbb{R}^{n_i} \to \mathbb{R}$ and $h_i : \mathbb{R}^{r_i+l_i} \to \mathbb{R}$, $i \in \mathcal{V}$, are proper, closed and convex functions;

*(iii) The set of solutions to problem (9.29) is non-empty. Furthermore, the intersection of $x_i \in$ **ri dom** g_i and $\mathbf{L}_i x_i \in$ **ri dom** h_i is also non-empty.*

Definition 9.8 For $(i, j) \in \mathcal{E}$, the edge step size/weight matrix is defined as follows:

$$\tilde{\mathrm{K}} = \mathbf{blkdiag}\{(\tilde{\kappa}_{(i,j)} I)_{(i,j)\in\mathcal{E}}\} \in \mathbb{R}^{l\times l}.$$

Furthermore, for each agent i, $i \in \mathcal{V}$, we define positive step sizes, $\tilde{\sigma}_i$ and $\tilde{\tau}_i$, which are associated with dual variables $\tilde{u}_i$ and $\tilde{\lambda}_i$, respectively. Moreover, we define

$$\begin{aligned}
\tilde{\Sigma} &= \mathbf{blkdiag}\{\tilde{\sigma}_1 I, \ldots, \tilde{\sigma}_m I, \tilde{\mathrm{K}}\} \in \mathbb{R}^{(r+l)\times(r+l)},\\
\tilde{\Gamma} &= \mathbf{blkdiag}\{\tilde{\tau}_1 I, \ldots, \tilde{\tau}_m I\} \in \mathbb{R}^{n\times n},\\
\tilde{Q} &= \mathbf{blkdiag}\{\tilde{\beta}_1 \tilde{Q}_1, \ldots, \tilde{\beta}_m \tilde{Q}_m\} \in \mathbb{R}^{n\times n}.
\end{aligned}$$

In order to resolve problem (9.29) in a distributed manner, the researchers in [17] first propose a notable distributed primal-dual algorithm named as synchronous TriPD-Dist and we summarize the concise and compact form of synchronous TriPD-Dist as follows:

$$\begin{cases}
\bar{u}^k = \mathbf{prox}_{H^{\otimes}}^{\tilde{\Sigma}^{-1}}\{u^k + \tilde{\Sigma}\mathbf{L}x^k\},\\
x^{k+1} = \mathbf{prox}_{G}^{\tilde{\Gamma}^{-1}}\{x^k - \tilde{\Gamma}\nabla F(x^k) - \tilde{\Gamma}\mathbf{L}^{\mathrm{T}}\bar{u}^k\},\\
u^{k+1} = \bar{u}^k + \tilde{\Sigma}\mathbf{L}(x^{k+1} - x^k),
\end{cases} \tag{9.31}$$

where $x^k \in \mathbb{R}^n$ is a primal variable and $u^k \in \mathbb{R}^{r+l}$ is an aggregated dual variable at iteration k; $\tilde{\Sigma} \in \mathbb{R}^{(r+l)\times(r+l)}$ and $\tilde{\Gamma} \in \mathbb{R}^{n\times n}$ are block-diagonal step sizes; $H^{\otimes}$ is the conjugate function of H. In the following, a generic convergence analysis on algorithm (9.31) is presented. To begin with, we make an important assumption that is an indispensable condition to the convergence of algorithm (9.31) in what follows.

Assumption 9.6 *(The step sizes of TriPD-Dist) The step sizes, $\tilde{\Sigma}$ and $\tilde{\Gamma}$, as defined in Definition 9.8, are assumed to be symmetric positive definite and further satisfy the condition as follows:*

$$0 < \tilde{\tau}_i < \frac{1}{\frac{\tilde{\beta}_i \left\| \tilde{Q}_i \right\|}{2} + \|\tilde{\sigma}_i L_i^{\mathrm{T}} L_i + \sum_{j \in \mathcal{N}_i} \tilde{\kappa}_{(i,j)} [\tilde{N}^{\mathrm{T}} \tilde{N}]_{ii} \|}, \tag{9.32}$$

where $\tilde{\beta}_i \geq 0$ is the Lipschitz continuous constant of ∇f_i with metric $\tilde{Q}_i \succ 0$. The notation $[H]_{ii}$ denotes the i-th row and i-the column element of matrix H.

Definition 9.9 We define the following operators:

$$T_A : (u, x) \to \left(\partial H^{\otimes}(u), \partial G(x)\right), \tag{9.33a}$$

$$T_M : (u, x) \to (-\mathbf{L}x, \mathbf{L}^{\mathrm{T}} u), \tag{9.33b}$$

$$T_C : (u, x) \to (0, \nabla F(x)), \tag{9.33c}$$

and two linear operators:

$$T_s = \begin{bmatrix} \tilde{\Sigma}^{-1} & 0 \\ 0 & \tilde{\Gamma}^{-1} \end{bmatrix}, \tag{9.34a}$$

$$T_H = \begin{bmatrix} \tilde{\Sigma}^{-1} & 0 \\ \mathbf{L}^{\mathrm{T}} & \tilde{\Gamma}^{-1} \end{bmatrix} = \begin{bmatrix} \tilde{\Sigma}^{-1} & \frac{1}{2}\mathbf{L} \\ \frac{1}{2}\mathbf{L}^{\mathrm{T}} & \tilde{\Gamma}^{-1} \end{bmatrix} + \begin{bmatrix} 0 & -\frac{1}{2}\mathbf{L} \\ \frac{1}{2}\mathbf{L}^{\mathrm{T}} & 0 \end{bmatrix} = T_p + T_\kappa, \tag{9.34b}$$

Then, it is straightforward to verify the following properties:

(i) The operators, T_M, T_s, T_p and T_κ are linear operators while operators T_A and T_C are nonlinear;
(ii) The operators, T_M and T_κ are monotone since $T_M^{\mathrm{T}} = -T_M$ and $T_\kappa^{\mathrm{T}} = -T_\kappa$ [17]. Moreover, we know that the operator, T_A, is maximally monotone [22, Proposition 20.23] and the operator, T_C, is cocoercive [22, Corollary 18.16]. Based on the definitions in (9.33) and (9.34), we write an equivalent and synchronous formulation of (9.31) as follows:

$$\begin{cases} \bar{U}^k = (T_H + T_A)^{-1} (T_H - T_M - T_C) U^k, \\ U^{k+1} = U^k + T_s^{-1} (T_H - T_M)(\bar{U}^k - U^k), \end{cases} \tag{9.35}$$

where $\bar{U}^k = [(\bar{u}^k)^{\mathrm{T}}, (\bar{x}^k)^{\mathrm{T}}]^{\mathrm{T}} \in \mathbb{R}^{r+l+n}$ and $U^k = [(u^k)^{\mathrm{T}}, (x^k)^{\mathrm{T}}]^{\mathrm{T}} \in \mathbb{R}^{r+l+n}$. Let U^* be the vector of a primal-dual solution to (9.29) and the set of primal-dual solutions to (9.29) is denoted as $\mathcal{U}$, thus $U^* \in \mathcal{U}$;

(iii) Under Assumption 9.6, it is not difficult to verify that the operator, T_p, is positive definite.

Lemma 9.10 (Convergence of Synchronous TriPD-Dist [17, Theorem 5.1]) *Suppose that Assumptions 9.2, 9.5 and 9.6 hold. Then, the sequence,* $\{U^k\}_{k \geq k_0}$, $k_0 \in \mathbb{N}$, *generated by synchronous updates of algorithm (9.35), is* T_s*-quasi-Fejér monotone relative to* $\mathcal{U}$, *i.e.,*

$$\|U^{k+1} - U^*\|_{T_s}^2 - \|U^k - U^*\|_{T_s}^2 \leq -\|U^{k+1} - U^k\|_{2T_d - T_s}^2, \tag{9.36}$$

where $2T_d - T_s$ *is symmetric positive definite under the sufficient condition (9.32) and the operator* T_d *is given by*

$$T_d = \begin{bmatrix} \tilde{\Sigma}^{-1} & -\frac{1}{2}\mathbf{L} \\ -\frac{1}{2}\mathbf{L}^{\mathrm{T}} & \tilde{\Gamma}^{-1} - \frac{L_f}{4}\tilde{Q} \end{bmatrix}, \tag{9.37}$$

with $\tilde{Q}$ *defined in Definition 9.8. Furthermore, the sequence,* $\{U^k\}_{k \geq k_0}$, *converges to some* $U^* \in \mathcal{U}$.

Based on Definitions 9.2–9.3, we next present the convergence analysis on the asynchronous updates of (9.31). Through relaxing the updates in (9.35), an equivalent asynchronous update of (9.31) is given as:

$$\begin{cases} \bar{U}^k = (T_H + T_A)^{-1} (T_H - T_M - T_C) U^k, \\ \tilde{U}^k = U^k + T_s^{-1} (T_H - T_M) (\bar{U}^k - U^k), \\ U^{k+1} = U^k + \sum_{i=1}^{m} v_i^{k+1} \mathbb{A}_i (\tilde{U}^k - U^k), \end{cases} \tag{9.38}$$

Lemma 9.11 (Convergence of Asynchronous TriPD-Dist [17, Theorem 5.2]) *Suppose that Assumptions 9.2, 9.3, 9.5 and 9.6 hold. Then, the sequence,* $\{U^k\}_{k \geq k_0}$, $k_0 \in \mathbb{N}$, *generated by asynchronous updates of algorithm (9.38), is* $\mathbb{M}^{-1}T_s$*-stochastic quasi-Fejér monotone relative to* $\mathcal{U}$, *i.e.,*

$$\mathbb{E}_k[\|U^{k+1} - U^*\|_{\mathbb{M}^{-1}T_s}^2] - \|U^k - U^*\|_{\mathbb{M}^{-1}T_s}^2 \leq -\|\tilde{U}^{k+1} - U^k\|_{2T_d - T_s}^2, \tag{9.39}$$

where $2T_d - T_s$ *is symmetric positive definite under the sufficient condition (9.32).*

Main Results

In this section, we present the convergence analysis of Algorithms 12–13 based on the above obtained results. To begin with, we provide a compact form of SynDe-DuPro algorithm. Via setting $\mathcal{X} = \prod_{i=1}^{m} \mathcal{X}_i$ and $\mathcal{M} = \prod_{(i,j)\in\mathcal{E}} \mathcal{M}_{(i,j)}$, we have

$$\begin{cases} \bar{w}^k = \text{prox}_{\delta^{\otimes}_{\mathcal{M}}}^{\mathrm{K}^{-1}}\{w^k + \mathrm{K}\mathcal{B}\lambda^k\}, \\ \lambda^{k+1} = \lambda^k - \Gamma(-Ax^k + b + \mathcal{B}^{\mathrm{T}}\bar{w}^k), \\ u^{k+1} = \text{prox}_{g^{\otimes}}^{\Sigma^{-1}}\{u^k + \Sigma x^k\}, \\ w^{k+1} = \bar{w}^k + \mathrm{K}\mathcal{B}(\lambda^{k+1} - \lambda^k), \\ x^{k+1} = \arg\min_{x\in\mathcal{X}}\{f(x) + x^{\mathrm{T}}(A^{\mathrm{T}}\lambda^{k+1} + u^{k+1})\}, \end{cases} \tag{9.40}$$

where the definitions of step sizes K, Γ, Σ can be referred to Definition 9.6. Moreover, we have the following definitions: $x^k = \mathbf{col}\{x_i^k\} \in \mathbb{R}^n$, $w^k = \mathbf{col}\{w_{(i,j)}^k\}_{(i,j)\in\mathcal{E}} \in \mathbb{R}^l$, $\bar{w}^k = \mathbf{col}\{\bar{w}_{(i,j)}^k\}_{(i,j)\in\mathcal{E}} \in \mathbb{R}^l$, $\lambda^k = \mathbf{col}\{\lambda_i^k\} \in \mathbb{R}^r$, $u^k = \mathbf{col}\{u_i^k\} \in \mathbb{R}^n$, $b \doteq \mathbf{col}\{b_i\} \in \mathbb{R}^r$, and the matrix $A \in \mathbb{R}^{r\times n}$ is the diagonal stacked form of $A_i \in \mathbb{R}^{\tilde{r}\times n_i}$. Intuitively, it is difficult to analyze algorithm (9.40) because the updates related to x^k are hard to deal with. To overcome the challenge, we introduce the following definition to keep converting problem (9.8) to the one we can handle.

Definition 9.12 For $\forall i \in \mathcal{V}$, we define vectors, $q_i = [\lambda_i^{\mathrm{T}}, u_i^{\mathrm{T}}]^{\mathrm{T}} \in \mathbb{R}^{\tilde{r}+n_i}$, and matrices, $B_1 = [I, 0] \in \mathbb{R}^{\tilde{r}\times(\tilde{r}+n_i)}$ and $B_2 = [0, I] \in \mathbb{R}^{n_i\times(\tilde{r}+n_i)}$ such that $\lambda_i = B_1 q_i$ and $u_i = B_2 q_i$. Then, it is natural to define

$$\tilde{D}_{ij} = [D_{ij}, 0] = \begin{cases} B_1, i < j, \\ -B_1, i > j, \end{cases}$$

and $\mathcal{A}_i q_i = A_i^{\mathrm{T}}\lambda_i + u_i$, where $\mathcal{A}_i = [A_i^{\mathrm{T}}, I] \in \mathbb{R}^{n_i\times(\tilde{r}+n_i)}$.

Based on the Definition 9.12, problem (9.8) can be equivalently arranged as:

$$\begin{aligned} \min_{q_1,\ldots,q_m} \; & \sum_{i=1}^{m} F_i^{\otimes}(q_i) + G_i^{\otimes}(q_i), \\ \text{s.t.} \; & \tilde{D}_{ij}q_i + \tilde{D}_{ji}q_j = 0, (i,j) \in \mathcal{E}, \end{aligned} \tag{9.41}$$

where $F_i^{\otimes}(q_i) = f_i^{\otimes}(-\mathcal{A}_i q_i) + (B_1 q_i)^{\mathrm{T}} b_i$ and $G_i^{\otimes}(q_i) = g_i^{\otimes}(B_2 q_i)$. For $\forall i \in \mathcal{V}$, functions $F_i^{\otimes} : \mathbb{R}^{\tilde{r}+n_i} \to \mathbb{R}$ are proper, closed, convex and $\sqrt{1 + \|A_i\|^2}/\mu_i$-

Lipschitz smooth. Functions $G_i^{\otimes} : \mathbb{R}^{\tilde{r}+n_i} \to \mathbb{R}$ are proper, closed and convex. Similar with (9.9)–(9.11), we first define a linear operator as $N_{(i,j)} : q \to \left[(\tilde{D}_{ij}q_i)^{\mathrm{T}}, (\tilde{D}_{ji}q_j)^{\mathrm{T}}\right]^{\mathrm{T}}$, $(i, j) \in \mathcal{E}$, where $q = \mathbf{col}\{q_i\} \in \mathbb{R}^{r+n}$ and its stacked form $N : \mathbb{R}^{r+n} \to \mathbb{R}^l$. Then, recalling the definition of the set $\mathcal{M}_{(i,j)}$ in (9.11), problem (9.41) is equivalent to

$$\min_q \sum_{i=1}^{m} F_i^{\otimes}(q_i) + G_i^{\otimes}(q_i) + \sum_{i=1}^{m} \sum_{(i,j)\in\mathcal{E}} \delta_{\mathcal{M}_{(i,j)}}\left(N_{(i,j)}q\right), \tag{9.42}$$

which gives a Lagrangian function as follows:

$$\begin{aligned} \Phi(\lambda, u, w) =& \sum_{i=1}^{m} \sum_{(i,j)\in\mathcal{E}} ((\tilde{D}_{ij}q_i)^{\mathrm{T}} w_{(i,j),i} - \delta_{\mathcal{M}_{(i,j)}}^{\otimes}\left(w_{(i,j)}\right)) \\ &+ \sum_{i=1}^{m} F_i^{\otimes}(q_i) + G_i^{\otimes}(q_i), \end{aligned} \tag{9.43}$$

where $w_{(i,j)} = [(w_{(i,j),i})^{\mathrm{T}}, (w_{(i,j),j})^{\mathrm{T}}]^{\mathrm{T}} \in \mathbb{R}^{\tilde{l}}$ is the edge variable corresponding to coupled edge constraint (9.8b); $\delta_{\mathcal{M}_{(i,j)}}^{\otimes}$ is the conjugate function of $\delta_{\mathcal{M}_{(i,j)}}$. Therefore, based on (9.43), for $j \in \mathcal{N}_i$, we briefly describe updates as follows:

$$\bar{w}_{(i,j),i}^k = \mathrm{prox}_{\kappa_{(i,j)}\delta_{\mathcal{M}_{(i,j)}}^{\otimes}} \left\{w_{(i,j)}^k + \kappa_{(i,j)}\left(N_{(i,j)}q^k\right)\right\}, \tag{9.44a}$$

$$q_i^{k+1} = \mathrm{prox}_{G_i^{\otimes}}^{\psi_i^{-1}} \{q_i^k - \psi_i(\nabla F_i^{\otimes}(q_i) + \sum_{j\in\mathcal{N}_i} \tilde{D}_{ij}^{\mathrm{T}} \bar{w}_{(i,j),i}^k)\}, \tag{9.44b}$$

$$w_{(i,j),i}^{k+1} = \bar{w}_{(i,j),i}^k + \kappa_{(i,j)}\tilde{D}_{ij}\left(q_i^{k+1} - q_i^k\right), \tag{9.44c}$$

where variables $\kappa_{(i,j)}$ and ψ_i are the step sizes with the former mentioned in Remark 9.4 and the latter defined as $\psi_i = \mathbf{diag}\{\tau_i, \sigma_i\}$.

Remark 9.13 We emphasize that the updates, (9.44a)–(9.44c), can be equivalently transformed into the updates in Algorithm 12 with some tedious decomposition which is placed in Sect. 9.5 available in the online supplementary file. It is clear that problem (9.42) is equivalent to (9.12). Moreover, via setting $\tilde{F}(q) = \sum_{i=1}^{m} F_i^{\otimes}(q_i)$, $\tilde{G}(q) = \sum_{i=1}^{m} G_i^{\otimes}(q_i)$, and $\tilde{H}(Nq) = \sum_{i=1}^{m} \sum_{(i,j)\in\mathcal{E}} \delta_{\mathcal{M}_{(i,j)}}\left(N_{(i,j)}q\right)$, it is natural to convert (9.42) into a general formulation as (9.29).

In the following, we give the compact form of (9.44a)–(9.44c) to conduct convergence analysis. Defining $\Psi = \mathbf{blkdiag}\{\psi_1 I, \ \ldots, \ \psi_m I\} \in \mathbb{R}^{(r+n)\times(r+n)}$, $\tilde{F} = \sum_{i=1}^{m} F_i^{\otimes}$, $\tilde{G} = \sum_{i=1}^{m} G_i^{\otimes}$ and $\tilde{H}^{\otimes} = \delta_C^{\otimes}$, then we have

$$\begin{cases} \bar{w}^k = \mathrm{prox}_{\tilde{H}^{\otimes}}^{\mathrm{K}^{-1}}\{w^k + \mathrm{K}Nq^k\}, \\ q^{k+1} = \mathrm{prox}_{\tilde{G}}^{\Psi^{-1}}\{q^k - \Psi\nabla\tilde{F}(q^k) - \Psi N\bar{w}^k\}, \\ w^{k+1} = \bar{w}^k + \mathrm{K}N(q^{k+1} - q^k)\,, \end{cases} \tag{9.45}$$

which concisely captures the updates of both SynDe-DuPro and AsynDe-DuPro algorithms. Before presenting the main theorems, we give some definitions as follows:

$$\begin{aligned}
&\mathbf{T}_A : (w, q) \to (\partial\tilde{H}^{\otimes}(w), \partial\tilde{G}(q)),\\
&\mathbf{T}_M : (w, q) \to (-Nq, N^{\mathrm{T}}w),\\
&\mathbf{T}_C : (w, q) \to (0, \nabla\tilde{F}(q)),\\
&\mathbf{U}^k = [(w^k)^{\mathrm{T}}, (q^k)^{\mathrm{T}}]^{\mathrm{T}} \in \mathbb{R}^{r+l+n},\\
&\mathbf{U}^* = [(w^*)^{\mathrm{T}}, (q^*)^{\mathrm{T}}]^{\mathrm{T}} \in \mathbb{R}^{r+l+n},\\
&\mathbf{T}_{\tilde{p}} = \begin{bmatrix} \mathrm{K}^{-1} & -\frac{1}{2}N \\ -\frac{1}{2}N^{\mathrm{T}} & \Psi^{-1} - \frac{Q}{4} \end{bmatrix},\\
&\mathbf{T}_s = \begin{bmatrix} \mathrm{K}^{-1} & 0 \\ 0 & \Psi^{-1} \end{bmatrix}\\
&\mathbf{T}_H = \begin{bmatrix} \mathrm{K}^{-1} & 0 \\ N^{\mathrm{T}} & \Psi^{-1}, \end{bmatrix} = \begin{bmatrix} \mathrm{K}^{-1} & \frac{1}{2}N \\ \frac{1}{2}N^{\mathrm{T}} & \Psi^{-1} \end{bmatrix} + \begin{bmatrix} 0 & -\frac{1}{2}N \\ \frac{1}{2}N^{\mathrm{T}} & 0 \end{bmatrix} = \mathbf{T}_p + \mathbf{T}_\kappa,\\
&\hat{U}^k = \mathbf{U}^k + \mathbf{T}_s^{-1}(\mathbf{T}_H - \mathbf{T}_M) \times ((\mathbf{T}_H + \mathbf{T}_A)^{-1}(\mathbf{T}_H - \mathbf{T}_M - \mathbf{T}_C) - I)\mathbf{U}^k,
\end{aligned}$$

where $\mathbf{U}^*$ is the vector of a primal-dual solution to (9.42) and the set of primal-dual solutions to (9.42) is denoted as $\mathcal{U}$, thus $\mathbf{U}^* \in \mathcal{U}$. Note that the definition of Q can be referred to Definition 9.6.

Remark 9.14 It is worth mentioning that the updates in (9.45) can be transformed from updates in (9.31) via the following replacements: $u \to w$, $x \to q$, $\tilde{\Sigma} \to \bar{\Sigma}$, $\tilde{\Gamma} \to \Gamma$, $\mathbf{L} \to N$ and $\tilde{Q} \to Q$. After these replacements, it can be verified that the properties of operators $\mathbf{T}_A$, $\mathbf{T}_M$, $\mathbf{T}_C$, $\mathbf{T}_s$, $\mathbf{T}_H$, $\mathbf{T}_p$ and $\mathbf{T}_\kappa$ are in line with their counterparts defined in Definition 9.9. Thus, we can still construct both synchronous and asynchronous updates based on the operators similar with (9.35) and (9.38), respectively. Therefore, the convergence analysis on both SynDe-DuPro and AsynDe-DuPro algorithms can be obtained by Lemmas 9.10–9.11.

Theorem 9.15 (Convergence of SynDe-DuPro Algorithm) *Suppose that Assumptions 9.1, 9.2 and 9.4 hold. Then, the sequence,* $\{\mathbf{U}^k\}_{k\geq k_0}$, $k_0 \in \mathbb{N}$, *generated by synchronous updates of Algorithm 12, is* $\mathbf{T}_s$*-quasi-Fejér monotone relative to* $\boldsymbol{\mathcal{U}}$, *i.e.,*

$$\|\mathbf{U}^{k+1} - \mathbf{U}^*\|_{\mathbf{T}_s}^2 - \|\mathbf{U}^k - \mathbf{U}^*\|_{\mathbf{T}_s}^2 \leq -\|\mathbf{U}^{k+1} - \mathbf{U}^k\|_{2\mathbf{T}_d-\mathbf{T}_s}^2, \tag{9.46}$$

where $2\mathbf{T}_d - \mathbf{T}_s$ *is symmetric positive definite under the sufficient condition (9.22). Consequently, the sequence,* $\{\mathbf{U}^k\}_{k\geq k_0}$, *converges to some* $\mathbf{U}^* \in \boldsymbol{\mathcal{U}}$.

Proof *As discussed in Remark 9.14, we can write SynDe-DuPro updates (9.45) in a totally same form as (9.35) with some uncomplicated replacements. Furthermore, one can easily prove that the properties of operators* $\mathbf{T}_A$, $\mathbf{T}_M$, $\mathbf{T}_C$, $\mathbf{T}_s$, $\mathbf{T}_H$, $\mathbf{T}_p$, *and* $\mathbf{T}_\kappa$ *are in line with their counterparts defined in Definition 9.9. Notice that (9.22) is a sufficient condition for* $2\mathbf{T}_d - \mathbf{T}_s$ *to be positive definite. We omit the detailed proof here, which follows directly from the proof in Lemma 9.10.*

Theorem 9.16 (Convergence of AsynDe-DuPro Algorithm) *Suppose that Assumptions 9.1–9.4 hold. Then, the sequence,* $\{\mathbf{U}^k\}_{k\geq k_0}$, $k_0 \in \mathbb{N}$, *generated by Algorithm 13, is* $\mathbb{M}^{-1}\mathbf{T}_s$*-stochastic quasi-Fejér monotone relative to* $\boldsymbol{\mathcal{U}}$, *i.e.,*

$$\mathbb{E}_k[\|\mathbf{U}^{k+1} - \mathbf{U}^*\|_{\mathbb{M}^{-1}\mathbf{T}_s}^2] - \|\mathbf{U}^k - \mathbf{U}^*\|_{\mathbb{M}^{-1}\mathbf{T}_s}^2 \leq -\|\mathbf{U}^k - \hat{U}^k\|_{2\mathbf{T}_d-\mathbf{T}_s}^2, \tag{9.47}$$

where $2\mathbf{T}_d - \mathbf{T}_s$ *is symmetric positive definite under the sufficient condition (9.22). Consequently, the sequence* $\{\mathbf{U}^k\}_{k\geq k_0}$ *converges almost surely to some* $\mathbf{U}^* \in \boldsymbol{\mathcal{U}}$.

Proof *Similar with Theorem 9.15, the AsynDe-DuPro updates (9.45) can also be written into a totally same form as (9.38) through conducting the uncomplicated replacements and adding some relaxed iterations as defined in Definitions 9.2–9.3. Therefore, we do not repeatedly present the proof which is similar to that of Lemma 9.11.* ∎

Appendix C: The Connection Between (9.44) and Algorithm 12

In this section, we connect the updates in (9.44) to the updates in Algorithm 12 and the main step is to decompose the update (9.44b). The details are given as:

$$q_i^{k+1}$$

$$=\text{prox}_{G_i^{\otimes}}^{\psi_i^{-1}}\left(q_i^k - \psi_i\left(\nabla F_i^{\otimes}(q_i) + \sum\nolimits_{(i,j)\in\mathcal{N}_i} \tilde{D}_{ij}^{\mathrm{T}} \bar{w}_{(i,j),i}^k\right)\right)$$

$$
= \begin{bmatrix} \arg\min_{\lambda_i} \left\{ \frac{1}{2\tau_i} \left\| \lambda_i - \left(\lambda_i^k - \tau_i \left(-A_i x_{i\,i}^k + b_i + \sum_{(i,j)\in\mathcal{N}_i} D_{ij}^{\mathrm{T}} \bar{w}_{(i,j),i}^k \right) \right) \right\|^2 \right\} \\ \arg\min_{u_i} \left\{ g_i^{\otimes}(u_i) + \frac{1}{2\sigma_i} \left\| u_i - \left(u_i^k + \sigma_i x_i^k \right) \right\|^2 \right\} \end{bmatrix}
$$

$$
= \begin{bmatrix} \lambda_i^k - \tau_i \left(-A_i x_i^k + b_i + \sum_{(i,j)\in\mathcal{N}_i} D_{ij}^{\mathrm{T}} \bar{w}_{(i,j),i}^k \right) \\ \mathrm{prox}_{\sigma_i g_i^{\otimes}} \left(u_i^k + \sigma_i x_i^k \right) \end{bmatrix},
$$

where ψ_i is defined in (9.44). Then, the updates in (9.44) are equivalent to

$$
\bar{w}_{(i,j),i}^k = \frac{1}{2} \left(w_{(i,j),i}^k + w_{(i,j),j}^k \right) + \frac{\kappa_{(i,j)}}{2} \left(D_{ij} \lambda_i^k + D_{ji} \lambda_j^k \right), \tag{9.48a}
$$

$$
u_i^{k+1} = \mathrm{prox}_{\sigma_i g_i^{\otimes}} \left(u_i^k + \sigma_i x_i^k \right), \tag{9.48b}
$$

$$
\lambda_i^{k+1} = \lambda_i^k - \tau_i \left(-A_i x_i^k + b_i + \sum_{(i,j)\in\mathcal{N}_i} D_{ij}^{\mathrm{T}} \bar{w}_{(i,j),i}^k \right), \tag{9.48c}
$$

$$
w_{(i,j),i}^{k+1} = \bar{w}_{(i,j),i}^k + \kappa_{(i,j)} D_{ij} \left(\lambda_i^{k+1} - \lambda_i^k \right). \tag{9.48d}
$$

To proceed, using Moreau decomposition [22] and introducing the local minimization of x_i^{k+1} yield

$$
\bar{w}_{(i,j),i}^k = \frac{1}{2} (w_{(i,j),i}^k + w_{(i,j),j}^k) + \frac{\kappa_{(i,j)}}{2} (D_{ij} \lambda_i^k + D_{ji} \lambda_j^k), \tag{9.49a}
$$

$$
u_i^{k+1} = u_i^k + \sigma_i x_i^k - \sigma_i \mathrm{prox}_{\sigma_i^{-1} g_i} \{ \sigma_i^{-1} u_i^k + x_i^k \}, \tag{9.49b}
$$

$$
\lambda_i^{k+1} = \lambda_i^k - \tau_i (-A_i x_i^k + b_i + \sum_{j\in\mathcal{N}_i} D_{ij}^{\mathrm{T}} \bar{w}_{(i,j),i}^k), \tag{9.49c}
$$

$$
w_{(i,j),i}^{k+1} = \bar{w}_{(i,j),i}^k + \kappa_{(i,j)} D_{ij} (\lambda_i^{k+1} - \lambda_i^k), \tag{9.49d}
$$

$$
x_i^{k+1} = \arg\min_{x_i \in \mathcal{X}_i} \left\{ f_i(x_i) + x_i^{\mathrm{T}} \left(A_i^{\mathrm{T}} \lambda_i^{k+1} + u_i^{k+1} \right) \right\}, \tag{9.49e}
$$

which completes the connection.

Chapter 10
Distributed Proximal Splitting Algorithm for Composite Constrained Convex Optimization

Abstract This chapter concentrates on a class of distributed convex optimization problems subject to local feasible sets, equality and inequality constraints, where the global objective function consists of a sum of locally smooth convex functions and nonsmooth regularization terms. To address this problem, a synchronous full-distributed primal-dual proximal splitting algorithm (Syn-FdPdPs) is presented, which avoids the unapproximable property of the proximal operator with respect to inequality constraints via logarithmic barrier functions. Following the proposed distributed protocol, each agent carries out local information exchange without any global coordination and weight balancing strategies introduced in most consensus algorithms. In addition, a randomized version of the proposed algorithm (Rand-FdPdPs) is conducted through subsets of activated agents, which further removes the global clock coordinator. Theoretically, with the help of asymmetric forward-backward-adjoint (AFBA) splitting technique, the convergence results of the proposed algorithms are provided under the same local step size conditions. Finally, the effectiveness and practicability of the proposed algorithms are demonstrated by numerical simulations on the least-square and least absolute deviation problems.

Keywords Distributed convex optimization · Randomized algorithm · Nonsmooth functions · Logarithmic barrier functions · Proximal operators

10.1 Introduction

In recent years, distributed optimization with network-structured objective functions and constraints has received much attention in the fields of machine learning [228, 229], sensor networks [138, 230], resource allocation problems [231, 232], and cooperative control [233, 234], etc. Generally speaking, one of the options to deal with these optimization problems is the centralized methods by collecting all the information and then computing through a central center. However, the centralized methods seem to be not amenable for large-scale networks due to the heavy communication costs. Additionally, privacy concern is another non-negligible

H. Li et al., *Network-System Research and Distributed Composite Algorithm Design*, Computational Intelligence Methods and Applications,
https://doi.org/10.1007/978-981-95-0911-9_10

issue [211]. Thus, their distributed counterparts have gradually become the research interest, in implementation of which each agent updates its own variables and shares partially private information with its neighboring agents.

There have been reported several important works for distributed convex optimization. For general convex objective functions, the typical work [9] developed a distributed sub-gradient descent algorithm with a diminishing step size, which converges with the rate $O(\ln k/\sqrt{k})$, where $k > 0$ is the iteration number. Based on this sub-gradient method, another work in [103] considered a convex optimization problem abiding by a feasible set constraint, and presented a projected sub-gradient algorithm through introducing a positive, diminishing and non-summable step size. To avoid the deficiency of slow convergence rate caused by the diminishing step size, many researchers recently have developed new approaches with fixed step sizes, e.g., gradient descent methods [51, 235], EXTRA [49] and DIGing [217], all of which explicitly derived the linear convergence rates for strongly convex functions with Lipschitz gradients. Meanwhile, some interesting works also focused on distributed randomized or asynchronous optimization methods. For example, the authors in [236] dealt with an unconstrained optimization problem by developing an algorithm based on the random sleep strategy. Bastianello et al. [13] developed a distributed asynchronous update version of the relaxed alternating direction method of multipliers [104].

Note that the algorithms [9, 103] do not consider the structure where the local objective function consists of a single smooth function and a nonsmooth one. More than that, these developed methods [49, 51, 217, 235, 236] only consider smooth functions cannot handle such smooth plus nonsmooth structure. To this end, proximal operators are utilized to address nonsmooth objectives and show more stable properties than that of sub-gradient counterparts [237]. For example, an excellent work in [54] employed proximal operators to propose a distributed proximal gradient algorithm (termed PG-EXTRA), which is an extension to its previous work [49]. Additionally, other examples that took advantage of such operators also include NIDS [18], DDPG [124], dual coupled diffusion [238], and the proximal primal-dual algorithm [239], etc.

However, it should be pointed out that: (i) Apart from local boxes for decision variables taken into account in [103], optimization problems studied in [9, 13, 18, 49, 51, 54, 124, 217, 235, 238, 239] did not consider any local constraints, such as equality and inequality constraints; (ii) The aforementioned algorithms standing on proximal iterations were unable to deal with minimization problems with more than two nonsmooth objective functions, since the sum of several proximal nonsmooth functions, such as the sum of two nonsmooth regularization functions, may not be proximal. The authors of [6] recently studied a more general convex optimization framework consisting of a smooth convex function and other two possibly nonsmooth functions, by means of the ingenious asymmetric forward-backward-adjoint (AFBA) splitting technique. This motivates us to investigate distributed methods for solving general constrained convex optimization problems. The main contributions of this chapter are stated as follows:

(i) This chapter focuses on a generalized form of nonsmooth composite constrained optimization problem, in which the local nonsmooth term involves an ℓ_1-norm regularization with a linear mapping. The considered regularization captures a wide range of applications in model fitting [228], compressed sensing [116] and 1D total variation [240], etc. Unlike the unconstrained problems [9, 18, 49, 51, 54, 124, 217, 235, 238, 239], local constraints containing feasible sets, equality and inequality constraints are investigated.

(ii) Inspired by interior-point optimization [241], an approximation is exploited to address the considered problem, where the inequality constraints are integrated into the cost function by introducing suitable barrier function terms. Moreover, it avoids the unapproximable property of proximal functions with respect to inequality sets.

(iii) Based on proximal operators, a synchronous full-distributed primal-dual proximal splitting algorithm (named Syn-FdPdPs) is proposed to solve the approximation problem. Different from the existing consensus-based algorithms [49, 51, 217, 235, 242], the proposed algorithm gets rid of the dependence of weight balancing strategies or graph Laplacians, and thus profits less conservative step sizes. To be specific, each agent possesses private uncoordinated step sizes, instead of taking diminishing [103, 243] or commonly sharing coordinated [238, 239] ones.

(iv) Considering the irreplaceability of a global coordinator clock in the implementation of Syn-FdPdPs, a randomized version of the synchronous one (named Rand-FdPdPs) is conducted, where subsets of agents are activated independently with certain probabilities and participate in the iterations. In this way, the global clock is no longer required and the robustness is improved.

(v) With the help of AFBA splitting technique, the convergence of proposed algorithms are proved by constructing quasi-Fejér monotone sequences. In particular, the sub-linear rate $O(1/k)$ of Syn-FdPdPs is established with respect to running-average successive difference.

10.2 Preliminaries

10.2.1 Notation

Let $\mathbb{N}$, $\mathbb{R}^n$ and $\mathbb{R}^{m\times n}$ be the sets of non-negative integers, n-dimension real vectors and $m \times n$ real matrices, respectively. Use 0 and I to respectively stand for the zero vector (or matrix) and identity matrix with appropriate dimensions. Denote by $\text{col}\{x_i\}_{i=1}^m$ the column vector stacked with $x_1,\ x_2,\ \cdots,\ x_m$, and $\text{blkdiag}\{X_i\}_{i=1}^m$ the block diagonal matrix composed of diagonal blocks $X_1,\ X_2,\ \cdots,\ X_m$. In addition, let $x_{i,j}$ be the j-th element of the vector x_i, and $X_{i,j}$ is the j-th row vector of the matrix X_i. For a positive definite matrix $V \in \mathbb{R}^{n\times n}$, its 2-norm and maximum eigenvalue are represented by $||V||$ and $\theta_{\max}(V)$, respectively. Moreover, the scalar product and induced norm are respectively defined by $\langle x, y\rangle_V = \langle x, Vy\rangle$ and $\|x\|_V = \sqrt{\langle x, x\rangle_V}$, where $x, y \in \mathbb{R}^n$, and $V \in \mathbb{R}^{n\times n}$ is positive definite. For a non-empty closed convex set $\mathbf{C}$, rint($\mathbf{C}$) denotes its relative interior, and $\iota_{\mathbf{C}}$ denotes its indicator function, which is defined by

$$\iota_{\mathbf{C}}(x) = \begin{cases} 0, & x \in \mathbf{C}, \\ +\infty, & x \notin \mathbf{C}. \end{cases} \tag{10.1}$$

For a proper, closed, convex function $f : \mathbb{R}^n \to \mathbb{R}$, the set of its sub-differential is given by

$$\partial f(x) = \{y \mid \forall z \in \mathbb{R}^n,\ f(x) + (z-x)^{\mathrm{T}} y \le f(z)\}, \tag{10.2}$$

and its conjugate is defined by $f^{\star}(v) = \sup_{x\in\mathbb{R}^n}\{v^{\mathrm{T}}x - f(x)\}$. For all $x, v \in \mathbb{R}^n$, the Fenchel-Young inequality is given by $v^{\mathrm{T}}x \le f^{\star}(v) + f(x)$, which contributes to the following inequality:

$$v^{\mathrm{T}}x \le \frac{1}{2}\|x\|_V^2 + \frac{1}{2}\|v\|_{V^{-1}}^2, \tag{10.3}$$

with the positive definite matrix $V \in \mathbb{R}^{n\times n}$. The proximal operator relative to f is given by

$$\operatorname{prox}_f^V(x) = \operatorname*{argmin}_{\xi\in\mathbb{R}^n}\{f(\xi) + \frac{1}{2}||x-\xi||_V^2\}. \tag{10.4}$$

In the special case where $f(\cdot) = \iota_{\mathbf{C}}(\cdot)$ and $V = I$, it holds that

$$\operatorname{prox}_{\iota_{\mathbf{C}}}(x) = \mathcal{P}_{\mathbf{C}}(x), \tag{10.5}$$

where $\mathcal{P}$ is a projection operator. On the other hand, when $\mathbf{C} = \{z \in \mathbb{R}^n \mid Az = a\}$ for $A \in \mathbb{R}^{s\times n}$ and $a \in \mathbb{R}^s$, it holds that

$$\mathcal{P}_{\mathbf{C}}(x) = x - A^{\dagger}(Ax - a), \tag{10.6}$$

where $A^{\dagger}$ is the Moore-Penrose pseudoinverse of A [244].

An operator (or set-valued mapping) $\mathcal{A} : \mathbb{R}^n \to \mathbb{R}^{\tilde{n}}$, from $\mathbb{R}^n$ to $\mathbb{R}^{\tilde{n}}$, is characterized by its graph, i.e., $\operatorname{gra}(\mathcal{A}) = \{(x,\ y) \in \mathbb{R}^n \times \mathbb{R}^{\tilde{n}} | y \in \mathcal{A}x\}$. Its domain, zeros and fixed points are denoted by $\operatorname{dom}(\mathcal{A}) = \{x \in \mathbb{R}^n | \mathcal{A}x \ne 0\}$, $\operatorname{zer}(\mathcal{A}) = \{x \in \mathbb{R}^n | 0 \in \mathcal{A}x\}$ and $\operatorname{fix}(\mathcal{A}) = \{x \in \mathbb{R}^n | x \in \mathcal{A}x\}$, respectively. The operator $\mathcal{A}$ is said to be monotone if $\langle x - \tilde{x},\ y - \tilde{y}\rangle \ge 0$ for any (x, y), $(\tilde{x}, \tilde{y}) \in \operatorname{gra}(\mathcal{A})$, and maximally monotone if and only if there exists no another graph of a monotone operator that strictly contains gra($\mathcal{A}$).

The probability space is denoted by $(\Omega, \mathcal{F}, \mathbb{P})$, where Ω, $\mathcal{F}$ and $\mathbb{P}$ are the sample space, σ-algebra and the probability measure, respectively.

10.2.2 Model of Optimization Problem

Consider the following constrained optimization problem:

$$\begin{aligned}&\min_{\tilde{x}\in\mathbb{R}^n} \sum_{i=1}^{m}(f_i(\tilde{x}) + \rho_i \|L_i\tilde{x} - l_i\|_1),\\ &\text{s.t.}\quad A_i\tilde{x} = a_i,\ i = 1, \cdots, m,\\ &B_i\tilde{x} \le b_i,\ i = 1, \cdots, m, \tilde{x} \in \bigcap_{i=1}^{m}\mathcal{X}_i,\end{aligned} \tag{10.7}$$

where $\tilde{x} \in \mathbb{R}^n$ $(n \in \mathbb{N})$ is the decision variable. Each agent privately holds the local objective function, $f_i : \mathbb{R}^n \to \mathbb{R}$, and the ℓ_1-norm $\|\cdot\|_1$ with a non-negative penalty factor ρ_i. The transformers, $L_i : \mathbb{R}^n \to \mathbb{R}^{r_i}$ $(r_i \in \mathbb{N})$, $A_i : \mathbb{R}^n \to \mathbb{R}^{s_i}$ $(s_i \in \mathbb{N})$ and $B_i : \mathbb{R}^n \to \mathbb{R}^{c_i}$ $(c_i \in \mathbb{N})$, are linear mappings, while $l_i \in \mathbb{R}^{r_i}$, $a_i \in \mathbb{R}^{s_i}$ and $b_i \in \mathbb{R}^{c_i}$ are constant vectors. $\mathcal{X}_i \subseteq \mathbb{R}^n$ is a closed and non-empty convex set. We assume that problem (10.7) is solvable, and further satisfies the following feasible conditions.

Assumption 10.1 (The Feasible Conditions) *The problem* (10.7) *is strictly feasible, i.e., there exists* $\tilde{x} \in \operatorname{rint}(\bigcap_{i=1}^{m}\mathcal{X}_i)$ *that satisfies* $A_i\tilde{x} = a_i$ *and* $B_i\tilde{x} < b_i$ *for all* $i = 1, \cdots, m$.

In order to evaluate the communication among agents, we introduce a local variable $x_i \in \mathbb{R}^n$ for $i = 1, \cdots, m$. Then, under Assumption 10.2, problem (10.7) can be equivalently written as the following distributed optimization:

$$\begin{aligned}\min_{x_1,\cdots,x_m}\ &\sum_{i=1}^{m}(f_i(x_i) + h_i(L_ix_i)),\\ \text{s.t.}\quad &A_ix_i = a_i,\ i = 1, \cdots, m,\\ &B_ix_i \le b_i,\ i = 1, \cdots, m,\\ &x_i \in \mathcal{X}_i,\ i = 1, \cdots, m,\\ &C_{ij}x_i + C_{ji}x_j = 0,\ (i, j) \in \mathcal{E},\end{aligned} \tag{10.8}$$

where $h_i(y_i) = \rho_i \|y_i - l_i\|_1$ for $y_i \in \mathbb{R}^{r_i}$, and the operator C_{ij} corresponding to each edge $(i, j) \in \mathcal{E}$ follows

$$C_{ij} = \begin{cases} I, & i < j, \\ -I, & i > j. \end{cases}$$

Remark 10.1 In the absence of the penalty factor ρ_i, the distributed manner of (10.7) is studied via the consensus method [242], in which an agent-based communication mode is employed, without highlighting the edges linking with neighboring agents. In contrast, the adopted coupled equality constraint in (10.8), derived from a general type of edge constraints [21, Equality (1)], can naturally induct the local exchange of information among agents by means of the edge variables.

Remark 10.2 Note that some specific forms of the linear mapping L_i appear in engineering applications, i.e., the feature matrices in machine learning and statistics, and the discrete gradient operator corresponding to the classical 'isotropic' total variation (TV) [240]. In addition, the local function h_i with the linear mapping L_i is in vogue encountered in [17, 245], allowing the proximal function of h_i to be handled explicitly. As the nonsmooth regularization term in (10.8), the proximal operator of h_i can be efficiently computed as follows:

$$\begin{aligned} \text{prox}_{\sigma_i h_i}(y_i) &= \underset{\bar{y} \in \mathbb{R}^{r_i}}{\text{argmin}} \left\{ \rho_i ||\bar{y} - l_i||_1 + \frac{1}{2\sigma_i} ||\bar{y} - y_i||^2 \right\} \\ &= [\phi_{i,1}, \cdots \phi_{i,r_i}]^{\mathrm{T}}, \end{aligned} \tag{10.9}$$

where $\sigma_i > 0$, $y_i = [y_{i,1}, \cdots y_{i,r_i}]^{\mathrm{T}} \in \mathbb{R}^{r_i}, l_i = [l_{i,1}, \cdots l_{i,r_i}]^{\mathrm{T}} \in \mathbb{R}^{r_i}$, and for $j = 1, \cdots, r_i$,

$$\phi_{i,j} = \begin{cases} y_{i,j} - \sigma_i^{-1} \rho_i, & y_{i,j} - l_{i,j} > \sigma_i^{-1} \rho_i, \\ l_{i,j}, & \left| y_{i,j} - l_{i,j} \right| \le \sigma_i^{-1} \rho_i, \\ y_{i,j} + \sigma_i^{-1} \rho_i, & y_{i,j} - l_{i,j} < -\sigma_i^{-1} \rho_i. \end{cases} \tag{10.10}$$

10.2.3 Communication Network

The communication network is captured by an undirected graph $\mathcal{G} = \{\mathcal{V}, \mathcal{E}\}$, where $\mathcal{V} = \{1, \cdots, m\}$ is the set of agents, and $\mathcal{E} \subseteq \mathcal{V} \times \mathcal{V}$ is the set of edges. An undirected edge described by the unordered pair (i, j) links neighboring agents i and j, which further implies that agents i and j can exchange information with each other. For $i \in \mathcal{V}$, the set of its all neighbors is defined as $\mathcal{N}_i$. It specifies that there is no any self-loop in $\mathcal{G}$, i.e., $(i, i) \notin \mathcal{E}$. Agents i and j are said to be connected if there is a path between i and j, and $\mathcal{G}$ is said to be connected if any two agents are connected. For the considered graph $\mathcal{G}$, we make the following assumption.

Assumption 10.2 *The undirected graph $\mathcal{G}$ is connected.*

10.2.4 Problem Development

This section describes proximal functions pertaining to the considered constraints, particularly to the inequality constraint. Before starting, we consider the linear operator:

$$N_{(i,j)} : x \mapsto (C_{ij}x_i, C_{ji}x_j),$$

where $x = \mathrm{col}\{x_i\}_{i=1}^m$. By stacking $N_{(i,j)}$, N is represented by

$$N : x \to \{N_{(i,j)}x\}_{(i,j)\in\mathcal{E}}.$$

For the involved (in)equality constraints in problem (10.8), we further define the following sets:

$$\mathcal{A}_i = \left\{x_i \in \mathbb{R}^n \,|A_i x_i = a_i \right\}, \tag{10.11a}$$

$$\mathcal{B}_i = \left\{x_i \in \mathbb{R}^n \,|B_i x_i \leq b_i \right\}, \tag{10.11b}$$

and

$$\mathcal{C}_{(i,j)} = \left\{(z_1, z_2) \in \mathbb{R}^n \times \mathbb{R}^n \,|z_1 + z_2 = 0\right\}. \tag{10.12}$$

Then, the goal of minimizing (10.8) is equivalent to solving for the unconstrained problem:

$$\min_{x_1,\cdots,x_m} \sum_{i=1}^{m} [f_i(x_i) + h_i(L_i x_i) + \iota_{\mathcal{A}_i}(x_i) + \iota_{\mathcal{B}_i}(x_i) + \iota_{\mathcal{X}_i}(x_i) + \sum_{(i,j)\in\mathcal{E}} \iota_{\mathcal{C}_{(i,j)}}(N_{(i,j)}x)], \tag{10.13}$$

Compared with the minimization problem associated with a nonsmooth term (e.g. [54]), such structure (10.13) is more complex and challenging due to several nonsmooth terms involved. Now, we employ proximal operators to measure these indicators. It can be verified that the proximal operators associated with $\iota_{\mathcal{A}_i}$ and $\iota_{\mathcal{X}_i}$ can be efficiently evaluated via (10.6) and (10.5), respectively. Recalling the definition $\mathcal{C}_{(i,j)}$ in (10.12), the projection of $(z_1, z_2) \in \mathbb{R}^n \times \mathbb{R}^n$ onto $\mathcal{C}_{(i,j)}$ is given by

$$\mathcal{P}_{\mathcal{C}}(z_1, z_2) = \frac{1}{2}(z_1 - z_2, z_2 - z_1), \tag{10.14}$$

which yields the accessibility of the proximal operator of $\iota_{\mathcal{C}_{(i,j)}}$. Note that, although the proximal operator is access to $\iota_{\mathcal{B}_i}$ for $\mathcal{B}_i$ being a halfspace [244, Chapter 6], it might remain a level of difficulty when given in more general cases. To bypass the difficulty, the next subsection makes use of an approximation approach called logarithmic barrier method.

10.2.4.1 Approximation Problem

To identify the relevant properties of the logarithmic barrier method, we analyze a simple example at first. Consider the indicator function $\iota_{\mathbf{C}}(x)$, where $\mathbf{C} = \{z \,|z < 0\}$. As discussed in [105], the indicator function can be approximated by a logarithmic barrier function:

$$\hat{\iota}_{\mathbf{C}}(x) = -\frac{1}{t}\log(-x),$$

where $t > 0$ is a weighting parameter that determines the accuracy of the approximation. The function $\iota_{\mathbf{C}}$ and approximation $\hat{\iota}_{\mathbf{C}}$ for several values of t are shown in Fig. 10.1: as t increases, the approximation becomes more accurate. On the other hand, both $\iota_{\mathbf{C}}$ and $\hat{\iota}_{\mathbf{C}}$ are convex and take on the value ∞ for $x > 0$. However, a distinguishing fact is that $\hat{\iota}_{\mathbf{C}}$ is differentiable and closed. Motivated by

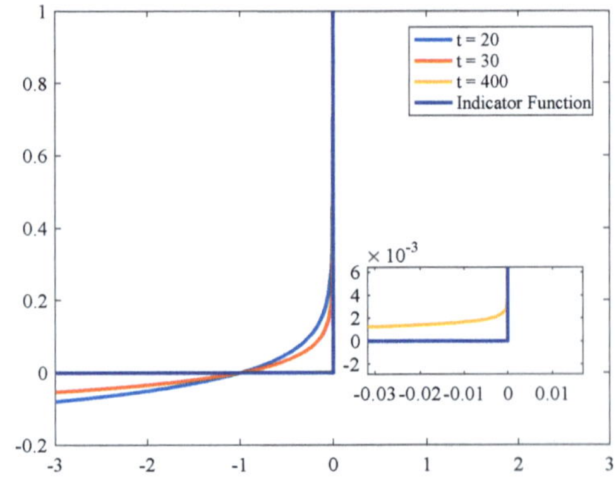

Fig. 10.1 Approximation performance for $t = 20, 30$ and 400

this idea, we define the local logarithmic barrier function:

$$\begin{aligned}\hat{\iota}_i(B_i x_i - b_i) &= -\frac{1}{\gamma_i}\mathbf{log}\big(-(B_i x_i - b_i)\big)\\ &= -\frac{1}{\gamma_i}\cdot\sum_{j=1}^{c_i}\log\big(-(B_{i,j}x_i - b_{i,j})\big).\end{aligned} \tag{10.15}$$

The domain of (10.15) is given by $\{z_i = B_i x_i - b_i \,|B_i x_i < b_i\}$, which is the set of points that satisfy the inequality constraints to (10.8) strictly.

In what follows, substitute $\hat{\iota}_i$ for ι_i in (10.13) and let

$$F_{\gamma_i}(x_i) = f_i(x_i) + \hat{\iota}_i(B_i x_i - b_i). \tag{10.16}$$

The goal is to approximate problem (10.13) by solving

$$\begin{aligned}\min_{x_1,\cdots,x_m} \sum_{i=1}^{m} [F_{\gamma_i}(x_i) &+ \iota_{\mathcal{X}_i}(x_i) + h_i(L_i x_i)\\ &+\iota_{\mathcal{A}_i}(x_i) + \sum_{(i,j)\in\mathcal{E}} \iota_{\mathcal{C}_{(i,j)}}(N_{(i,j)}x)].\end{aligned} \tag{10.17}$$

Under Assumption 10.1, the set of solutions to (10.17) is non-empty. In what follows, we further make a key assumption.

Assumption 10.3 *Consider a convex and closed set $\Omega_i \subseteq \mathbb{R}^n$. The local function f_i is proper and convex, and has β_i-Lipschitz continuous gradients, i.e., for any $x_i,\ y_i \in \Omega_i$,*

$$\|\nabla f_i(x_i) - \nabla f_i(y_i)\|_{Q_i^{-1}} \le \beta_i \|x_i - y_i\|_{Q_i}, \tag{10.18}$$

The local logarithmic barrier function $\hat{\iota}_i$ has $\hat{\beta}_i$-Lipschitz continuous gradients, i.e., for any $x_i,\ y_i \in \Omega_i$,

$$\left\|\nabla\hat{\iota}_i(x_i) - \nabla\hat{\iota}_i(y_i)\right\|_{V_i^{-1}} \le \hat{\beta}_i \|x_i - y_i\|_{V_i}, \tag{10.19}$$

where Q_i and V_i are positive definite.

Note that the local feasible set $\mathcal{X}_i$ in (10.8) is convex and closed, meaning the accessibility of estimating Lipschitz gradients of $\hat{\iota}_i$ when $\hat{\beta}_i$ is properly positive. In addition, Assumption 10.3 implies that $\hat{\iota}_i$ and f_i are continuously differentiable, the local composite function F_{γ_i} can be thus considered as a smooth term and its Lipschitz gradients are also able to be derived (see Lemma 10.5).

10.2.4.2 Accuracy of Approximation

In this section, the quality of the approximation (10.17) is discussed. In order to construct the dual problem, we introduce three sets of dual variables: λ_i and u_i corresponding to agent i, and $w_{(i,j)} = \text{col}\{w_{(i,j),i}, w_{(i,j),j}\}$ corresponding to each edge constraint, where $w_{(i,j),i}$ is held by agent i, and $w_{(i,j),j}$ by agent j. Then the dual problem associated with (10.17) is formulated as

$$\min_{\lambda,u,w} \sum_{i=1}^{m} \Phi_i(\lambda_i, u_i, w_{(i,j)}), \tag{10.20}$$

where $\lambda = \text{col}\{\lambda_i\}_{i=1}^m$, $u = \text{col}\{u_i\}_{i=1}^m$, and w is a stacked vector by stacking $w_{(i,j)}$ for all $(i, j) \in \mathcal{E}$. The local function Φ_i is given by

$$\begin{aligned}\Phi_i(\lambda_i, u_i, w_{(i,j)}) =& (F_{\gamma_i} + \iota_{\mathcal{X}_i})^\star(-L_i^{\mathrm{T}}\lambda_i - u_i - (N^{\mathrm{T}}w)_i)\\ &+ h_i^\star(\lambda_i) + \iota_{\mathcal{A}_i}^\star(u_i) + \sum_{(i,j)\in\mathcal{E}} \iota_{\mathcal{C}_{(i,j)}}^\star(w_{(i,j)}),\end{aligned} \tag{10.21}$$

with $\left(N^{\mathrm{T}}w\right)_i = \sum_{j\in\mathcal{N}_i} C_{ij} w_{(i,j),i}$. Using $(x_i^*, \lambda_i^*, u_i^*, w_{(i,j)}^*)$ to be the optimal point of (10.17) and (10.20), we then have

$$\begin{aligned}&\sum_{i=1}^{m} \Phi_i(\lambda_i^*, u_i^*, w_{(i,j)}^*)\\ =& \sum_{i=1}^{m}(-F_{\gamma_i}(x_i^*)) + \sum_{i=1}^{m}(-L_i{}^{\mathrm{T}}\lambda_i^* - u_i^* - (N^{\mathrm{T}}w^*)_i)^{\mathrm{T}}x_i^*\\ &+ \sum_{i=1}^{m}\left(\langle\lambda_i^*, L_i x_i^*\rangle + \langle u_i^*, x_i^*\rangle\right) - \sum_{i=1}^{m} h_i(L_i x_i^*)\\ &+ \sum_{i=1}^{m}\sum_{(i,j)\in\mathcal{E}}\left\langle w_{(i,j)}^*, N_{(i,j)}x_i^*\right\rangle \qquad (10.22)\\ =& -\sum_{i=1}^{m}(F_{\gamma_i}(x_i^*) + h_i(L_i x_i^*))\\ =& -\sum_{i=1}^{m}(f_i(x_i^*) + \hat{\iota}_i(B_i x_i^* - b_i)) - \sum_{i=1}^{m} h_i(L_i x_i^*)\\ =& -\sum_{i=1}^{m}(f_i(x_i^*) + h_i(L_i x_i^*)) + \sum_{i=1}^{m}\frac{\mathbf{log}(b_i - B_i x_i^*)}{\gamma_i}.\end{aligned}$$

Using Fenchel-Rockafellar duality theory [22] yields that the pair $(x_i^*, \lambda_i^*, u_i^*, w_{(i,j)}^*)$ is the primal-dual solution to (10.17) and (10.20). Let $\Phi^* = -\sum_{i=1}^{m} \Phi_i \times (\lambda_i^*, u_i^*, w_{(i,j)}^*)$ be the optimal value of the approximation (10.17), and f^* the optimal value of (10.8), respectively. Note that the difference between the optimizations (10.17) and (10.13) is that all inequality constraints of (10.8) are moved to the objective of (10.16) in the form of local logarithmic barrier terms. It follows from [105, Chapter 11] that x_i^* is the feasible solution to problem (10.13), while $(\lambda_i^*, u_i^*, w_{(i,j)}^*)$ is its dual feasible pair. According to (10.22), one concludes that

$$f^* \leq \sum_{i=1}^{m} f_i\left(x_i^*\right) + h_i\left(L_i x_i^*\right), \tag{10.23}$$

which implies that the accuracy between Φ^* and f^* is derived as

$$f^* - \Phi^* \leq \sum_{i=1}^{m} \frac{\mathbf{log}(b_i - B_i x_i^*)}{\gamma_i}. \tag{10.24}$$

Intuitively speaking, it follows from (10.24) that the accuracy ε^* will be closer to 0 as γ_i increases for each $i = 1, \cdots, m$. This chapter fixes the values of γ_i, $i = 1, \cdots, m$, the consideration of which is common in related works [246, 247].

10.3 Algorithm Development

This section develops a synchronous full-distributed primal-dual proximal splitting algorithm (Syn-FdPdPs) and its randomized version (Rand-FdPdPs) for problem (10.17).

10.3.1 Syn-FdPdPs Algorithm

In the following, the steps of the algorithm are presented one by one in detail. Besides the local primal variable x_i, each agent $i \in \mathcal{V}$ stores dual variables λ_i and u_i, along with auxiliary variables $\bar{\lambda}_i$ and $\bar{u}_i$. Each edge constraint is estimated by the dual edge variable $w_{(i,j)} = \mathrm{col}\{w_{(i,j),i}, w_{(i,j),j}\}$ and auxiliary variable $\bar{w}_{(i,j)} = \mathrm{col}\{\bar{w}_{(i,j),i}, \bar{w}_{(i,j),j}\}$, where $w_{(i,j),i}$ and $\bar{w}_{(i,j),i}$ are kept by agent i, while $w_{(i,j),j}$ and $\bar{w}_{(i,j),j}$ are kept by neighboring agents $j \in \mathcal{N}_i$. It should be pointed out that each agent carries out locally information exchange with its neighboring agents, i.e., agent i shares private data $w_{(i,j),i}$ and $C_{ij} x_i$ with $j \in \mathcal{N}_i$, and receives $w_{(i,j),j}$ and $C_{ji} x_j$ from $j \in \mathcal{N}_i$.

Overall, the distributed protocol performs two operations: the local proximal gradient and correction operations. For no ambiguity occurring, we introduce an auxiliary variable $\bar{x}_i$ for x_i. By employing a local proximal gradient step, the updates of auxiliary variables including $\bar{x}_i$, $\bar{w}_{(i,j)}$, $\bar{u}_i$ and $\bar{\lambda}_i$ follow that

$$\bar{w}_{(i,j)} = \mathrm{prox}_{\omega_{(i,j)}\iota^*_{\mathcal{C}_{(i,j)}}}\left(\bar{w}_{(i,j)} + \omega_{(i,j)} N_{(i,j)} x\right), \tag{10.25}$$

$$\bar{\lambda}_i = \mathrm{prox}_{\sigma_i h_i^*}\left(\lambda_i + \sigma_i L_i x_i\right), \tag{10.26}$$

$$\bar{u}_i = \mathrm{prox}_{\mu_i \iota^*_{\mathcal{A}_i}}\left(u_i + \mu_i x_i\right), \tag{10.27}$$

$$\bar{x}_i = \mathrm{prox}_{\tau_i \iota_{\mathcal{X}_i}}\left(x_i + \tau_i d_i\right), \tag{10.28}$$

where μ_i, σ_i, τ_i and $\omega_{(i,j)}$ are constant step sizes, while d_i as the local update direction involves

$$d_i = -\nabla F_{\gamma_i}(x_i) - \bar{u}_i - L_i^{\mathrm{T}} \bar{\lambda}_i - \sum\nolimits_{j \in \mathcal{N}_i} C_{ij} \bar{w}_{(i,j),i}, \tag{10.29}$$

with the local gradient $\nabla F_{\gamma_i}(x_i)$ being given by

$$\nabla F_{\gamma_i}(x_i) = \nabla f_i(x_i) + \frac{1}{\gamma_i} \cdot B_i^{\mathrm{T}} \cdot \mathrm{col}\left\{\frac{1}{b_{i,j} - B_{i,j} x_i}\right\}_{j=1}^{c_i}. \tag{10.30}$$

For designing the fully distributed algorithm, we next compute the above proximal operators explicitly. It is easy to check that $\mathrm{prox}_{\tau_i \iota_{\mathcal{X}_i}}(\cdot)$ can be estimated through (10.5). With the employment of Moreau decomposition [22], one decomposes (10.25)–(10.27) into

$$\begin{aligned}
\bar{w}_{(i,j)} &= w_{(i,j)} + \omega_{(i,j)} N_{(i,j)} x - \omega_{(i,j)} \mathcal{P}_{\mathcal{C}_{(i,j)}}\left(w_{(i,j)} + \omega_{(i,j)} N_{(i,j)} x\right), \\
\bar{\lambda}_i &= \lambda_i + \sigma_i L_i x_i - \sigma_i \mathrm{prox}_{\mu_i^{-1} h_i}\left(\sigma_i^{-1} \lambda_i + L_i x_i\right), \\
\bar{u}_i &= u_i + \mu_i x_i - \mu_i \mathcal{P}_{\mathcal{A}_i}\left(\mu_i^{-1} u_i + x_i\right).
\end{aligned} \tag{10.31}$$

Note that $\mathrm{prox}_{\mu_i^{-1} h_i}(\cdot)$ and $\mathcal{P}_{\mathcal{A}_i}(\cdot)$ can be evaluated via (10.10) and (10.6), respectively. Using the projection result in (10.14), we are able to compute $\mathcal{P}_{\mathcal{C}_{(i,j)}}(\cdot)$ and obtain the following explicit form of the component $\bar{w}_{(i,j),i}$ of $\bar{w}_{(i,j)}$:

$$\bar{w}_{(i,j),i} = \frac{1}{2}\left(w_{(i,j),i} + w_{(i,j),j}\right) + \frac{\omega_{(i,j)}}{2}\left(C_{ij} x_i + C_{ji} x_j\right), \tag{10.32}$$

which highlights the local communication of information between agents i and j. As a result, the desired results of proximal operators are obtained. To proceed, at each iteration, we take once correction step for dual variables, $w_{(i,j)}$, u_i and λ_i,

Algorithm 14 : Syn-FdPdPs algorithm

Initialization: Each agent $i \in \mathcal{V}$ initializes $x_i^0 \in \mathcal{X}_i$, $\lambda_i^0 \in \mathbb{R}^{r_i}$ and $w_{(i,j),i}^0 \in \mathbb{R}^{e(i,j)}$ for $j \in \mathcal{N}_i$, and then chooses proper step sizes $\omega_{(i,j)}$, σ_i, μ_i and τ_i.

Local Updates: Each agent $i \in \mathcal{V}$ repeats, for $j \in \mathcal{N}_i$

1: **for all** $k = 0, 1, \cdots$ **do**

2:

$$\bar{w}_{(i,j),i}^k = \frac{1}{2}\left(w_{(i,j),i}^k + w_{(i,j),j}^k\right) + \frac{\omega_{(i,j)}}{2}\left(C_{ij}x_i^k + C_{ji}x_j^k\right), \tag{10.33}$$

$$\bar{\lambda}_i^k = \lambda_i^k + \sigma_i L_i x_i^k - \sigma_i \text{prox}_{\sigma_i^{-1}h_i}\left(\sigma_i^{-1}\lambda_i^k + L_i x_i^k\right), \tag{10.34}$$

$$\bar{u}_i^k = A_i^+\left(A_i(u_i^k + \mu_i x_i^k) - \mu_i a_i\right), \tag{10.35}$$

$$d_i^k = -\nabla F_{\gamma_i}\left(x_i^k\right) - \bar{u}_i^k - L_i^{\mathrm{T}}\bar{\lambda}_i^k - \sum_{j\in\mathcal{N}_i} C_{ij}^{\mathrm{T}}\bar{w}_{(i,j),i}^k, \tag{10.36}$$

$$x_i^{k+1} = \mathcal{P}_{\mathcal{X}_i}\left(x_i^k + \tau_i d_i^k\right); \tag{10.37}$$

$$\hat{x}_i^{k+1} = x_i^{k+1} - x_i^k, \tag{10.38}$$

$$w_{(i,j),i}^{k+1} = \bar{w}_{(i,j),i}^k + \omega_{(i,j)}C_{ij}\hat{x}_i^{k+1}, \tag{10.39}$$

$$\lambda_i^{k+1} = \bar{\lambda}_i^k + \sigma_i L_i \hat{x}_i^{k+1}, \tag{10.40}$$

$$u_i^{k+1} = \bar{u}_i^k + \mu_i \hat{x}_i^{k+1}. \tag{10.41}$$

3: Broadcast $C_{ij}x_i^{k+1}$ and $w_{(i,j),i}^{k+1}$ to each neighbor $j \in \mathcal{N}_i$.

4: **end for**

respectively. Meanwhile, let $(\cdot)^k$ denote the k-th iteration and assign $\bar{x}_i^k$ to x_i^{k+1} directly. Therefore, a pseudo-code of local updates of the fully distributed algorithm is given in Algorithm 14.

Remark 10.3 It can be seen that Algorithm 14 is fully distributed. On the one hand, the local variables (i.e., x_i^k, u_i^k and λ_i^k) are individually maintained by agents, while the local edge variables $w_{(i,j),i}^k$ are shared with themselves neighbors at k-th iteration. On the other hand, each agent i privately managers the local constant positive step sizes σ_i, μ_i and τ_i, which is distinguished from the dynamic or coordinated-wise ones [9, 13, 51, 103, 235]. The edge step-size $\omega_{(i,j)}$, kept by agent i and its neighbors j, can be viewed as inherent parameters or weights of the communication network, capturing the quality of the communication.

Remark 10.4 Notice that the consensus-based algorithms [49, 51, 217, 227, 235] are studied under a strict requirement on doubly stochastic weight matrices with positive definite property. One question arising immediately is how to properly assign the weights to the neighboring agents of each agent i. The edge-based communication adopted in Algorithm 14 removes the weights and further reveals that two agents of each edge exchanging information with each other lie in equal status.

10.3.2 Rand-FdPdPs

In the synchronous implementation, it is inevitable to rely on a global clock coordinator, which may be dragged down by the slowest agent. Meanwhile, the clock coordinator is expensive and demanding to maintain in the whole network. To overcome this limitation, a randomized version of the synchronous one is conducted via a class of random activation mechanisms, which is summarized in Algorithm 15.

Algorithm 15 : Rand-FdPdPs algorithm

Initialization: Each agent $i \in \mathcal{V}$ initializes $x_i^0 \in \mathcal{X}_i$, $\lambda_i^0 \in \mathbb{R}^{r_i}$ and $w_{(i,j),i}^0 \in \mathbb{R}^{e(i,j)}$ for $j \in \mathcal{N}_i$, and then chooses proper step sizes $\omega_{(i,j)}$, σ_i, μ_i and τ_i.

1: **for all** $k = 0, 1, \cdots$ **do**
2: Each agent $i \in \mathcal{V}$ is activated independently with a probability $p_i > 0$.
3: The group of activated agents perform the Steps 10.33–10.41 in Algorithm 14, while the others without being activated at k-th iteration do not participate in the updates and keep the states unchanged.
4: Broadcast $C_{ij}x_i^{k+1}$ and $w_{(i,j),i}^{k+1}$ to each neighbor $j \in \mathcal{N}_i$.
5: **end for**

Under the randomized scheme, each agent is allowed to awaken with an independent probability. In other words, there is a subset of randomly activated agents participating in the updates and exchange updated information with neighboring agents, while inactivated ones stay in previous states. Then, the slow agents can be suspended per iteration to some extent. Substantially, as a randomized block-coordinate model, Algorithm 15 removes the clock coordinator and improves the robustness of the network.

10.4 Convergence Analysis

In this part, we discuss a monotone inclusion involving three operators, which is helpful to guarantee the later convergence analyses. Then, under some sufficient assumptions, the main convergence results for the proposed algorithms are obtained.

10.4.1 Monotone Inclusion

We start this section by establishing the local Lipschitz-continuous property of F_{γ_i}.

Lemma 10.5 *Suppose Assumption 10.3 holds. Recall the composite function F_{γ_i} in* (10.16). *For each agent i, the local gradient ∇F_{γ_i} is Lipschitz-continuous with some positive constant φ_i and positive definite matrix R_i, i.e., for any $x_i, y_i \in \mathbb{R}^n$,*

$$\left\| \nabla F_{\gamma_i}(x_i) - \nabla F_{\gamma_i}(y_i) \right\|_{R_i^{-1}} \leq \varphi_i \|x_i - y_i\|_{R_i}. \tag{10.42}$$

Proof From Assumption 10.3 on the Lipschitz-continuous properties of f_i and $\hat{\iota}_i$, we respectively have

$$\begin{aligned} \|\nabla f_i(x_i) - \nabla f_i(y_i)\|^2_{Q_i^{-1}} &\leq \beta_i^2 \|x_i - y_i\|^2_{Q_i R_i^{-1} R_i} \\ &= \beta_i^2 \theta_{\max}\left(Q_i R_i^{-1}\right) \|x_i - y_i\|^2_{R_i}, \end{aligned} \tag{10.43}$$

and

$$\begin{aligned} &\left\| \nabla\hat{\iota}_i(B_i x_i - b_i) - \nabla\hat{\iota}_i(B_i y_i - b_i) \right\|^2_{V_i^{-1}} \\ \leq\ &\hat{\beta}_i^2 \gamma_i^{-2} \theta_{\max}\left(B_i^{\mathrm{T}} V_i B_i R_i^{-1}\right) \|x_i - y_i\|^2_{R_i}, \end{aligned} \tag{10.44}$$

where $R_i = \max\{Q_i, V_i\}$. Using the basic inequality

$$\|a + b\|^2_{\tilde{R}} \leq \xi \|a\|^2_{\tilde{R}} + \frac{\xi}{\xi - 1} \|b\|^2_{\tilde{R}}, \forall \xi > 1, \tag{10.45}$$

and combining (10.43) with (10.44), we obtain

$$\begin{aligned} &\left\| \nabla F_{\gamma_i}(x_i) - \nabla F_{\gamma_i}(y_i) \right\|^2_{R_i^{-1}} \\ \leq &\xi_i \|\nabla f_i(x_i) - \nabla f_i(y_i)\|^2_{Q_i^{-1}} \\ &+ \frac{\xi_i}{\xi_i - 1} \left\| \nabla\hat{\iota}_i(M_i x_i - w_i) - \nabla\hat{\iota}_i(M_i y_i - w_i) \right\|^2_{V_i^{-1}} \\ \leq &\varphi_i^2 \|x_i - y_i\|^2_{R_i}, \end{aligned} \tag{10.46}$$

where $\xi_i > 1$, and φ_i is defined as:

$$\varphi_i = \sqrt{\xi_i \beta_i^2 \theta_{\max}\left(Q_i R_i^{-1}\right) + \frac{\xi_i \hat{\beta}_i^2 \gamma_i^{-2}}{\xi_i - 1} \theta_{\max}\left(M_i^{\mathrm{T}} V_i M_i R_i^{-1}\right)}. \tag{10.47}$$

Therefore, we conclude that ∇F_{γ_i} is Lipschitz-continuous. ■

By Lemma 10.5, the selection of step sizes is shown in the following assumption.

Assumption 10.4 (The Step Size Conditions) *For agent* $i \in \mathcal{V}$*, let the weight parameter* $\gamma_i > 0$*, and the step sizes* μ_i*,* σ_i *along with* $\omega_{(i,j)}$ *are constant and strictly positive. Furthermore, the step size* τ_i *satisfies*

$$0 < \tau_i < \frac{2}{\varphi_i + 2\left(\sum_{j\in\mathcal{N}_i}\omega_{(i,j)} + \mu_i + \sigma_i \left\|L_i^{\mathrm{T}}L_i\right\|\right)}, \tag{10.48}$$

where φ_i *is a constant parameter and its value can be referred to Lemma 10.5, and* L_i *is shown in problem* (10.7)*. The other comments of local step sizes* τ_i*,* μ_i*,* σ_i *and* $\omega_{(i,j)}$ *are referred to Remark 10.3.*

Next, we consider a more general optimization problem. For ease of exposition, let $L = \text{blkdiag}\{L_i\}_{i=1}^m$, $\mathcal{A} = \prod_{i=1}^m \mathcal{A}_i$, $\mathcal{C} = \prod_{(i,j)\in\mathcal{E}} \mathcal{C}_{(i,j)}$ and $\mathbf{L} = [N^{\mathrm{T}}, I, L^{\mathrm{T}}]^{\mathrm{T}}$. Further, we set

$$\begin{aligned} F(x) &= \sum_{i=1}^m F_{\gamma_i}(x_i), h(Lx) = \sum_{i=1}^m h_i(L_i x_i), \\ \iota_{\mathcal{X}}(x) &= \sum_{i=1}^m \iota_{\mathcal{X}_i}(x_i), \iota_{\mathcal{A}}(x) = \sum_{i=1}^m \iota_{\mathcal{A}_i}(x_i), \\ \iota_{\mathcal{C}}(Nx) &= \sum_{i=1}^m \sum_{(i,j)\in\mathcal{E}} \iota_{\mathcal{C}_{(i,j)}}(N_{(i,j)}x), \end{aligned} \tag{10.49}$$

and

$$\tilde{h}(\mathbf{L}x) = h(Lx) + \iota_{\mathcal{C}}(Nx) + \iota_{\mathcal{A}}(x).$$

Then the compact form of (10.17) is given by

$$\min_x \; F(x) + \iota_{\mathcal{X}}(x) + \tilde{h}(\mathbf{L}x). \tag{10.50}$$

Rewriting (10.20) compactly, we obtain

$$\min_\chi \; (F + \iota_{\mathcal{X}})^\star(-\chi^{\mathrm{T}}\mathbf{L}) + \tilde{h}^\star(\chi), \tag{10.51}$$

where $\tilde{h}^\star(\chi) = h^\star(\lambda) + \iota_{\mathcal{C}}^\star(w) + \iota_{\mathcal{A}}^\star(u)$ and $\chi = \text{col}\{w, u, \lambda\}$.

We denote the primal-dual solution by (χ^*, x^*), and the set of primal-dual solutions by $\mathcal{S}$. Indeed, as the optimal points of (10.50) and (10.51), (χ^*, x^*) satisfies that

$$\begin{cases} 0 \in \nabla F(x) + \partial\iota_{\mathcal{X}}(x) + \mathbf{L}^{\mathrm{T}}\chi, \\ 0 \in \partial\tilde{h}^\star(\chi) - \mathbf{L}x. \end{cases} \tag{10.52}$$

Define the compact variable $U = \mathrm{col}\{\chi, x\}$ and following operators:

$$\begin{aligned} A &: (\chi, x) \to (\partial \tilde{h}^{\star}(\chi), \partial \iota_{\mathcal{X}}(x)), \\ M &: (\chi, x) \to (\mathbf{L}^{\mathrm{T}}\chi, -\mathbf{L}x), \\ C &: (\chi, x) \to (0, \nabla F(x)). \end{aligned} \tag{10.53}$$

Then, the condition (10.52) can be cast into the form of the monotone inclusion:

$$0 \in AU + MU + CU, \tag{10.54}$$

which moves forward the following analysis.

10.4.2 Analysis of Syn-FdPdPs Algorithm

Before analyzing the convergence of Algorithm 14, there are important definitions that need to be introduced.

Definition 10.6 (Step Size Matrices)

(i) For each edge $(i, j) \in \mathcal{E}$, define the edge weight matrix:

$$W = \mathrm{blkdiag}\left\{\left(\omega_{(i,j)} I\right)_{(i,j)\in\mathcal{E}}\right\}.$$

(ii) For the private step sizes, μ_i, τ_i and σ_i, define the step size matrices:

$$\begin{aligned} J &= \mathrm{blkdiag}\left\{\mu_i I\right\}_{i=1}^{m}, \\ \Sigma &= \mathrm{blkdiag}\left\{\sigma_i I\right\}_{i=1}^{m}, \\ \Gamma &= \mathrm{blkdiag}\left\{\tau_i I\right\}_{i=1}^{m}. \end{aligned}$$

(iii) Consider the compact variable $U = \mathrm{col}\{\chi, x\}$, define the matrices:

$$\begin{aligned} \Lambda &= \mathrm{blkdiag}\{W, J, \Sigma\}, \\ S &= \mathrm{blkdiag}\{\Lambda^{-1}, \Gamma^{-1}\}. \end{aligned}$$

Driven by Definition 10.6, the compact form of Algorithm 14 can be written as

$$U_{k+1} = \mathcal{T} U_k, \tag{10.55}$$

where the operator $\mathcal{T}$ is given by

$$\mathcal{T} : (\chi, x) \to \left(\bar{w} + WN(\bar{x} - x), \bar{u} + V(\bar{x} - x), \bar{\lambda} + \Sigma L(\bar{x} - x), \bar{x}\right), \tag{10.56}$$

and the variables $\bar{w}$, $\bar{u}$, $\bar{\lambda}$ and $\bar{x}$ follow

$$\begin{aligned}
\bar{w} &= \mathrm{prox}_{\iota_{\mathcal{C}}^{\star}}^{W^{-1}} (w + WNx), \\
\bar{u} &= \mathrm{prox}_{\iota_{\mathcal{A}}^{\star}}^{J^{-1}} (u + Jx), \\
\bar{\lambda} &= \mathrm{prox}_{h^{\star}}^{\Sigma^{-1}} (\lambda + \Sigma Lx), \\
\bar{x} &= \mathrm{prox}_{\iota_{\mathcal{X}}}^{\Gamma^{-1}} \left(x - \Gamma\left(\nabla F(x) + \bar{u} + L^{\mathrm{T}}\bar{\lambda} + N^{\mathrm{T}}\bar{w}\right)\right).
\end{aligned} \tag{10.57}$$

The iteration (10.55), as the compact operator form of Algorithm 14, remains difficulties in analyzing its convergence behavior directly, since the operator $\mathcal{T}$ in (10.56) has a complex structure that involves the primal-dual variables (i.e., x, w, u, λ) and auxiliary variables (i.e., $\bar{x}, \bar{w}, \bar{u}, \bar{\lambda}$). Recently, the method AFBA is introduced [6], which focuses on the monotone inclusion involving a maximally monotone, a co-coercive and a monotone term, e.g., the structure one (10.54). Its main idea is to split a compact operator, like $\mathcal{T}$, into several simplified sub-operator that are endowed with the properties of positive definiteness or monotonicity. Based on this line, we consider the linear operator:

$$H = \underbrace{\begin{bmatrix} \Lambda^{-1} & \frac{1}{2}\mathbf{L} \\ \frac{1}{2}\mathbf{L}^{\mathrm{T}} & \Gamma^{-1} \end{bmatrix}}_{P} + \underbrace{\frac{1}{2}\begin{bmatrix} 0 & -\mathbf{L} \\ \mathbf{L}^{\mathrm{T}} & 0 \end{bmatrix}}_{\mathcal{K}}. \tag{10.58}$$

Recalling the operators A, M and C in (10.53), the relationship (10.57) can be reformulated as

$$\bar{U} = (A + H)^{-1} (H - M - C)\, U, \tag{10.59}$$

where $\bar{U} = \mathrm{col}\{\bar{\chi}, \bar{x}\}$ and $\bar{\chi} = \mathrm{col}\{\bar{w}, \bar{u}, \bar{\lambda}\}$. Furthermore, the operator $\mathcal{T}$ can be split into

$$\mathcal{T}U = U + S^{-1} (H - M) \left(\bar{U} - U\right). \tag{10.60}$$

It can be checked that the operator A is maximally monotone [22, Proposition 20.23]; the operators M is monotone because of its skew-symmetry (i.e., $M^{\mathrm{T}} = -M$), and the operator C is co-coercive [22, Corollary 18.17]. A key consideration for splitting the operator H into the special form (10.58) yields the monotonicity of $\mathcal{K}$ (since $\mathcal{K}^{\mathrm{T}} = -\mathcal{K}$) and the symmetric positive definiteness of P (from Schur complement under Assumption 10.4), which makes it accessible to estimate the convergence of the compact operator form (10.55) of Algorithm 14.

Next, we show how to deal with the considered inclusion form (10.54) by means of the AFBA-based splitting scheme (10.58)–(10.60). Utilize U^* to denote the fix point of $\mathcal{T}$. Then, recalling the operator $H = P + \mathcal{K}$ in (10.58) and substituting U^* (resp. $\bar{U}^*$) for U (resp. $\bar{U}$) in (10.59) and (10.60) give

$$\begin{cases} (P + \mathcal{K} - M - C)\,U^* \in (A + P + \mathcal{K})\,\bar{U}^*, \\ 0 = S^{-1}\,(P + \mathcal{K} - M)\left(\bar{U}^* - U^*\right). \end{cases} \tag{10.61}$$

Since M and $\mathcal{K}$ are monotone, and S and P are positive definite under Assumption 10.4, one concludes from the second line of (10.61) that

$$\bar{U}^* = U^*,$$

plugging the result of which into the first line of (10.61) obtains

$$0 \in AU^* + MU^* + CU^*. \tag{10.62}$$

Hence, the desired result for solving (10.54) is achieved and a fact that $U^* \in \mathcal{S}$ if $U^* \in \operatorname{fix} \mathcal{T}$ is also released.

In light of the mentioned splitting scheme (10.58)–(10.60), we state the property of $\mathcal{T}$ via the following lemma.

Lemma 10.7 *Suppose that Assumptions 10.2 and 10.3 hold. According to Lemma 10.5, consider the block diagonal matrix* $R = \operatorname{blkdiag}\{\varphi_i R_i\}_{i=1}^m$. *Recall the operator* $\mathcal{T}$ *defined in* (10.56). *Then, for any* $U^* \in \mathcal{S}$, *it holds that*

$$\left\langle U - U^*, \mathcal{T}U - U \right\rangle_S \leq \langle U - \mathcal{T}U, \mathcal{T}U - U \rangle_{\tilde{P}}, \tag{10.63}$$

where $\tilde{P}$ *is given by*

$$\tilde{P} = \begin{bmatrix} \Lambda^{-1} & -\frac{1}{2}\mathbf{L} \\ -\frac{1}{2}\mathbf{L}^{\mathrm{T}} & \Gamma^{-1} - \frac{1}{4}R \end{bmatrix}.$$

Proof From U and $\bar{U}$ in (10.59), we have that

$$H\bar{U} - HU + MU = -CU - A\bar{U}, \tag{10.64}$$

which contributes to

$$\begin{aligned}&\left\langle \bar{U}-U^{*},(H-M)\left(\bar{U}-U\right)\right\rangle \\ =&-\left\langle \bar{U}-U^{*},A\bar{U}-AU^{*}\right\rangle-\left\langle \bar{U}-U^{*},M\bar{U}-MU^{*}\right\rangle-\left\langle \bar{U}-U^{*},CU-CU^{*}\right\rangle \\ \leq&\left\langle U^{*}-\bar{U},CU-CU^{*}\right\rangle,\end{aligned} \tag{10.65}$$

where the equality (10.62), and the inequality holds because of the monotonicity of A and skew-symmetry of M. Further, it follows from [22, Corollary 18.17] that ∇F is co-coercive, i.e., for any $x, y \in \mathbb{R}^{mn}$,

$$\|\nabla F(x)-\nabla F(y)\|_{R^{-1}}^{2} \leq \langle x-y,\nabla F(x)-\nabla F(y)\rangle . \tag{10.66}$$

Noting the operator C in (10.53), we can show that

$$\begin{aligned}&\left\langle U^{*}-\bar{U},CU-CU^{*}\right\rangle \\ \leq&\left\|\nabla F(x)-\nabla F\left(x^{*}\right)\right\|_{R^{-1}}^{2}+\frac{1}{4}\|x-\bar{x}\|_{R}^{2} \\ &-\left\langle x-x^{*},\nabla F(x)-\nabla F\left(x^{*}\right)\right\rangle \\ \leq&\frac{1}{4}\|x-\bar{x}\|_{R}^{2},\end{aligned} \tag{10.67}$$

where we have used (10.3) ($V = 2R^{-1}$) in the first inequality, and (10.66) in the second inequality, respectively.

On the other hand, recalling the operator $\mathcal{T}$ in (10.60) yields

$$S(\mathcal{T}U-U)=(H-M)\left(\bar{U}-U\right). \tag{10.68}$$

Therefore, combining (10.65), (10.67), and (10.68) to get

$$\begin{aligned}&\left\langle U-U^{*},\mathcal{T}U-U\right\rangle_{S} \\ \leq&-\left\langle \bar{U}-U,P\left(\bar{U}-U\right)\right\rangle \\ &+\left\langle \bar{U}-U^{*},(H-M)\left(\bar{U}-U\right)\right\rangle \\ \overset{(10.65)}{\leq}&-\left\langle \bar{U}-U,P\left(\bar{U}-U\right)\right\rangle+\left\langle U^{*}-\bar{U},CU-CU^{*}\right\rangle \\ \overset{(10.67)}{\leq}&-\left\langle \bar{U}-U,P\left(\bar{U}-U\right)\right\rangle+\frac{1}{4}\|x-\bar{x}\|_{R}^{2}.\end{aligned} \tag{10.69}$$

where the first inequality follows from (10.58) and the skew-symmetry of M and $\mathcal{K}$. Note that (10.68) further indicates

$$(H - M)^{-1} S (\mathcal{T}U - U) = \bar{U} - U. \tag{10.70}$$

Then, combining (10.59), (10.60) and (10.70) obtains

$$-\langle \bar{U} - U, P(\bar{U} - U)\rangle + \frac{1}{4}\|x - \bar{x}\|_R^2 = \langle U - \mathcal{T}U, \mathcal{T}U - U\rangle_{\tilde{P}}. \tag{10.71}$$

Thus, (10.69) together with (10.71) gives (10.63). This completes the proof. ∎

Next, Theorem 10.8 reports the convergence behavior of Algorithm 14.

Theorem 10.8 *Suppose Assumptions 10.2 and 10.3 hold. Considering Algorithm 14, the sequence $\{U_k\}_{k\in\mathbb{N}}$, generated by* (10.55)*, is quasi-Fejér monotone with respect to $\mathcal{S}$, i.e.,*

$$\|U_{k+1} - U^*\|_S^2 \le \|U_k - U^*\|_S^2 - \|U_{k+1} - U_k\|_{2\tilde{P}-S}^2. \tag{10.72}$$

Then, $\{U_k\}_{k\in\mathbb{N}}$, converges to some $U^* \in \mathcal{S}$.

Proof Note that, for any $a, b, c \in \mathbb{R}^n$, and positive definite matrices $V \in \mathbb{R}^{n\times n}$, it holds that

$$2\langle a - b, c - a\rangle_V = \|c - b\|_V^2 - \|a - b\|_V^2 - \|c - a\|_V^2. \tag{10.73}$$

Hence, combining (10.55), (10.63) and (10.73) yields

$$\begin{aligned} &2\langle U_k - U^*, U_{k+1} - U_k\rangle_S \\ &= \|U_{k+1} - U^*\|_S^2 - \|U_{k+1} - U_k\|_S^2 - \|U_k - U^*\|_S^2 \\ &\le -\|U_k - U_{k+1}\|_{2\tilde{P}}^2. \end{aligned} \tag{10.74}$$

Therefore, (10.72) is obtained by rearranging the inequality in (10.74). Observe that $2\tilde{P} - S$ is positive definite under Assumption 10.4. Consequently, we conclude that the sequence $\{U_k\}_{k\in\mathbb{N}}$ is quasi-Fejér monotone with respect to $\mathcal{S}$, while $\{U_k\}_{k\in\mathbb{N}}$ is bounded [22, Theorem 5.33]. Let $\hat{U}$ be a cluster point of $\{U_k\}_{k\in\mathbb{N}}$, i.e., $U_{k_l} \to \hat{U}$, which implies $\hat{U} \in \mathcal{S}$. The convergence of the sequence $\{U_k\}_{k\in\mathbb{N}}$ follows [22, Lemma 2.47]. ∎

This theorem provides rigorous guarantee in convergence to one of the solutions to problem (10.17). Recalling the compact variable $U = \text{col}\{\chi, x\}$ and the dual one $\chi = \text{col}\{w, u, \lambda\}$, the convergence of the sequence $\{U_k\}_{k\in\mathbb{N}}$ implies that $\{x_k\}_{k\in\mathbb{N}}$ converges the optimal solution x^*.

On the other hand, the sub-linear rate $O(1/k)$ for Syn-FdPdPs can be derived via Theorem 10.8. Since the individual terms $\|U_k - U^*\|_S^2$ converge to 0 when k goes to $+\infty$. So, we sum (10.72) over $k = 0$ through $+\infty$ and apply the telescopic cancellation, which yields:

$$\begin{aligned}\sum_{k=0}^{+\infty} \|U_k - U_{k+1}\|_{2\tilde{P}-S}^2 &= \sum_{k=0}^{+\infty} \left(\left\|U_k - U^*\right\|_S^2 - \left\|U_{k+1} - U^*\right\|_S^2 \right) \\ &= \left\|U_0 - U^*\right\|_S^2 < \infty.\end{aligned}$$

Furthermore, utilizing [54, Proposition 1] results in

$$\frac{1}{k} \sum_{\xi=0}^{k} \left\|U_\xi - U_{\xi+1}\right\|_{2\tilde{P}-S}^2 = o\left(\frac{1}{k}\right). \tag{10.75}$$

Remark 10.9 The $O(1/k)$ indicates that FdPdPs needs at most $O(1/\epsilon)$ iterations in order to reach an accuracy of ϵ. Up to now, this chapter only estimates the converge rates (10.75). There exists an open question on the monotonicity of $\|U_k - U_{k+1}\|_{2\tilde{P}-S}^2$. If it holds, then $o(1/k)$ convergence rates will apply to the sequence itself.

10.4.3 Analysis of Rand-FdPdPs Algorithm

In this part, we carry out the convergence behavior of Algorithm 15. For $i \in \mathcal{V}$, define the diagonal matrix δ_i consisting of 0–1 diagonal elements, which only picks out the involved variables $w_{(i,j),i}$, λ_i, u_i and x_i from U, i.e., U can be rewritten as

$$U = \sum_{i=1}^{m} \delta_i U. \tag{10.76}$$

To assess the active state of the k-th iteration, we introduce the m-dimensional vector ϱ_k with 0–1 elements, i.e., $\varrho_i^k = 1$ represents i-th block updates. Next, let the following assumption hold.

Assumption 10.5 (The Activation Mechanism) *Let $\Theta = \{0, 1\}_m$ denote the set of binary strings of length m, the elements of which are combined to form an m-dimensional vector. The sequence $\{\varrho_k\}_{k\geq 0}$ contains Θ-valued vectors with the fixed independent probability*

$$p_i = \mathbb{P}\left(\varrho_i^1 = 1\right) > 0,\ i = 1,\ 2,\ \cdots,\ m.$$

For the sake of simplicity, let the notation, $\mathbb{E}_k(\cdot)$, briefly denote the conditional expectation $\mathbb{E}(\cdot\,|\mathcal{F}_k)$, where $\mathcal{F}_k$ is the filtration yielded by the sequence $\{\varrho_1, \cdots, \varrho_k\}$. Therefore, by combining (10.56) and (10.76), the compact form of Algorithm 15 is given by

$$U_{k+1} = U_k + E_{k+1}\left(\mathcal{T}U_k - U_k\right), \tag{10.77}$$

where $E_{k+1} = \sum_{i=1}^{m} \varrho_i^{k+1}\delta_i$. The next theorem establishes the convergence results for Algorithm 15.

Theorem 10.10 *Let Assumptions 10.2–10.5 hold. Considering Algorithm 15, the sequence $\{U_k\}_{k\in\mathbb{N}}$, generated by* (10.77)*, is stochastic quasi-Fejér monotone with respect to $\mathcal{S}$, i.e.,*

$$\mathbb{E}_k\Big[\|U_{k+1}-U^*\|^2_{\Pi^{-1}S}\Big] \le \|U_k-U^*\|^2_{\Pi^{-1}S} - \|\mathcal{T}U_k-U_k\|^2_{2\tilde{P}-S}. \tag{10.78}$$

where $\Pi = \sum_{i=1}^{m} p_i\delta_i$ is the probability matrix. Furthermore, the sequence, $\{U_k\}_{k\in\mathbb{N}}$, converges to some $U^* \in \mathcal{S}$.

Proof According to (10.76), it indicates that $\sum_{i=1}^{m}\delta_i = I$, which contributes to

$$\begin{cases} \delta_i\delta_j = 0, \ i \ne j, \\ \delta_i\delta_j = \delta_i, i = j, \end{cases}$$

from which it follows that

$$E_k \cdot E_k = \sum_{i=1, i\ne j}^{m} \varrho_i^k\delta_i \cdot \varrho_j^k\delta_j + \sum_{i=1}^{m} \left(\varrho_i^k\delta_i\right)^2 = E_k. \tag{10.79}$$

On the other hand, the conditional expectation of E_{k+1} is given by

$$\begin{aligned} \mathbb{E}_k\left(E_{k+1}\right) &= \sum_{\vartheta\in\Theta} \mathbb{P}\left(\varrho_{k+1} = \vartheta\right) \sum_{j=1}^{m} \varrho_j^k\delta_j \\ &= \sum_{j=1}^{m}\sum_{\vartheta\in\Theta} \mathbb{P}\left(\varrho_{k+1} = \vartheta\right)\cdot \varrho_j^k\delta_j \\ &= \sum_{j=1}^{m}\sum_{\vartheta\in\Theta, \vartheta_j=1} \mathbb{P}\left(\varrho_{k+1} = \vartheta\right)\cdot \vartheta_j\delta_j \\ &= \sum_{j=1}^{m} p_j\delta_j = \Pi. \end{aligned} \tag{10.80}$$

Then, combining (10.77), (10.79) and (10.80), we have

$$\begin{aligned}
&\mathbb{E}_k\left[\left\|U_{k+1}-U^*\right\|^2_{\Pi^{-1}S}\right] \\
&= \mathbb{E}_k\left[\left\|U_k-U^*+E_{k+1}\left(\mathcal{T}U_k-U_k\right)\right\|^2_{\Pi^{-1}S}\right] \\
&= \left\|U_k-U^*\right\|^2_{\Pi^{-1}S} \\
&\quad+\langle \mathcal{T}U_k-U_k, \mathbb{E}_k\left[E_{k+1}\left(\mathcal{T}U_k-U_k\right)\right]\rangle_{\Pi^{-1}S} \\
&\quad+2\big\langle U_k-U^*, \mathbb{E}_k\left[E_{k+1}\left(\mathcal{T}U_k-U_k\right)\right]\big\rangle_{\Pi^{-1}S} \\
&= \left\|U_k-U^*\right\|^2_{\Pi^{-1}S}+\left\|\mathcal{T}U_k-U_k\right\|^2_S \\
&\quad+2\big\langle U_k-U^*, \mathcal{T}U_k-U_k\big\rangle_S.
\end{aligned} \tag{10.81}$$

Utilizing (10.63) yields

$$\begin{aligned}
&\left\|\mathcal{T}U_k-U_k\right\|^2_S+2\big\langle U_k-U^*, \mathcal{T}U_k-U_k\big\rangle_S \\
&\leq -\left\|\mathcal{T}U_k-U_k\right\|^2_{2\tilde{P}-S}.
\end{aligned} \tag{10.82}$$

Thus, (10.78) holds by combining (10.81) with (10.82). Furthermore, the convergence of $\{U_k\}_{k\in\mathbb{N}}$ follows from (10.77) utilizing the Robbins-Siegmud Lemma [69] and arguing as in [23, 24]. ■

Remark 10.11 The diagonal structure of S and Π^{-1} are exploited in Theorem 10.10. Recall the diagonal step size matrix S in Definition 10.6. Assumption 10.5 indicates that the diagonal probability matrix Π contributes to the diagonal structure of its inverse Π^{-1}. Thus, S and Π^{-1} can commute, i.e., $\Pi^{-1}S = S\Pi^{-1}$, which is necessary for the Fejér monotonicity in (10.78). Additionally, the block-coordinate technique plays a critical role in Algorithm 15. To be specific, it allows more than one agent to be randomly activated. Such a setting is more practical than single activation one, showing more flexibility compared with the single waking-up scheme and the subsets of activated block coordinates that are uniformly selected. The local activation probability p_i assumed in Assumption (10.5) is completely independent of the others, without additional considerably strict conditions, like the condition that $\sum_{i=1}^{m} p_i = 1$.

Remark 10.12 Note that the property of $\mathcal{T}$ in Lemma 10.7 potentially drives the establishment of Fejér monotonicity via Theorems 10.8 and 10.10. The local step size conditions for convergence of Algorithm 15 is the same as that of Syn-FdPdPs, where the local Lipschitz constants φ_i is involved in Lemma 10.5, rather than a global constant in some distributed methods [13, 49, 51, 54, 235, 238]. As can be shown from Assumption (10.4), the step sizes, σ_i, μ_i and $\omega_{(i,j)}$, are taken in a wide range, i.e., they only keep positive. As for the step size τ_i, corresponding to primal variable x_i, obeys an explicit upper bound that depends only on the local parameters,

φ_i, σ_i, μ_i, $\omega_{(i,j)}$, and the private linear mapping L_i in problem (10.7). All these parameters are known by agent i and their selections are local. That is the meaning of the fully distributed algorithm.

10.5 Numerical Examples

In this section, the effectiveness of the proposed algorithms is examined through several illustrative examples and their performance are compared with the existing methods.

10.5.1 Case Study I: Performance Examination

Each agent i holds its local objective function $0.5||D_i\tilde{x}-d_i||^2+\rho_i||L_i\tilde{x}-l_i||_1$, where $\tilde{x} \in \mathbb{R}^4$ is the common decision variable, D_i and L_i are 1×4 real matrices, while d_i and $l_i \in \mathbb{R}$ are four-dimensional constant vectors, the components of which are generated randomly in $(-15, 15)$. The penalty factor ρ_i for each agent i is set to 1. Then, we employ the proposed algorithms to solve the optimization problem:

$$\begin{aligned}
\min_{\tilde{x}\in\mathbb{R}^4} \quad & \sum_{i=1}^{m} \left(\frac{1}{2}\|D_i\tilde{x} - d_i\|^2 + \rho_i\|L_i\tilde{x} - l_i\|_1\right), \\
\text{s.t.} \quad & 3\tilde{x}_1 + 3\tilde{x}_2 + 2\tilde{x}_3 + \tilde{x}_4 = 6, \\
& 4\tilde{x}_1 - \tilde{x}_2 - \tilde{x}_3 - \tilde{x}_4 \leq 2, \\
& -2 \leq \tilde{x}_q \leq 2, \quad q = 1, 2, 3, 4.
\end{aligned} \tag{10.83}$$

In light of (10.8), the local linear operators A_i and B_i for all i are respectively given by

$$A_i = [3, 3, 2, 1], \ \ B_i = [4, -1, -1, -1],$$

and the scalars $a_i = 6$ and $b_i = 2$. In this simulation, the step sizes, $\omega_{(i,j)}$ and μ_i, are generated randomly in the interval $(m, m+1)$, while σ_i is selected randomly from the interval $(m/||L_i^{\mathrm{T}}L_i||, (m+1)/||L_i^{\mathrm{T}}L_i||)$. According to Assumption 10.4, we set

$$\tau_i = \frac{1.6}{\varphi_i + 2\left(\sum_{j\in\mathcal{N}_i}\omega_{(i,j)} + \mu_i + \sigma_i \left\|L_i^{\mathrm{T}}L_i\right\|\right)},$$

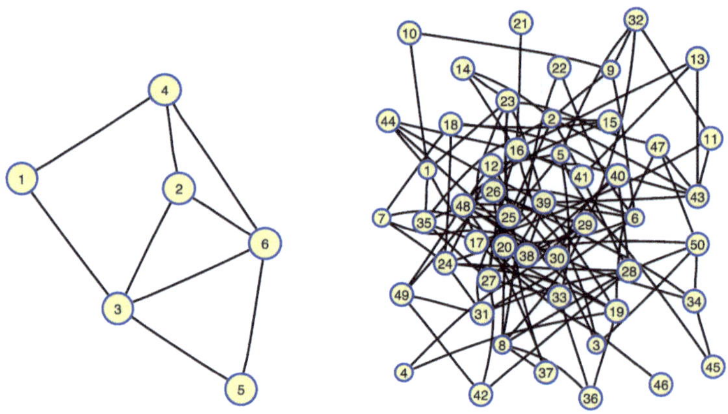

(a) (b)

Fig. 10.2 Undirected networks. (**a**) 6-agents network. (**b**) 50-agents network

with $\beta_i = \|D_i^{\mathrm{T}} D\|$, $\hat{\beta}_i = 4$ and $\xi_i = 2$ in (10.47). At the same time, Q_i and R_i are assumed to be the identity matrix. Moreover, the weighting parameter γ_i is chosen as $\exp(i+9)$, which is sufficiently large to some degree. Besides, in the implementation of Rand-FdPdPs, agents 1–4 are activated independently with the probabilities $p_i = 0.5, i = 1, \cdots, 4$, and agents 5 and 6 with 0.3 and 0.4, respectively. Furthermore, all initial values are set to 0.

For comparison purposes, we consider other two approaches to address problem (10.83). One is the distributed primal-dual sub-gradient algorithm [92], in which the primal and dual variables share a common step size. Another one is the consensus algorithm developed in [242], where the agent-based communication mode is adopted. Note that both of the considered algorithms with global clock coordinators employ coordinated step sizes.

The algorithms are conducted over two undirected networks, i.e., 6-agents and 50-agents, as shown in Fig. 10.2. For the 6-agents network, the transient behaviors of all dimensions of x_i^k are depicted in Fig. 10.3, showing that the proposed algorithms can successfully solve the considered problem (10.83) and expectedly obtain its optimal solution, $[0.0091,\ 1.4850, 0.2446, 1.0286]^{\mathrm{T}}$, which is in line with that of the consensus and sub-gradient methods. Figure 10.4 describes the accuracy of the approximation under different selections of the weighting parameters, showing that the larger γ_i results in the better accuracy.

On the other hand, the transient behaviors of x_i^k over the 50-agents network are described in Fig. 10.5. It is important to emphasize that the optimal solution in 50-agents network may be different from that of the first scenario (6-agents network) because of the random generations of the involved matrices or vector in local function f_i, but the proposed algorithms still achieve desired results that obtained via the consensus method. Finally, Fig. 10.6 indicates that the proposed algorithms are superior to the other two algorithms in terms of convergence speed, through evaluating the relative errors $\sum_{i=1}^{m} \|x_i - x_i^*\| / \sum_{i=1}^{m} \|x_i^*\|$.

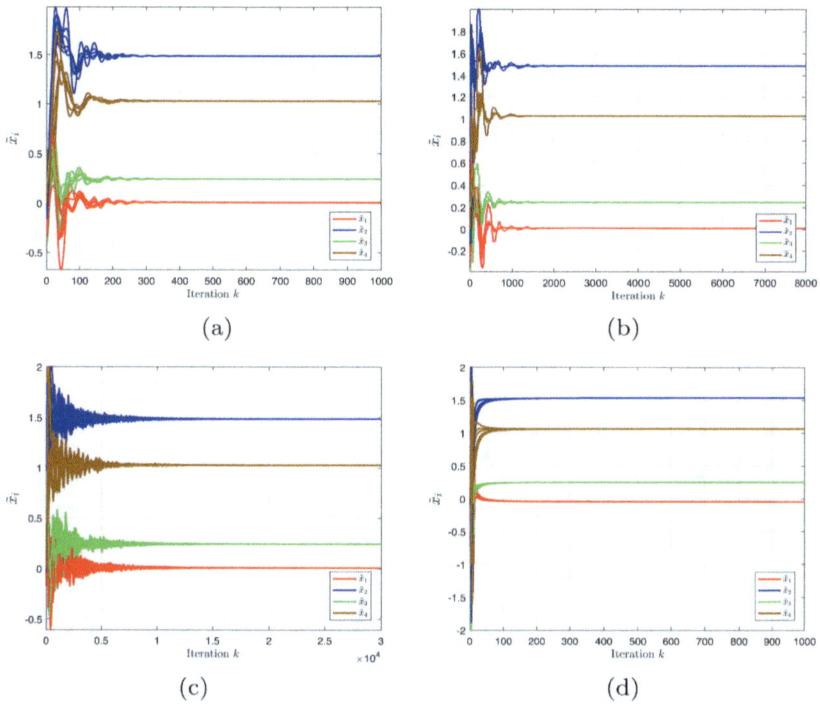

Fig. 10.3 Transient behaviors of x_i^k with 6 agents. (**a**) Syn-FdPdPs. (**b**) Rand-FdPdPs. (**c**) Consensus algorithm [242]. (**d**) Sub-gradient algorithm [92]

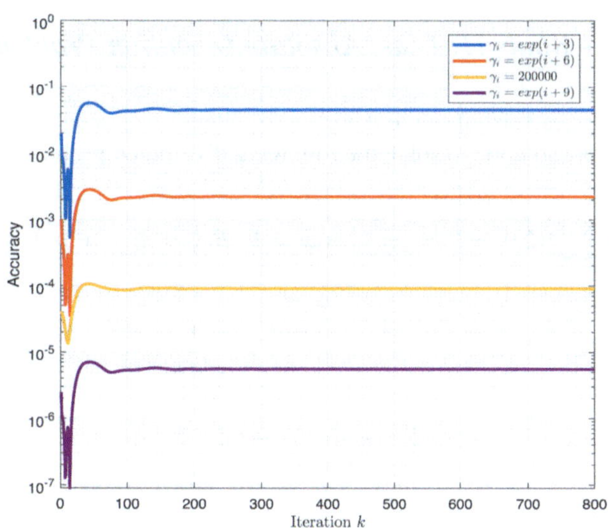

Fig. 10.4 Accuracy for different selections of $\gamma_i > 0$

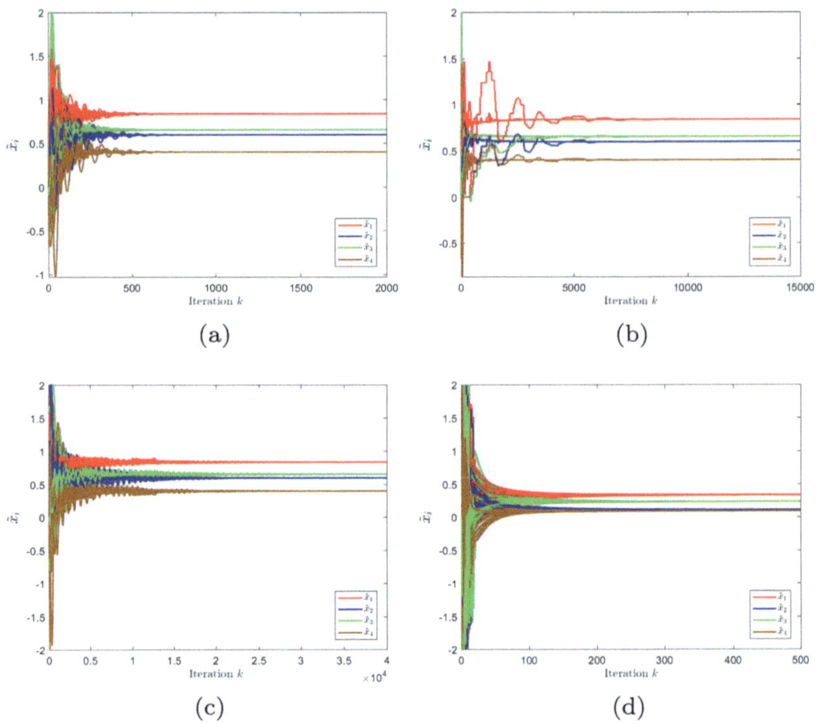

Fig. 10.5 Transient behaviors of x_i^k with 50 agents. (**a**) Syn-FdPdPs. (**b**) Rand-FdPdPs. (**c**) Consensus algorithm [242]. (**d**) Sub-gradient algorithm [92]

10.5.2 Case Study II: Least Absolute Deviation Problem

This case combines least absolute deviation problem mentioned in [242, 248] with local constraints and aims to solve the following distributed problem:

$$\min_{\tilde{x}\in\mathbb{R}^3} \sum_{i=1}^{m} ||L_i\tilde{x} - l_i||_1, \text{ s.t. } A_i\tilde{x} = 1,\ B_i\tilde{x} \leq 5,\ \ \tilde{x} \in \bigcap\nolimits_{i=1}^{m} \mathcal{X}_i,$$

where $A_i = [1, 1, 1]$, $B_i = [1\ , -1\ , -1]$ and $\mathcal{X}_i = \{\tilde{x} \in \mathbb{R}^3 \,|{-5} \leq \tilde{x}_1, \tilde{x}_2, \tilde{x}_3 \leq 5\}$. The vector $l_i = [-2, 1.1, 4.2, -0.5, 2.1]^{\mathrm{T}}$ and the linear matrix L_i is given by

$$L_i = \begin{bmatrix} 1.1 & 4 & 7 & -3.1 & 5.5 \\ 2 & 5.1 & 8 & -4 & 6.9 \\ 3.1 & 6 & 8.9 & -5 & 8.1 \end{bmatrix}^{\mathrm{T}}.$$

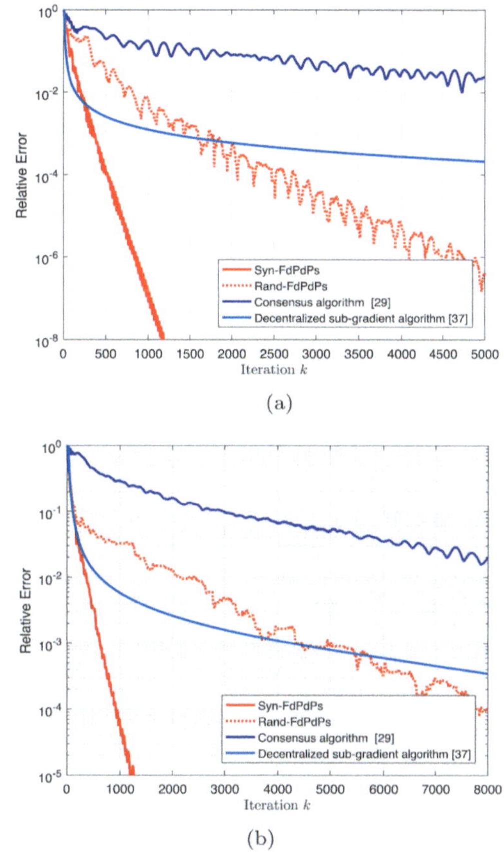

Fig. 10.6 Convergence performance comparison. (**a**) 6-agents network. (**b**) 50-agents network

Note that this problem has a unique optimal solution $\tilde{x}^* = [2, 1, -2,]^{\mathrm{T}}$. As shown in Fig. 10.7, consider the following 60-agents network. Set the step sizes, $\omega_{(i,j)}$, μ_i and σ_i as 1, while τ_i as the same selection of Case I. The activation probability of each agent is 0.8. Furthermore, all initial values are set to 0. The Fig. 10.8 indicates that both Syn-FdPdPs and Rand-FdPdPs obtain the optimal solution after certain iterations, which shows the effectiveness of proposed algorithms.

10.6 Conclusion

In this chapter, two full-distributed primal-dual proximal splitting algorithms have been developed for convex optimization problems abiding by feasible sets, linear equality and inequality constraints over undirected networks, which bypass the

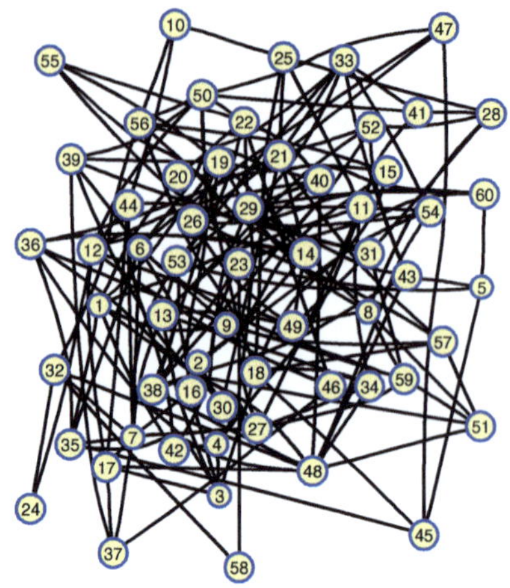

Fig. 10.7 The 60-agents network

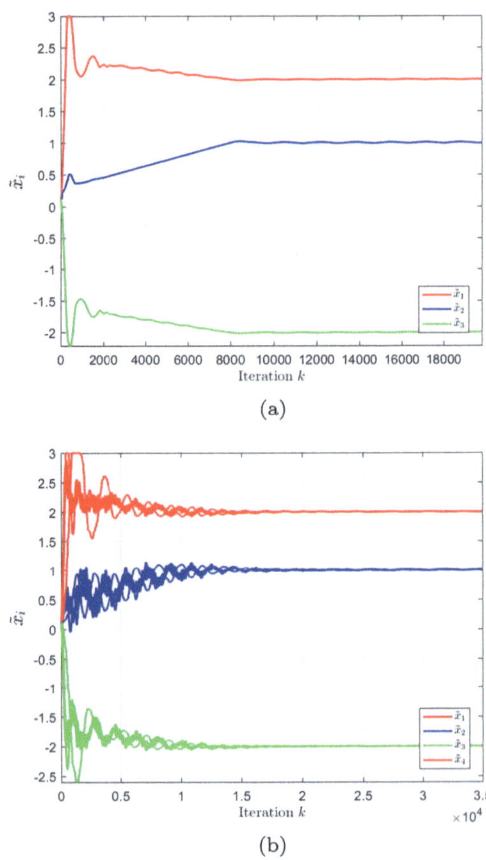

Fig. 10.8 Transient behaviors of x_i^k of least absolute deviation problem. (**a**) Syn-FdPdPs. (**b**) Rand-FdPdPs

unapproximable property of the proximal function of inequality constraints via logarithmic barrier functions. Distinguish features of the proposed algorithms include taking the uncoordinated step sizes and avoiding the selection of balance weights. In addition, to remove the global coordinator, a randomized algorithm based on the block-coordinate technique has been presented.

Chapter 11
Conclusions

Distributed computation and optimization of large-scale networked systems are ubiquitous in all aspects of the interconnected world today. These applications range from signal processing and control systems to various areas of artificial intelligence. The emergence of big data applications has further stimulated researchers' interest in distributed optimization. On the one hand, large datasets push centralized computing to its limits, and the need for distributed algorithms emerges naturally. On the other hand, transmitting data collected in a distributed manner to a center is too costly or may violate privacy. This book is dedicated to the optimization problem of information distribution over networked systems. Each agent in the network possesses private local information and solves the global optimization problem collaboratively through local computation and information exchange. To this end, this book provides an in-depth exploration of issues related to distributed optimization of networked systems mainly based on randomized block-coordinate methods, primal-dual fixed point methods, randomized asynchronous iterative methods, triple proximal splitting methods, dual operator splitting methods, primal-dual forward-backward splitting methods model predictive control methods, dual proximal gradient methods, primal-dual proximal splitting methods, and so on. The research in this book is completed step by step in accordance with four parts: -abstracting the distributed optimization problems according to the actual application-designing the distributed optimization algorithms according to the problem models-analysis of the convergence performance of the algorithm-verification by the actual applications.

In the future, the following topics deserve further study. First, most of the existing distributed optimization methods are mainly focused on the case where the objective function is convex, however, the objective function of more practical optimization problem models such as machine learning, especially deep learning, is mainly non-convex. Therefore, it will be a very meaningful topic to comprehensively consider the actual non-convex optimization problems and ensure that the algorithm has a better convergence performance. Second, in practical application scenarios, the dynamics of the network topology (e.g., agents joining/withdrawing, link

H. Li et al., *Network-System Research and Distributed Composite Algorithm Design*, Computational Intelligence Methods and Applications,
https://doi.org/10.1007/978-981-95-0911-9_11

disruption/reconstruction) has become a key factor constraining the performance of distributed algorithms. However, the current distributed optimization algorithms are still insufficient to consider the network dynamics, mainly focusing on performance validation in static or low-frequency dynamic scenarios, and lack of systematic analysis of the combined effects of high topology dynamics, agent heterogeneity and communication unreliability. Therefore, the design of high-performance distributed optimization algorithms to effectively cope with more complex and dynamic network environments is an important theoretical guidance for solving practical problems. Last but not least, the distributed optimization process requires agents to interact with each other with real information, which may leak some interaction data. These data often contain a large amount of sensitive information, such as biometric data, economic status, location trajectories, health data, etc. Once these sensitive information are leaked, it may bring personal or property security threats to the data providers. Therefore, privacy security has become one of the key issues that must be considered in the distributed optimization, and there is an urgent need to carry out the corresponding research of privacy-preserving distributed optimization to reduce the risk of privacy leakage.

References

1. H. Zou and T. Hastie, "Regularization and variable selection via the elastic net," *Journal of the Royal Statistical Society Series B: Statistical Methodology*, vol. 67, no. 2, pp. 301–320, 2005.
2. E. Y. Sidky, J. H. Jorgensen and X. C. Pan, "Convex optimization problem prototyping for image reconstruction in computed tomography with the Chambolle-Pock algorithm," *Physics in Medicine and Biology*, vol. 57, no. 10, pp. 3065–3091, 2012.
3. M. Yuan and Y. Lin, "Model selection and estimation in regression with grouped variables," *Journal of the Royal Statistical Society Series B: Statistical Methodology*, vol. 68, no. 1, pp.$\tilde{4}$9–67, 2006.
4. P. L. Combettes and J. C. Pesquet, "Primal-dual splitting algorithm for solving inclusions with mixtures of composite, Lipschitzian, and parallel-sum type monotone operators," *Set-valued and Variational Analysis*, vol. 20, no. 2, pp. 307–330, 2012.
5. L. Condat, "A primal-dual splitting method for convex optimization involving lipschitzian, proximable and linear composite terms," *Journal of Optimization Theory and Applications*, vol. 158, no. 2, pp. 460–479, 2013.
6. P. Latafat and P. Patrinos, "Asymmetric forward-backward-adjoint splitting for solving monotone inclusions involving three operators," *Computational Optimization and Applications*, vol. 68, no. 1, pp. 57–93, 2017.
7. P. Chen, J. Huang and X. Zhang, "A primal-dual fixed point algorithm for minimization of the sum of three convex separable functions," *Fixed Point Theory and Applications*, vol. 2016, pp. 1–18, 2016.
8. M. Yan, "A new primal-dual algorithm for minimizing the sum of three functions with a linear operator," *Journal of Scientific Computing*, vol. 76, no. 3, pp. 1698–1717, 2018.
9. A. Nedić and A. Ozdaglar, "Distributed subgradient methods for multi-agent optimization," *IEEE Transactions on Automatic Control*, vol. 54, no. 1, pp. 48–61, 2009.
10. D. Jakovetić, J. Xavier and J. M. F. Moura, "Fast distributed gradient methods," *IEEE Transactions on Automatic Control*, vol. 59, no. 5, pp. 1131–1146, 2014.
11. J. C. Duchi, A. Agarwal and M. J. Wainwright, "Dual averaging for distributed optimization: Convergence analysis and network scaling," *IEEE Transactions on Automatic control*, vol. 57, no. 3, pp. 592–606, 2012.
12. Y. Tian, Y. Sun and G. Scutari, "Achieving linear convergence in distributed asynchronous multi-agent optimization," *IEEE Transactions on Automatic Control*, vol. 65, no. 12, pp. 5264–5279, 2020.

H. Li et al., *Network-System Research and Distributed Composite Algorithm Design*, Computational Intelligence Methods and Applications,
https://doi.org/10.1007/978-981-95-0911-9

13. N. Bastianello, R. Carli, L. Schenato and M. Todescato, "Asynchronous distributed optimization over lossy networks via relaxed ADMM: Stability and linear convergence," *IEEE Transactions on Automatic Control*, vol. 66, no. 6, pp. 2620–2635, 2021.
14. S. A. Alghunaim, E. K. Ryu, K. Yuan and A. H. Sayed, "Decentralized proximal gradient algorithms with linear convergence rates," *IEEE Transactions on Automatic Control*, vol. 66, no. 6, pp. 2787–2794, 2021.
15. J. Xu, Y. Tian, Y. Sun and G. Scutari, "Distributed algorithms for composite optimization: unified framework and convergence analysis," *IEEE Transactions on Signal Processing*, vol. 69, pp. 3555–3570, 2021.
16. P. Latafat, L. Stella and P. Patrinos, "New primal-dual proximal algorithm for distributed optimization," *55th IEEE Conference on Decision and Control (CDC)*, pp. 1959–1964, 2016.
17. P. Latafat, N. M. Freris and P. Patrinos, "A new randomized block-coordinate primal-dual proximal algorithm for distributed optimization," *IEEE Transactions on Automatic Control*, vol. 64, no. 10, pp. 4050–4065, 2019.
18. Z. Li, W. Shi and M. Yan, "A decentralized proximal-gradient method with network independent step sizes and separated convergence rates," *IEEE Transactions on Signal Processing*, vol. 67, no. 17, pp. 4494–4506, 2019.
19. J. Xu, S. Zhu, Y. C. Soh and L. Xie, "Augmented distributed gradient methods for multi-agent optimization under uncoordinated constant step sizes," *54th IEEE Conference on Decision and Control (CDC)*, pp. 2055–2060, 2015.
20. C. A. Micchelli, L. Shen and Y. Xu, "Proximity algorithms for image models: denoising," *Inverse Problems*, vol. 27, no. 4, pp. 045009, 2011.
21. G. Zhang and R. Heusdens, "Bi-alternating direction method of multipliers over graphs," *International Conference on Acoustics, Speech, and Signal Processing*, pp. 3571–3575, 2015.
22. H. H. Bauschke and P. L. Combettes, "Convex analysis and monotone operator theory in hilbert spaces," Cham, Switzerland: Springer, 2011.
23. P. Bianchi, W. Hachem and F. Iutzeler, "A coordinate descent primal-dual algorithm and application to distributed asynchronous optimization," *IEEE Transactions on Automatic Control*, vol. 61, no. 10, pp. 2947–2957, 2016.
24. P. L. Combettes and J. C. Pesquet, "Stochastic quasi-Fejér block-coordinate fixed point iterations with random sweeping," *SIAM Journal on Optimization*, vol. 25, no. 2, pp. 1221–1248, 2015.
25. N. S. Aybat, Z. Wang, T. Lin and S. Ma, "Distributed linearized alternating direction method of multipliers for composite convex consensus optimization," *IEEE Transactions on Automatic Control*, vol. 63, no. 1, pp. 5–20, 2018.
26. R. Tibshirani, M. Saunders, R. Rosset, J. Zhu and K. Knight, "Sparsity and smoothness via the fused lasso," *Journal of the Royal Statistical Society Series B: Statistical Methodology*, vol. 67, no. 1, pp. 91–108, 2005.
27. J. Wu, T. Yang, D. Wu, K. Kalsi and K. H. Johansson, "Distributed optimal dispatch of distributed energy resources over lossy communication networks," *IEEE Transactions on Smart Grid*, vol. 8, no. 6, pp. 3125–3137, 2017.
28. B. Jin, H. Li, W. Yan and M. Cao, "Distributed model predictive control and optimization for linear systems with global constraints and time-varying communication," *IEEE Transactions on Automatic Control*, vol. 66, no. 7, pp. 3393–3400, 2021.
29. P. L. Combettes and J. C. Pesquet, "Proximal splitting methods in signal processing," *Fixed-Point Algorithms for Inverse Problems in Science and Engineering*, Springer, New York, vol. 49, pp. 185–212, 2011.
30. P. Tseng, "A modified forward-backward splitting method for maximal monotone mappings," *SIAM Journal on Control and Optimization*, vol. 38, no. 2, pp. 431–446, 2000.
31. B. Mercier and G. Vijayasundaram, "Lectures on topics in finite element solution of elliptic problems," *Springer*, 1979.
32. J. Eckstein and D. P. Bertsekas, "On the Douglas-Rachford splitting method and the proximal point algorithm for maximal monotone operators," *Mathematical Programming*, vol. 55, no. 1, pp. 293–318, 1992.

33. P. Chen, J. Huang and X. Zhang, "A primal-dual fixed point algorithm for convex separable minimization with applications to image restoration," *Inverse Problems*, vol. 29, no. 2, pp. 025011, 2013.
34. A. Krol, S. Li, L. Shen, and Y. Xu, "Preconditioned alternating projection algorithms for maximum a posterior ect reconstruction," *Inverse Problems*, vol. 28, no. 11, pp. 115005, 2012.
35. A. Chambolle and T. Pock, "A first-order primal-dual algorithm for convex problems with applications to imaging," *Journal of Mathematical Imaging and Vision*, vol. 40, no. 1, pp. 120–145, 2011.
36. R. I. Bot and E. R. Csetnek, "An inertial forward-backward-forward primal-dual splitting algorithm for solving monotone inclusion problems," *Numerical Algorithms*, vol. 71, no. 3, pp. 519–540, 2016.
37. F. Alvarez, "On the minimizing property of a second order dissipative system in Hilbert spaces," *SIAM Journal on Control and Optimization*, vol. 38, no. 4, pp. 1102–1119, 2000.
38. F. Alvarez and H. Attouch, "An inertial proximal method for maximal monotone operators via discretization of a nonlinear oscillator with damping," *Set-Valued Analysis*, vol. 9, no. 1, pp. 3–11, 2001.
39. Q. Li and N. Zhang, "Fast proximity-gradient algorithms for structured convex optimization problems," *Applied and Computational Harmonic Analysis*, vol. 41, no. 2, pp. 491–517, 2016.
40. M. Wen, J. Peng, Y. Tang, C. Zhu, and S. Yue, "A preconditioning technique for first-order primal-dual splitting method in convex optimization," *Mathematical Problems in Engineering*, vol. 2017, no. 1, pp. 3694525, 2017.
41. T. Pock and A. Chambolle, "Diagonal preconditioning for first order primal-dual algorithms in convex optimization," *IEEE International Conference on Computer Vision*, pp. 1762–1769, 2011.
42. W. Huang and Y. Tang, "Primal-dual fixed point algorithm based on adapted metric method for solving convex minimization problem with application," *Applied Numerical Mathematics*, vol. 157, pp. 236–254, 2020.
43. D. Chen, Y. Zhou and L. Song, "Fixed point algorithm based on adapted metric method for convex minimization problem with application to image deblurring," *Advances in Computational Mathematics*, vol. 42, no. 6, pp. 1287–1310, 2016.
44. J. E. Dennis, Jr. and J. J. More, "Quasi-Newton methods, motivation and theory," *SIAM Review*, vol. 19, no. 1, pp. 46–89, 1977.
45. H. Chen, H. C. Wu, S. C. Chan and W. H. Lam, "A stochastic Quasi-Newton method for large-scale nonconvex optimization with applications," *IEEE Transactions on Neural Networks and Learning Systems*, vol. 31, no. 11, pp. 4776–4790, 2020.
46. A. Nedic and A. Olshevsky, "Distributed optimization over time-varying directed graphs," *IEEE Transactions on Automatic Control*, vol. 60, no. 3, pp. 601–615, 2015.
47. H. Li, Q. Lü and T. Huang, "Distributed projection subgradient algorithm over time-varying general unbalanced directed graphs," *IEEE Transactions on Automatic Control*, vol. 64, no. 3, pp. 1309–1316, 2019.
48. A. Nedic and A. Olshevsky, "Stochastic gradient-push for strongly convex functions on time-varying directed graphs," *IEEE Transactions on Automatic Control*, vol. 61, no. 12, pp. 3936–3947, 2016.
49. W. Shi, Q. Ling, G. Wu and W. Yin, "EXTRA: An exact first-order algorithm for decentralized consensus optimization," *SIAM Journal on Optimization*, vol. 25, no. 2, pp. 944–966, 2015.
50. A. Nedic, "Asynchronous broadcast-based convex optimization over a network," *IEEE Transactions on Automatic Control*, vol. 56, no. 6, pp. 1337–1351, 2011.
51. J. Xu, S. Zhu, Y. C. Soh and L. Xie, "Convergence of asynchronous distributed gradient methods over stochastic networks," *IEEE Transactions on Automatic Control*, vol. 63, no. 2, pp. 434–448, 2018.
52. N. Parikh and S. Boyd, "Block splitting for distributed optimization," *Mathematical Programming Computation*, vol. 6, no. 1, pp. 77–102, 2014.
53. P. Bianchi and W. Hachem, "A primal-dual algorithm for distributed optimization," *53rd IEEE Annual Conference on Decision and Control (CDC)*, pp. 4240–4245, 2014.

54. W. Shi, Q. Ling, G. Wu and W. Yin, "A proximal gradient algorithm for decentralized composite optimization," *IEEE Transactions on Signal Processing*, vol. 63, no. 22, pp. 6013–6023, 2015.
55. R. Xin and U. A. Khan, "Distributed heavy-ball: A generalization and acceleration of first-order methods with gradient tracking," *IEEE Transactions on Automatic Control*, vol. 65, no. 6, pp. 2627–2633, 2020.
56. G. Qu and N. Li, "Accelerated distributed Nesterov gradient descent," *IEEE Transactions on Automatic Control*, vol. 65, no. 6, pp. 2566–2581, 2020.
57. M. Eisen, A. Mokhtari and A. Ribeiro, "A primal-dual quasi-Newton method for exact consensus optimization," *IEEE Transactions on Signal Processing*, vol. 67, no. 23, pp. 5983–5997, 2019.
58. A. Mokhtari, W. Shi, Q. Ling and A. Ribeiro, "DQM: Decentralized quadratically approximated alternating direction method of multipliers," *IEEE Transactions on Signal Processing*, vol. 64, no. 19, pp. 5158–5173, 2016.
59. A. Mokhtari, W. Shi, Q. Ling and A. Ribeiro, "A decentralized second-order method with exact linear convergence rate for consensus optimization," *IEEE Transactions on Signal and Information Processing over Networks*, vol. 2, no. 4, pp. 507–522, 2016.
60. A. Mokhtari, Q. Ling and A. Ribeiro, "Network Newton distributed optimization methods," *IEEE Transactions on Signal Processing*, vol. 65, no. 1, pp. 146–161, 2017.
61. F. Mansoori and E. Wei, "Superlinearly convergent asynchronous distributed network newton method," *56th IEEE Annual Conference on Decision and Control (CDC)*, pp. 2874–2879, 2017.
62. R. L. Raffard, C. J. Tomlin and S. P. Boyd, "Distributed optimization for cooperative agents: Application to formation flight," *43rd IEEE Conference on Decision and Control (CDC)*, pp. 2453–2459, 2004.
63. T. Schouwenaars, J. How and E. Feron, "Decentralized cooperative trajectory planning of multiple aircraft with hard safety guarantees," *AIAA Guidance, Navigation, and Control Conference and Exhibit*, pp. 1–14, 2004.
64. X. Shi, J. Cao and W. Huang, "Distributed parametric consensus optimization with an application to model predictive consensus problem," *IEEE Transactions on Cybernetics*, vol. 48, no. 7, pp. 2024–2035, 2018.
65. Q. Wang, Z. Duan, Y. Lv, Q. Wang and G. Chen, "Distributed model predictive control for linear-quadratic performance and consensus state optimization of multiagent systems," *IEEE Transactions on Cybernetics*, vol. 51, no. 6, pp. 2905–2915, 2021.
66. L. Bai, M. Ye, C. Sun and G. Hu, "Distributed economic dispatch control via saddle point dynamics and consensus algorithms," *IEEE Transactions on Control Systems Technology*, vol. 27, no. 2, pp. 898–905, 2019.
67. Q. Lü, X. Liao, H. Li and T. Huang, "Achieving acceleration for distributed economic dispatch in smart grids over directed networks," *IEEE Transactions on Network Science and Engineering*, vol. 7, no. 3, pp. 1988–1999, 2020.
68. A. Beck, "*First-order methods in optimization*," Philadelphia, PA: Society for Industrial and Applied Mathematics, 2017.
69. H. Robbins and D. Siegmund, "A convergence theorem for non negative almost supermartingales and some applications," *Optimizing Methods in Statistics*, New York: Academic Press, pp. 233–257, 1971.
70. H. Li, Q. Lü, G. Chen, T. Huang and Z. Dong, "Distributed constrained optimization over unbalanced directed networks using asynchronous broadcast-based algorithm," *IEEE Transactions on Automatic Control*, vol. 66, no. 3, pp. 1102–1115, 2021.
71. T. Doan and A. Olshevsky, "On the geometric convergence rate of distributed economic dispatch/demand response in power systems," *arXiv preprint arXiv:1609.06660*, 2016.
72. P. Yi, Y. Hong and F. Liu, "Distributed gradient algorithm for constrained optimization with application to load sharing in power systems," *Systems & Control Letters*, vol. 83, pp. 45–52, 2015.

73. X. He, D. W. C. Ho, T. Huang, J. Yu, H. Abu-Rub and C. Li, "Second-order continuous-time algorithms for economic power dispatch in smart grids," *IEEE Transactions on Systems, Man, and Cybernetics: Systems*, vol. 48, no. 9, pp. 1482–1492, 2018.
74. K. Li, Q. Liu, S. Yang, J. Cao and G. Lu, "Cooperative optimization of dual multiagent system for optimal resource allocation," *IEEE Transactions on Systems, Man, and Cybernetics: Systems*, vol. 50, no. 11, pp. 4676–4687, 2020.
75. L. Carlone, V. Srivastava, F. Bullo and G. C. Calafiore, "Distributed random convex programming via constraints consensus," *SIAM Journal on Control and Optimization*, vol. 52, pp. 629–662, 2014.
76. S. Yang, J. Wang and Q. Liu, "Consensus of heterogeneous nonlinear multiagent systems with duplex control laws," *IEEE Transactions on Automatic Control*, vol. 64, no. 12, pp. 5140–5147, 2019.
77. S. Yang, Q. Liu and J. Wang, "Distributed optimization based on a multiagent system in the presence of communication delays," *IEEE Transactions on Systems, Man, and Cybernetics: Systems*, vol. 47, no. 5, pp. 717–728, 2017.
78. J. Xu, Y. Tian, Y. Sun and G. Scutari, "Accelerated primal-dual algorithms for distributed smooth convex optimization over networks," *International Conference on Artificial Intelligence and Statistics*, pp. 2381–2391, 2020.
79. Y. Xu, M. Fang, Y.-J. Pan, K. Shi and Z.-G. Wu, "Event-triggered output synchronization for nonhomogeneous agent systems with periodic denial-of-service attacks," *International Journal of Robust and Nonlinear Control*, vol. 31, no. 6, pp. 1851–1865, 2021.
80. B. Johansson, T. Keviczky, M. Johansson and K. H. Johansson, "Subgradient methods and consensus algorithms for solving convex optimization problems," *47th IEEE Conference on Decision and Control (CDC)*, pp. 4185–4190, 2008.
81. B. Huang, L. Liu, H. Zhang, Y. Li and Q. Sun, "Distributed optimal economic dispatch for microgrids considering communication delays," *IEEE Transactions on Systems, Man, and Cybernetics: Systems*, vol. 49, no. 8, pp. 1634–1642, 2019.
82. M. Zhu and S. Martinez, "On distributed convex optimization under inequality and equality constraints," *IEEE Transactions on Automatic Control*, vol. 57, no. 1, pp. 151–164, 2012.
83. H. Li, Q. Lü, X. Liao and T. Huang, "Accelerated convergence algorithm for distributed constrained optimization under time-varying general directed graphs," *IEEE Transactions on Systems, Man, and Cybernetics: Systems*, vol. 50, no. 7, pp. 2612–2622, 2020.
84. T. Erseghe, "A distributed and scalable processing method based upon admm," *IEEE Signal Processing Letters*, vol. 19, no. 9, pp. 563–566, 2012.
85. J. F. Mota, J. M. Xavier, P. M. Aguiar and M. Puschel, "Distributed optimization with local domains: Applications in MPC and network flows," *IEEE Transactions on Automatic Control*, vol. 60, no. 7, pp. 2004–2009, 2015.
86. E. Wei and A. Ozdaglar, "On the $O(1/k)$ convergence of asynchronous distributed alternating direction method of multipliers," *IEEE Global Conference on Signal and Information Processing (GlobalSIP)*, pp. 551–554, 2013.
87. Y. Xu, J. Sun, G. Wang and Z.-G. Wu, "Dynamic triggering mechanisms for distributed adaptive synchronization control and its application to circuit systems," *IEEE Transactions on Circuits and Systems I: Regular Papers*, vol. 68, no. 5, pp. 2246–2256, 2021.
88. Z. Ye, D. Zhang and Z.-G. Wu, "Adaptive event-based tracking control of unmanned marine vehicle systems with DoS attack," *Journal of the Franklin Institute*, vol. 358, no. 3, pp. 1915–1939, 2021.
89. X. He, H. Wen and T. Huang, "A fixed-time projection neural network for solving L_1-minimization problem," *IEEE Transactions on Neural Networks and Learning Systems*, vol. 33, no. 12, pp. 7818–7828, 2022.
90. D. Yuan, A. Proutiere and G. Shi, "Distributed online optimization with long-term constraints," *IEEE Transactions on Automatic Control*, vol. 67, no. 3, pp. 1089–1104, 2022.
91. Z. Denkowski, S. Migórski and N. S. Papageorgiou, *An Introduction to Nonlinear Analysis: Theory*. New York, NY, USA: Springer-Verlag, 2003.

92. D. Yuan, S. Xu and H. Zhao, "Distributed primal-dual subgradient method for multi-agent optimization via consensus algorithms," *IEEE Transactions on Systems, Man, and Cybernetics, Part B (Cybernetics)*, vol. 41, no. 6, pp. 1715–1724, 2011.
93. Z. Qiu, S. Liu and L. Xie, "Distributed constrained optimal consensus of multi-agent systems," *Automatica*, vol. 68, pp. 209–215, 2016.
94. X. He, T. Huang, J. Yu, C. Li and Y. Zhang, "A continuous-time algorithm for distributed optimization based on multiagent networks," *IEEE Transactions on Systems, Man, and Cybernetics: Systems*, vol. 49, no. 12, pp. 2700–2709, 2019.
95. X. Zeng, P. Yi and Y. Hong, "Distributed continuous-time algorithm for constrained convex optimizations via nonsmooth analysis approach," *IEEE Transactions on Automatic Control*, vol. 62, no. 10, pp. 5227–5233, 2017.
96. S. Liang, X. Zeng and Y. Hong, "Distributed nonsmooth optimization with coupled inequality constraints via modified Lagrangian function," *IEEE Transactions on Automatic Control*, vol. 63, no. 6, pp. 1753–1759, 2018.
97. W. Jia, N. Liu, and S. Qin, "An adaptive continuous-time algorithm for nonsmooth convex resource allocation optimization," *IEEE Transactions on Automatic Control*, vol. 67, no. 11, pp. 6038–6044, 2022.
98. Y. Wei, H. Fang, X. Zeng, J. Chen and P. Pardalos, "A smooth double proximal primal-dual algorithm for a class of distributed nonsmooth optimization problems," *IEEE Transactions on Automatic Control*, vol. 65, no. 4, pp. 1800–1806, 2020.
99. B. C. Vũ, "A splitting algorithm for dual monotone inclusions involving cocoercive operators," *Advances In Computational Mathematics*, vol. 38, no. 3, pp. 667–681, 2013.
100. M. Hong and T. H. Chang, "Stochastic proximal gradient consensus over random network," *IEEE Transactions on Signal Processing*, vol. 65, no. 11, pp. 2933–2948, 2017.
101. Q. Shi and M. Hong, "Penalty dual decomposition method for nonsmooth nonconvex optimization-part I: algorithms and convergence analysis," *IEEE Transactions on Signal Processing*, vol. 68, pp. 4108–4122, 2020.
102. Q. Lü, X. Liao, H. Li and T. Huang, "A computation-efficient decentralized algorithm for composite constrained optimization," *IEEE Transactions on Signal and Information Processing over Networks*, vol. 6, pp. 774–789, 2020.
103. S. Liu, Z. Qiu and L. Xie, "Convergence rate analysis of distributed optimization with projected subgradient algorithm," *Automatica*, vol. 83, pp. 162–169, 2017.
104. D. Davis and W. Yin, "Convergence rate analysis of several splitting schemes," *Splitting Methods in Communication, Imaging, Science, and Engineering*, Cham: Springer International Publishing, pp. 115–163, 2016.
105. S. Boyd and L. Vandenberghe, *"Convex Optimization"*, Cambridge, U.K. Cambridge Univ. Press, 2004.
106. Z. Li, Y. Tang, J. Fang and T. Huang, "Formation control of multi-agent systems with orientation noises," *IEEE Transactions on Network Science and Engineering*, vol. 8, no. 1, pp. 305–317, 2021.
107. L. Liu and G. Yang, "Distributed optimal economic environmental dispatch for microgrids over time-varying directed communication graph," *IEEE Transactions on Network Science and Engineering*, vol. 8, no. 2, pp. 1913–1924, 2021.
108. R. Xin, S. Kar and U. A. Khan, "Decentralized stochastic optimization and machine learning: A unified variance-reduction framework for robust performance and fast convergence," *IEEE Signal Processing Magazine*, vol. 37, no. 3, pp. 102–113, 2020.
109. C. Ababei and M. G. Moghaddam, "A survey of prediction and classification techniques in multicore processor systems," *IEEE Transactions on Parallel and Distributed Systems*, vol. 30, no. 5, pp. 1184–1200, 2019.
110. J. Qin, Y. Wan, X. Yu and Y. Kang, "A Newton method-based distributed algorithm for multi-area economic dispatch," *IEEE Transactions on Power Systems*, vol. 35, no. 2, pp. 986–996, 2020.

111. D. Wang , J. Zhou, Z. Wang and W. Wang, "Random gradient-free optimization for multiagent systems with communication noises under a time-varying weight balanced digraph," *IEEE Transactions on Systems, Man, and Cybernetics: Systems*, vol. 50, no. 1, pp. 281–289, 2020.
112. D. Wang, J. Yin and W. Wang, "Distributed randomized gradient-free optimization protocol of multiagent systems over weight-unbalanced digraphs," *IEEE Transactions on Cybernetics*, vol. 51, no. 1, pp. 473–482, 2021.
113. J. Zhang and K. You, "AsySPA: an exact asynchronous algorithm for convex optimization over digraphs," *IEEE Transactions on Automatic Control*, vol. 65, no. 6, pp. 2494–2509, 2020.
114. Y. Zhu, G. Wen, W. Yu and X. Yu, "Continuous-time distributed proximal gradient algorithms for nonsmooth resource allocation over general digraphs," *IEEE Transactions on Network Science and Engineering*, vol. 8, no. 2, pp. 1733–1744, 2021.
115. A. Nedic, A. Ozdaglar and P. A. Parrilo, "Constrained consensus and optimization in multi-agent networks," *IEEE Transactions on Automatic Control*, vol. 55, no. 4, pp. 922–938, 2010.
116. G. Mateos, J. Bazerque and G. Giannakis, "Distributed sparse linear regression," *IEEE Transactions on Signal Processing*, vol. 58, no. 10, pp. 5262–5276, 2010
117. H. Eiselt and V. Marianov, *"Foundations of Location Analysis"*, New York, NY, USA: Springer, 2011.
118. J. Darko, L. Folsom, N. Deshpande and H. Park, "Distributed constraint optimization problem for coordinated response of unmanned aerial vehicles and ground vehicles," *55th Annual Conference on Information Sciences and Systems*, pp. 1–6, 2021.
119. X. Zeng, J. Chen and Y. Hong, "Distributed optimization design of iterative refinement technique for algebraic riccati equations," *IEEE Transactions on Systems, Man, and Cybernetics: Systems*, vol. 52, no. 5, pp. 2833–2847, 2022.
120. N. S. Aybat and E. Y. Hamedani, "A distributed ADMM-like method for resource sharing over time-varying networks," *SIAM Journal on Optimization*, vol. 29, no. 4, pp. 3036–3068, 2019.
121. S. A. Alghunaim, K. Yuan and A. H. Sayed, "A linearly convergent proximal gradient algorithm for decentralized optimization," in *Advances in Neural Information Processing Systems*, pp. 2848–2858, 2019.
122. J. Dass, V. Sarin and R. N. Mahapatra, "Fast and communication-efficient algorithm for distributed support vector machine training," *IEEE Transactions on Parallel and Distributed Systems*, vol. 30, no. 5, pp. 1065–1076, 2019.
123. E. Esser, X. Zhang and T. F. Chan, "A primal-dual fixed point algorithm for multi-block convex minimization," *Journal of Computational Mathematics*, vol. 34, no. 6, pp. 723–738, 2016.
124. I. Notarnicola and G. Notarstefano, "Asynchronous distributed optimization via randomized dual proximal gradient," *IEEE Transactions on Automatic Control*, vol. 62, no. 5, pp. 2095–2106, 2017.
125. D. Bertsekas, *"Nonlinear programming"*. Belmont, Massachusetts: Athena Scientific, 2016.
126. J. Zhang, K. You and K. Cai, "Distributed dual gradient tracking for resource allocation in unbalanced networks," *IEEE Transactions on Signal Processing*, vol. 68, pp. 2186–2198, 2020.
127. K. Sadeghi, A. Banerjee and S. K. Gupta, "A system-driven taxonomy of attacks and defenses in adversarial machine learning," *IEEE Transactions on Emerging Topics in Computational Intelligence*, vol. 4, no. 4, pp. 450–467, 2020.
128. K. Huang, H. Jiang and X. Y. Zhang, "Field support vector machines," *IEEE Transactions on Emerging Topics in Computational Intelligence*, vol. 1, no. 6, pp. 454–463, 2017.
129. Q. Jia, L. Guo, Y. Fang and G. Wang, "Efficient privacy-preserving machine learning in hierarchical distributed system," *IEEE Transactions on Network Science and Engineering*, vol. 6, no. 4, pp. 599–612, 2019.
130. Y. Li, G. Liu, G. Lu, L. Jiao, N. Marturi and R. Shang, "Hyper-parameter optimization using MARS surrogate for machine-learning algorithms," *IEEE Transactions on Emerging Topics in Computational Intelligence*, vol. 4, no. 3, pp. 287–297, 2019.

131. I. Loris and C. Verhoeven, "On a generalization of the iterative softthresholding algorithm for the case of non-separable penalty," *Inverse Problems*, vol. 27, no. 12, pp. 125007, 2011.
132. D. Davis and W. T. Yin, "A three-operator splitting scheme and its optimization applications," *Set-Valued and Variational Analysis*, vol. 25, no. 4, pp. 829–858, 2017.
133. P. L. Combettes and V. R. Wajs, "Signal recovery by proximal forward-backward splitting," *Multiscale Modeling & Simulation*, vol. 4, no. 4, pp. 1168–1200, 2005.
134. P. L. Combettes and I. Yamada, "Compositions and convex combinations of averaged nonexpansive operators," *Journal of Mathematical Analysis and Applications*, vol. 425, no. 1, pp. 55–70, 2015.
135. C. X. Zong, Y. C. Tang and Y. J. Cho, "Convergence analysis of an inexact three-operator splitting algorithm," *Symmetry*, vol. 10, no. 11, pp. 563, 2018.
136. Y. C. Tang, G. R. Wu and C. X. Zhu, "An inner-outer iteration method for solving convex optimization problems involving the sum of three convex functions," *Scientia Sinica Mathematics*, vol. 49, pp. 831–858, 2019.
137. P. D. Lorenzo and S. Barbarossa, "A bio-inspired swarming algorithm for decentralized access in cognitive radio," *IEEE Transactions on Signal Processing*, vol. 59, no. 12, pp. 6160–6174, 2011.
138. M. Rabbat and R. Nowak, "Distributed optimization in sensor networks," *3rd International Symposium on Information Processing in Sensor Networks*, pp. 20–27, 2004.
139. Z. Tang, D. J. Hill and T. Liu, "A novel consensus-based economic dispatch for microgrids," *IEEE Transactions on Smart Grid*, vol. 9, no. 4, pp. 3920–3922, 2018.
140. G. Chen, F. L. Lewis, E. N. Feng and Y. Song, "Distributed optimal active power control of multiple generation systems," *IEEE Transactions on Industrial Electronics*, vol. 62, no. 11, pp. 7079–7090, 2015.
141. A. H. Sayed, "Adaptation, learning, and optimization over networks," *Foundations and Trends in Machine Learning*, vol. 7, no. 4–5, pp. 311–801, 2014.
142. K. Yuan, Q. Ling and W. Yin, "On the convergence of decentralized gradient descent," *SIAM Journal on Optimization*, vol. 26, no. 3, pp. 1835–1854, 2016.
143. P. Latafat, A. Bemporad and P. Patrinos, "Plug and play distributed model predictive control with dynamic coupling: A randomized primal-dual proximal algorithm," *2018 European Control Conference*, pp. 1160–1165, 2018.
144. P. Combettes, "Solving monotone inclusions via compositions of nonexpansive averaged operators," *Optimization*, vol. 53, no. 5–6, pp. 475–504, 2004.
145. N. Ogura and I. Yamada, "Non-strictly convex minimization over the fixed point set of an asymptotically shrinking nonexpansive mapping," *Numerical Functional Analysis and Optimization*, vol. 23, no. 1–2, pp. 113–137, 2002.
146. H. Li, E. Su, C. Wang, J. Liu, Z. Zheng, Z. Wang and D. Xia, " A primal-dual forward-backward splitting algorithm for distributed convex optimization," *IEEE Transactions on Emerging Topics in Computational Intelligence*, vol. 7, no. 1, pp. 278–284, 2023.
147. H. Li, H. Cheng, Z. Wang and G. C. Wu, "Distributed nesterov gradient and heavy-ball double accelerated asynchronous optimization," *IEEE Transactions on Neural Networks and Learning Systems*, vol. 32, no. 12, pp. 5723–5737, 2021.
148. T. C. Aysal, M. E. Yildriz, A. D. Sarwate and A. Scaglione, "Broadcast gossip algorithms for consensus," *IEEE Transactions on Signal Process*, vol. 57, no. 7, pp. 2748–2761, 2009.
149. D. Gabay and B. Mercier, "A dual algorithm for the solution of nonlinear variational problems via finite element approximation," *Computers & Mathematics with Applications*, vol. 2, no. 1, pp. 17–40, 1976.
150. P. Di Lorenzo and G. Scutari, "Distributed nonconvex optimization over networks," *IEEE 6th International Workshop on Computational Advances in Multi-Sensor Adaptive Processing*, pp. 229–232, 2015.
151. P. Di Lorenzo and G. Scutari, "Next: In-network nonconvex optimization," *IEEE Transactions on Signal and Information Processing over Networks*, vol. 2, no. 2, pp. 120–136, 2016.

152. S. Boyd, N. Parikh, E. Chu, B. Peleato and J. Eckstein, "Distributed optimization and statistical learning via the alternating direction method of multipliers," *Foundations and Trends in Machine Learning*, vol. 3, no. 1, pp. 1–122, 2011.
153. T. H. Chang, M. Hong, W. C. Liao, and X. Wang, "Asynchronous distributed ADMM for large-scale optimization-Part I: Algorithm and convergence analysis," *IEEE Transactions on Signal Processing*, vol. 64, no. 12, pp. 3118–3130, 2016.
154. Z. Peng, Y. Xu, M. Yan and W. Yin, "ARock: An algorithmic framework for asynchronous parallel coordinate updates," *SIAM Journal on Scientific Computing*, vol. 38, no. 5, pp. A2851–A2879, 2016.
155. P. Yi and L. Pavel, "Asynchronous distributed algorithms for seeking generalized Nash equilibria under full and partial-decision information," *IEEE Transactions on Cybernetics*, vol. 50, no. 6, pp. 2514–2526, 2019.
156. Z. Wang, F. Liu, Y. Su, P. Yang and B. Qin, "Asynchronous distributed voltage control in active distribution networks," *Automatica*, vol. 122, pp. 109269, 2020.
157. T. Wu, K. Yuan, Q. Ling, W. Yin and A. H. Sayed, "Decentralized consensus optimization with asynchrony and delays," *IEEE Transactions on Signal and Information Processing over Networks*, vol. 4, no. 2, pp. 293–307, 2018.
158. J. Zhang and X. Xia, "A model predictive control approach to the periodic implementation of the solutions of the optimal dynamic resource allocation problem," *Automatica*, vol. 47, no. 2, pp. 358–362, 2011.
159. X. Zhuan and X. Xia, "Development of efficient model predictive control strategy for cost-optimal operation of a water pumping station," *IEEE Transactions on Control Systems Technology*, vol. 21, no. 4, pp. 1449–1454, 2012.
160. X. Xia, J. Zhang, and A. Elaiw, "An application of model predictive control to the dynamic economic dispatch of power generation," *Control Engineering Practice*, vol. 19, no. 6, pp. 638–648, 2011.
161. J. Richalet, A. Rault, J. Testud, and J. Papon, "Model predictive heuristic control," *Automatica*, vol. 14, no. 5, pp. 413–428, 1978.
162. D. M. Prett and R. Gillette, "Optimization and constrained multivariable control of a catalytic cracking unit," *Joint Automatic Control Conference*, pp. 73, 1980.
163. S. Qin and T. Badgwell, "A survey of industrial model predictive control technology," *Control Engineering Practice*, vol. 11, no. 7, pp. 733–764, 2003.
164. S. Alam and B. Natarajan, "Stability of agent based distributed model predictive control over a lossy network," *IEEE Transactions on Signal and Information Processing over Networks*, vol. 1, no. 4, pp. 235–246, 2015.
165. B. Zhu, H. Tazvinga, and X. Xia, "Switched model predictive control for energy dispatching of a photovoltaic-diesel-battery hybrid power system," *IEEE Transactions on Control Systems Technology*, vol. 23, no. 3, pp. 1229–1236, 2014.
166. C. Garcia, D. Prett, and M. Morari, "Model predictive control: theory and practice-a survey," *Automatica*, vol. 25, no. 3, pp. 335–348, 1989.
167. E. Camponogara and L. Barcelos de Oliveira, "Distributed optimization for model predictive control of linear-dynamic networks," *IEEE Transactions on Systems, Man, and Cybernetics - Part A: Systems and Humans*, vol. 39, no. 6, pp. 1331–1338, 2009.
168. E. Camponogara and H. F. Scherer, "Distributed optimization for model predictive control of linear dynamic networks with control-input and output constraints," *IEEE Transactions on Automation Science and Engineering*, vol. 8, no. 1, pp. 233–242, 2011.
169. G. Zhang and R. Heusdens, "Distributed optimization using the primal-dual method of multipliers," *IEEE Transactions on Signal and Information Processing over Networks*, vol. 4, no. 1, pp. 173–187, 2018.
170. H. Raja and W. Bajwa, "Cloud k-svd: A collaborative dictionary learning algorithm for big, distributed data," *IEEE Transactions on Signal Processing*, vol. 64, no. 1, pp. 173–188, 2015.
171. D. Wang and W. Wang, "Necessary and sufficient conditions for containment control of multi-agent systems with time delay," *Automatica*, vol. 103, pp. 418–423, 2019.

172. D. Wang, Z. Wang, C. Wen and W. Wang, "Second-order continuous-time algorithm for optimal resource allocation in power systems," *IEEE Transactions on Industrial Informatics*, vol. 15, no. 2, pp. 626–637, 2019.
173. H. Wai, Z. Yang, Z. Wang and M. Hong, "Multi-agent reinforcement learning via double averaging primal-dual optimization," *Advances in Neural Information Processing Systems*, pp. 9649–9660, 2018.
174. T. Sherson, R. Heusdens and W. Kleijn, "On the distributed method of multipliers for separable convex optimization problems," *IEEE Transactions on Signal and Information Processing over Networks*, vol. 5, no. 3, pp. 495–510, 2019.
175. K. Tsianos and M. Rabbat, "Efficient distributed online prediction and stochastic optimization with approximate distributed averaging," *IEEE Transactions on Signal and Information Processing over Networks*, vol. 2, no. 4, pp. 489–506, 2016.
176. D. Yuan, D. Ho and S. Xu, "Regularized primal-dual subgradient method for distributed constrained optimization," *IEEE Transactions on Cybernetics*, vol. 46, no. 9, pp. 2109–2118, 2015.
177. P. Lin, W. Ren and Y. Song, "Distributed multi-agent optimization subject to nonidentical constraints and communication delays," *Automatica*, vol. 65, pp. 120–131, 2016.
178. P. Liu and U. Ozguner, "Distributed model predictive control of spatially interconnected systems using switched cost functions," *IEEE Transactions on Automatic Control*, vol. 63, no. 7, pp. 2161–2167, 2017.
179. P. Trodden and J. Maestre, "Distributed predictive control with minimization of mutual disturbances," *Automatica*, vol. 77, pp. 31–43, 2017.
180. Y. Gao, L. Dai, Y. Xia and Y. Liu, "Distributed model predictive control for consensus of nonlinear second-order multi-agent systems," *International Journal of Robust and Nonlinear Control*, vol. 27, no. 5, pp. 830–842, 2017.
181. Z. Sun, L. Dai, Y. Xia and K. Liu, "Event-based model predictive tracking control of nonholonomic systems with coupled input constraint and bounded disturbances," *IEEE Transactions on Automatic Control*, vol. 63, no. 5, pp. 608–615, 2017.
182. W. Ren, K. Moore and Y. Chen, "High-order consensus algorithms in cooperative vehicle systems," *IEEE International Conference on Networking, Sensing and Control*, pp. 457–462, 2006.
183. W. He and J. Cao, "Consensus control for high-order multi-agent systems," *IET Control Theory & Applications*, vol. 5, no. 1, pp. 231–238, 2011.
184. Y. Xin and Z. Cheng, "R-consensus control for higher-order multi-agent systems with digraph," *Asian Journal of Control*, vol. 15, no. 5, pp. 1524–1530, 2013.
185. R. Olfati-Saber, J. Fax, and R. Murray, "Consensus and cooperation in networked multi-agent systems," *Proceedings of the IEEE*, vol. 95, no. 1, pp. 215–233, 2007.
186. Y. Xin and Z. Cheng, "Brief paper R-consensus control for discrete-time high-order multi-agent systems," *IET Control Theory & Applications*, vol. 7, no. 17, pp. 2103–2109, 2013.
187. R. Olfati-Saber and R. M. Murray, "Consensus problems in networks of agents with switching topology and time-delays," *IEEE Transactions on Automatic Control*, vol. 49, no. 9, pp. 1520–1533, 2004.
188. W. Ren, K. L. Moore, and Y. Chen, "Information consensus in multivehicle cooperative control," *IEEE Control Systems Magazine*, vol. 27, no. 2, pp. 71–82, 2007.
189. L. Cheng, Z. Hou, M. Tan, and X. Wang, "Necessary and sufficient conditions for consensus of double-integrator multi-agent systems with measurement noises," *IEEE Transactions on Automatic Control*, vol. 56, no. 8, pp. 1958–1963, 2011.
190. W. Ren, "On consensus algorithms for double-integrator dynamics," *IEEE Transactions on Automatic Control*, vol. 53, no. 6, pp. 1503–1509, 2008.
191. J. Qin, W. X. Zheng and H. Gao, "Coordination of multiple agents with double-integrator dynamics under generalized interaction topologies," *IEEE Transactions on Systems, Man, and Cybernetics, Part B*, vol. 42, no. 1, pp. 44–57, 2012.

192. R. Olfati-Saber and A. Megretski, "Nonlinear Control of Underactuated Mechanical Systems with Application to Robotics and Aerospace Vehicles," *Massachusetts Institute of Technology*, 2001.
193. J. Kaloust, "Nonlinear autopilot control design for a 2-dof helicopter model," *IEEE Proceedings - Control Theory and Applications*, vol. 144, no. 4, pp. 612–616, 1997.
194. Z. Zuo, B. Tian, M. Defoort and Z. Ding, "Fixed-time consensus tracking for multiagent systems with high-order integrator dynamics," *IEEE Transactions on Automatic Control*, vol. 63, no. 2, pp. 563–570, 2018.
195. F. Sun, Z.-H. Guan, X.-S. Zhan and F.-S. Yuan, "Consensus of second-order and high-order discrete-time multi-agent systems with random networks," *Nonlinear Analysis: Real World Applications*, vol. 13, no. 5, pp. 1979–1990, 2012.
196. H. Rezaee and F. Abdollahi, "Average consensus over high-order multi-agent systems," *IEEE Transactions on Automatic Control*, vol. 60, no. 11, pp. 3047–3052, 2015.
197. W. Yu, G. Chen, W. Ren, J. Kurths and W. X. Zheng, "Distributed higher order consensus protocols in multiagent dynamical systems," *IEEE Transactions on Circuits and Systems I: Regular Papers*, vol. 58, no. 8, pp. 1924–1932, 2011.
198. H. Zhang and F. L. Lewis, "Adaptive cooperative tracking control of higher-order nonlinear systems with unknown dynamics," *Automatica*, vol. 48, no. 7, pp. 1432–1439, 2012.
199. J. Huang, H. Fang, L. Dou and J. Chen, "An overview of distributed high-order multi-agent coordination," *IEEE/CAA Journal of Automatica Sinica*, vol. 1, no. 1, pp. 1–9, 2014.
200. H. Zhang, F. L. Lewis and A. Das, "Optimal design for synchronization of cooperative systems: state feedback, observer and output feedback," *IEEE Transactions on Automatic Control*, vol. 56, no. 8, pp. 1948–1952, 2011.
201. H. K. Khalil, "Nonlinear systems third edition", *Prentice Hall*, 2002.
202. P. Wieland, J.-S. Kim, H. Scheu and F. Allgower, "On consensus in multi-agent systems with linear high-order agents," *IFAC Proceedings Volumes*, vol. 41, no. 2, pp. 1541–1546, 2008.
203. F. Jiang, L. Wang and Y. Jia, "Consensus in leaderless networks of high-order-integrator agents," *American Control Conference*, pp. 4458–4463, 2009.
204. W. Ren, K. L. Moore and Y. Chen, "High-order and model reference consensus algorithms in cooperative control of multi vehicle systems," *Journal of Dynamic Systems, Measurement, and Control*, vol. 129, pp. 678–688, 2006.
205. W. Jinhuan and C. Daizhan, "Consensus of multi-agent systems with higher order dynamics," *Chinese Control Conference*, pp. 761–765, 2007.
206. J. Hu, Y. Yan, H. Li, Z. Wang, D. Xia and J. Guo, "Convergence of an accelerated distributed optimisation algorithm over time-varying directed networks," *IET Control Theory and Applications*, vol. 15, no. 1, pp. 24–39, 2021.
207. T. Yang et al. Distributed energy resource coordination over timevarying directed communication networks, *IEEE Transactions on Control of Network Systems*, vol. 6, no. 3, pp. 1124–1134, 2019.
208. T. Yang, D. Wu, W. Ren, H. Wang, Y. Hong and K. H. Johansson, "Cooperative optimal coordination for distributed energy resources," *IEEE 56th Annual Conference on Decision and Control (CDC)*, pp. 6334–6339, 2017.
209. D. Wu, T. Yang, A. A. Stoorvogel and J. Stoustrup, "Distributed optimal coordination for distributed energy resources in power systems," *IEEE Transactions on Automation Science and Engineering*, vol. 14, no. 2, pp. 414–424, 2017.
210. W. Liu, L. Chen, Y. Chen and W. Zhang, Accelerating federated learning via momentum gradient descent, *IEEE Transactions on Parallel and Distributed Systems*, vol. 31, no. 8, pp. 1754–1766, 2020.
211. H. Li, X. Liao, T. Huang and W. Zhu, Event-triggering sampling based leader-following consensus in second-order multi-agent systems, *IEEE Transactions on Automatic Control*, vol. 60, no. 7, pp. 1998–2003, 2015.

212. H. Brendan McMahan, E. Moore, D. Ramage, S. Hampson and B. Ag uera yArcas, Communication-efficient learning of deep networks from decentralized data, *Proceedings of the 20th International Conference on Artificial Intelligence and Statistics*, vol. 54, pp. 1273–1282, 2017.
213. J. A. P. Lopes, C. L. Moreira and A. G. Madureira, "Defining control strategies for MicroGrids islanded operation," *IEEE Transactions on Power Systems*, vol. 21, no. 2, pp. 916–924, 2006.
214. H. Li, Z. Wang, G. Chen and Z. Y. Dong," Distributed robust algorithm for economic dispatch in smart grids over general unbalanced directed networks," *IEEE Transactions on Industrial Informatics*, vol. 16, no. 7, pp. 4322–4332, 2020.
215. M. Basu, Dynamic economic emission dispatch using nondominated sorting genetic algorithm-II, *International Journal of Electrical Power & Energy Systems*, vol. 30, no. 2, pp. 140–149, 2008.
216. M. Assran, N. Loizou, N. Ballas and M. Rabbat, Stochastic gradient push for distributed deep learning, *Proceedings of the 36th International Conference on Machine Learning*, vol. 97, pp. 344–97:353, 2019.
217. A. Nedic, A. Olshevsky and W. Shi, Achieving geometric convergence for distributed optimization over time-varying graphs, *SIAM Journal on Optimization*, vol. 27, no. 4, pp. 2597–2633, 2017.
218. D. Jakovetic, A unification and generalization of exact distributed first-order methods, *IEEE Transactions on Signal and Information Processing over Networks*, vol. 5, no. 1, pp. 31–46, 2019.
219. P. Latafat and P. Patrinos, Multi-agent structured optimization over message-passing architectures with bounded communication delays, *IEEE Conference on Decision and Control (CDC)*, 2018, pp. 1688–1693.
220. C. Xi and U. A. Khan, Distributed subgradient projection algorithm over directed graphs, *IEEE Transactions on Automatic Control*, vol. 62, no. 8, pp. 3986–3992, 2017.
221. Y. Yuan, H. Li, J. Hu and Z. Wang, Stochastic gradient-push for economic dispatch on time-varying directed networks with delays, *International Journal of Electrical Power & Energy Systems*, vol. 113, pp. 564–572, 2019.
222. J.-B. Hiriart-Urruty and C. Lemarechal, Conjugacy in Convex Analysis, Berlin, Germany: Springer, 1993.
223. S. Boyd, A. Ghosh, B. Prabhakar and D. Shah, Randomized gossip algorithms, *IEEE Transactions on Information Theory*, vol. 52, no. 6, pp. 2508–2530, 2006.
224. O. Fercoq and P. Bianchi, A coordinate-descent primal-dual algorithm with large step size and possibly nonseparable functions, *SIAM Journal on Optimization*, vol. 29, no. 1, pp. 100–134, 2019.
225. D. Dua and Graff, UCI Machine Learning Repository, School Inf. Comput. Sci., Univ. California, California, Irvine, CA, USA, (2019)
226. T. Athay, R. Podmore and S. Virmani, A practical method for the direct analysis of transient stability, *IEEE Transactions on Power Apparatus and Systems*, vol. PAS-98, no. 2, pp. 573–584, 1979.
227. A. Salim, L. Condat, K. Mishchenko and P. Richtarik, Dualize, split, randomize: Fast nonsmooth optimization algorithms, *Journal of Optimization Theory and Applications*, vol. 55, no. 4, pp. 922–938, 2010.
228. V. Smith, S. Forte, C. Ma, M. Takac and M.I. Jordan, M. Jaggi, CoCoA: a general framework for communication-efficient distributed optimization, *Journal of Machine Learning Research*, vol. 18, pp. 230, 2016.
229. B. Wang, Z. Li and X. Yan, Multi-subspace factor analysis integrated with support vector data description for multimode process monitoring, *Journal of the Franklin Institute*, vol. 355, no. 15, pp. 7664–7690, 2018.
230. L. Jiang, L. Yan, Y. Xia, Q. Guo, M. Fu and L. Li, Distributed fusion in wireless sensor networks based on a novel event-triggered strategy, *Journal of the Franklin Institute*, vol. 356, no. 17, pp. 10315–10334, 2019.

231. T. Wang, X. He, T. Huang, C. Li and W. Zhang, Collective neurodynamic optimization for economic emission dispatch problem considering valve point effect in microgrid, *Neural Networks*, vol. 93, pp. 126–136, 2017.
232. G. Shao, R. Wang, X.-F. Wang and K.-Z. Liu, Distributed algorithm for resource allocation problems under persistent attacks, *Journal of the Franklin Institute*, vol. 357, no. 10, pp. 6241–6256, 2020.
233. T. Meng, Z. Lin and Y.A. Shamash, Distributed cooperative control of battery energy storage systems in DC microgrids, *IEEE/CAA Journal of Automatica Sinica*, vol. 8, no. 3, pp. 606–616, 2021.
234. C. Wang, S. Xu, D. Yuan, Y. Chu and Z. Zhang, Cooperative convex optimization with subgradient delays using push-sum distributed dual averaging, *Journal of the Franklin Institute*, vol. 358, pp. 7254–7269, 2021.
235. Y. Niu, H. Wang, Z. Wang, D. Xia and H. Li, Primal-dual stochastic distributed algorithm for constrained convex optimization, *Journal of the Franklin Institute*, vol. 356, no. 16, pp. 9763–9787, 2019.
236. C.-X. Shi and G.-H. Yang, Multi-cluster distributed optimization via random sleep strategy, *Journal of the Franklin Institute*, vol. 356, pp. 5353–5377, 2019.
237. D.P. Bertsekas, Incremental proximal methods for large scale convex optimization, *Mathematical Programming*, vol. 129, no. 2, pp. 163, 2011.
238. S.A. Alghunaim, K. Yuan and A.H. Sayed, A proximal diffusion strategy for multiagent optimization with sparse affine constraints, *IEEE Transactions on Automatic Control*, vol. 65, no. 11, pp. 4554–4567, 2020.
239. J. Xu, Y. Sun, Y. Tian and G. Scutari, A unified contraction analysis of a class of distributed algorithms for composite optimization, *IEEE 8th International Workshop on Computational Advances in Multi-Sensor Adaptive Processing (CAMSAP)*, pp. 485–489, 2019.
240. A. Chambolle, T. Pock, An introduction to continuous optimization for imaging, *Acta Numerica*, vol. 25, pp. 161–319, 2016.
241. Y. Nesterov, A. Nemirovskii, Interior-point polynomial algorithms in convex programming, SIAM, Philadelphia, 1994.
242. Y. Zhao, Q. Liu, A consensus algorithm based on collective neurodynamic system for distributed optimization with linear and bound constraints, *Neural Networks*, vol. 122, pp. 144–151, 2020.
243. X. Ren, D. Li, Y. Xi and H. Shao, Distributed subgradient algorithm for multi-agent optimization with dynamic stepsize, *IEEE/CAA Journal of Automatica Sinica*, vol. 8, no. 8, pp. 1451–1464, 2021.
244. N. Parikh, B. Stephen, Proximal algorithms, *Foundations and trends in Optimization*, vol. 1, no. 3, pp. 123–231, 2014.
245. N. Komodakis, J.C. Pesquet, Playing with duality: an overview of recent primal-dual approaches for solving large-scale optimization problems, *IEEE Signal Processing Magazine*, vol. 32, no. 6, pp. 31–54, 2015.
246. L. Feller, C. Ebenbauer, Relaxed logarithmic barrier function based model predictive control of linear systems, *IEEE Transactions on Automatic Control*, vol. 62, no. 3, pp. 1223–1238, 2017.
247. S. Bellavia, J. Gondzio and M. Porcelli, An inexact dual logarithmic barrier method for solving sparse semidefinite programs, *Mathematical Programming*, vol. 178, no. 3, pp. 109–143, 2019.
248. A. Cichocki, R. Unbehauen, Neural networks for solving systems of linear equations. II. Minimax and least absolute value problems, *IEEE Transactions on Circuits and Systems II: Analog and Digital Signal Processing*, vol. 39, no. 9, pp. 619–633, 1992.

MIX
Papier aus verantwortungsvollen Quellen
Paper from responsible sources
FSC® C105338

If you have any concerns about our products,
you can contact us on
ProductSafety@springernature.com

In case Publisher is established outside the EU,
the EU authorized representative is:
Springer Nature Customer Service Center GmbH
Europaplatz 3, 69115 Heidelberg, Germany

Printed by Libri Plureos GmbH
in Hamburg, Germany